Greek Labour Relations in Transition in a Global Context

Labour, Education & Society

Edited by György Széll,
Heinz Sünker, Anne Inga Hilsen
and Francesco Garibaldo

Volume 34

PL ACADEMIC RESEARCH

Dimosthenis Daskalakis

Greek Labour Relations in Transition in a Global Context

PL ACADEMIC RESEARCH

Bibliographic Information published by the Deutsche Nationalbibliothek
The Deutsche Nationalbibliothek lists this publication in the Deutsche Nationalbibliografie; detailed bibliographic data is available in the internet at http://dnb.d-nb.de.

Library of Congress Cataloging-in-Publication Data
Daskalakis, Dimosthenis, 1959- author.
Greek labour relations in transition in a global context / Dimosthenis Daskalakis.
pages cm. — (Labour, education & society ; volume 34)
Includes bibliographical references and index.
ISBN 978-3-631-66657-9
1. Industrial relations—Greece. 2. Labor—Greece. 3. Labor policy—Greece. 4. Greece—Economic conditions—1974- I. Title.
HD8650.5.D37 2015
331.09495—dc23

2015026974

Translation – Editing: Aikaterini Nikolarea

ISSN 1861-647X
ISBN 978-3-631-66657-9 (Print)
E-ISBN 978-3-653-06091-1 (E-Book)
DOI 10.3726/978-3-653-06091-1

PL Academic Research is an Imprint of Peter Lang GmbH.

Peter Lang – Frankfurt am Main · Bern · Bruxelles · New York · Oxford · Warszawa · Wien

This publication has been peer reviewed.

www.peterlang.com

Table of Contents

Preface

Every national industrial relations system is determined by the degree of the state intervention and the operation of collective labour institutions, more particularly those of collective bargaining, which for some authors and researchers, such as Flanders, are almost identical with the subject of labour – industrial relations.

In Greece, the national industrial relations system traces its origins to Metaxas' dictatorship, just before World War II. It was then that for the first time the dictatorial regime attempted to organize a national system of industrial relationships in order to control it. Its main choices were, first, to appoint management to the unions that were controlled by the dictatorial government and, second, to create a tripartite mechanism that could regulate payments in Greece for the first time. In this mechanism participated: employers' representatives, union representatives appointed by the government and the Minister of Labour. On the one hand, that tripartite shape, as a mechanism to regulate payments, can be considered as "ancestor", in a sense, of the institution of collective bargaining. On the other hand, the fact that in this mechanism there was participation of union representatives appointed by government and representatives of the state itself may be pure falsification of the institution of collective bargaining. Thus, the dictatorial regime attempted to organize and control the national system of industrial relations.

Of a similar character – that is, of tripartite composition – there were bodies that were established to regulate payments were established after World War II, during the Greek Civil War and after that. The fierce statism that characterized industrial relations in Greece continued the subsequent years, that ism in the 1950s, 1960s and the 1970s. The first, however, effort to develop an effective system of collective bargaining is dated back in the mid-1950s. It was then that for the first time a system of collective bargaining was essentially created in Greece. However, it was a system that had many problematic aspects and was operating within a context of keen statism and conflict. At the time, the country was coming out of a tough Civil War; there were fierce political and social conflicts; an economy – devastated by World War II – was trying to get rebuilt with the aid of Marshall Plan; there were great waves of internal migration from the countryside to the big city centers and outside of Greece to the developed countries. Basic characteristic of that period was that there was distrust between the state and its social partners, distrust that was being manifested in various forms of intense statism and a collective bargaining system, which – although it was established at the time for the first time – was faking and negating the very essence of collective autonomy and the institution of collective bargaining with its provisions and its operation.

During the specific period, the national industrial relations system showed various peculiarities. The management of the trade union movement seemed to depend on the State. A lot of socio-historical and political studies refer to interventions of a foreign agent too. The dependence of the trade union movement on the state is conspicuous in the finances of trade unions. There was state control over the funding of trade unions through the well-known ODEPES (initials in Greek for "Special Resources Management Agency of Labour Unions"). The situation changed in the early 1980s when the agency ODEPES was abolished, there were provided financial independence both of trade unions and reliable procedures to appoint independent management in trade unions so the independence of the trade union movement would be ensured (Law 1264/1982 "About democratization of the trade union movement"). Furthermore, there was generalized statism in the Greek industrial relations system which was being manifested more particularly in diverse provisions and the operation of the institution of collective bargaining, something that was regulated by Law 3339/1955. Such provision was the Minister's right to be able to judge the validity of a collective employment agreement (CEA), that is, to exercise control over the legality of the content of an attached CEA. Another provision by which statism was manifested was the general distrust between the state and its social partners, as expressed in the regulations of Law 3339/1955.

A feature of that period's model was the paucity of the content of the collective bargainin that practically regulated payments. This system led to the development of centralized collective bargaining and arrangements and contributed to maintaining the fragmentation of the trade union movement, since it was placing its emphasis on bargaining for the same occupation. Moreover, it did not provide the opportunity for collective bargaining and conclusion of collective employment agreements (CEAs) at a company level other than public utilities. More specifically, things were controlled in public companies. Management was appointed by the government, whereas there was the respective government and party control both over the trade union management and public companies through the customer's appointment system. Therefore, if things were not uncontrollable in public companies, there could be collective bargaining. In contrast, in private companies at company level, both collective bargaining and conclusion to collective bargaining agreements were impossible; in private economy and private sector there could be no state control. Thus, the mistrust between the state and social partners was manifested in the absence of provisions for company level bargaining. Typical of how much economic and social reality actually exceeded the current framework is the fact that after the dictatorship, particularly after 1974, in a number of private companies in which a keen wave of factory unionism was flourished – "enlightened employers" in partnership with trade unions drew "written agreements" that were recorded in the history of Greek labour relationships as "cooperation agreement" This agreement, however, was neither provided by the institutional context of collective bargaining nor had the power of collective contract from a legal point of view; it was simply a "debt effect".

Furthermore, all that system of collective bargaining was accompanied by provisions for suspension of strike and regulation of collective labour disputes with a model of compulsory state arbitration. This is especially the point that had been criticized by social partners for many years. The primary and secondary administrative arbitration tribunals – which were set up by a decision of the respective Labour Minister, that is, the state character of the mechanism that was providing arbitration services – were a fact that it could not guarantee the settlement and regulation system of collective labour disputes, a function without interference from the state. At the same time, a critical issue was the obligatoriness of arbitration, namely the fact that any collective labour dispute would lead to arbitration anyway. As a result, arbitration came to replace collective bargaining while this model was in operation. Instead of taking responsibility for bargaining of essence and mutual concessions – in view of the risk of being exposed to the "basis" they represented, the negotiating parties rather wanted bargaining to fail so that it would be sent to the automatic referral to arbitration, and then they jointly (with the other party) protested against the 'bad' arbitration system.

The operation of such a model resulted in maintaining a situation within which the parties – employees and employers – had a negative attitude towards accountability, mutual commitments as well as towards substantial dialogue. That situation led in practice to a complete falsification and cancellation of the institution of collective bargaining. In reality, neither collective bargaining nor collective labour agreements were held as a product of collective bargaining. On the contrary, collective bargaining was held only typically so that its failure would also be typically determined and the cases would "automatically" be brought to state compulsory arbitration so that decisions of compulsory implementation were to be made. The statistics of the specific period confirm this dramatic reality, since 98% of collective bargaining was not producing collective employment agreements (CEAs); it was producing rather arbitration decisions.

Undoubtedly, it can be argued that until the 1980s government interventions resulted in a strong statism prevailing in the Greek industrial relations system. Nevertheless, something that differentiates much the 1980s was the fact that, at the time, there was a wave of institutional reforms in Greek labour relations favouring employees in regulating labour issues.

On the contrary, the policy of the period between 1990 and 1993, which was oscillating between voluntarism and neoliberalism, aimed to overthrow the previous status quo. Additionally, it should be acknowledged that the state after 1993 – with its interventions that seem to meet the model of democratic bargained neocorporatism – formed a new institutional balance between state intervention and collective autonomy in industrial relations, a balance that allowed the operation of the labour market to be based not only on stable social protection but also on a flexible legal framework through which industrial relations could move and operate.

This situation, however, seems to be upset so dramatically – and of dubious constitutionality – if not directly unconstitutional, as eminent jurists hold – in the past two years, that is, after the Memorandum.

Since the 1980s pretty much fixed rules for a variety of issues have been developed among others – certainly with variations depending on the overall political and ideological direction of each government; these issues included the status of breach of the employment contract and the employee's compensation, gender equality in industrial relations (Law 1414/84), Sanitation and Safety Conditions of the Employees (Law 1568/85), the protection of special categories of people (Law 1648/86), the operation of Employees' Councils (Law 1767/88) or free collective bargaining (Law 1876/90).

Balanced regulations were also formed so that flexible forms of employment and working time would be explored, and, more specifically: (1) the introduction of part-time employment, with a written agreement between employers and employees; (2) the implementation of the system of four (4) working groups by companies of continuous operation, with employees' consent; (3) the establishment of a job rotation system (Paragraph 7, Article 13, Decree 2961/1954); (4) provision for companies of continuous operation, when they have to hire additional personnel who would be employed in two rotating shifts for twelve hours a day so that the company operates during Saturday and Sunday; and (5) new balanced shop opening hours were established, which provided large flexibility.

It should be noted that, in recent years, important initiatives have been taken up, which have been truly implemented, such as: the development of institutions and social dialogue processes between employees and employers or between employees and the state; and the empowerment both of the institution of employees' councils and free collective bargaining. Thus, the same interested parties, employees and employers, can regulate not only employees' wages but also almost all issues that concern them. Moreover, there was a development of institutions of conflict mitigation and resolution of labour disputes, such as: the new Organisation for Mediation and Arbitration (O.M.E.D. in Greek), new reliable mediation procedures, a mixed system of arbitration which is of an auxiliary character (which is neither entirely voluntary nor entirely obligatory) and new procedures of public dialogue. At the same time, the Economic and Social Committee (O.K.E. in Greek; ESC) was formed, a key institutional agency conducting social dialogue for all major financial and social issues and being a key corporatist institutional version to achieve social bargain and social consensus at national level. This agency is a key mechanism and institution that pursues and achieves consensus and policies of social contract, as with this kind of institutions there can be detected seeds of alternative procedures of corporatist enrichment of political decision-making mechanisms within modern parliamentary democracies. Finally, a three-member Administration (involving state, employers and employees) was also appointed to the National Organization for the Occupation of the Work Force (OAED in Greek).

It is of particular importance the fact that in recent years there has been a good rapport between employees and employers, a fact that has both led to the conclusion of biennial national general collective employment agreements (EGSSE in Greek) and ensured conditions of labour peace in recent years.

The new law on collective bargaining passed by the Ecumenical Government in March 1990, since only then it was possible to create the appropriate balance that allowed the modification of the institutional framework. The new framework introduced an entirely new concept of collective bargaining and collective labour disputes. Even the title that the new Law had: "On free collective bargaining" indicates that the legislator has no longer in mind – as s/he did previously – collective disputes but primarily the dialogue between the parties through collective bargaining so that economic interests are regulated and settled and disputes get prevented.

By force of the Memorandum it could be argued that the changes that have been made, especially in collective labour relations, have not only brought individual changes but also led to an overall readjustment and reregulation of the labour market in Greece, which has brought drastic and immediate results. What should be emphasized is that the new Memorandum is only of horizontal cuts in wages and pensions, which may well be reversed in the future. It deconstructs the whole system of collective bargaining and cancels employees' right of recourse to arbitration. Working conditions in the private sector cease being the subject of bargaining between social partners; they are regulated either by the employer through individual contracts or by governmental intervention. Even the minimum wage of National General Collective Employment Agreement (EGSSE) is also canceled, since it can be decreased whenever the Troika or the government requires it.

Chapter 1: Industrial Relations

1.1 Clarifications of Terminology and Methodology

In international bibliography the terms "labour relations", "industrial relations" and "professional relations" are used interchangeably, whereas in the Anglo-Saxon literature the term "industrial relations" is mainly used. This term, however, traditionally does not denote the employee-employer relation at an individual level; it rather indicates strictly the organizational dimension of the relationship between employers and employees at a collective level. The term "industrial relations" has formed a research and study field whose object is the web of rules that regulate labour relations as a specific category of social relations between employers and employees within an employment context, namely, the total of behaviours and interactions between the two parties within the framework of production and employment.

The initial definition of the field of "industrial relations" features as a core issue, as it is reasonable, since this definition determines the research range of "industrial relations". Another issue of particular importance is that the definition restricts the field about the formal and informal aspects, rules, terms, conditions, and relationships underlying the regulation of traditional employment. However, over the past decades a number of developments have fundamentally redefined the scope of this field of study. The developments in industrial relations, which have been designated as "modern anomalies", have played a decisive role to this direction.

More specifically, the decline of organised trade unions, the development of companies without trade unions, the extension of flexible and informal employment and the destabilization of normal employment model are such phenomena. In addition, the rapid development of human resources management, both as a set of practical applications and as a field of scientific study, as well as the re patriation of quantitative methods and labour economics, which have put labour relations within the framework of labour market, have fundamentally reframed the object of industrial relations.

Consequently, the definition of the object of industrial relations has been broadened, and is now a common place (: *a locus* or *a topos*) including not only labour regulation but also the wider context by and within which employment relationships can be determined. There is always a core assumption in industrial relations that employment relationships are competitive and contentious, since there are power relations between employers and employees involved around and within the employment context, whereas many times the State gets into this relationship as a third actor, as a protagonist, a regulator or an employer. In the past, the object of industrial relations used to get focused exclusively on the collective dimensions of employment, whereas nowadays individual dimensions and views are integrated in the study of industrial relations by some researchers of a particular orientation, especially that of the field of human resources management.

Now regarding a sociological approach to industrial relations, it calls into play its own specialised theoretical and methodological approaches; it is essentially a part of the wider field of industrial sociology or, rather more correctly, part of a specific field of study and research with its own specialised theories and approaches. Nevertheless, the universal, integrated and overall approach to industrial relations and their phenomena is interdisciplinary by its very nature. Some scholars consider industrial relations in terms of reciprocal collaboration between employees and employers, some other approach industrial relations in terms of conflict of interest among social groups; and some other scholars consider industrial relations in terms of class conflict. Based on these underlying premises and accepting them as ideological, three main approaches to the interpretation of industrial relations have been formed: the monist, the pluralist and the radical approach.

First, the **monist approach** could be summarised in that initiatives, decisions and "leadership" are interconnected and emanate exclusively from management that is based on hierarchy. This hierarchy is also the unique legalised and acceptable agency of rights and power within an organization. This particular view adopts an "organic analogy", where, on the one hand, the company is considered "the body of an organism" and the management as the head, whereas, on the other hand, employees are considered members that should execute the orders of the "head", without thinking of or reacting to them. The coordinated collective action of the members of an organism, that is, the employees' collective trade-union action makes the organism to lose co-ordination of its operation, while conflict is presented and is dealt with as a dysfunctional and disruptive phenomenon.

Second, the **pluralist approach** addresses those groups that operate within a company in order to dictate them how to "behave" to each other. Within the context of this approach, the two parties – employers and employees – are not dealt with as classes but rather as two parties which, despite the fact that they may be different and have conflict of interests, both have rights and, definitely, common interests and responsibilities. This point of view recognizes the existence and interference of the element of conflict in industrial democracy, to which it also contributes the role of regulation of conflicting situations or even their transformation into beneficial ones for both the company and economy, through institutionalization of and mechanisms of solution to collective employment differences as well as corporatism.

Third, the **radical approach** considers that precisely because of the very nature of the capitalist society the clash of social classes do exist and is expressed in the work place. Within this framework, conflict appears inevitable, as the absence of a field of common interests between these two classes: that of capital and that of employment. Consequently, on the one hand, collective bargaining manipulates rather than solves conflict; on the other hand, an overall participation is dealt with as an element of employees' disorientation from their particular class interests.

1.2 Determining Factors and Trends in Historical Research

The beginnings of industrial relations as a scientific field can be traced back in the first work by the Webbs at the end of the 19th century. Of course, some other previous texts as those by the British Social Science Association can also be considered as research in industrial relations. During their early stage, labour relations were identified with industrial democracy, since the research of the same scientific field began fifty years later (Daskalakis, 1989a, p. 73). From Marx to the Webbs and Commons and until the end of World War II, the questioning on issues that are nowadays considered as part of the field of industrial relations that are focused rather on theoretical questions that dealt mainly with labour movement and trade unions.

During the period that followed, the point of relative interest was bifocal: industrial peace and industrial conflict. From 1930 to 1960 various researches were carried out into the structure of trade unions, the structure and the operation of industrial relations in individual industries, political activities of trade unions and into collective bargaining in industries as well as in private and nationalised companies. In the 1940s there was a great variety of studies in Europe and, more specifically, in the United Kingdom (UK), most of which were based on theoretical constructs from finances and political sciences and attempted to analyse "whatever was relevant and was offered easily" (Daskalakis, 1989a, p. 73). From the 1950s onwards, a clear shift of research focus from trade unions to collective bargaining occurred and, at the end of the same decade, there was a particular turn to theoretical issues. At the same time, specialities such as industrial sociology and psychology came to being and the Human Relations School (HRS) started being adopted by European researchers, with the result that some issues that traditionally interested the research of industrial relations were ignored. During the following decade, more specific and effective efforts for the development of a theoretical framework of the field were made (Daskalakis, 1989a). More specifically, the Oxford School became known – with basic proponents Flanders and Bains – and focused its research on the group rather on the employee as an individual. Meanwhile, in the USA industrial relations started being studied as a special scientific field from World War II onwards. It was about 1945 that the first appeals for an interdisciplinary approach to industrial relations were made.

Until roughly the end of the 1950s, special emphasis was placed on the examination of processes and outcomes of collective bargaining. However, during that entire period, a variety of studies used various theoretical analytical forms, "borrowed" mainly from political science and sociology in Europe and from finances and psychology in the USA. Nonetheless, none of those studies seemed to have contributed substantially to the formation of a specialised general theory, something that happened a bit later at the level of inductive theories (Daskalakis, 1989a). More specifically, in 1958, Dunlop's Systems Theory appeared, giving the spark for a wider problematization on the definition and the focal point of labour relations. Later and more specifically about the middle of the 1960s, came to light the approach of organizational behaviour, which also approached labour issues from its own particular point of view. At about the beginning of the 1970s, issues on which the research interest was focused were: industrial democracy, collective bargaining and social contract (Daskalakis, 1989a, p. 73). At the same time, research in Europe was influenced primarily by sociology, whereas in the USA various existing general paradigms in the field of social sciences shifted the research focus on the employee as an individual (Daskalakis, 1989a).

Basic factor in the formation of the European research into industrial relations that determined the direction, physiognomy and its features was the controversy over industrial relations as an independent discipline. There were researchers who insisted that the field did not constitute an independent discipline and hence there was no need for a general theory to be formulated. On the contrary, they claimed that it was an umbrella field that incorporated many disciplines. That view was supported more in the USA. However, this view was not the only element that differentiated the research in these two geographical areas of the planet. In the USA, psychology and finances were adopted more as research background, whereas in Europe it was sociology and, more particularly, specific case studies. At a European level, the research covered a variety of theoretical approaches to labour relations. At the beginning of the 20th century, the institutional approach emerged among economists of the time.

Much earlier there had been the classical Marxist view that considered that industrial relations come out of relations of production. Later, pluralist view came to fore, according to which there are conflicting but interdependent interests between management-employers and labour force. Of special importance was Dunlop's Systems Theory which focused its attention on actors, context and a body of rules that act upon, influence and regulate employment relations. Finally, some theories based on social sciences came out and tried to explain the changes in processes and results of collective bargaining (Daskalakis, 1989a).

At the same time in the course of European research into labour relations and from a historical point of view, both the "traditional opposition" between industrial relations and the approach to "behaviour in organizations" were recorded. However, the most serious factor in the formation of the characteristics and the content of the research into industrial relations at a European level may have been the process of a series of studies that resulted from the interest of governments and the need for a policy making. At that point, what featured was the experience from the UK that was relevant to the creation and the operation of a series of institutions (Donovan Commission, 1965–68) that were connected with the course of the research. It could therefore be claimed that, at a European level, the research in its course had as general features the range and the variety of approaches and the study of the field of industrial relations. That was the result of a web of interrelated factors as the controversy over whether this field is a discipline, the wide problematization on the need for a specialised general theory, different scientific backgrounds and views as well as the absence of specific commonly acceptable strategy. Thus, the research – given its casual connection with policy making – made mainstream features: the empirical orientation, the pragmatic and applied nature and the pluralist institutional approach, with emphasis on procedural and institutional aspects (Donovan Commission, 1965–68).

The serious lack of a theoretical framework has repeatedly been an issue for the researchers of industrial relations; for this reason, the issue of the formation of a theory has been a principal issue for the last decades. Thus, to cover this gap – that is, the lack of theory – many efforts have been made, of which some being more or less successful; some have widened and some have narrowed the horizon and the object of industrial relations. The questioning that has been developed up to now on the formation of theory is really as vast as important theory itself is for the existence of industrial relations as a discipline. A systematic effort to form a theory of labour relations was made first by Dunlop (Dunlop, 1958). Indeed, Dunlop's theory can be considered as one of the most important ones, since its theoretical proposition has been the "mainstream paradigm" and the core of modern respective scientific problematization. The evaluation of Dunlop's theory can be of special importance; first, within the framework of the overall research features of labour relations and from a historical perspective; second, when compared to other competitive or supplementary theoretical constructs and their ability to interpret real phenomena; and, third, within the wide scientific debate to what kind of contribution this very theory has made (Dunlop, 1958).

In the entire historical course of the research into industrial relations, there have been serious differences in approaches. European research, as already mentioned, was based mainly on sociology and inductive qualitative method, whereas in the USA the research was based on economics, psychology and inductive quantitative method. The different scientific points of view and backgrounds have been expressed through specific theoretical constructs on which various studies were based. The first efforts to study issues that are nowadays considered that they belong to the field of industrial relations are date back to Marx up to the end of World War II and focus primarily on issues on political and trade-union activity of the collective formations of the working class (Blain and Gennard, 1970, pp. 389–390). From a historical point of view, the Marxist approach is mentioned first; this approach examines work and employee both individually and collectively within the framework of a more general analysis of the capitalist system, productive relations, work distribution, dominant opposition of capital-work and leads to the "expectation of" a revolution for a radical social transformation. However, among the pioneers[1] of industrial relations are considered, on the one hand, in the UK Sidney and Beatrice Webb, on the other hand, in the US John Commons[2]. At the end of the 19th century, the Webbs' studies were the first complete contribution to the issues of industrial relations. These writers became renown in international bibliography from their two monumental works, *The History of Trade Unionism and Industrial Democracy*, of which the latter refers to trade-unionism, as a form of collective action and power of the employees, whereas the former refers to the development of British trade unions (Blain and Gennard, 1970, p. 389). The Webbs – inspired by Marx, although they were closely connected with the traditional Marxist point of view, as far as

1 The aforementioned writers were directly involved in industrial relations matters at the time; for example, Commons was a member of the Commission on Industrial Relations in the US from 1912 to 1915, whereas Slitchter was an expert in labour and management issues and worked in many private and public agencies.

2 Many writers contributed to the study of industrial relations. In addition to the abovementioned writers, Jacob Hollander, George Barnett and Summer Slichter at Harvard University (after 1930) are also considered as pioneers in the field. Dunlop, 1958.

its background is concerned – differ greatly from this, as they considered that the transition to the socialist society is more a result of a progressive development than of a revolution. In their work, these writers describe trade unions as a formation, which, by mediating employees' demands, are transformed into a collective will and a demanding, trade-union and political power. This collective will and power, through collective bargaining that is an alternative regulatory mechanism, is crystallized in rules, and result in settlements and regulations that condition work relations that are a product of this collective process of correlation of powers (Flanders, 1968, pp. 1–2) It is within this framework when employees are organised collectively are more powerful (Webbs, 1902, pp. 35–36) – rather when they bargain individually with their employee, a process in which the employee is impotent and becomes a pray to market forces. The Webbs set off the process of collective bargaining as the means with which, *inter alia*, trade unions achieve their main objectives, that is, how to maintain or improve employees' living conditions.

But if the Webbs were the pioneers of industrial relations in the UK, J. Commons was the pioneer of industrial relations in the USA and represented the institutional tradition, rejecting the traditional approach of classical economists and the view of work as a commodity in the market; he focused mainly on the collective action. Many years later, two schools of thought came into being: the School of Human Relations and Taylorism or the School of Scientific Management. On the one hand, the School of Human Relations appeared within the context of industrial sociology. This school put special emphasis not on individuals but on employees as a group as well as on the convergence of objectives between employers and employees. This approach dealt particularly with the issue of labour satisfaction – which, being dealt with as an outcome of a "prudent management" – was considered that it could lead to high productivity.

On the other hand, Taylorism, that is, the School of Scientific Management put emphasis on two issues: first, on the research into the employee as an individual, and, second, on the claim that there is no need for the existence of trade unions. This view tries to intermingle economic motives with techniques of industrial mechanics, so that a better way of organization of the work is generated, aiming to achieve high productivity and through this labour satisfaction. These were the first theoretical constructs on which a series of studies and a large part of research (Webbs, 1902, pp. 35–36) were based. The "genuine", however, research into industrial relations that focused its interest primarily on the study of collective formations and inclined to regard "conflict" both as inevitable and beneficial, appeared in a later period. A little later, the approach to organizational behaviour emerged. Having its roots in the School of Human Relations and

Scientific Management, this approach dealt with the issue of conflict – the most important among the labour issues – as a disruptive but also as an avoidable element (Webbs, 1902, pp. 35–36).

After World War II, industrial relations began to be dealt with as a particular scientific field, the nature of which imposed interdisciplinary study of and research into the interpretation and comprehension of its phenomena (Webbs, 1902, p. 48). At this point, we will be focused on Behrent and Barbash's approaches, who in their effort to define and describe industrial relations, claimed that industrial relations need to be studied as a separate discipline. J. Barbash (1964, pp. 66–78) considers that industrial relations consist of four elements: rationalism of the company, the sector of organization, people's irrational behaviour and the values of the wider society (Barbash, 1964, p. 66). These components of industrial relations, since they concern social and cultural models, affect employees' processes of decision-making and management and widen essentially the range of industrial relations out of the narrow industrial and labour environment to the wider politico-economic and social field (Barbash, 1964, pp. 71–72). On the one hand, rationalism refers to the effort of the company to maximize profit (Barbash, 1964, pp. 66–67) as well as to impose bureaucratic methods of organization and management on the labour force. On the other hand, irrationalism of management is expressed with the tendency to adopt meta-bureaucratic methods, whereas that of employees is expressed both as an effort to resist and avoid of the employer's control which is imposed with the methods of management and organization and as a different conceptualization of the value of work as much from employees as from the management and employers. Finally, the intense conflict is deterred due to the compromise to which both parties resort and because of both parties' willingness to achieve their objectives (Barbash, 1964, pp. 68–71).

Attempting to define industrial relations to a great extent based on quotes, definitions and views of teaching materials, Behrend (1963, pp. 383–394) held the thesis that two trends were being formed. Whereas the first trend, coined as "industrial relations", refers to collective relations, organised and disorganised or informal groups, which are involved in the performance of work, the second trend, together with the above-mentioned collective dimensions, co-examines individual relations, something that makes this approach the more comprehensive of the two. For this reason, Behrend proposes an approach to industrial relations which, based on this comprehensive version, would take into consideration the internal and external conditions of the company and would cover all formal and informal (individual and collective) mixed relations, as it suits to an independent discipline that Behrend himself aspired industrial relations to become (1963, pp. 383–394).

In the 1950s, the research into industrial relations showed a rapid development. In addition to the fact that the centre of research interest began to be shifted onto collective bargaining – the most characteristic of which were the cases of theories set forth by N. Chamberlain (Blain and Gennard, 1970, pp. 390–391) and A. Flanders – a whole series of researches did follow through which a lot of valuable efforts were made so that a general theory that would be able to lend theoretical and methodological framework to industrial relations is formed and transform industrial relations from a field of study and research into an independent discipline (Blain and Gennard, 1970, pp. 390–391). Other valuable efforts were those by J. Dunlop and, later, by Laffer as well as by Clegg and Bain. Nevertheless, of particular importance there were two contributions to the formation of a general theory of industrial relations. At a European level, it was the so-called Oxford School (Clegg, 1975, p. 309) and J. Dunlop's systems theory that determined to a great extent the theoretical and methodological model that has been the mainstream model in the field of industrial relations for the last fifty years (Daskalakis, 1989a, p. 71).

R. Hyman, a distinguished Marxist theorist in industrial relations, has directly argued about the pluralist approach. More specifically, Hyman has pointed out and insisted on analysing the issue of the employee's "freedom"; a freedom with double significance: "freedom" to work or not to work and freedom from the means of production. After industrialization and urbanization, while – as Marx first claimed, people have been alienated from the land and, at the same time, are not householders of capital or the means of production – are "free" to work or not to work in the capitalist production; that is, they have the freedom that is mainly an one-way street, to sell – as every merchandise is sold – their working force in the labour market for a wage in order to ensure that they have enough to live on. This working force will be sold against compensation and will be utilized in terms determined by the powerful side of this bargaining, that is, capital. On the other hand, employees – as they are "free" from the means of production, with their work on means of production of somebody else's property – produce goods that will be sold as merchandise in the market, with result their exchange value being greater than the value of their use. At the same time, the employee's working time is divided into the paid one – during which the employee creates value equal to the needs of reproduction of working force – and into the unpaid one – during which a surplus value is created and is reaped by the capitalist. As this situation is the foundation of modern industrial relations, these cannot be studied, claims Hyman – who is consistent with his Marxist origins – overlooking the nature of capitalist society and capitalist way of production (Blain and Gennard, 1970, p. 389) that determine the modern form of work, supplying society and industrial relations with conflicts that are related to and derive from the structure of production relations.

One further feature of the research and, consequently, of the scientific context within which Dunlop's theory was developed and elaborated is the wide exchange of opinions and ideas on the necessity of a general theory, the different opinions of individual researchers and the entire theoretical schools on this issue as well as on how all these points of view are connected with the hypothesis of the existence of industrial relations as an independent discipline. This situation that includes a diversity of opinions even on the very nature of industrial relations, because of its particular importance, is proclaimed an element that should be objectively highlighted. It should be noted that the thesis that industrial relations are not an independent discipline but a field of scientific study was often supported by researchers. There have been characteristic cases where the absence of a general theory was considered an inevitable fact that was due to the lack of specific identity of the object of industrial relations or that the absence of theory is not only a fact but also a situation desirable as industrial relations are simply an art; that is, there was a situation that was characterized no only by the lack of theory but also by the existence of negative views, since there was a record of researchers' negative inclination for their least involvement in theoretical discussion. Given this context, it shouldn't come as a surprise that the gap at the theoretical level was being reproduced. Nevertheless, the existence of a theory is decisive for the existence of a discipline, since it is only this that ensures its two decisive components: its cohesion, which is reflected in the identity of its object (of study) and its particular methodology (Daskalakis, 1989a).

At the same time, however, there were lots of researchers that acknowledged the importance of theory and placed emphasis on its necessity. For example, Flanders' position was explicit: "the use of theories of other disciplines has never aimed to provide a complete picture of the nexus of institutions of particular field" (Daskalakis, 1989a). A similar position took H. Behrend: "each discipline has approached the field with its own emphasis and biases, using its own tools, methods and linguistic properties. In my opinion, this has led to a "poor communication over the borders". Consequently, it shouldn't come as a surprise the fact that the discipline of industrial relations uses methodological tools of other disciplines, since, from an epistemological point of view, communication among disciplines and their methodologies is desirable.

The view that denied the need for a general theory of industrial relations and considered them simply as field of study including other disciplines created problems. The implementation of various incoherent with each other methodological tools, values and affairs leads at best to a picture of diversity, heterogeneity and absence of internal cohesion in industrial relations. It potentially constitutes a source of competition among disciplines, causes fragmentation in the discipline and restricts greatly the researcher since s/he is practically not in a position to know the variety of problematization and conclusions of other disciplines. Industrial relations need "their own theories, their own models and systems" (Daskalakis, 1989a); they need "a general theory of interdisciplinary nature" (Daskalakis, 1989a) and such an effort was made by Dunlop with his systemic model. From the above-mentioned references it is conspicuous that, from a historical point of view, the absence of a general theory has been a major feature of industrial relations, a fact that led to a host of heterogeneous approaches with different starting points, methods and objectives, the fragmentation of the field, and, finally, to the controversy over the very same nature of industrial relations as a discipline (Daskalakis, 1989a).

1.3 Dunlop's Systems Theory – Criticism and Creative Responses to it

That was the scientific context within which Dunlop's theoretical proposition, the "systems theory of industrial relations" was developed. Dunlop used the theoretical concept "system" that had often been used in the past both in Europe and in the USA, as a *"device"*. Of course, it is a fact that as a lot of other researchers so Dunlop was influenced by Parsons' views on the interaction between the general social system and the economic sub-system. Under this influence, industrial relations were considered as a sub-system of a wider social system that, however, operates with similar reasoning to that of economics. As it is also supported by the proponent of the theory, these two systems are not the same. Nevertheless, both have an analytical content related to modern industrial society and, finally, both systems overlap each other. There is, however, a serious distinct element: each of these two systems is the object of a different discipline - that of economics and that of labour relations respectively – which also has different analytical tools.

The system of industrial relations consists of three groups of agencies-protagonists-actors: employees and their collective representation, employers and their collective representation, the state and government-owned agencies related to labour issues. These agencies interact in an environment consisting of technology, market of products and labour and power relations in the wider society. The interaction among these agencies-protagonists-actors takes place "under the rule of a commonly acceptable ideology, which results from the very same interaction among the agencies; that is, it is created totally by the system and, in its turn, it contributes to preserving its cohesion. As Dunlop himself clarifies, "the system" is possible to be referred to different from each other levels of industrial relations, which however in no case can be selected arbitrarily. On the contrary, they will have "a reasonable degree of cohesion as well as a formal and essential independence from each other" (Daskalakis, 1989a). Even if they are likely to vary totally or partly in their internal components, these systems at various levels cannot be differentiated in their formal structure and internal logic.

The target of this system is to create rules commonly acceptable from both parties – that is, employers and employees – so they can manage the labour community. The total "nexus of" these rules, as the proponent of it calls and delimits it, is the general focus of theoretical analysis of the discipline of labour relations. Considering that in a dynamic society rules "will change constantly as a consequence of changes in the environment" (Daskalakis, 1989a), Dunlop stresses that "duty of the theory is" (Daskalakis, 1989a), specifically, "to interpret why rules change responding to external changes that influence the system" (Daskalakis, 1989a).

As far as the formation of a theory is concerned, other efforts were also made, being however, very different from each other regarding the point of view adopting on the object of industrial relations. For example, Laffer suggested that a major issue in industrial relations is bargaining relations between employers and employees. According to criticism that has already been made against it, a serious fault of this theory could be the omission of norms that come in the form of customs. At this point, it should be claimed that Laffer's theory seems similar to Dunlop's systemic model, despite the fact that the former criticises the latter in that Dunlop's model ignores informal sides, customs and practices. It is a theoretical and methodological problem that narrows the point of view and hence the object of industrial relations, which, however, is still intensified more in the framework of Laffer's theory, which also ignores the rules that are set unilaterally by trade unions, employers or the state (Daskalakis, 1989a).

Another effort was made by Margerison. According to Margerison, the focal point of the study of industrial relations cannot be other but "the nature and the development of conflict" (Daskalakis, 1989a), which is illustrated at two levels: first, at the level of the company and, second, outside of it. Margerison sees interfering conflicting factors and three types of conflict being shaped: the distributive conflict; the structural conflict; and the human conflict, which are possible to be solved through another three distinctive types of processes that correspond to: collective bargaining, the structure of social system and to management respectively. It is conspicuous that such an approach – rejecting the proposition of systemic model to get focused on "determining rules" – gives emphasis on conflict. Nevertheless, the problem with this approach seems to be in the fact that, although it takes into consideration sociological factors and gives more emphasis on them than on the systemic model, takes economics and the rest of variables for granted (Daskalakis, 1989a).

As important for the formation of the theory of industrial relations it is acknowledged the contribution of a good number of researchers who belong to and are expressed through the so-called Oxford School. The tendency observed in this School is towards "normative-regulating institutions of labour". This approach, as much as that by Dunlop, focuses on the existence of rules of industrial labour relations, but advances even more distinguishing, on the one hand, the rules between procedural and essential, and, on the other hand, the labour normative regulation and settlement between internal and external. The two approaches, that of Oxford School and that by Dunlop, are often considered as a theoretical framework, while they have – despite their similarities – serious differences. Moreover, Dunlop's approach gives special emphasis on the role of wider influences on determining rules, whereas the Oxford School focuses on the processes of formation of the rules through collective bargaining, which it considers a prominent political institution. It is clear how much stress this last approach lays on political factors and dimensions of analysis, rather on economic, sociological and ideological factors, the importance of which, on the contrary, Dunlop overstresses. These can be considered as the most important theoretical trends, each of which seems to have a sore spot, preventing industrial relations from achieving a round universal and complete view of the field of study (Daskalakis, 1989a).

Dunlop's work is the first complete effort to form a general theory of industrial relations which can be universally accepted. Despite the critique that – rightly so – it has attracted, on the one hand, Dunlop's work has set its limits analytically, cohesively and systematically – widening indeed – the field of study and research of the discipline. On the other hand, it has given this field of study a theoretical and methodological framework (Blain and Gennard, 1970, pp. 392–393), ensuring that those elements of industrial relations that are the essential components of the epistemological and methodological identity of an independent discipline are in this framework.

In Europe, Dunlop's theory – either because of its wider point of view, and hence its analytical possibilities, or because of its Parsons' origins – became an object of study of a wide exchange of views among the researchers of the field. The point that attracted most criticism is related to the difficulty in determining the "system" within the framework of a systemic theory, since it is the most essential point of the theory under discussion. Dunlop attributes a classificatory character to the term "system". Thus, Dunlop's systems theory uses a conceptual construct, “the system”, to classify factors that determine the rules of industrial relations, at three levels: at the national level, at the level of the industrial sector and at the level of the company. The systemic approach proceeds to call into play the concept of “system”, despite the fact that many times it has been claimed that the use of the particular concept in industrial relations is inappropriate, as it is a conceptual category mainly structural, which simply describes the relations between the parts of an entity, being unable, however, to interpret the dynamics of its behaviour. Most criticisms are drawn upon the lack of an explicit definition of the concept of system by Dunlop. Blain and Gennard claimed that the introduction of “system” that Dunlop attempts to provide industrial relations, since it is not accompanied by his own definition of it, is very likely to have problems inherent to Parsons’ analysis. They considered that, within the context of this theoretical scheme of the study of social systems, there is an explicit analytical uncertainty. Dunlop’s theory has been reproached that “it inherited” serious epistemological problems from Parsons’ analysis of social systems. Parsons, being rooted in Pareto’s analysis, tried to create a concept from the viewpoint of social action (Blain and Gennard, 1970, pp. 392–393), with regard to the study and the description of the social system, which, however, had as result the introduction of an analytical ambiguity to this concept.

This aforementioned discussion about Dunlop’s terminological ambiguity is likely to emanate from the simultaneous use of the term “system” both as a scientific research tool and as an empirical phenomenon that needs to be studied and explained. Since the concept remained unclear from Dunlop himself, the instigator of the systemic theory, it is claimed that the problem will indeed be maintained as for how much the concept of “system” is used as tool of a scientific research or as an empirical phenomenon that requires an explanation. If “system” is considered and defined as a sum of concepts that are dynamically interconnected with each other rather than with external variables, then industrial relations can be studied as a system that is structured from internal variables connected with a common reference specifically to industrial relations. From this point of view, system is more a conceptual construct than an empirical phenomenon, and its study should be focused on human behaviour (Blain and Gennard, 1970). A number, however, of distinguished researchers, such as Gill, Eldridge and Bain, distinguishing Dunlop’s origins from Parson’s theory, postulated the use of the concept of system in industrial relations simply as an analytical model and classificatory system and not as a theoretical framework or an element of social action (Blain and Gennard, 1970).

The questioning in the “weaknesses” of Dunlop’s approach does not seem however to end here, but certainly, because of its origins, it also goes to how it deals with concepts such as ideology and conflict. More specifically, Dunlop asks as follows: "certain societies are characterized by a high degree of intensity and conflict and by one high tendency of disputes and radicalism. Thus, in social relations and experiences that such societies have created, these characteristics are likely to be reflected in the workplace", and adds that he attempts "to release the problematization of industrial relations from bias, if not from the negative aspect of labour peace and conflict" (Blain and Gennard, 1970). One more point that, in connection with the previous one, attracted criticisms, concerns ideology which Dunlop dealt with as a decisive factor that interferes at two levels. First, at the individual's level, where it determines not only the role of each agency but also the individual's opinion on the role of others, and, second, on a wider scale, where it interferes directly with setting rules (Blain and Gennard, 1970, pp. 398–400), without, however, being explained sufficiently how this precisely happens. This specific thesis expressed by Dunlop, that is, the issue of both conflict and ideology, to the extent, that the former escapes from the view of the systemic model and the latter internalises the former, was objected to by many researchers.

Noted is the position that Hyman took, who characteristically, claims that: "the issue of the existing structure of property and control in the production, which are inevitably sources of conflict, are omitted as external elements of the research", "if one accepts Dunlop's definition of the system of industrial relations is as one shares (with him) conservative sociologists' traditional reference to the issue of class" and, finally, that "all the interest of Dunlop's approach falls onto how the real framework of social relations is stabilised". Moreover, critical towards Dunlop is Eldridge too, who considers that "in sociology the sources of conflict and collaboration of social method and instability should have equally valid claims in questioning". Furthermore, as far as the issue of conflict is concerned, Eldridge claims that "even where there are common values, these encompass the element of conflict", a fact that is confirmed into practice with examples such as the recognition of the right to go on strike, which is an institutional recognition and regulation of conflict. Similar to Eldridge's critique is that by Clegg and Bain, who consider that out of Dunlop's theory comes that a system of labour relations is "naturally static inclined to be completed and is forced to continue it". Therefore, it is conspicuous that the range of criticism and its orientation towards the subject are connected with the particular view that every perspective holds for the sociological issue of conflict in modern industrial societies and its origins. Hyman's perspective connected with the traditional opinion considering that conflict has its origins in capitalist relations of production and the dominant opposition between labour and capital, practises a criticism that essentially leads to rejection (Blain and Gennard, 1970).

On the contrary, other writers' approaches lead to a perspective that combines a critical analysis with a creative synthesis, a fact that in itself is positive independently from the theoretical and analytical sufficiency of the approach. For example, Eldridge considers Dunlop's reference to "power" as a starting line for the study of conflict. Through the analytical view of flexible approach, Clegg and Bains as well as Margerison consider that Dunlop's systems theory deals only with the resolution of conflict ignoring the conditions of its genesis. In other words, they claim that there is an emphasis only on rules but not on the processes that produce them, whereas rules and processes are both of equal analytical value (Blain and Gennard, 1970).

The point, however, that is in fact pivotal, since a criticism of wide range is directed towards and converge on it, concerns behavioural variables that seem to be completely absent from Dunlop's framework (Blain and Gennard, 1970). The basis of criticism at this point is not only the researcher's subjective analysis but also Dunlop's thesis that "the variables of human relations should be limited to a smaller role in each complete explanation of the behaviour in industrial relations" (Blain and Gennard, 1970).

As far as this factor of behavioural variables is concerned, Heneman comments that "Dunlop omits major theoretical schemes and variables from social and behavioural sciences and, more specifically, from psychology" (Blain and Gennard, 1970). Somers adds the omission of human relations and that of interactions among small groups, to conclude finally that "Dunlop has nothing to say for such complex things" (Blain and Gennard, 1970) Behrend's criticism of the same subject insists on claiming that "there is no dividing line between various kinds of relations, between personal and collective, formal and informal, that is, that there is a consistent interaction between them" (Blain and Gennard, 1970). Clegg and Bain consider that variables as the behavioural one cannot be omitted *a priori* because in a lot of cases they are of particular importance. Thus, if they are omitted, it is not possible for a "complete analysis and explanation of the behaviour in labour relations" to be achieved, as Dunlop would wish. Blain and Gennard claim that Dunlop sees these institutions interfere with the system of industrial relations through a view that stresses their structural rather than their dynamic dimension. So, to the lack of "processes" there is added the absence of behavioural features, customs and practices of "non-codified rules", which are factors determining in their turn their "processes".

Finally, there are still some points of the systemic model, such as the emphasis on the importance of the environment, which is an advantage of this approach over, for example, the School of Human Relations, which, as it claims, uses agencies-protagonists in a "vacuum". Nevertheless, Dunlop has suffered from a negative criticism of a diametrically opposite view: the dominance of environment in his theory. There has been, of course, certain other argumentation according to which Dunlop's systems theory is unable to explain changes of wide scale and be tested empirically (Blain and Gennard, 1970).

The criticism of Dunlop's theory appears in general to converge with the following main points: First, regarding the definition of system. The use of "system" as a framework of analysis and classification has been considered as a choice that finally releases the system from potentially restrictive elements of origins connected with the theory of social action, while at the same time it enables it to operate as a "means of classification" of mass of events relevant to the study of industrial relations" (Blain and Gennard, 1970). The second point of the converging criticism concerns the absence from the model of those elements and factors that could add a breath of dynamism in the system. This view points out that, despite the fact that Dunlop uses the term actors-protagonists – a term that internalises the dynamism of a particular energetic dimension – instead of the more passive term "participants" and at the same time gives emphasis on dynamic factors as the environment, finally, his systemic model does not seem to escape from being over-dominated by "structure" and from being static, as well as it suffers from the total absence of any dynamic dimension (Blain and Gennard, 1970).

However, Dunlop's theory, apart from being a common place (: *locus* or *topos*) of criticism, has also been the starting point and background for forming other theoretical frameworks. Kerr, Harbison and Meyers are a good example of this, since, in their common effort, they extended Dunlop's work by shifting the emphasis from the theoretical to the operational dimension of the system. Of important value it is also Kerr's work, and, more specifically, this part of his criticism on which he insists that Dunlop's theory cannot be empirically confirmed. This happens because Kerr applied the theoretical part of Dunlop's systemic model to a lot of cases. There are also, however, other cases of researchers. Flanders, who, it should be noted that, first, as the main exponent perhaps of the Oxford School, differs significantly from Dunlop, and, second, that he uses the theoretical concept "system" in a different way from Dunlop, exclusively to define the institutional structure of British industrial relations and to show "how these were disrupted". On the contrary, Dunlop considers "system" as an entity. Nevertheless, both Dunlop and Flanders consider that, while industrial relations are being studied, it should not be taken into consideration all the relations in the organization but only those that are related to labour (Jackson, 1985, pp. 1–5) implying that this is the reason why the study of unstructured or informal relations should be omitted. Even if there are important differences in Dunlop's Systems Theory,

Flanders' theoretical construct, which considers industrial relations as the study of institutions of normative regulation – settlement of labour – that is, the study of institutional relations in the organization – is a work based on Dunlop's theory (Daskalakis, 1995a). This is, however, legitimate to say if the more general physiognomy of the so-called "Oxford School" is taken into consideration.

Oxford School, which resulted from the research and teaching work of a number of scientists in the respective university (Jackson, 1985, Ch. 5, p. 114), shaped the so-called institutionalised approach in the study of industrial relations – which, together with Dunlop's Systems Theory and its revised version – is the mainstream theoretical and methodological paradigm in the field today. Whereas, however, Dunlop places special emphasis on economic and social factors and, more particularly, on technology, on the job market, social status, ideology (Blain and Gennard, 1970, pp. 396–397) and on the wider correlation of forces within the society, the Oxford School focuses on the importance of political and institutional factors, power and political processes. Within these two frameworks, of decisive importance for the formation of rules in industrial relations are, in the case of systemic theory, wider influences, while in the framework of the Oxford School collective bargaining (Daskalakis, 1989a) that are dealt with as a primarily political institution (Blain and Gennard, 1970, p. 396). Thus, collective bargaining and especially their rules are proclaimed by this school as the decisive factor of normative labour regulation[3] and, more generally, that of normative institutions of industrial relations, which are the focal point of research interest of the field within the framework of the Oxford School.

Afterwards, Walker, in his effort to develop a framework for labour studies, also adopted Dunlop's approach to a "set of rules" and a "system", thus leading industrial relations closer to a complete theory. Kochan, McKersie and Capelli maintained a critical perspective on Dunlop. They consider that there are "abnormalities" that "cannot be explained with the existing theories" in modern industrial relations, and stress the importance of the role of management (Blain and Gennard, 1970). Nevertheless, they admit that they do not refute Dunlop; instead, they claim that there is a need for a simple "shift of paradigm" from usual changes they occur at regular intervals in the context of every discipline (Daskalakis, 1989a).

---

3 Within the context of the Oxford School of thought, labour regulation is divided into internal and external, depending on the existence or not of conditions of autonomy for the change of rules, without exercising any external influences. Furthermore, regulatory institutions and rules can be divided into substantive and procedural.

Finally, there are two serious theoretical constructs that are quite similar and tend to improve the integration, within the framework of Dunlop's systemic model. The first theoretical construct is that by A.N.J. Blain and J. Gennard who, having analyzed Dunlop's theory, postulate two essential improvements that multiply the research and methodological value of the systemic approach. The first improvement concerns the integration of the variable of "processes" that is possible to offer a dynamic dimension to the system. The second theoretical construct concerns the acknowledgment of psychological influences and the integration of behavioural factors in the system as elements that determine the very same variable of "processes".

The other theoretical construct is connected with Clegg and Bain and their effort to improve Dunlop's systems theory. More specifically, they postulate: "first, there should be included in the study of industrial relations structural and behavioural and "non-structural" variables and relations, institutions, rules, but also the processes of regulation of work issues, both the solution and the generation of conflict situations so that, finally, the study of all aspects of regulation of labour issues is achieved, which is also the object of industrial relations" (Daskalakis, 1989a). Second, Clegg and Bain consider that if there is a system of industrial relations, this should be surely an "open" system, so that it operates as an analytical tool and not as a category that has been drawn upon the approach to "social action"; and, third, although the two researchers insist that their work does not depend on the concept of system, they admit that their theoretical construct is structured and based on Dunlop and Flanders (Daskalakis, 1989a).

To sum up, it can be said that Dunlop's systems theory has made an essential contribution to industrial relations and, more specifically, to the development of their theory. Although there are critiques that they have already been presented, whose main points concern specific and real weaknesses of Dunlop's work, however, the systemic theory managed to make a contribution to the development of a theory of industrial relations, and this is acknowledged by every side and perspective. As a result of Dunlop's work, it can also be considered the creation of a theoretical core for the study of the field as an independent discipline. In the systemic model there are elements that lead to the departure from the controversy over the very same existence of industrial relations as discipline. This theoretical scheme has become the general framework for the inversion of the fragmented and heterogeneous image that the study of industrial relations has presented historically. The theoretical content and analytical framework not only unify the issues, the object and the methodological tools of industrial relations, but also enables them to get further enlarged, compared to the limits and the restrictions of the past and to other theoretical constructs. Finally, despite the fact that Dunlop's theory has weaknesses, it presents tendencies of integration and is susceptible to improvements that can lead to constructs that are sufficient for analysing and explaining of phenomena and particularities of industrial relations in modern industrial societies (Daskalakis, 1989a).

1.4 Modern Research Directions

Nowadays, an important factor is that the data as practised in industrial relations are connected with the development of new phenomena, "modern abnormalities", as characterized, and concern an abundance of factors. As such phenomena can be considered the declining course of trade unions, the decline of their power or even their complete absence from certain kinds of companies, the changes both in the role of management and in those values that determine its policy, as well as summoning up of new kinds of organization of employment, alternative experimentations and new forms of labour relations. The particular points on which the research interest is focused are culture and values, since they seem to determine important phenomena of labour relations both at national and interstate level (Daskalakis, 1989b).

These new elements in the practice of labour relations and the experience from the historical course of the research have raised awareness of certain research issues; that is, it is not possible for these either to be exclusively dictated by methodology or to be arbitrarily selected. Their selection should be made based on a particular strategy connected with undertaking a unified general theory being interdisciplinary in nature and confirmable empirically in the character. Such an effort, at the level of the formation of a theoretical process can indeed provide a suitable theoretical framework that can cover all the phenomena of practice of labour relations and also offer essential methodological tools for their analysis. Thus, since the development of the theory influences or even determines the research direction and the selection of its issues, a very important direction in modern labour research should be precisely an effort at this level (Daskalakis, 1989b).

Dunlop's systems theory combined with the improvements that it is susceptible to has widened the horizon of industrial relations and has already been the "mainstream paradigm". And this occurs because the interdisciplinary approach which brings into play the methodological demand for a universal view and a compromise between traditionally conflicting views on "industrial relations" and the theory of "organizational behaviour", despite the fact that at first there are unbridgeable contrasts, since, on the one hand, "labour relations" focus their interest on collective entities, whereas, on the other hand, the "organizational behaviour", with origins in the schools of scientific management and human relations, focus on the relation of employer-employee as individuals-private citizens. Central point of differentiation of these two approaches also constitutes a conflict, a component that, on the one hand, the approach of behaviour in organizations considers it as disruptive and, thus, avoidable, whereas, on the other hand, industrial relations considers it as inevitable and sometimes as a useful one. Thus, nowadays the relative appeal for integration goes both directions. And this is a central point for the direction of modern research, provided that it can offer a theory with the essential quality and necessary dimensions can cover, analyse and understand modern industrial relations. Despite the fact this objective seems difficult to be achieved, there have already been important efforts made towards this direction (Daskalakis, 1989b).

All the aforementioned effort is connected with the general sense that labour relations should widen their horizons. Within this framework and context, one more research direction is that of comparative studies. Since comparative research consists of the study of the same or similar phenomena in different countries, the promotion of such a kind of research can offer answers to a lot of and serious issues. An important question within the framework of comparative studies concerns the existence or not of certain country models in industrial relations and what specific elements give them such a role. In this sense, country models and, consequently, in the centre of interest of labour researchers were: Great Britain at the end of the 19th century, Germany before World War II, the USA in the 1940s and the 1950s, Sweden after the 1960s, Western Germany after the 1970s, and, finally, Japan after the 1980s. However, it should be totally clear that the nature and character of comparative studies are not to be used to implement policy making and the practice of labour relations in a mechanistic fashion from country to country. Comparative studies are not possible to operate as a system of "import-export", because very simply every policy can turn out to be effective only within its own specific context in which is also embedded. Nevertheless, the conclusions of the comparative research can be used for the evaluation of policy in various countries (Daskalakis, 1989b).

In the current economic situation, the usefulness of such a kind of studies is also connected with the issue of convergence or divergence of the systems of social, economic and political organization. During the 1960s, there was the impression that between the systems of the USA and the USSR there had begun to emerge a convergence, since under the impact of industrialization, the decisions in both countries seemed to be made by some bureaucratic elite, who were being exclusively determined by their own values. Today, the questioning of convergence of systems comes to the fore transformed. More specifically, since 1980

Shalev's convergence theory appeared, which based on Kerr's *Industrialism and Industrial Man*, and developed a problematization about the potential convergence between developed and developing countries (Daskalakis, 1989b).

The most serious problem perhaps within the framework of comparative research is that there are inherent methodological problems, and the main issue is what can be usefully comparable. So, although comparative studies up to now have been very empirically oriented, if they are well processed they can draw useful conclusions with precision, comparing "methods and ways with which particular operations of labour relations are carried out in various countries" (Daskalakis, 1989b). In this way, it is possible that these studies can contribute to and help in comprehending better a variety of phenomena at a national level, making more valid generalizations and in participating in forming a theory of labour relations that can be empirically tested (Daskalakis, 1989b).

A third dimension of modern research into labour relations is connected with phenomena as the drop in massiveness of trade unions, which is at a level much lower than that in the 1920s, as well as the fact of the division of bigger and more traditional companies in the north and smaller and newer companies in the south. In the latter's case, there is the phenomenon of absence of trade unions, which, whereas in the past it was ignored as depending on the individual's space, nowadays there are serious reasons that this phenomenon is integrated in and interpreted by labour relations. This is a phenomenon that is encountered in a number of heterogeneous companies, that is, from big and powerful to widely heterogeneous companies or in other companies of no importance. Although this phenomenon is not as widely widespread in Europe as in the USA, however, today it appears in Europe too, mainly in small companies or in those of high technology that cover an important rate of employment of employees. Of these companies, the former are referred to in the bibliography as a new – *laisser faire* type of companies; they cover a big part of the employment and have been influenced by the levels of the increase in unemployment. According to estimations, their prospects do not inspire any optimism. Suffice to say that since the end of the 1980s (and in four years) roughly one third (1/3) of these companies had already shrunk at 50% and that, according to predictions and calculations of the period – which were confirmed later – most had no chance to develop in the following decade (Daskalakis, 1989b).

The second category is about companies of high technology that employ small percentage of labour force. As far as this category of companies is concerned, the discipline encounters certain problems of their methodological classification, to which it should be made a reference even parenthetically. Nevertheless, we believe that three elements are of vital importance for distinguishing this kind of companies, the elements of which can also constitute criteria: the existence in these companies of: (a) a high percentage of research expenses; (b) technological innovations; and of (c) specialised professional and scientific administrative, technical and research staff. Regarding these companies, the respective research has shown that they have an unprecedented dimension: that of complete absence of trade unions. There are also other findings related to the paternalistic character of their management, the existence of new forms of organization of labour in their production and the fastest rate of distribution of their phenomenon. Within the research framework, these last conclusions do not seem to be particularly reliable, since there have been lately elements of the opposite direction. Thus, the undisputable conclusion is the absence of trade unions and until now this phenomenon cannot be combined positively and exclusively with any other elements and data (Daskalakis, 1989b).

It can be claimed that nowadays there have already been formalised three directions of particular importance in modern research into labour relations, overlapping each other. The effort at the theoretical level can offer the analytical framework and methodological tools so that the study of comparative aspects of labour relations and, particularly, those of the development of new practices can be done. At the same time, the research at the level of comparative studies can essentially contribute to understanding better the details of various phenomena, making valid generalizations and thus to forming a theory. These different perspectives, the nature of labour relations, relative discussions about theory, the need for a research strategy that is connected with the hypothesis of the structure of theory, various scientific approaches and backgrounds, the connection of research with the needs of policy making have determined the issues and the content of research. Nowadays, both levels at which scientific issues are raised in relation to the nature and the theory of labour relations from a more general and specific point of view, as well as the pressure that recent developments exert undeniably on practices of space shape a tendency of integration of theoretical approach and, hence, a widening of horizon of labour relations, methodology and that of research directions.

1.5 Usefulness and Dangers of Comparative Studies

The comparative analysis of labour problems and labour institutions paves the way for solutions different from those that we have known in Greece. It allows us to avoid the erroneous handlings of other countries and it gives us ideas of how to solve some of our problems. It is, consequently, encouraging that Greek labour researchers (lawyers, sociologists, economists etc.) and people in charge of professional organizations of employers and employees show interest in the international experience in labour relations of various origins and scientific backgrounds. It should certainly be stressed that in very few countries of Europe a similar "opening" up to the international experience with that observed in our country can be sensed. Being characteristic of small countries – as Greece – the "opening" up to the international experience facilitates a progressive harmonization of national social systems (Daskalakis, 1995a), which should accompany the integration of the European economic and monetary union. Thus, in order for a comparative study of labour relations to be useful and efficient, it should be carried out with a critical view and complete knowledge of traps that wait for the scholar who studies foreign institutions superficially (Daskalakis, 1989b).

Two are the major dangers that the comparative scholar (a comparatist) encounters. The first is related to terminology. The difficulty here is not only of translation, that is, how to transfer and render a term from a language into another. It lies mainly on the different signification that the same term in different societies and cultural context carries. Indeed, the concepts of a national system of labour relations are charged with values, experiences, mainstream ideological preferences operating in a given society. The only way for this difficulty to be overcome is to reflect both in what this term refers to and the particular role it plays in the operation of the given national system. As Otto Kahn – Freund, the wise scholar of labour law and labour relations in Europe, has observed there is in the field we deal with a "magic of" words, in which one should resists with all one's might if one wants to avoid the trap of dangerous parallelisms and unsuccessful transferences. The second danger lurking in the course of comparative study is the known tendency of many researchers to decontextualise an institution or a mechanism or a legal rule and proceed, based on this limited base, to make a comparison between two national systems without taking into consideration the social, economic, legal, political and cultural context in its entirety. The existence of an institution, a mechanism, a legal rule in a society is not accidental and, consequently, is not automatically transferred. It is the fruit of multiple and complex local conditions (historical, geographic, economic, social and other) and corresponds to particular characteristics of a society in which it was first born and to the correlation of social forces within the given society (Daskalakis, 1995a).

Chapter 2: The Development of the Labour Market Policy between 1980 and 2000

2.1 Modernization of the Labour Market in the light of Employment Guidelines and the European Union Enlargement

Despite the fact that Astable macro-economic environment and economic growth prevailed in the European Union (EU) since the early 1990s, the rates of unemployment have not shown any improvement. Unemployment is still at high levels. Therefore, planning and implementation of a comprehensive employment policy, supported by a highly effective internal market, will form the basis for a sustainable development and create a new dynamic climate of credibility which is necessary for a recovery in terms of employment. Significant factors for the creation of conditions of sustainable development are the improvement of competitiveness and, thus, of growth, along with preservation of Social Cohesion.

Modernization of the European labour markets is of quintessential importance. It is an urgent process that will enable us to support these new national employment policies that are compatible with the Employment Guidelines, agreed on in the Extraordinary Jobs Summit that took place in Luxembourg. Modernization of labour markets and restructuring of their operation should be based on:

1. the formation of a stable and dynamic macro-economic environment, which will favour the increase of employment;
2. structural changes in labour relations;
3. a fair process of social adjustment; and on
4. the Extraordinary Jobs Summit in Luxembourg that decided to take a second – after Amsterdam – significant step towards Social Europe. After this historical decision, European countries have a lot to do.

Nowadays, the EU is moving forward with common targets and common policy directions. So, the creation of new jobs will not be recorded in the peoples' conscience as a declaration of good intentions but rather as a clear and visible target that is to be attained by specific policies and reliable prospects. It is obvious that, along with national economic policies, progressive convergence and harmonization in the European Monetary Union (EMU) initiative as well as EU specific policy priorities can build the Social Pillar of Europe. Given the political conjecture at the economic and social level in the EU, its enlargement with the adhesion of 10 Central and Eastern European countries gives them the opportunity to work on adapting the 'aquis communautaire' (i.e. 'the Community acquis' or simply known as 'acquis') to economic and social level, thus creating a social protection and security safety net for their citizens. By implementing policies aiming at 'mature' crucial issues, the EU member-states will be able to prepare their economic and social institutions and, especially, their social partners for a new balance between social justice and economic effectiveness. Social Dialogue is a predominant element towards such a target. It should be fully understood that the role and duties of social partners increase and become more and more important that social policy should be exercised at national and community level. Social partners should try to acquire the necessary information, as soon as possible, and establish structures of scientific-technical assistance and documentation so to be able to carry out reliably the new duties and obligations they undertake.

In Greece, Social Dialogue on 'Development – Competitiveness and Employment' was held and carried out with great success, ending up with an 'agreement of trust between the Government and the social partners concerning the move towards 2000'. It was an important process for both the Government and social partners. The three parties agreed on important measures that our Government undertook to introduce and implement. A summary of that agreement in English was available to the participants in that Summit. In the context of the enlarged European Union, it is important for the states to develop their own Social Dialogue structures and activities in such a way that allows social partners to prepare for their effective participation in all processes involved. In the whole process, public authorities share a great part of responsibility for the attainment of these goals, because they should offer various opportunities to employers' and employees' organizations for bilateral or trilateral Social Dialogue. The implementation of community legislation in the social field requires internal ability to implement correctly legal standards and the "aquis communautaire". A basic element to develop that ability is the appropriate and prompt preparation of the public sector and public institutions. The legal "aquis communautaire" covers certain issues of labour law, such as employment conditions, health and safety at work, equal opportunities between men and women, free movement of employees, social security co-ordination etc. However, the impact on the entire society is an issue that should be addressed by national authorities. I should underline the impressive 10 years' experience on negotiations between the Government and Social Partners, provided by the Hungarian Ministry of Labour. Such political choices and governmental practices could ensure the easier, friendlier and without social frictions integration of the "aquis communautaire" in national law. It could also guarantee modernization of the labour market, achievement of higher levels of employment and social protection, higher living standards as well as economic and social cohesion and solidarity, which are requirements for a welfare society.

The Greek government has been very sensitive about the unemployment problem for long time now. In 1996, it introduced: the new structural policy for employment reflected in a 1996 law – that is law 2434/96. So, it created a solid background that is today enabling us to adapt the EU Employment Guidelines. With our participation at a European level, we took all the necessary information. So, policies that they did not diverge from the guidelines we have been following. The national policy for employment has been trying to give a combined solution. It tries to promote development, restructuring of economy as well as social protection and social cohesion. Nevertheless, a great effort needs to be made so serious problems, such as unemployment, could be dealt with. Same policies may function differently in different socio-economic environments. Thus, the steps we should take may be risky.

All the society must be activated: local government, entrepreneurs, employees and the unemployed. Our national policy is based on the following pillars:

- a plan for macroeconomic stabilization, investment initiatives, entrepreneurship, modernization of small and medium sized enterprises and restructuring of the technological and productive base of the Greek economy;
- promotion of a strong investment stream in the private and public sector by creating new opportunities for production and employment, especially from small and medium sized enterprises and self-employment;
- adoption of institutional changes in economy and the labour market which could make socially acceptable the flexible work patterns;
- implementation of integrated policies;
- employment must be the crossroad where various structural policies are met. Therefore, we promote active rather than passive measures, investments in human capital through life-long education and vocational training, restructuring public and private sector as well as the regulation for the new forms of employment;
- identification of special target groups such as young people, long-term unemployed and disabled employees in Risk of Unemployment; and
- restructuring finances with the aid of EU programmes so employment policies are assisted more effectively.

Promoting flexibility in the labour market and organizing work in the productive process favour the development of enterprises, entrepreneurship and the increase of employment as well. The Greek Government has been taking a faster pace to this direction. Its policy includes measures for:

- Self-employment for the creation of new jobs in dynamic sectors;
- Small and Medium sized Enterprises (SMEs) Networks;
- reinforcement of vocational training programmes for the personnel of private enterprises;
- integrated interventions to prevent unemployment of the employed in enterprises under reconstruction;
- special programmes for middle aged employees who are in danger of unemployment; and
- a crucial point in the policy for adaptability, that is, a web of measures that concerns radical restructuring of public enterprises.

To this direction, there has already been a legal framework and in many public enterprises the administration has already been in a process of a dialogue with trade unions in order to take its final decisions.

Small and medium sized enterprises (SMEs) are the backbone of the Greek economy. The development of entrepreneurship mainly concerns these enterprises. In this sector the Greek Government's objectives are to:

- develop new enterprises;
- reinforce the viability of the existing enterprises;
- favour entrepreneurial initiative through self-employment in new dynamic sectors; and to
- reinforce employment through local development, which will be assisted by entrepreneurship and social partners' participation. In Greece, unemployment is unevenly distributed among sexes, ages and geographical areas.

The problem is related to the weakness more in finding than in losing employment. The distribution of unemployment benefits is not a solution to the problem. Long-term unemployed people are 58% of the total unemployment, whose 75% are young people. In order to face young people's unemployment, the programme "Young people in active life" is promoted. Through this programme all young people up to 27 years old, according to their studies and skills, are offered at least one opportunity for professional inclusion, combining training, professional experience and employment or the opportunity to obtain working experience through their direct inclusion into employment or self-employment. The programme covered 50,000 people in 1998 and 200,000 people during the three years of its operation. 25% percent of long-term unemployed concerns 15,000 people from 28 up to 64 years old. Each had the opportunity of a two-month trial employment and then a 16-month employment, containing supplementary training and working experience in local government, in social services or in private agencies. To combat long-term unemployment integrated packages of measures are also implemented in case of personnel reduction and laid-offs, while laid-off people older than 58 years old have been assisted to get a pension.

Our main priority was to improve employability by introducing active policies to the labour market and develop all necessary structures so to assist such policies. The active participation of the social partners at national and local level was a basic precondition for employment recovery. In this field there was an important development. The social dialogue for "development competitiveness and employment" ended with a "confidence pact towards 2000" between the government and the social partners. The experimental implementation of local employment pacts in seven areas which were under deindustrialization and faced high unemployment rates, the function of specialized information offices for employers and unemployed and the establishment of "a special fund for the employment and the vocational training", funded by employers' and employees' contributions, were important efforts that supported the measures facilitating labour market inclusion, which the Greek Government promoted: lifelong learning, continuing adaptation of skills, improving the quality of the school system and technical vocational training have been priorities for the Greek Government. Main element of our policy is the coordination of primary education with vocational training and lifelong continuing education. In Greece, equal opportunities between sexes have been established institutionally for many years now. In practice, however, there have been many inequalities, which, as in many European countries, originated from the cultural background.

The current policy of the Greek Government for "equal opportunities" is defused to the whole spectrum of measures we implement to combat unemployment and create employment opportunities. Our macroeconomic effort and structural policy aims at high and sustainable development, competitiveness and at decreasing unemployment. Its primary aim was to increase employment.

2.1.1 Labour Market Modernization

2.1.1.1 First Pillar: Inclusion in the labour market

In Greece unemployment is unevenly distributed among sexes, ages and geographical areas. The problem is more related to the weakness in finding than in losing employment. The distribution of unemployment benefits is not a solution to the problem. Long-term unemployed people are 58% of the total unemployment, 75% of which are young people. In order to face young people's unemployment, the programme "Young people in active life" is promoted.

Through this programme all young people up to 27 years old, according to their studies and skills, are offered at least one opportunity for professional inclusion, combining training, professional experience and employment or the opportunity to obtain working experience through their direct inclusion into employment or self-employment. The programme covered 50,000 people in 1998 and 200,000 persons during the three years of its operation. 25% percent of the long-term unemployed concerns 15,000 people from 28 up to 64 years old. Each had the opportunity of a two-month trial employment and then a 16-month employment, containing supplementary training and working experience in local government, in social services or in private institutions. To combat long-term unemployment integrated packages of measures are also implemented in case of personnel reduction and laid-offs, while laid-off people older than 58 years old have been assisted to get a pension.

Our main priority for improving employability is to activate policies for the labour market. Nowadays, we are developing all necessary structures so such policies are assisted. Such structures are:

- The integrated information system in manpower employment organization (National Organization for the Occupation of the Work Force or OAED in Greek);
- Special interchangeable card for many uses by the employed and the unemployed;
- Employment Promotion Centres (KPA in Greek);
- The National Observatory of Employment (EPA in Greek);
- The National Institute of Labour (EIE in Greek); and
- The National Resource Center for Vocational Guidance (EKEP in Greek).

All these structures assist the active measures that can motivate the unemployed for their inclusion in the labour market. Social partners' active participation at national and local level is a basic requirement for the recovery in employment. In this field, there has been an important development. The social dialogue for "development competitiveness and employment" ended with a "confidence pact towards 2000" between the Government and the social partners. The experimental implementation of local employment pacts, the function of information offices for employers and unemployed and the establishment of "a special fund for the employment and the vocational training", funded by employers' and employees' contributions, are important efforts that support the measures facilitating the labour market inclusion which the Greek Government of those days promoted.

2.1.1.2 Second Pillar: Entrepreneurship

The small and medium sized enterprises are the backbone of the Greek economy. The development of entrepreneurship mainly concerns these enterprises. In this sector the Greek Government's objectives are to:

- develop new enterprises;
- reinforce the viability of the existing enterprises;
- favour the entrepreneurial initiative through self-employment in new dynamic sectors; and to
- reinforce the employment through local development, which will be assisted by the entrepreneurship and the participation of social partners.

The measures promoted include:

- a modernized "development and growth" Act;
- special treatment for the areas with intense unemployment problems;
- simplification of administrative procedures;
- development of scientific and technological parks;
- reduction of tax barriers;
- experimental implementation of Local Employment Pacts (TSA in Greek);
- technology transfer and employment incentives for young researchers and technicians;
- subsidies for partial coverage of the non-wage labour cost;
- subsidies for projects modernizing small and medium sized enterprises; and
- an establishment of three new credits: a monetary institution for the assistance of small and medium sized enterprises.

In Greece wherever there are many small and medium sized enterprises, they make a significant contribution to the development of entrepreneurship and the reinforcement of employment, two crucial initiatives that the summit of Luxembourg decided to assist:

- The first is an action plan of the European Investment Bank, which will be activated to support small and medium sized enterprises.
- The second is an outcome of an agreement between the European Parliament and the Commission and includes restructuring of the budget so that small and medium sized enterprises are reinforced and, in return, they will create new jobs.

2.1.1.3 *Third Pillar: Adaptability*

The promotion of flexibility in the labour market, the work organization and in the productive process favors the development of enterprises, the entrepreneurship and the increase of employment as well. The Greek Government is taking a faster pace to this direction. It has been preparing a new act to regulate the following issues:

- expansion of part time employment in Public Enterprises;
- reorganization and rearrangement of working time;
- limitation of overtime;
- regulation and social protection of atypical employment;
- gradual reduction of the employment of high income pensioners;
- enactment of Local Employment Pacts;
- reinforcement of the labour inspectorates in the Ministry of Labour; and
- adoption of the Directive 93/104 E.C of the Council concerning the organization of working time.

The policy of Greek Government in this sector also includes measures for:

- Self-employment for the creation of new jobs in dynamic sectors;
- Small and Medium sized Enterprises Networks;
- reinforcement of vocational training programs for personnel of private enterprises;
- integrated interventions to prevent the unemployment of the employed in enterprises under reconstruction;
- special programmes for middle aged employees who are in danger of unemployment; and
- a crucial point in the policy for adaptability is a web of measures that is planned for the next three years, concerning the radical restructuring of public enterprises. To this direction the legal framework has already been in place, and the administration of many public enterprises has already been in a process of dialogue with trade unions in order to take its final decisions during next months.

2.1.1.4 *Fourth Pillar: Equal Opportunities*

In this pillar there are included policies to reconcile work and family life, counteract sex discrimination and to facilitate socio-economic integration of persons with special needs. The policy of Greek Government in this sector is defused to the whole spectrum of measures that is implemented so that unemployment can be combated and employment opportunities can be created. However, special measures have been taken to assist mothers and persons with special needs to keep their jobs.

On the one hand, the measures taken for mothers focus on:

- establishment of women's entrepreneurship information centre;
- improvement of baby-sitting services;
- provision for all day kindergarden; and on
- provision for mobile units for child care.

On the other hand, the measures for persons with special needs include:

- preparation of a new act that offers special protection for the employment of persons with special needs and for members of families with more than four children;
- through integrated interventions, the National System of Social Care has had as its target:
  - to include persons with special needs; and
  - to promote institutions for the vocational training and the special technical support of these groups.

2.2 Institutional Interventions in Labour Relations

At an institutional level, if it is considered that the statism of the 1980s and the then governmental interventions had as result to "turn the scales" in favour of the working side as far as the regulation of labour relations is concerned, and that, on the contrary, the policy of the period between 1990 and 1993 – which oscillated between voluntarism and neoliberalism – aimed at the inversion of the previous status quo, then it should be supposed and recognized that since 1993 the state with its interventions – which seem to correspond to the model of democratic negotiating neocorporatism – has shaped an institutional balance in labour relations between governmental intervention and collective autonomy; a balance which allows the operation of the labour market to be based on steady social protective but also, at the same, flexible legal frameworks within which labour relations move and act.

Thus nowadays, there are *inter alia* standard rules concerning:

- employees' Hygiene and Safety Conditions (Law 1568/85);
- the operation of Employees' Councils (Law 1767/88);
- free collective bargaining (Law 1876/90);
- equality of two sexes in labour relations (Law 1414/84);
- protection of special categories of persons (Law 1648/86); and
- arrangement of the work contract and the employee's compensation.

There are also regulations that anticipate the use of flexible forms of employment and organization of working time, and, more specifically:

- establishment of part-time employment, with a written agreement between employers and employees;
- implementation of the system of four (4) sets of employees by enterprises of continuous operation, with the employees' consent;
- establishment of shift work (Paragraph 7, Article 13 Legislative, Decree 2961/1954);
- possibility of enterprises to operate continuously, provided that they employ special personnel so they are occupied in two consecutive shifts for twelve hours a day, if they are to operate on Saturday and Sunday; and
- there are also new shops hours of operation that provide great potential of flexibility.

It should be noted that important initiatives have been undertaken and put into practice successfully. Institutions and processes of social dialogue between employees and employers or even the state have been developed. The operation of the institution of councils of employees and free collective bargaining has been strengthened. Thus, the interested parties themselves – that is, employees and employers – can regulate not only the wages but also almost all the issues that concern them.

Institutions of conflict mitigation and resolution of labour differences have been developed, such as: the new Organization for Mediation and Arbitration (OMED), new reliable processes of mediation – the mixed system of the complementary character (neither absolutely voluntary nor obligatory) of arbitration – and new processes of public dialogue. Moreover, the Economic and Social Committee (OKE) was established, which is an institutional body of social dialogue conduct for all great social issues at a national level, while there has been appointed a Tripartite Administration in the National Organization for the Occupation of the Work Force (OAED) in which the State, employers and employees participate. Of particular importance is the development that has been observed over the recent years and the good climate that there has been cultivated between employees and employers, a fact that not only has led to biennial national general collective labour agreements but also has ensured conditions of labour peace for the last few years.

2.3 New Structural Policy on Employment

Considering unemployment as one of the most important problems of the Greek society, the State – after having consulted the Economic and Social Committee

(OKE), that is, the institutional body of the social dialogue conduct at a national level – developed a new structural policy on how to face unemployment and how to increase employment that was included in the National Multiannual Employment Programme which was submitted to the European Union.

This policy concerned the implementation of a "Package of Measures", where the structural characteristics of the Greek job market, the international experience and the five key areas of Essen European Summit for the promotion of employment had been taken into consideration.

Since 1993 the policy on the labour market has been focused mainly on modernizing institutionally various sectors and enhancing professional training, by establishing specialised institutions, such as the National Institute of Labour (EIE), the National Accreditation Center for Continuing Vocational Training (EKEPIS), National Resource Center for Vocational Guidance (EKEP) and the National Observatory of Employment (EPA).

The aforementioned institutional structural interventions are included in a constituted multidimensional policy of employment for a better operation of the labour market and for combating unemployment. The structural and, consequently, long-term character of the social phenomenon of unemployment has led to measures that go beyond traditional policies on employment that have been ineffective. They concern both actions for the use of new opportunities offered by rapid growth and development and the promotion of technological changes in the productive processes for Employment, Growth and Development as well as for the Quality of our life.

Law 2434 in 1996 was the corollary of the implemented new structural policy on the confrontation of unemployment and the increase of employment. With this Law, what was sought, through a series of structural character innovations, was the transformation of long-term unemployment into a long-term potential for every citizen to have access to employment. In other words, a turn into new active policies on employment was taken. Basic elements of the new structural policy on employment are:

- placing emphasis not on passive but rather on new social and active measures;
- encouraging new jobs creation, while businessmen are subsidised;
- interconnecting effectively actions of professional orientation and / or vocational guidance with training and the labour market;
- facilitating employees' professional and geographic mobility;
- taking special measures for unemployment in geographically, developmentally and nationally sensitive regions;
- developing vocational counselling services;

- modernizing, decentralizing and establishing the tripartite constitution of the administration of the National Organization for the Occupation of the Work Force (OAED);
- institutionalizing and implementing special additional accompanying social measures for the laid-off in case that enterprises are restructured;
- making social partners participate actively in political decisions on employment at local and regional level;
- upgrading and extending Employment Promotion Centres (KPA in Greek);
- studying and following up systematically the labour market and those factors that influence it;
- connecting training with employment with new special programmes; and
- integrating the computerised system of briefing labour supply and demand and making a direct and effective collabouration of Centres for Vocational Training (KEK) with the Employment Promotion Centres (KPA), aiming to link training with employment.

Finally, innovation of particular importance has been the intention to utilize new institutions such as the National Observatory of Employment (EPA) and the Employment Card for all the domestic and immigrant labour force, with which there could be a complete depiction of the situation and changes in the labour market as well as control and restriction of the black market and illegal immigration.

2.4 Social Dialogue

2.4.1 Institutionalization of Social Dialogue at National Level

The idea of social dialogue, the institutionalization and encouragement of which the State had promised has henceforth acquired "flesh and bones" through the operation of institutions that have been come out to serve it. The first important step for the support of social dialogue that has been taken in the past few years has been the creation of its "back bone", that is the Law on collective bargaining and the OMED (i.e. Organization for Mediation and Arbitration) on the prevention and the resolution of conflicts and collective differences. Then, the establishment of Economic and Social Committee (OKE) was a next step that essentially generalised the use and the value of social dialogue. The OKE constitutes the main central institutional body of social dialogue conduct that was founded with Law 2232/94. It constitutes an institution that corresponds to the Western European and Scandinavian model of social collaboration. For the last decades in most Western European countries several institutions have been established and operating, which are differentiated as for:

- the composition (for example, they can be bilateral or tripartite or they include independent experts);
- the Chair (for example, the Body can be elected or can be appointed by the Government);
- the responsibilities (advisory or decisive);
- the types of issues it deals with; and
- the outcomes (in certain cases of such a type of bilateral or tripartite composition bodies it is possible that they may seek either to form a "general" consent round an issue or to make a binding agreement (for an example, social contract or even regulations, such as collective labour agreements or clauses which, after they have been agreed between employers and employees, are legislated afterwards by the Government).

Thinking of establishing the OKE began to be developed around 1986. After two failed efforts to establish such a type of bodies – one at the end of 1970, when the Council of Social and Economic Policy (SKOP in Greek) was created, and another one in 1982 with the establishment of National Council of Development and Productivity (ESAP) – nowadays we have already had in use the OKE. The OKE is a Private Entity Law (NPID in Greek), whose work is the formulation of a justified opinion on issues of particular importance that are related to labour relations, social insurance, tax measures and to the more general socio-economic policy. On the aforementioned issues the expression of the OKE's opinion is obligatory before corresponding laws are to be voted for. The OKE's opinion is asked by the responsible governmental body every time. The OKE consists of a Chair and other members that come from three groups.

The first group consists of: the Association of Greek Industrialists (SEB in Greek), General Confederation of Professional Graftsmen and Traders in Greece (GSEBEE in Greek), National Confederation of Hellenic Commerce (EESE in Greek), Union of Greek Banks, Pan-Hellenic Union of Hotel keepers, Union of Greek Ship owners, Association of SA Technical Companies and LTD.

The second group consists of third degree employees' organizations: Greek General Confederation of Labour (GSEE) and Greek Supreme Civil Servants' Confederation (ADEDY), whereas the third group also consists of third degree organizations of farmers and cooperatives – that is, of GESASE (General Confederation of Agricultural Associations in Greece), PA.SE.GE.S (Pan-Hellenic Confederation of Unions of Agricultural Co-operatives) – representatives of consumers, Central Union of Municipalities and Communities of Greece (KEDKE), Technical, Economic and Geotechnical Chamber, representatives of free professionals, lawyers and doctors. In order for the OKE's operation and work to be facilitated, committees from its members are set up. There is also an Executive Committee. The expression of OKE's opinions is followed by a specific procedure determined by the law. The OKE has one (1) Chair and three (3) Vice-Presidents, one from each group of members. It also has a Secretary-General, who is the senior officer of its services.

Today, the complexity, the particularity and the interweaving of economic and social problems impose more than ever before a convergence through the utilization of a dialogue of substance and the responsible attitude and participation of all productive and social factors so that critical choices can be determined. These choices primarily differentiate how the political power is exercised, how mechanisms and processes of formation of social, legal and political choices are changed and show how innovations influence substantially the political constitution of society per se are imposed. In modern pluralist societies the traditional way of exercising political power through unilateral decisions has not been acceptable any more. The OKE and social dialogue, generally, are basic choices that should be fully encouraged and developed. Within this framework, social partners will cease to play shrinking and traditional roles. By undertaking these new responsible roles, they will be able to shape and make jointly important choices, get upgraded and become basic factors in the modern socio-political scene. Social dialogue – including social negotiation, associated universal confrontation of economic and social demands at all levels, agreements, disagreements – is the only process to weave convergence, find socially acceptable solutions for all the critical aspects of the Modern Greek society. Every effort should be made so that policy-making for development, modernization, social cohesion, central options for employment, training, working time, labour relations, labour market can become the object of a fruitful without prejudices and predetermined results tripartite social dialogue

2.4.2 Developments in the Practice of Social Dialogue

In recent years the process of social dialogue in our country has been determined by many parameters. An important factor has initially been the fact that the state "bureaucracy"- whereas until recently it was unable to accept this new development – has already started to adapt to new data introduced by social dialogue both in decision-making processes and in the institutional and political constitution of society. Nevertheless, of particular importance was a rampant practice followed by some social partners – which had been exerting a negative influence on social dialogue though. Furthermore, a decisive role played the peculiar way that social dialogue was understood by the civilian personnel of the Greek parties that resulted repeating reviled social practices in the name of social dialogue. Consequently, nowadays, any reasonable criticism about the effectiveness of social dialogue and the basic institution that serves it – that is, the OKE – cannot lead to question either the institution or its decisions.

Since 1993 the state has promised social dialogue. It has pointed out the need for development of an extended framework of participation corresponding to modern needs. It has announced in advance the operation of institutions of equal participation that would be the "backbone" of social dialogue, the field of "negotiation" of social contract and the safety pin guaranteeing a democratic, transparent and reliable course of development and modernization. In other words, it has proposed institutions that can ensure social agreements, development and social cohesion; that is, institutions that alter essentially the traditional mechanisms of decision-making as well as generally the institutional and political constitution of the Modern Greek society. These institutions are not the development of a doctrine; they are rather a framework of socialization of the political power and incitement of the society, which is an alternative model to that which, deifying the market in other national cases, sought to impose a general deregulation with unilateral decisions.

Every time the course of social dialogue is influenced decisively by the situation that prevails in the political limelight of each country; that's why in recent years Greece has shown some features that have reflected the picture of a modern struggle between two mainstream trends. On the one hand, the trend that has been seeking to encourage social dialogue and the institutionalization of the social are great issues that all responsible social partners ought to face jointly, so that every citizen's participation in generating and distributing the national product is ensured. Towards this direction social dialogue is the basic "key-choice" that the State has decided to encourage, develop and utilize at each level in the past few years.

Social dialogue, social negotiation, the interconnected and universal confrontation of economic and social problems and requests at all levels are the only process to form socially acceptable solutions for all critical issues of the Modern Greek society. This alternative process of regulation of socio-economic issues seems to be the most reliable from the outdated "recipes" both of statism and neoliberalism nowadays.

2.5 Collective Bargaining

Law 1876/90 "About Free Collective Bargaining" has introduced a series of important innovations in the institutional organization of the collective autonomy in Greece. More specifically:

- It has extended the implementation of collective bargaining. Thus, nowadays private sector employees, rural economy employees, employees in the public sector with a private entity law relationship and employees of the wider public sector are covered by the law. Furthermore, the new law covers employees based on forms concealing a relation of dependence.
- It has extended the object of collective bargaining and collective labour agreements (sse). So, whereas in the past the object of collective bargaining was practically only wages, nowadays, through this bargaining, the directly interested parties – that is, employees and employers – can have a universal supervision of issues of mutual interest and regulate all economic and social issues that concern them. Yet, beyond these important issues, they can also regulate other procedural issues regarding their in-between relations.
- It has been anticipated that collective bargaining is conducted by the "most representative" organizations, so that there will be as much genuine representation of collective interests as it can be.
- For the first time, four types of collective labour agreements have been anticipated: national, general, industry-based, occupation-based (national or local) and enterprise-based. Furthermore, with the provisions on the influx of collective labour agreements (sse), there have been institutional conditions of the development of a national system of collective bargaining with elements of decentralization, which is based mostly on industry- and enterprise-based collective bargaining, downplays occupation-based collective labour agreements, whereas at the same time it utilizes central bargaining that lead to the contract of National General Collective Bargaining Labour Agreements (EGSSE).
- The State compulsory arbitration has been abolished, which had been criticized for decades; new procedures and reliable resolution mechanisms and regulation of collective labour disputes were created. More specifically, it was anticipated the establishment of an independent body, the Organization for Mediation and Arbitration (OMED), the operation of an independent Body of Mediators-Arbitrators and, first and foremost, the use of mediation procedure, which is an extension and help rather than a substitution of collective bargaining, assisting the arbitration process by implementing a mixed system of arbitration that is neither absolutely compulsory nor completely voluntary. These innovations have provided the institution of collective bargaining in Greece with new potential, integrating elements from the experience of Western Europe countries. The important thing is that Law 1876/90 had been the first and only example of "Negotiated Legislation" in Greece by that time, which was eventually passed through the Greek Parliament – since all

interested parties and all political parties had agreed upon – in March 1990. The framework of collective bargaining established by Law 1876/90 responds to new needs and modern trends dictated by the recent European experience. This framework also meets most of the points raised in "The framework of social dialogue on the development, competitiveness and employment" conducted in 1997 and came to the "Pact of Confidence towards 2000".

More specifically, the fact that the whole system of collective bargaining of Law 1876/90 also utilizes National General Collective Bargaining Labour Agreements (EGSSE) serves the objectives of the creation of a "co-decided fiscal policy framework at a national level," the continuation of the EGSSE operation as a fundamental institution of social protection, guaranteeing the minima at the national level and the potential to widen the dynamism of EGSSE insofar as it establishes a framework of co-negotiation and co-regulation of all major issues that businesses and employees face, such as issues of reorganization of working time, part time etc.

Moreover, the fact that Law 1876/90 widens the scope of collective bargaining virtually in all matters of mutual interest of employees and facilitates the introduction of many innovations, such as clauses that would expand employment. The existing institutional framework rightly plays emphasis on decentralization – that is, on industry- and enterprise-based agreements, s.s.e. – the conditions of which prevail in the event of concurrence of the terms of occupation-based agreements, while – if there is a concurrence of industry-based with the occupation-based agreement, the more favourable to the employee regulation prevails. Industry-based and collective labour agreements (sse), as dictated by the European experience, are usually "pilot" regulations for similar businesses of a sector.

However, in the current context within which the phenomenon of restructuring is very usual, it does not always appear *en masse* in all sectors, but in many cases in individual companies, the European experience of "Concession Bargaining" and Agreements going "hand in hand" dictate that it should be useful to disentangle the power of enterprise-based and collective labour agreements (sse) from that of industry-based so that employers and the company's union are able to amend clauses and tailor them to the needs of the specific company. There can be a similar rationale so to both introduce a new type of Social Agreements that can be concluded by labour unions and local agencies of employers, especially, as far as the pockets of unemployment and regions in crisis and deindustrialization are concerned. This new form of agreement, if not introduced by legislation, will simply have a "debt effect". In any case, it is perfectly reasonable that legislative intervention in changing the institutional framework of collective bargaining should not be made but only with the consent of the interested parties. Moreover, the minimum protection of employees should be guaranteed by the EGSSE, and, therefore, clause of any kind of contract – that is, enterprise-based, occupation-based or local new type of agreement – should not include conditions worse than those in the EGSSE. Whereas, finally, concluded clauses related to employment, as, for example, introduction to flexible forms of employment, social work and their pay, should be such that they cannot compete with full-time employment and with its whole institutional system of protection as a whole, but they should only be complementary, meaning that there shouldn't be a generalized implementation of such measures.

The existing institutional framework of collective bargaining provides great potential. It restores the collective autonomy to its natural regulating dimensions. At a time that trade unionism is abating, if it is considered that the tendency of decentralization of collective bargaining is not a major advantage for trade unions, the central bargaining and the EGSSE can be an eminent institution of consolidation of social protection. More specifically, the utilization of central bargaining and the EGSSE can contribute to the formation of a National Social Agreement which will also turn out to be particularly beneficial for the Greek economy and enterprises within the framework of the implementation of the Convergence Programme. In other words, it will be proven to be a mechanism of "interconnected" and "universal" confrontation with great financial and social issues as well as a guarantee of the minimum limits of social protection. Consequently, the question in relation to all this problematization does not concern so much the state or the institutional framework in effect. On the contrary, it concerns primarily the interested parties that should make policies, which will give dynamism to the existing institutional framework of collective bargaining, and will utilize it to promote their collective interests.

2.6 Basic Choices of the Labour Market Policy

In our days, economy and society face two great challenges: on the one hand, how to increase in real terms the competitiveness of economy and enterprises, and, one the other hand, how to face unemployment and how to increase employment. These two are great challenges that concern both the employee and the businessman. These challenges are two important issues that can be dealt with together. Consequently, the labour market policy and labour relations should be supported both by the state planning and the cooperation between employees and employers. Apart from the social, such an orientation also has economic value since it ensures greater effectiveness in the operation of the market.

Basic element of this policy should be the utilization of a corresponding to modern needs widened framework of participation, with the first institution being the Economic and Social Committee (OKE), which can be the "backbone" of social dialogue, social agreements and convergences. In addition, another basic element of this policy is the attribution of a sovereign role to social partners within the context of the modern political and social democracy, the processes of social dialogue, the negotiation of modernization and the formation of Social Agreements. Finally, an equally important parameter of this policy is the full utilization of all potentials and the flexibility of free collective bargaining for the interconnected confrontation of financial and social demands at all levels, so that, within the scope permitted by legislative regulations, combined and co-articulated issues can be dealt with; these issues are such as: employment safety, further employment flexibility, the organization and the structure of employment combined with the decrease in working time and unemployment, the introduction of new technologies, the organization of labour, changes in labour production, increase in productivity, improvement of the collaboration of social partners and labour satisfaction, investments. Moreover, there is a whole series of other issues: those of finances, enterprises and those of employees, for most important of which a National Social Agreement should be signed.

Collective bargaining can be utilized so that the following issues can be regulated within the scope permitted by the law:

- A restriction of multiple employment in sectors with redundant labour force or even for employees and pensioners whose income exceeds certain limits;
- the encouragement of geographic and professional mobility;
- the establishment of special "solidarity contributions" from employers and employees with permanent employment, so that compensations, unemployment benefits and expenses for training and social support of the unemployed or individuals with precarious or discontinuous employment are covered;
- Agreements on reduction of working time instead of wage increase, when productivity increases, provided that, wage suffices, and there are specific commitments for creation of new jobs, of course;
- "Social plans", if enterprises are being reformed;
- Playing complementary role, the utilization of new institutions, such as Local Employment Pacts (TSAs), and the social work especial of young unemployed in work of social usefulness – as, for an example, old people's protection, cultural and educational excursions in the country, the protection of forest wealth, maintenance work of infrastructures and community space, etc. – for

symbolic payment or even in combination with training and professional orientation programmes;
- the specialization of the implementation of measures of active policies for employment;
- a further regulation of quantitative labour flexibility; and
- an emphasis on qualitative elements of the labour and production flexibility, productivity and its modernization, an emphasis on professional training.

As mentioned above, provided that the state has ensured fixed operation rules of the labour market, basic conditions of quantitative labour flexibility, effective mechanisms of achievement of social bargaining and convergences as well as a completed framework of structural policy for unemployment and active policies for employment should be met. Consequently, it directed the further action and its interventions, first, towards the institutionalization of measures and, more specifically, tax exemptions for the "reduction of non-wage labour cost" – especially for some vulnerable or marginal population groups as well as the adoption of an income policy aiming to portect employees' real income. The stabilization of economy and the approach of the convergence programme should be combined with a policy that would guarantee employees' and pensioners' real income, which has accepted powerful blows and, specifically, reduction at 19,5% of real earnings between 1984–1995. In 1996, private sector employees ceased seeing their income being decreased year after year. They got an increase that was above inflation. But for civil servants, who carried the bigger weight, regulations were made that guaranteed their real income and led to real higher increases in 1996.

Considering the experience of the decade 1984–95, contrary to the tactic of unilateral governmental imposition of legislative restrictions in increases, there was an effort for social dialogue and free collective bargaining to be utilized so that salaries and wages would be regulated, both in the private and public sector. The proposal that submitted – that is, the principle "projected inflation + national productivity" should be valid for the National General Collective Bargaining Labour Agreements (EGSSE) – was considered satisfactory. Furthermore, another particularly important direction of the modern governmental intervention is the re-adjustment of certain aspects of the institutional nexus of the organization of labour relations and the labour market so that the identified modern needs or traditionally existing abnormalities could be dealt with.

We live in an era of great changes and transformations. The intensified international competition, the rapid introduction of new technologies and the globalization of economy have been altering the technological, productive and labour model that we have known up to now. The new model that has been formed involves reversals in the structures of technology, production, employment, society as well as in the systems of labour relations, social insurance and professional and/or vocational training. Within this context, on the one hand, the difficulties of enterprises and economies increase, on the other hand, social achievements (social acquis) of previous decades have been destibilized. At the same time, some other traditionally existing "abnormalities" and informal or marginal situations in the labour market have occurred, which are latent phenomena whose extent depends on the size of the underground economy. They are informal forms of employment whose operation moves on the fringe of law or circumvent it with multiple negative social and economic repercussions for employees, insurance funds and for economy.

Thus, there is a *de facto* issue of changes in the institutional organization of labour relations and the labour market. It is not necessary that these changes may aim at deregulation or flexibility that involves a decline in social protection. On the contrary, they can aim to reset aspects of the institutional nexus of organization of labour relations and the labour market, so that this nexus, on the one hand, can cover informal situations, and, on the other hand, it can respond to the new production, technological and labour model, with specifications that will also satisfy the needs of enterprises so to be more competitive in the modern environment. Nevertheless, they should respond to the demand of consolidation of every citizen's social and labour rights, in a world of intensifying insecurity and uncertainty. Finally, if we consider market flexibility as a demand made primarily by enterprises today, the aforementioned data dictate that this is satisfied to a large extent. The existence of a stable legal framework of the operation of the labour market and labour relations means that the rules of game are "clean" and with duration, a fact that facilitates enterprises to decide upon adopting flexible policies that decrease the cost of labour factors.

The same result, more or less, has the existence of labour peace and the consolidation of confidence and collaboration between the parties that have been ensured by the recent EGSSE and the new mechanisms of conflict resolutions, which make the strike the utmost means, whereas the provisions in effect have already regulated certain forms of quantitative labour flexibility, as part-time employment, the 4th shift, working time management and overtime. Finally, the new law, 1876/90, on the collective bargaining provides new great regulatory potentials in the institution, a fact that strengthens the flexibility of Labour Law, since its flexibility goes with its conventionalization. At the same time, the whole nexus of measures of the new Structural Policy on Unemployment and Active Policies on Employment that are promoted for implementation strengthens substantially the potential to increase qualitative and functional flexibility and upgrade professional qualifications and the mobility of labour force.

2.7 Flexibility and its Regulation

2.7.1 Calling on for More Flexibility

For long time production and the labour market have been suffering, with continuously increasing rate and intensity, the repercussions of new international conditions that have been set and continue being developed by the globalization of economic relations. More specifically, their main feature is the need for providing terms of convergence into the relations between labour and capita; a need that is imposed by new conditions of competition. Further on, new technologies redefine employees' behaviour, with result the initiatives that new technologies require, the responsibilities they shoulder and the new organization they impose give new content in labour relations. Finally, changing needs in the market organization make necessary for a more flexible organizational structure in the personnel of enterprises, whereas the effort to satisfy consumption and other needs pushes the same employees in the search of new types of labour relations. Nevertheless, it should not be overlooked the produced social reconstruction of the class of employees, a fact that, on the one hand, facilitates the tendency to split interests and highlight individualised behaviour – with evident the development of "regional labour" in the form of home employment or freelancing – and, on the other hand, it disrupts their traditional cohesion and solidarity.

All these factors shape and determine a new situation in front of which the persistence in maintaining the traditional system of regulation of labour relations seems to be a clear quixotic affair; this means, that the relevant regulatory interventions should not be restricted only to regulations considering the employee simply as a contracting party, but they should rather be based on the employee's capacity as a member of the labour market, so to cover employment as a whole. Therefore, these regulations should form an elasticity (a flexibility) while dealing with labour relations, to a degree according to circumstances, so to become means of modernization; that is, employees' means of self-determination, with flexibility and variety of choices they are also provided with in their private life. However, in order for such an elasticity to become the means of modernization and not to become simply a refusal of what they have acquired, it should be accompanied by full consolidation of employees' fundamental rights, based on the principle equivalence of social protection, meaning that in order for social policy to survive it should be directed towards new forms of protection and new type of balance of interests, in such a way that social cohesion continues being the most fundamental term of the socio-economic development, supplied not from the traditional perception of incompatibility of interests between labour and capital, but from the modern idea of negotiation of conflicting interests in labour relations.

2.7.2 Regulation of Atypical Forms of Employment

In Greece, the state is the main source of labour relations law and the only unique and exclusive source of insurance legislation, except for few exceptions. Today, the modernization of atypical forms of work – such as, for example, project contracts, fixed-term contracts, availability, consecutive, independent seasonal, illegal work, sub-contract/housework (fason) and shiftwork – involves legislative interventions initiated by the state, which will create regulations where there are none – a lot of forms are completely unregulated, whereas it will supplement regulations, where required, or, otherwise, it will change totally. The framework of these legislative regulations should aim to subordinate atypical forms of employment, which are unregulated or insufficiently regulated, to the regulating field of social legislation (Labour and Insurance Law). Moreover, these regulations should be an integrated nexus of policies, aiming to generate, first, minimum guarantees for every employee in these forms of employment, second, the consolidation the "individual and social rights", (wages, labour conditions, safety, professional and/or vocational development, quality of labour life, and, third, the prevention of de-unionization of labour relations. Whereas, finally, these regulations should be the minimum at national level, which will guarantee employees' minimum rights, leaving some room for creation of conventional regulations, with collective agreements that will be flexible so to satisfy the needs of production sectors, regions or enterprises, without, however, affecting social, labour and insurance rights.

In any case, the critical issue is not the acceptance or the rejection of these forms of employment, but rather the formation of institutional safeguards with suitable specifications. Another critical issue concerns the environment in which these forms of employment will function; more specifically, what the context of labour market organization is as a whole. The whole intervention on the labour market regulation should be such so that neither to generate conditions of absolute inelasticity, which impede enterprises being the productive body of national economy, nor to create situations of complete liberalization and deregulation, something that would lessen the employees' negotiation power and protection in this. Finally, a important political issue is that a policy on atypical forms of employment should be accompanied by the promotion, on permanent base, of a policy of social solidarity, reduction of inequalities and poverty, and creation of new jobs, aiming at full-time employment; that is, it is required a coherent policy that will render these forms a "vestibule" not for the entry of the regional employee in a situation of poverty or social exclusion but rather for his/her reentry in the labour market and in the full-time employment.

2.7.3 Social Protection of the Regular Model of Employment and that of an Atypical Employment

The social protection of labour from labour and insurance legislation is initially limited to dependent labour. Consequently, there is need for a simultaneous completion of Labour and Insurance Law. The structure of labour and insurance legislation based on the concept of dependent labour has as consequence that the projected social protection – that of labour and insurance – is not extended to other forms of employment and, particularly, to the independent work, project contracts, sub-contract/housework (fason) and to other similar forms. All these contracts are the main sources of atypical employment and bypass of social protection.

Under the current circumstances of crisis that the reduction of labour cost is sought, these forms of employment are getting great extent. Thus, a legislative intervention is needed so that the criterion of labour dependence can be relaxed in order for the already used forms of employment and those that will appear later to be covered; that is, an adjustment to modern circumstances and projections for the new labour forms (such as telecommuting or telework) is required. So, it should be defined explicitly in the legislation that labour legislation is implemented in every form of paid work, independently from the contract with which this is covered. Some steps towards this direction were taken in the past with Law 1414/84 "on the implementation of gender equality in labour relations" that are essentially harmonized with Paragraphs 2 and 22, Paragraph 1[b], Article 4 of Constitution, International Labour Agreement N.100 and the Directive of 76/207/1976 of European Economic Community. Based on Law 1414/84, the principle of gender equality in labour relations was decided that it is applicable to all employees, with relation of dependent labour as well as to those who are "freelancers". Moreover, based on Law 1835/1989, the implementation of this principle is valid for "independent work". The regulations of two previous laws create cracks in the absolute use of the concept of dependent work in the Greek Labour Law and, of course, they can become a model; that is, in a similar way, other issues of labour relations can be regulated.

In insurance legislation, it is necessary that the clause of the main occupation should be nullified and be replaced with a quantitative criterion of minimum work, suitably adapted not only to the benefits of every sector but also to the particularity of every form of atypical employment. Especially, concerning these employees who have signed a fixed-term contract or sub-contract/housework (fason):

- they should be subjected to a coverage of a socially protective legislation;
- the concept of dependence of provided labour should be replaced by the more flexible concept of economic subordination, a fact that should give the opportunity to these employees to be subjected to a coverage of a socially protective legislation;
- trade unionism should be encouraged, overcoming difficulties and real obstacles, a fact that will facilitate the development of collective bargaining;
- the reaction of trade unions against every effort to regulate legislatively atypical forms of labour. Trade unions should accept the intervention of legislative regulations, which will establish some minimum standards for the interest of employees; and
- the implementation of the recommended regulations will contribute to resource input to insurance funds, resources that are being lost nowadays.

2.7.4 Regulation of Part-time Employment

The institution of part-time employment in Greece in contrast with other Western European countries has limited implementation. Before Law 1892/90, the concept of both hourly-paid and part-time employment was known in Greece. More specifically, working time limits could be regulated with a contract within the context of legal schedule. The verification of part-time employment also resulted from the situation of the personnel of an enterprise, or other data of public services (Laws 515/70 and 1037/71). Despite the fact that as the base of labour relations was considered the monthly salary and the wage, there was a legal framework for the wages of part-time employment based on hourly-paid wages (Law 133/75) that was calculated based on match wage with employment. Law gave the same opportunities to some part-time employees as to full-time employees. More specifically, they were eligible to annual holiday, compensation for overtime and in case of being laid off, if they had signed a dependent labour contract. Finally, there was provided insurance coverage, if they were employed at least the half of statuary working time.

Various legislative interventions in Europe sought initially to officialise the "neglected institutionally" part-time employment as a regular form of employment. They tried both to raise the unfavourable law treatment that resulted for part-time employees from the use of this form of employment and deter the use of this form of employment from being used as competitive measure against full time employment. With Law 1892/90 it was for the first time that total regulation of part-time employment was laid down. More specifically, with Paragraph 1, Article 38 of the above-mentioned Law every form and type of working hour is recorded, assumes either the form reduced working hour or the form of shiftwork or is estimated as open-ended or fixed-term employment. "In this way, part-time employment is established as voluntary." The relation between full-time and part-time employment as far the substitution of the one from the other is regulated with the prediction of cancelling the termination of the contract, when this is due to the employee's refusal to accept the proposal of part-time employment (Paragraph 2, Article 38), as predicted by this Law. With Paragraphs 3 and 4 of the same Article, an equal treatment of part-time employees is established, based on the principle of proportionality with regard to full-time employees, as far the estimation of their earnings, their annual holiday with the pay and the benefit of holiday. With Paragraph 5, the employee's right to deny any additional work is guaranteed, provided that s/he also has another employment or s/he has family obligations. This allows the employee to call upon any of his/her obligations that is considered family as long as it is connected with the particular employment. With the provision, the legislator accepts that part-time employment is not adopted only for the needs of the enterprise but also as a means for the employee's needs. Finally, with Paragraph 6, Article 38 it is recognized that the part-time employee is on equal terms and has priority to be hired in a full-time position in the same enterprise. However, this provision is insufficient, since the legislator forgot to determine how this right is implemented by the interested employee. Finally, with Article 39 the social insurance of part-time employees is established

The main criticism that GSEE made of the regulation of part-time employment from Law 1892/90 was focused on the fact that, although the social insurance of part-time employees (Article 39, Law 1892190) is established, it is still incomplete. The main problem that emerges is that of pension. What would happen with those who "they are forced" in a part-time employment during the last years of their employment? It is vague and unclear how unemployment compensation for part-time employees would be calculated. More specifically, it was supported that there are no provisions that would guarantee:

- a minimal time limit of employment, a fact that involves the implementation of hourly-paid employment;
- the smooth professional development of the part-time employee and there are no regulations on the consolidation of the collective dimension of labour

relations; that is, not only the departure but also the development of part-time within the context of the law 1892/90 regulations are restricted to individual labour law;

- the role that the trade union or the employees council can play in the introduction, monitoring and development of part-time employment. The trade union's intervention in the regulation of part-time employment appears only potentially in Article 2 of Law 1876/90, as this was supplemented with Paragraph 8, Article 40 of Law 1892/90.

Today, it can be claimed that the regulation of Law 1892/90 on part-time employment was sufficient. Thus, any further discussion about part-time employment should concern how one gets a position in the State and the wider public sector. In this case, an open-ended issue is the role that industry-based trade unions play in determining:

- administrative units to which part-time employment will be introduced;
- specific positions of part-time employment;
- cases in which contracts of part-time employment are not open-ended ones;
- a maximum number of part-time employees on all employees;
- a limit of overtime, daily and weekly labour;
- a threshold of hours worked "going downwards" (i.e. decreased); and
- terms of a potential change of a part-time employee into a full-time one.

Finally, something of particular importance – which would assist the use not only of part-time employment but also of other special forms of employment, would guarantee at the same time the employees' rights and facilitate the mobility of labour force – would be the creation of a national list of professions, the creation of levels of quality, seniority and grade development a profession as well as the creation of a matching between the ranks of professions, with special provisions for moving from one rank of a profession to another rank of another profession. Although it was regulated by Law 1892/90 in a particularly flexible and socially protective way, part-time employment did not begin to be used enough or it was used without "being declared". Hence, it needs being encouraged so to be used "officially", that is, to "registered", in order to be used to a great extent in such a way that it serves the needs both of enterprises and individuals or the needs of special demographic categories. It should be encouraged in a way that it enhances both the competitiveness of enterprises and employment, and, at the same time, in a way that it functions complementary but not competitively to full-time employment.

Consequently, in order for part-time employment (a) to be encouraged, it should cost as much as or less than full-time employment; for example, two part-time employees of 4-hour labour cost – with regard to wage and employer's contributions to social insurance – as much or less than an 8-hour full-time employee (only if it is for less, then it is competitive!!!); and (b) to function complementarily but not competitively to full-time employment, the maximum number of part-time employed on the total of personnel of enterprise should be considered. It is conspicuous that these measures make sense only when they are introduced together. The introduction of only one of the two measures leads to the opposite direction. Moreover, part-time employment – which is a real situation and which is connected with the most recent developments in the organization of employment – needs a more systematic and more complete legal treatment, so that, on the one hand, greater guarantee and protection of employees is achieved than the one that is provided by the provisions being in effect, especially those of Article 38 of Law 1892/90 and, on the other hand, there should be a clear extension of this form of employment in the DEKOs (: Public Utility Organizations) and in the rest of NPID (: Private Entity Law) of the public sector.

With the proposed regulations in the issue of part-time the following new interventions are made:

First, should the danger of full-time employment be substituted by part-time employment be deterred and should the issue be watched by the responsible Labour Inspections, there should be a restriction as the number of part-time employees and is provided that their total number is not allowed to exceed 20% of the total number of full-time employees in the enterprise. Moreover, it is considered as abusive the breach of contract of a full-time employee without a cause, if within six months (from this breach) a position and a specialty are covered by a part-time employee. Whereas, finally, it is determined that the relative to contract of part-time employment, if it is not submitted within eight (8) days in the respective Labour Inspection, is considered that it covers relation of full-time employment.

Second, the part-time employee's right of priority to be hired as full-time in the enterprise in which s/he is employed is clarified, and s/he is provided with certain participative potentials. More specifically, it is provided that part-time employees are provided with the same social services available to the other employees of the enterprise, as well as they can participate in professional training activities that the enterprise initiate, under conditions similar to those concerning full-time and contract of indefinite duration (e.g. permanent contract) employees. It is also provided that the employer informs the representatives of employees about the number of part-time employees in relation to the development of the employees as a whole, as well as about the prospects of hiring full-time employees.

Third, it is clarified that collective autonomy, at the level of enterprise-level collective labour agreement within the enterprise, can regulate again some issues of part time employment with primary lawful power.

Fourth, it is clearly provided the implementation of part-time employment in the DEKOs and in the rest of organizations of the wider public sector.

2.7.5 Working Time

Concerning the working time regulation, Law 1892190 gives the possibility – after the employer has come to enterprise collective bargaining or agreements with the employee council, and on interval until 3 months – that the employees' working time is increased up to 9 hours a day and 48 hours a week and that decreased working time is to be provided for the next quarter. A requirement for the introduction of this measure is that for one semester the mean of working hours should not exceed 40 hours a week, without overtime being due for the period during which the schedule is increased (Paragraph a, Article 4). Extending the measure, it could be provided legislatively that the working time regulation from one hour plus (+) or one hour minus (-) daily could become two hours plus (+) one hour minus (-) daily. This measure should be combined with abolishing overworking and with reducing drastically the amount of overtime.

Moreover, still greater flexibilization in the working time regulation (longer-shorter working time daily/weekly and for a period for more than three months up to ten months) should be provided legislatively that it can be achieved with business or written agreement between the employer and the employee council.

Henceforth, working time constitutes the leading factor so that the developments in the entire spectrum of labour relations can be determined. At an EU level, priority is given to the redistribution of working time, based on periods of wider time duration. The objective of these regulations is that the state will have the opportunity to achieve economic and social objectives which are interrelated with each other. The recommended regulations, combined with the relative Directive, provide more specifically:

- discretion for enterprises to organize the working time in such a way that it better serves their operational and economic needs, that is, the working time regulation could adapt to market condition and to product demand, aiming at competitiveness;
- clear delineation and guarantee of full-time employment and its regular salary;
- improved conditions of protection of employees' hygiene and safety, since the maximum allowed working time a week is 48 hours;

- cracking down on "grey economy" and, more specifically, on illegal overtimes;
- socially fairer distribution of existing volume of employment; and
- reinforcement of employment as a whole and the potential for creation of new jobs.

With the new regulations in the issues of working time the following innovative interventions are proposed the following:

First, it can be determined for a period up to two months the increased number of working hours up to (9) hours a day and up to forty-eight (48) a week and the decreased number of working hours for the next respective period, provided that the mean of working hours for the total time period, which is not allowed to exceeds four (4) months, amounts in 40 hours a week. This means that the employer, practising his/her managerial right, has the discretion to organise the working time according to the operational and economic needs of his/her enterprise.

Second, it can be determined for a period up to three (3) months and in cases there are technical reasons or reasons of work management for a period up to six (6) months, with business collective labour agreements or with agreements between the employer and the employee council, an increased number of working hours up to ten (10) hours a day and up to forty-eight hours (48) a week and a decreased number of working hours during the next consecutive period, provided that the mean of working hours for total time, which is not allowed to exceed six (6) or twelve (12) months respectively, it amounts in 40 hours a week. This means that such a regulation of the working time can be realized only after a collective labour agreement. Finally, for the two above mentioned cases, for regulation that is to say, the time of work or straightly by the law or via collective labour agreements (: sse in Greek), it is also provided that the remuneration paid for the case by case total time interval, it is equal with the corresponding wage for work of 8 hours daily and 40 hours weekly, without allowing fluctuation. Accordingly, with this regulation the wage cost of work is decreased and both the competitiveness of enterprises and total employment are strengthened, without full-time employment and its wages being touched.

2.7.6 The Establishment and Operation of Private Employment Agencies

On the occasion of the warning letter sent by the European Committee, that is based on Article 169 of the Treaty of the European Union, and in view of the relative decision of the Court of Justice of the European Union (CVRIA) and the opinion of its General Public Prosecutor, as well as relative observations made by the National Organization for the Occupation of the Work Force (OAED) and Revised International Convention 96, it was considered that henceforth the conditions had matured so that the first legal step to forecast the establishment and operation of private employment agencies (IGEE) in our country. While the relevant provisions were being adopted, it was considered that the prominent role of public employment agencies should be, among others, provided, that is, the relevant services of the Occupation of the Work Force (OAED), the collabouration of public and private employment agencies as well as that the monitoring of the two categories of employment services – public and private – should belong to the Ministry of Labour and Social Insurance. Furthermore, it was considered that the establishment of the IGEE – which should concern activities mainly of provisional or extraordinary work, and the establishment and issue of special state authorization that has a time limit – be indefinitely revocable and renewable. And, finally, it was considered that the issue should be associated with the subscription of certain basic conditions, such as:

- the subscription of Greek citizenship in the business person;
- the non-conviction of the business person irrevocably for fraud, theft, misappropriation, counterfeiting, marketing, possession and use of drugs, white slavery, smuggling or for crime against morals; and
- the mediation of the IGEE occurs without any economic tax for the employee, that is, for the person who offers his/her work, while the amount of remuneration eligible for the IGEE for such a mediation paid by the enterprises that ask for work is determined by ministerial decision.

Among the first things to do it was the special new Law to provide, with ministerial decision: first, strict penal and administrative sanctions for the offenders owners of IGEE; second, the terms, the conditions, the supporting documents and the process on issuing authorization, pre-conditions for its revocation, bodies and how to monitor the IGEE's operation as well as any other necessary details; and, third, in every case, when the labour market is disturbed, the state can take adequate measures, after it has consulted with its social partners, for its regularization.

2.7.7 Local Employment Pacts

In order to deal with unemployment problems and problems of social exclusion, it was thought that Local Employment Pacts (TSAs) could be contracted and implemented in various areas of the country, following the respective European experience. The Local Employment Pact would constitute a voluntary affiliation form of collaboration of social partners, social productive and public agencies of an area. In the Local Pact of Employment there would contract freely the most representative trade-union organizations of employees and employers of the area; they could also participate or join public authorities, unions of persons as well as natural and legal persons of any legal form. The TSAs would aim to create new jobs, guarantee the existing employment and to combat against unemployment. More specifically, they would aim to:

- enforce local development and create jobs as constant and viable as possible, especially in sectors, places and activities that are dynamic and have prospect;
- create jobs immediately with new activities at a local level, by developing the institution of social work and local initiatives of employment;
- upgrade professional skills of human resources and connect professional training with real needs of the area;
- support labour rehabilitation of the unemployed, especially of the long-term unemployed and those who are threatened with social exclusion; and to
- encounter the consequences of industrial reformation by undertaking actions and initiatives that are commonly accepted by those who signed a contract, the participants or those who joined these initiatives.

In order to deal with the specific needs of the area and, more specifically, with unemployment, development, utilization of wealth-production sources as well as the achievement of social peace and the general interest of the area, the Local Employment Pact (TSA), based on provided procedures, could regulate issues related to:

- the guarantee and the creation of jobs so the unemployment problem of the regional population and, more specifically, those of the most vulnerable social groups (young, women, long-term unemployed, aged people);
- the education and the training of human resources potential and their connection with the needs of local labour market;
- the policy on development, investment and management, the enlargement of flexibility in the local job market, the utilization of available local resources and the reduction of non-wage cost of labour;
- the aid of administrative services of the area so they achieve better organization, operation and co-ordination in relation to planning and the support of the implementation of the TSA;
- the name, the legal form, their duration, the way of organization, operation and financing of the TSA;

- the rights and the obligations of the parties that sign a contract or participate or join the Local Employment Pact as well as the processes of resolution of differences that may by chance emerge between them; and
- the interpretation of the terms of the Local Employment Pact (TSA) as well as the processes and the terms of its modification. The terms of the TSA would engage all those who are in contract or participate in or join it, and they would be outlaws, should they breach the terms of National General Collective Bargaining Labour Agreements (EGSSE). With common decisions made by Ministers of National Economy, Work and Social Insurance and by the relevant Minister – which would be published following the opinion of Economic and Social Committee (OKE) – issues of organization, operation, financing and monitoring of Local Employment Pacts (TSAs) could be regulated.

2.8 Concluding Remarks

In Greece with Law 1892/90 new regulations have been established; these regulations reorganised the labour market by introducing new for the country institutions, such as part-time employment, additional work groups and flexible management of working time. The introduction of part-time employment is established, more specifically, on a voluntary basis; it is based on the principle of proportionality of rights with the full-time employees (authorizations, benefits etc.). It is provided annulment for the breach of contract for full-time employment that may follow the employer's proposal and the employee's refusal to accept transformation of his/her relation into part-time employment, whereas at the same time the coverage of this form of social security is guaranteed.

Concerning the working time management, the opportunity is given – after the collective labour bargaining or agreement between the employer and the employee council has been signed – and for a three-month period – that the employees' working time can be increased up to nine hours a day (and 48 hours a week) without any overtime being due for the period when the schedule is increased, whereas it is provided decreased time of employment for the next period, under the condition that during the semester of the operation of the measure the mean of working hours will not exceed forty-eight hours a week. Furthermore, all enterprises, no matter what sector they belong to, are able to differentiate their operation by using "additional work groups". Thus, it has been established that for a 24-hour work – 2 shifts on the weekend multiplied by 12 hours each – will be granted a wage equal to that of the full-time employee who works for forty-eight hours a week.

At the same time, with the same Law regulations were introduced that made flexible the opening hours of shops and the work of their personnel. This new schedule, combined with the rest of regulations of the Law, has shaped a framework that fundamentally differentiates the management framework of the labour market and the operation of wages. These data – combined with the high levels of the illegal employment of immigrants which is proportional to invisible activities and "grey economy", the extensive use of employment on contractual basis (which occur in the state and in the wider public sector) and fixed-term contracts, as well as the great weaknesses of control mechanisms of work – have had as a result the violation in practice the legislative and jurisprudential framework that considers their repeated renewal as a contract of indefinite period (e.g. permanent contract) and, of course, the *de facto* guarantee of a much higher degree of flexibility in the labour market than that the existing institutional framework formally provides. In 1996–1997, in order to improve the organization of the labour market, the government undertook social dialogue to legislate to the same direction issues of working time regulation as well as part-time employment, aiming to encourage it.

Moreover, the government has been preoccupied with the Local Employment Pacts (TSAs) as voluntary forms of collaboration, without, however, raising their existing labour relations and wages; the introduction of restrictions in pensioners' employment, the institutionalization of the operation of private employment agencies, the reorganization of control mechanisms of labour and the initiation of a policy that: (a) encourage the reduction of working time without reducing the wage, after an agreement between of the employer and employees has been reached; (b) improve the totality of the institutional and organizational infrastructure of support of policies of the labour market and energetic policies of employment, which have been undertaken by the new National Plan of Action; and (c) promote new innovative programmes that connect training and employment, alternative forms of social work as well as environmental and cultural employment.

In the Greek labour market, the following bodies also intervene: (a) the National Organization for the Occupation of the Work Force (OAED), covering the unemployment insurance, allocating apprenticeship schools, managing programmes of business-to-business training and the combined programmes of training and employment, dealing with recording immigrant employees; it is also on the verge of developing a Pan-Hellenic network of Employment Promotion Centres (KPA). (b) The Organization for Mediation and Arbitration (OMED) for the resolution and regulation of collective differences at work, influencing heavily the levels of wage formation. (c) The National Resource Centre for Vocational Guidance (EKEP). (d) The National Accreditation Centre for Continuing Vocational Training (EKEPIS), which is responsible for certifying agencies that conduct programmes, instructors and evaluators of training programmes; (e) the Tripartite National Labour Institute, INE – GESEE (: Labour Institute – Greek General Confederation of Labour), which carry out mainly research work; and (f) the National Observatory of Employment (EPA), dealing primarily with the follow-up and recording of developments in the labour market for research purposes and facilitating policy-making. In addition to the aforementioned agencies, there are employers' organizations and agencies that have a decisive intervention in policy-making for the labour market such as: the SEB (: Association of Greek Industrialists), the EESE (: National Confederation of Hellenic Commerce), GSEBEE (: General Confederation of Professional Graftsmen and Traders in Greece) and the GSEE (: Greek General Confederation of Labour).

The organization and operation of the labour market in Greece, whereas in the previous decades they were determined almost exclusively by the state intervention, have already got another image. The regulation of many issues, after the force of Law 1876/90 "about free collective bargaining", has been passed on the operation of this mechanism, whose objective is not only the wage but also a wider spectrum of issues. This development is facilitated by a lot of factors such as the provisions of the new Law that *de facto* give priority in the enterprise- and industry-based collective labour agreements, which are also downgraded, the new model of mediation and arbitration that aims mainly to encourage rather than substitute the direct dialogue of the parties, in contrast with what was in effect in the past, within the framework of a kind of obligatory and state controlled arbitration, the combination of this potentially decentralised system of negotiations by maintaining a position of strong central national general collective bargaining that guarantees the minimum levels of wage and becomes "the pilot" in the formation of the amount of allocated increases, the establishment of an Economic and Social Committee (OKE), the activation of *ad hoc* procedures for the conduct of a bilateral and tripartite dialogue at a national level as well as the progressive replacement of the conflicting situation that existed between employees and employers, from a will and culture of dialogue and collabouration, a fact that is confirmed by the declining number both of so many lost working hours due to strikes and collective differences that are solved neither with bargaining nor with mediation, but they rather lead to arbitration. These data reveal that the labour market – from a model of conflict and statism that was in effect in the previous decades – has been moving to a more consensual model corresponding to that of the democratic negotiated corporatism, within its context the state tends to limit gradually its role in establishing the "rules of game". Within this context, the trend of conventionalization of the norms of the regulation of the labour market keeps pace with the trend of its ever growing minimization.

Chapter 3: Trade Unionism in the Modern Changing Environment

3.1 Introduction

As time of the first appearance of the collective type of formations of employees and the various forms of trade union action, including bargaining, could be considered the middle of last century – with the only possible exception of Great Britain where industrialization preceded chronologically. The large industrial plant that gradually replaced the craft production resulted in large population inflow to urban centres, where there were such facilities. The development of mass production structures in those units generated oversupply of jobs to which much of the workforce flowed, which overwhelmed urban centres. Furthermore, employment of a large number of employees in a common workplace – and dealing with these related problems – had as a result their collective organization so they could vindicate better employment conditions from a less disadvantaged position (Ntasios, 1991a, pp. 17–18).

The revolutionary events that unfolded in almost all Europe in 1848, both dealing the ringleaders of those events as conspirators and the influence of ideas of liberalism, led almost one after the other the European states to impose restrictions on the freedom of association of both employees and employers that had been in effect for decades and were removed in the late 19th century (Karakatsanis, 1985).

Nowadays, trade union freedom (Aliprantis, 1979 p. 523, and esp. ft 4) is considered as part of freedom of association (Giugni, 1983, p. 11; Mitsou, 1981, pp. 6–7), and it is not – as the latter – general right of every social group. More specifically, trade unionism (Goutos, 1988, p. 13 ff)and trade union freedom, which was launched by employees and then extended to other professional groups[4] requires different social and economic interests which show controversy, competition (Mitropoulos, 1985, p. 5; Daubler, 1980, pp. 682–683) and need for coalition of every group, that is, a need for organization, action and representation to promote common, social and economic interests (Koukiadis, 1981, pp. 225–226). Trade union freedom – apart from its primary individual (Leventis, 1976, p. 137 ff) dimension – does have a collective dimension (Koukiadis, 1982,

4 Mitsou, 1982, pp. 5–7 & 13. Although disputed in theory, it has been argued that trade unionism is only an employee's right; see in particular Travlos-Tzanetatos, 1988, p. 232.

esp. p. 10; Spyropoulos, 1956, p. 7) and texture, which is nowadays expressed as the key element of modern democratic constitutions (Svolos and Vlachos, 1954, p. 94). It is specialized in freedoms and rights: establishment, organization and operation of trade unions, the conduct of collective trade union activities, collective bargaining and strike[5]. This freedom of trade union action is now generally the background of the development of mechanisms of how to conduct social dialogue, how social actors can participate in dealing with "major" social and economic issues[6], as well as of the overall development of socio-political process within the context of every modern pluralistic policy and social democracy (Koukiadis, 1981, pp. 230–238).

3.1.1 Citizen's Social Rights

The primary and formal recognition and protection of collective trade union freedoms and rights have been achieved in recent decades through international contracts as well as through constitutional and legislative texts by individual states. In particular, although trade union freedoms and, more specifically, collective autonomy and collective bargaining began to be recognized as fundamental social institution (Ntasios, 1991a, p. 20) after World War I, their official international recognition (Spyropoulos, 1955, p. 1 & p. 57 ff) and legal rights at a large scale occurred only after World War II; then individual national regulations followed.

Today's experience suggests that legislation per country bore at each stage a relation to socio-political, economic and production conditions; more specifically, a relation to the level of industrial development, the level of development of trade unions and labour relations. There was a common finding for all countries that the practice and the dynamics of trade union freedoms, collective autonomy and collective bargaining preceded respective legislative regulations (Ntasios, 1991a, pp. 19–20).

In some cases of national laws, the consolidation of freedom of trade unionism is not clearly identified, but its protection results from the consolidation of

5 Vais, 1978, p. 299 ff. See also, Karakatsanis, 1980, p. 21 ff. As argued, the direct object of the principle of freedom of association is no longer the union of the organization as such, but rather the union of action, i.e., action aimed to protect the interests of the union members. More specifically, see, Giugni, 1983), p. 13.

6 Mitropoulos, 1985, p. 45, where the author argues that trade unions action is a broad field "starting from the labour post/position and reaches the maximum level of macroeconomic planning and economic policy". See also, Travlos-Tzanetatos, 1984, p. 30.

freedom of association. However, freedom of trade unionism and the related or resulting freedoms – namely collective autonomy, collective bargaining and the right to strike – are explicitly guaranteed in constitutions, allowing the common legislator to specify how to exercise these rights and freedoms as well as how to form an analytical nexus of protection of the trade union action, without, however, excluding the cases in which provisions are absent. Moreover, national laws provide exceptions and restrictions to those rights for employees in the public sector, and, more specifically, for public servants as well as for employees in police and armed forces. The treatment of trade union freedom and the freedoms associated with it by individual national legal systems, without showing strong similarities to partly specialized regulations, presents a systematic convergence to some "major issues", while these rights and freedoms are regulated. First, a large volume of international labour agreements and other worldwide or Europe-wide documents and agreements has been established, and most of them have bound the majority of European countries. In Greece such documents or agreements ratified by Law are an integral part of national law and prevail over any contrary provision of law. Nowadays, it is recognized that the essence of the principle of trade union freedom lies in the trade union action whose aim is to pursue common economic and social interests.

Extremely important expression of trade union representation and effective means of achieving the aforementioned objectives is collective bargaining through which the collective autonomous self-regulatory power of the parties is expressed (Leventis, 1981, pp. 37 -38). In this sense, all institutional developments that ensure trade union freedom or freedom of association is of crucial importance for any form of trade union action, for collective bargaining and strike. As the International Labour Organization claims, a key condition for successful collective bargaining is that both employees and employers should enjoy fully freedom of association and, more specifically, based on the principles adopted by the "Convention, 1948, concerning Freedom of Association and the Right to Organize" as well as "the Convention, 1949, concerning the Right to Organize and Collective Bargaining" (ILO 1977, p. 11).

3.2 Social and Historical Background

As it comes out of the social history[7] of the labour movement, modern forms of collective labour relations and collective protest, which differ significantly from

7 Concerning social history as an alternative approach and trend of critical questioning for traditional historiography, see Koukoules, 1985, pp. 17–24.

their precedent, emerge with the Industrial Revolution. The "victory of the machine" resulted in substantial changes in the production process and the very organization of labour process[8]. The replacement even partly of the employee, and his/her physical strength, from the first machines gradually abolished craftsmen's production. Nevertheless, it was generating large units of mass industrial production, employment opportunities for young craftsmen and demand for unskilled people, while it was marginalizing other specialties and groups of employees. The entrance of women, children and the rural population into the production, population concentration in urban centres[9], the extension of the workday, work intensification, employment of large numbers of employees in common workplace and their treatment of common labour problems formed the context within which – always in relation to general socio-economic conditions – the first forms (Foster, 1978, pp. 26–33, 52–59) of collective "behaviour" of employees and employers and collective organization; initially, (Karakatsanis, 1985, p. 18) appeared only that of employees aiming to claim a less disadvantaged position and better work conditions.

At that time – in the late 18th and early 19th century, the early forms of modern labour relations can be detected, and, more specifically, the already organized opposition between employees and employers, which was articulated at local and professional level and later at sectoral and national level, dealing with wages and employment conditions with collective protest and strike (Geary, 1988, pp. 30–56).

In the pre-industrial era, collective claims took the form of riots during which an amorphous social crowd with mixed social composition, "the mob" – reacting spontaneously and without specific and stable organizational framework – exercised direct pressure and violent reactions so to satisfy the demands for food security and relief in relation to taxation and conscription. Phenomena of such uprisings occurred in Europe mainly between 1770 and 1850, with variations by country depending on the level of its industrialization (Tilly, 1970, pp. 25–30). From the beginning of the 19th century to about 1850, while pre-industrial forms were being maintained, other forms of early trade union protest were emerging, which were transitional types of expressing the problems with adaptation to industrialization.

---

8 Travlos-Tzanetatos, 1977, pp. 37–48. See also, Filias, 1978, pp. 135–141, where the author makes a comprehensive description of the developments that shaped the socio-economic conditions of that period.

9 See also, Filias, 1978, pp. 135–141, where the author makes a comprehensive description of the developments that shaped the socio-economic conditions of that period.

During that phase, however, whereas the local reference to the protest was being preserved, its sporadic, disorganized – to a great extent – violent character and its social base ceased consisting mainly of rural populations; it was restricted to employees' skills that the new productive reality of industrialization had marginalised. Moreover, whereas the objectives of pre-industrial protest concerned food, taxation and conscription and were often directed against machines (Foster, 1978, pp. 29–30) (luddites) and the very industrial production, the objectives of the early trade union protest referred to concrete economic or political demands whose satisfaction was to be fulfilled with riots rather than with strikes, something that was encountered in the next phase. That was the phenomenon of "bargaining through riots", which, however, did not seek to cancel the very same of industrial production line but rather to differentiate the terms of its operation (Abendrot, 1976, p. 14).

Especially after 1850, when the industrial mode of production had already been established in the Continent too, the origins of the phenomena of modern labour relations can be found; these relations articulated specific economic and political demands, the employees' collective organization, the collective confrontation between employees and employers as well as to the realization of strikes and collective bargaining (Geary, 1988, pp. 30–42). The hostility towards the new industrial order and the anti-industrial protest that had emerged from the early trade union movement took the form of clear demands to ban the import of machinery (Abendrot, 1976, p. 13), which were made explicit through slogans against machines and industrial plants.

The means of pressure were riots themselves. However, violence was gradually being replaced by strikes. The diffused and scattered riots were replaced by a specified context of collective rivalry between employees and employers, with means that were very organized, that is, trade unions and strikes instead of violence; their objective was not industrial society itself any more but employment conditions, power structures or property relations (Abendrot, 1976, p. 14). It is conspicuous that social and political conditions rather than production and economic conditions determined the advent of modern organized labour movement and, after a while, the forms of collective action of employees in the early 19th-century Continental Europe.

The first forms of collective organization of employees (Geary, 1988, pp. 62–74; Moskov, 1988, pp. 281–333), which had the form of discussion clubs, cultural associations, production and consumer cooperatives and "friendly associations" were followed both by the emergence of the classical form of trade union organization – that is, of trade union – in order to improve employees' economic position, and by a later appearance of purely labour political parties, which usually had a close relationship with trade unions. Despite the fact that, from a historical point of view, there can be no absolute distinction between politics and the action of organized labour movement formations, trade unions preceded and differed significantly from political organizations of the labour movement, which - having been influenced by French Enlightenment, English philosophy and by German idealist philosophy – had made sometimes reformative and sometimes revolutionary demands.

Trade unions as such first developed in areas where there was organizational tradition of guilds after the imposed bans that had been lifted (ILO 1975, pp. 13–18). In Great Britain, trade unionism appeared in the 18th century and was legitimized in 1824 (Jackson, 1985, pp. 29–32), whereas at the beginning, it developed on similar professional and later on sectoral basis, when the first peaceful collective bargaining appeared. In France, trade unionism, although it initially appeared in 1830, developed primarily after 1864, when the institutionalized repression of the right of association was banned, which was the result of the 1848 revolution. In Germany, the relaxation of prohibitory laws on the right of association during the decades of 1850 and 1860 (Karakatsanis, 1985, p. 17) led to a revival of trade unionism, which was at an embryonic stage before 1848. In the rest of Europe, where there was a delay in industrialization, there was also a delay in the development of trade unionism, organized industrial action and in bargaining. In the Balkan countries, and, especially in Greece, bargaining occurred only during the last decades of the 19th century (Kremalis, 1976, p. 17), since the past bargaining was conducted through unrest, to a great extent, with pre-industrial features of direct violence. What should be clarified is that the first trade unions included skilled employees, with high expectations and organizational traditions.

Those trade unions did not include unskilled employees who were introduced to unionize and went on bargaining only in the late 19th century (Ntasios, 1991a, p. 39), and more particularly, after the long strike of the dock employees in Great Britain. The demands of the bargaining that were structured and expressed clearly concerned about wages, the duration of the workday, the relaxation of labour discipline and authoritarianism of foremen. From a historical perspective, the result of the organized pressure, demands, strikes and bargaining and, generally, of the organized action of the trade union movement after 1850 was that concessions were achieved by employers and states, which were: factory councils, sponsored welfare institutions, consumer associations, reduction of child labour and provision of education. Typical examples are: the 1842 Law for mining in Great Britain that made concessions in terms of social policy; in France, the 1894 Law on miners' social insurance and the 1898 Law for the protection against accidents. Finally, what was the most significant in Great Britain (Abentrot, 1976, p. 20) was the 1847 Law with which the ten-hour workday was established, and in France the 1848 Law imposed a maximum limit of twelve (12) hours in a workday.

In the history of labour relations in Great Britain, even at the early stage of their development prior to the decriminalization of the strike, there had been lots of cases in which employers were forced to talk with the organized employees, and accepted the agreements, known as "Gentlemen's agreement", which, although unwritten, were practically mutually respected. Unlike Britain, France, Italy, Belgium and in the Continent generally there have been historically recorded cases of breach of agreements, which led to labour unrest. Typical is case of the first known collective agreement signed in Lyon, France, in 1831, which was broken by employers and led to widespread unrest (Ntasios, 1991a, p. 18).

Through different paths that were the respect of agreements and the creation of customary law for Great Britain, whereas the dynamic imposition of a surging and militant labour movement for France, Italy and Belgium, the institution of collective bargaining recorded its presence in the late 19th century. That development marked the simple prevalence of the practice of collective agreements, without, however, their being recognized legally or regulated, something that commenced after World War I (Karakatsanis, 1985, p. 7). At this early stage, collective agreements were a kind of employers' concession to their employees, had a character of private contracts of contract law, thus creating respectively rights and obligations for both parties. At this stage such arrangements were mentioned to have taken place in France (27 December 1892) and in Germany, whereas the unwritten "gentlemen's agreements" had already been recognized and were the basis of production from the courts of customary law in Great Britain during the same period (Ntasios, 1991a, pp. 17–20).

3.3 Development of Trade Unionism in Greece

The development of the Greek trade union movement was determined by the particularities of socio-economic, political and institutional development of the Greek society. The characteristics of a society such as the Modern Greek one – which became a nation much later than most European states, with an economy where industrialization was delayed by far, anachronistic structures, the burdening role of rural production as well as the particularities of local communities being maintained for a long time (Babounis, 2007), with the particularities it showed during the process of urbanization as well as the intense presence of authoritarian structures and institutional underdevelopment until quite recently, it is obvious that all the aforementioned are reflected both in the appearance, constitution and the development of trade union organizations in Greece, which - despite their important similarities with other European countries – illustrated, however, some obvious national peculiarities. Up to recently, these differences were due to the fact that labour rights in Greece were prohibited during dictatorship (1967–1974) (Spyropoulos, 1985a), and have been restored in their normal dimensions only during the last decades.

The Greek trade union movement was constituted where there was a meeting, that is, where there was industrial employment, according to the data of period. International radical currents and movements, progressive political theories from Europe, intellectuals, sociologists and various radicals transmitted and propagated new ideas and perceptions, thus influencing the employees of that period. Greek working associations appeared in the last quarter of the 19th century, from 1875 onwards, when an increasing part of population that was redundant in the countryside moved to urban centres and began to take the form of a class of landless wage labourers. Meanwhile, the constant employment in these industrial and commercial centres created a permanent working class. The history of Greek trade union movement begins after the appearance of first original factories in Athens, Piraeus, Syros, Volos and elsewhere, after 1860. In the race to get industrialised, Greece remained far behind certain Northern European countries where metropolitan centres of capitalism had been developed. Greece's delay being included in the capitalistic world had strong effects on the development of Greek capitalism.

The first association of employees, according to written testimonies, was established by the carpenters of the ship yards of the island of Syros. In the same year, that fraternity went on its first strike as an effort to deal with the consequences of crisis, which had decreased the purchasing force of their wage at 30%. A strike in Athens and Piraeus followed in 1882 and the big strike of miners in Lavrion and in other mining centres occurred in 1883. Those strikes had taken place before any working associations were established in those cities, while other strikes were taking place. Regular were the demands for wage increases, reduction of working time to ten (10) hours, protection from accidents and for medical care benefits. In the meantime, in Ermoupolis, Syros, the first centre of trade union action was organized because of the presence of ship yards. Over there did the first working association make its first appearance, the Union of Carpenters of Syros Ship yards, while the creation of various associations followed in the cities of Athens, Piraeus and Patras. At the same time – and more specifically in 1883 – the Association of Industrialists was established. Between 1880 and 1890 various associations in various sectors were being established. The typographers of

Athens, cigarettes makers and tailors went on strike. In 1893, the May Day was celebrated in the Pillars of Olympian Zeus for the first time. In the last few years of the 19th century, the employees of almost all arts and crafts linked and created what is known as "working centres" and their federations. In 1906, the big association of Lavrion miners was established, with 5000 members, while the first associations of tobacco employees appeared. In 1908, the first working centre was established, the working centre in Volos.

In reality, the first working organizations remained charitable associations and supportive societies up to 1910, giving much of importance to their members' prosperity especially since they established supportive funds. On 6 March 1910, the Kileler incident occurred – during which there were clashes between the local militia and farmers who were protesting against the extended privileges of landowners and the limitation of their own rights – and the working centre of Athens was established (on 21 March). In 1910, a Central Organization of Working Associations was established in Athens. The first indications for an effective unity of employees were shown on 3 December 1908. The 28 working organizations, up to that moment, organized "mass demonstrations against the taxation of those working and professional classes who were not able to afford it" (http://trade unions.macedonia.gr/tue). In 1911, the Pan-Hellenic Working Federation was established, which was dissolved a few years later. In 1914, the Law on Collective Contracts entered into force and between 1914 and 1916 a series of strikes was called, which, however, continued up to 1920.

World War I did not prevent the quick development of the Greek trade unionism. In 1917, there were 206 working associations with 44,230 members in total. In 1918, the fermentations for a central organization of trade unions in Greece emanated from the Working Centre of Thessaloniki, in which the Greek-Jewish Trade Union Social Federation was the dominant force. Venizelos[10] encouraged the establishment of the General Confederation of Greek Labour (GCGL; GSEE in Greek), hoping that it would dominate, since many of its head trade unionists were partisans of his party at the moment. Venizelos still realized that in Greece there was no powerful Socialist movement, which he could have at his side in the international peace conferences, as other countries did, strengthening thus his claims. Thus, in the end of 1918 – with the initiative of the working centres of Thessaloniki, Athens, Piraeus and Volos – the first Pan-Hellenic Working Congress was convened, which led to the establishment of the GSEE. With the

10 He was a famous politician and the Prime Minister of Greece during the first three decades of the 20th century.

establishment of the GSEE, the working movement took henceforth a concrete form. The first Pan-Hellenic Working Congress assembled in Athens in October 1918. In its meetings 214 associations (Katsanevas et al., (1995) with 180 representatives that represented 65.000 organized employees took part. In the Congress there were three political trade union trends: left wing socialists, right wing socialists and reformists (Delkos, 2009). Up to the establishment of the GSEE there had been only one Federation. After the end of the first Pan-Hellenic Working Congress a lot of Federations were established, those of: Tanning Employees, Shoe Makers, Mill Employees, Pasta Makers, Bakers, Press etc. More specifically, ten (10) federations were established. Nevertheless, the industry-based federal organization failed and the organization dominated in working centres. In 1919, there was a split in the GSEE, whereas in 1920 two Conferences took place in which the GSEE, communists and non-communists participated. In 1926, the basic trade union organizations of public servants were established, while the 3rd GSEE Conference also took place, which was united and unionist. The three trends that were then emerging were the communists, the socialists and the reformists. The most domineering trends were the last two ones, while the communist participants withdrew from the GSEE conference denouncing it as "opportunistic" (Katsanevas et al., 1995).

Between 1936 and 1945 (Katsanevas et al., 1995), during the Metaxas Dictatorship, the national system of labour relations was organized in such a way that it could be controlled. Hence, the trade unionism passed in the absolute governmental control. Free political and trade union organizations were controlled; thousands of trade unionists were expelled, jailed and exiled, while a number of strike mobilizations were organized. At the time, there were open political, party and judicial interferences in the changes of the GSEE administration and, more generally, in the trade unionism, whereas prosecutions, condemnations, imprisonments and exiles of trade unionists were very frequent. It was the consolidation of the area of so-called "paternalistic unionism".

With the end of World War II, the 8th Pan-Hellenic Congress of the GSEE took place, during which the administration of the GSEE devolved to the control of the executives of the Communist Party of Greece. In 1948, Fotis Makris became the Secretary-General of the GSEE and maintained this position for roughly twenty years (Katsanevas et al., 1995). In 1948, the 9th Congress of the GSEE was held, in which 1,544 representatives from 1,441 associations, 62 working centres and 11 federations participated. In 1950, the 10th Congress of the GSEE took place, in which 1,936 representatives from 1,603 associations participated. At that time, strides were being made both for the development of industrial trade unionism and the establishment of federations, while the issue of trade union contribution was being regulated. In those both Congresses trade unions and trade unionists were absent for ideological reasons. Despite the fact that F. Makris had already left (he left in 1964), the situation in the Greek trade union movement had yet to be smoothed out. In February 1962, the collaboration among the Pan-Hellenic Federation of Accountants, the Federation of Electricity and the Federation of Press was carried forward; those federations were united to face the prospective proposal put forward by the Labour Ministry with which actuarial and trade union rights would have been offended. Then, a lot of other associations adhered to that collabouration until they reached the number the 115; therefore, they remained in the history with this name, whereas their full name was "115 Collaborating Labour Organizations" or SEO 115. In the movement of 115, communists, socialists, social democrats and other progressive trade unionists played the leading part and became aware that labour trade union movement needed democratization (www.GCGL.gr).

Up to 1974, the police control of trade union organizations was very hard[11]. Essentially, trade union parties appeared in the trade union movement after dictatorship (1967–1974). In 1976, the then government brought forward to Parliament the Bill "About professional associations and unions and the guarantee of trade union freedom" so to deal with the strike wave, which – despite the vigorous reaction of the Opposition – was voted with very few modifications and constituted Law 330 of 1976; a Law which was criticized for its unconstitutionality. The government's continuous effort to control the trade unions, which is recorded historically, appeared particularly intense in the previous decades. The delay in the development of democratic institutions which was evident in Greece even during parliamentary periods in the twentieth century, the lapse of the Greek Civil War (1944–1949), a long period of "post-Civil War climate" and dictatorships with very important repercussions for the public life of country, the operation of the state that was based on relation networks of a cliental type had resulted in maintaining extensive paternalism and governmental interventionism in the system of labour relations and, more specifically, in the trade union movement of employees, with the consequence that any meaning of autonomy was cancelled and fundamental democratic rights and freedoms were infringed on. The re-establishment of democracy in 1974 did not resolve the problem of

11 Among others, the police required the possession of the so-called "certificate of social conscience", which was necessary for someone who wanted to obtain a passport, to get enrolled in higher education or to be assigned a public appointment. The police interference, however, did not prevent strikes and demonstrations and violent actions by employees, peasants and students.

democratization of the trade union movement of employees. On the contrary, that was achieved only when Law 1264 of 1982 was passed and placed in force for the democratization of the trade union movement (Katsanevas, 1995), which led to the clearing-out of trade union registrations and the organization of a true Congress of the GSEE in 1983, while "this positive development was interrupted from the interior crisis of the controlling party in 1985, and the essential split of the GSEE for three years" (Kouzis, 2005).

3.4 Institutional Safeguard

Nowadays, the trade union right is protected in principle and can be found among the economic and social rights, to which the Universal Declaration of Human Rights (UDHR) refers; the UDHR was adopted by the United Nations and signed in Paris in 1948. More specifically, the individual trade unionist freedom is ensured[12] and particularly the right of each person to establish with other people trade unions and to participate in them in order to protect his/her interests. The International Covenant on Economic, Social and Cultural Rights (ICESCR) which was adopted and signed by the United Nations in New York on 19 December 1966, among the aforementioned rights with which the ICESCR provides general protection (Articles 2,3,4,5), it recognizes and protects the right to work (Article 6), whereas at the same time it urges and commits the contracting parties to safeguard the right to associate (Paragraph1, Article 8) and not to restrict with legislative measures (Paragraph 3, Article 8) the right to form or join trade unions (Paragraph 1, subpar. a, Article 8), the right to free exercise of trade union activity (Paragraph 1, subpar. c, Article 8) and the right to strike (Paragraph 1, subpar. d, Article 8).

The right to form and join trade unions, and the rights coming from this – that is, the right to participate in trade union activities and the right to be collectively autonomous – are also safeguarded by:

(a) The Convention Relating to the Status of Refugees (CRSR) was approved at a special United Nations Conference in Geneva on 28 July 1951 and binds upon the contracting states that treat refugees that reside in their territory

12 See Paragraph 4, Article 23 of the Universal Declaration. Koukiadis, 1981, pp. 273–274, where the author notes that Paragraph 4, Article 23 of the Universal Declaration refers only to the positive but not to the negative freedom of association. See also, Koukoules and Tzanetakos, 1986.

at least equally to the citizens of foreign states in relation to associations and professional trade unions (Article 15).

(b) The Convention Relating to the Status of Stateless Persons, which was signed in New York on 28 September 1954 and with which the contracting states committed themselves that they will treat stateless persons that stay in their territory at least equally to the foreigners in relation to professional organizations.

(c) The Convention of Council of Europe "For the Protection of Human Rights and Fundamental Freedoms", which was signed in Rome on 4 November 1950, and its Protocol in Paris on 20 March 1952 – which guarantees the right of everyone[13] to freedom of association with others (including the right to form and to join trade unions for the protection of his/her own interests (Paragraph 1, Article 11) – claim that no restrictions shall be placed on the exercise of these rights other than such as are prescribed by law and are necessary in a democratic society in the interests of national security or public safety, for the prevention of disorder or crime, for the protection of health or morals or for the protection of the rights and freedoms of others[14].

(d) The European Economic Community, EEC Treaty and the Treaty establishing the European Atomic Energy Community (Euratom), which among others refers to social sector (Paragraph 1, Article 118) and declares that among other things the mission of the Committee is to collaborate with the member states in issues related to the right to associate (or join trade unions) and to collective bargaining between employees and employers. At the same time, it declares (Article 118 B)that the Committee seeks to develop the dialogue among social partners at a European level, which – if they themselves agree– would lead to conventional relations[15].

A monument both for the institution of collective bargaining and for the course of the European Community, more generally, was the European Social Charter, which was signed in Turin, Italy, on 18 October 1961. This text declares the right of employees and employers to go into partnership freely within the framework

---

13 This right is recognized regardless of gender, race, color, language, religion, political or other opinion, national or social origin, membership in a national minority, property, birth or other status (Article 14).

14 Paragraph 2, Article 11. The imposition of lawful restrictions on the exercise of the right for members of the armed forces, police or administrative departments of each state is not prohibited.

15 Article 118 B was added to Article 2 of the Single European Act.

of national or international organizations in order to defend their economic and social interests, and guarantees their right to collective bargaining. Based on this (i.e. the European Social Charter) the contracting states – aiming to guarantee and promote employees and employers' trade union freedom – undertook the obligation to adopt their national legislation accordingly so that it neither offends nor is implemented in an offensive way – this freedom.

There is special reference to the right to collective bargaining and to the obligations that the contracting states undertook (Article 9) so to encourage the joint consultation of employees and employers (Paragraph 1, Article 6), promote the establishment of bargaining processes so that employment conditions can be governed with collective agreements (Paragraph 2, Nr 6), and to encourage the establishment of appropriate reconciliation and arbitration procedures so that labour differences can be regulated[16]. In a much more direct way, a guarantee of the trade union freedom, the right to collective autonomy and collective bargaining are also provided by international labour conventions.

During its 31st Session, the International Labour Conference – after it had taken into consideration the Preamble to the International Labour Organization (ILO) Constitution and the Declaration of Philadelphia – decided to accept a series of proposals and principles for the trade union freedom, drawing up and voting International Labour Convention (No 87)[17], in which it incorporated them. According to the International Labour Convention (No 87), each member state was committed to take all the necessary and appropriate measures so that the free exercise of employees' and employers' right to join organizations is safeguarded. At the same time, the member states of the ILO were committed to implement this convention in their legislation, thus providing their employees and employers a full protective framework, and, more specifically, that employees and employers may exercise freely the right to organize (Part II, Article 11) and organize their administration and activities and to formulate their programmes (Paragraph 2, Article 3), to join organizations of their own choice without previous authorization (Paragraph 2, Article 3), that the public authorities shall refrain from any interference which would restrict this right (the right to associate) or impede the lawful exercise thereof (Paragraph 2, Article 3), which should be exercised in such a way that it should respect the law of the land and should

16 Paragraph 3, Article 6. However, the contracting states that are subject to the obligations that could arise from collective agreements recognize the right of employees and employers for collective action and, therefore, the right to strike in cases of conflict of interest (Paragraph 4, Article 6).

17 It was adopted in San Francisco in 1948.

not offend other persons or organized collectivities (Paragraph 1, Article 8 Paragraph 1, Article 8).

A much more direct reference not to the right to association in general but rather to the right to organize and collective bargaining does make the International Labour Convention (No. 98), which was voted in Geneva in 1949 during the 32nd Session of the International Labour Conference. The Convention, which does not address or affect the status of public servants (Article 6) eclares that employees should be protected from any action or discrimination that can adversely affect the freedom of association (Paragraph 1, Article 1) and introduces specific principles and rules for protection of the right to organize and trade union activities (Paragraph 2, subpar. a & b, Article 1). Most importantly, however, it dictates contracting states to take measures to encourage collective bargaining between employees and employers as well as the regulation of collective labour relations and employment[18].

Finally, it should be noted that, in the most indirect way, protection of trade union freedom is also provided by the International Labour Convention (No. 141) for the "organizations of rural employees as an effective means of ensuring the participation of these employees in economic and social development"[19], which provides that establishment and development – on a voluntary basis – of strong and independent trade union or rural employees should be facilitated, so to – without any discrimination – participate in economic and social development and in the benefits resulting therefrom (Article 4). Moreover, it urges that the principles of freedom of association (Paragraph 2, Article 3), free and voluntary in character establishment of rural employees' independent organizations shall be maintained (Paragraphs 1 and 2, Article 3), provided that rural employees and their respective organizations shall respect the law of the land (Paragraph 4, Article 3).

There are further references to the freedom of association in: (a) the International Labour Convention (No. 135) in 1971 – where "employees' representatives ... shall enjoy effective protection against any act prejudicial to them" (Article 1), which – with R143 Employees' Representatives Recommendation in the same year (1971) – provides a safety net for those who exercise trade union activities; and (b) in the International Labour Convention (No. 151) in

18 Article 4. However, it excludes the contract provided by the safeguards, the armed forces and police, leaving the crucial role for the rights of employees in these sectors in national legislation.

19 It was adopted in Geneva in June 1975, during the 60th Session of the General ILO Conference.

1978 "concerning Protection of the Right to Organize and Procedures for Determining Conditions of Employment in the Public Service" – combined with R (159) – Labour Relations (Public Service) Recommendation, 1978 (No. 159) – "concerning Procedures for Determining Conditions of Employment in the Public Service" – have shaped a nexus of regulations declaring that public servants (public employees) need to enjoy the same rights as the rest of employees. For this reason, these Conventions and Recommendations provide general protection to the individual and collective trade union freedom, to trade union activities (Article 6) and encouragement for collective bargaining, as a regulation "machinery" of labour relations of those who work in public services, with the exception of the Armed Forces and the Police for which national laws or regulations play a determining role in regulating trade union rights.

Precursor, however, of the foundation and guarantee of the relevant to freedom of association rights – not only those of rural employees but also those of all employees – are: the International Labour Convention, 1921 (No. 11) "concerning the Rights of Association and Combination of Agricultural Employees", the International Labour Convention, 1947 (No. 84) "concerning the Right of Association in Non-Metropolitan Territories", and, of course, the Treaty of Versailles (The Preamble (Part XIII) and Article 427 of the Treaty), within the context of which the first international official recognition of freedom of association (or trade union) was made.

Thus, nowadays the freedom of association (that is of trade union) and its resulting rights, such as the right to trade union action, strike, collective autonomy and collective bargaining are usually guaranteed constitutionally and legislatively, much more seldom customarily, in the legal order of most European states. Nevertheless, in order for trade union action to be practised effectively, it presupposes: (a) the guarantee of institutional terms of existence and operation of trade unions; (b) the guarantee of trade union objectives; and (c) the guarantee of mechanisms, tools and procedures that are required for the achievement of trade union objectives (Travlos–Tzanetatos, 1991).

In Greece, up to the force of the 1975 Constitution, the Constitution that was in effect periodically[20] contained no provisions on which legislation relevant to collective labour relations, the right to associate, to collective action and collective autonomy should be founded (Mitsou, 1982, p. 8). Up to 1975, the Collective Labour Law was formed in the fringes of the constitutional legal order, a fact that was interpreted by some positively and affirmatively and by some others

---

20 See the Greek Constitutions of the years 1822, 1844, 1911 and 1952.

negatively. More specifically, up to 1975, labour trade unionism and "the freedom to a trade union" was being based on the interpretations of "the freedom of association"[21] given by labour lawyers, constitutionalists and courts occasionally, which was considered to include obviously the freedom to join a trade union[22]. That was the background on which the creation of first working professional associations had already based since 1879.

The 1975/86 Constitution, contrary to the previous Constitutions[23], guaranteed in a direct way the freedoms of association and trade union (Koukiadis, 1981, p. 261) and, more specifically, both the basic right to associate (join a trade union) (Paragraph 1, Article 23) and the total of relevant and others rights with the particular provisions for collective labour conventions (Paragraph 2, Article 22) and strike (Paragraph 2, Article 23). At the same time, the state for first time was compelled to take all the essential measures for the free exercise of trade union freedoms. More specifically, for the free exercise of trade union freedom, the state took essential measures according to Paragraph 1, Article 23 of the Constitution and the provisions of Law 1264 of 1982. The objective of trade union organizations is to safeguard and promote the labour, financial, security, social and trade union interests of employees (Paragraph 1, Article 4, Law 1264/1982). The freedom of association (to join a trade union) is protected against potential interferences of the employer's side. The government bodies have the obligation to ensure the establishment and the autonomous operation of trade union organizations (Article 14, Law 1264/1982). Employers cannot participate in trade union organizations (Paragraph 3, Article 4, Law 1264/1982). After Law 1915 of 1990 had been in force – which regulated certain issues, such as the finances of trade union organizations (Articles 7 & 8, Law 1915/1990) and the conditions and the terms of the right to strike (Articles 1, 2, 3, 4 & 5, Law 1915/1990) – some relevant restrictions were imposed.

---

21 See Article 11 in Greek Constitutions of the years 1864, 1911 and 1952.

22 Following the tactics of the previous Greek Constitution, the Greek Constitution of 1952, does not provide direct and independent guarantee of freedom of association. Nevertheless, it explicitly prohibited the strike to civil servants and public officials (Paragraph 4, Article 11), which was interpreted as a recognition of the right to strike for wage earners with dependent employment contract. Shortly after, the jurisprudence of the Supreme Court recognized the right to strike (AP 670/1953) and lock out (AP 431/1959); see, Mitsou, 1982, pp. 13–14.

23 For the purpose of freedom of association under the Constitution of the year 1975, see Leventis, 1981, p. 29.

The consolidation of the total of trade union freedoms in a direct and general way led the constitutional legislator to the explicit report of special cases and provisions which impose restrictions to the right to association (i.e. to join a trade union) for only certain categories of employees (Paragraph 3, Article 23), as civil servants and in certain cases such as employees of public enterprises.

3.5 Modern Trade Unions

"The trade union movement is an expression of collective representation of employees, aiming to satisfy their interests against the policy of the capital and draws its emergence and development upon the historical and social development that contributed to the parallel development of the capitalistic way of production and to creation of the labour world" (Kouzis, 2005). According to the classic definition by Sidney and Beatrice Webb, trade union organizations, "are a permanent union of employees the aim of which is to maintain or improve their employment conditions and their life" (Katsanevas, 1994). A formal and generally acceptable definition of trade unions is that of mass voluntary organizations of employees whose work is to represent, defend and promote their members' interests[24].

An important issue concerns the reasons why employees join an association or a trade union. Some important motives for employees' participation in trade unions are considered the following: improvement of employment conditions and reinforcement of bargaining force while claiming wages and increases; protection of job positions from dismissals and unilateral acts of administration as well as from the unilateral change of terms and employment conditions; guarantee of a sense of solidarity, common spirit and community; guarantee of participation in training programmes, social activities of recreation, in various forms collective or co-operative social protection – those of consumption or investment; contribution to pressure groups that put pressure on the governments concerning the reallocation of wealth and the formation of labour and social legislation. Respectively, the reasons that push them to trade unionism is that it satisfies financial and social needs, guarantees security and employment, guarantees welfare, satisfies needs related to the personality development as well as it

24 This definition, however, is very general, extremely vague and could refer to very different approaches to the union phenomenon, since it does not specify the type of organization, the interests represented and the terms and conditions of successful action unions; see, Paleologos, 2006.

fulfils the feeling of achievement or even that of self-realization; trade unionism both satisfies political objectives and gives the sense of a political participation.

As principal objectives of trade unions are considered: the pursue of fair wages and salaries, the guarantee of a healthy and safe working environment, the promotion of the safety of labour and employment from arbitrary dismissal, the benefit of legal and other support to employees as well as the exercise of political influence on the governments. According to Law 1264 of 1982 and Constitution, in Greece trade union organizations aim to safeguard and promote labour, financial, actuarial, trade union and social interests of employees. Among these interests there are issues that are purely related to labour and the regulation of working terms, that is, related to recruitment employment, terms and employment conditions, salary, the termination of employment relationship, financial issues related to income and, more generally, to employees' financial situation, social security issues, trade union issues concerning how to exercise the right to association, generally, and in an enterprise specifically, as well as wider social issues concerning employees' interest as members of the particular association.

In order to achieve these objectives, trade unions have at their disposal a lot of means beyond the formal forms of trade union action. Indicatively, these are: collective bargaining, as an in effect permanent dynamic political correlation of power and bargaining with employers that is not completed when increases and wages are simply agreed upon. Moreover, there are various forms of trade union representation and trade union actions, among which are threat and strike, which can function as the outmost means.

In the recent years, trade unions – trying to get connected with the wider social needs, that is, with the needs of the members of society as consumers – advance the practice of boycotting at the expense of specific products. As in most developed countries, the practice of collective bargaining has been projected onto a macro-social and macroeconomic level, and has assumed the form of mechanisms of social bargaining so that political corporatism is implemented. Thus, trade unions are not simply agencies of trade union claim of issues related, in a narrow sense and exclusively, to work, but they have been transformed into bureaucratic structures with identified and conspicuous position and role within the context of the whole institutional building of modern pluralist parliamentary democracies. Thus, trade unions, as such structures, mediate politically wider interests of specific social classes and groups, playing in this way a vital role in institutionalizing and regulating social conflicts in modern societies.

Because of their participation in this kind of bodies and procedures, they play a preponderant role – not just a narrow trade union but a political and social role – and for this reason trade unions can exert influence on governments, provided that they allocate processed policies and to the degree that they are not incorporated in the government's objectives. This new framework, however, presupposes both trade union executives' training, and the utilization, through this knowledge, of institutional possibilities that collective autonomy provides, which has often led – as the experience of many European countries shows – to collective or co-operative forms of social protection, welfare as well as to forms of investment or consumption, such as professional insurance funds, mutual funds, health care funds, real estate, housing and consumption cooperatives.

In modern, that is, societies, trade unions go beyond their basic labour and trade union objectives and aim at objectives of a wider social and political character. Thus, trade union organizations – despite the fact that they are of non-profit character, nevertheless, without aiming at any profit – can be consumers and credit cooperatives or organize activities or places of cultural activities and recreation or conduct seminars so their members are trained. They can also create special funds so to serve certain objectives of solidarity and mutualism of their members or even to provide legal support to their members[25]. Furthermore, although the ability of trade union organizations has been disputed to have political aims, it is conspicuous that their pursued goals – such as social, actuarial and trade union rights, income reallocation, policy making or social justice – are ofhave a more widely social and undeniably political character but they do not cease to be legal. At the same time, as mentioned above, trade unions – and this is something crucially important – often seek to promote the interests not only of their members but of wider groups or categories of employees or even of social groups that do not belong to the active labour force.

Usually, in various countries there are the following types of trade union. First, there are trade unions that are categorized based on the occupation. It is the oldest form of trade unionism since it is considered mainly a residue of corporate pre-industrial structures. The background of trade union organizations of this form is the profession or the speciality of their members, a criterion with which they become members of the trade union.

In this sense, this type of organizations contribute to maintaining or enhancing specific specialities, whereas in certain cases and countries they may exert influence on or even control in the entry of employees in the specific profession

25 Trade unions are entitled to refer to administrative and other authorities on all matters related to their purpose, their members on industrial relations and their members' general interests. They must report on and cite administrative and judicial authorities violations of labour and insurance laws and regulations or organizations related to the same unions or their members (Leventis, 1986).

Another type of trade unions is general organizations that are joined by employees of independent speciality, profession or sector of economic activity in which they are occupied. These general organizations can be of national, local or enterprise level, where relatively high rates of participation of unskilled employees and blue collar employees can be observed.

Another type of trade unions are the industry-based ones that are also the most usual form of trade union organizations, in which participate employees of a specific sector of economic activity independent from profession or speciality of each employee or enterprise in which this employee is occupied, provided that this enterprise belongs to a particular sector. Today, there is the trend of the development both of industry-based trade unions and industry-based collective bargaining. Often certain industry-based trade unions, in which employees are organized, such as those of banking or financial and Stock Exchange sector – in contrast with industrial industry-based trade unions, which are considered mainly "blue collar" trade unions – are called "white collar" trade unions; as such a lot of trade unions of public servants are usually considered too.

Finally, there are international federations, that is, independent international trade unions, which connect national trade unions from different countries, such as Educational International, International Transport Employees' Federation or International Metalworkers' Federation (IMF), that focus their activities in developing actions of strategic reflection, education and activities of trade union solidarity at supranational and international scale.

The formal organizational structure of employees' trade union movement is structured at three levels: the first degree, the second degree and the third degree level. At the first degree level, there are the first degree trade union organizations that constitute unions of individuals and are the base of the trade union movement. These are distinguished in enterprise-based, industry-based and similar occupation-based (Katsanevas, 1994) ones. Despite the fact that it has surely been supported that the first degree trade union organizations are distinguished (Koukiadis, 1997) in associations, in simple unions and branches, the main form of this employees' trade union movement is corporatist.

The first degree level associations are established freely, have full legal and organizational independence, are scattered in the entire country and are estimated to be about seven thousands, even if their precise number remains unknown. The second degree level consists of second degree level organizations, which are created from two or more first degree level organizations.

The second degree level consists of two types of trade union organizations: working centres and federations, which organize simultaneously the first degree level associations. Federations organize the first degree level associations based on employees' profession or the sector to which they belong and form a vertical form of organization. The working centres organize the associations with local criterion independently from sectors and professions recommending a horizontal form of organization; that is, they organize first degree associations of certain region at a second degree level, independently from professional sector (Katsanevas, 1994).

The third degree level trade union organizations belong to the third degree level, which constitute the leading trade union institutions and are created by the union of two or more second degree level organizations. In Greece there are two big third degree level organizations: (1) the GSEE for employees of private and wider public sector (i.e. public enterprises); and (2) the ADEDY[26] for civil servants (Paleologos, 2006; Kouzis, 2005); these two organizations are the main expression of the Greek trade union movement.

The third degree level trade union organizations of employees in an employment relationship are constituted by the legal entities of Federations and Working Centres (Theodorou, 1983). These are confederations that consist of at least second degree level organizations. Each federation and working centre has the right to become member of only one confederation. In Greece, only one confederation has prevailed, the Greek General Confederation of Labour (GSEE in Greek or GGCL), which, formally at least, joins roughly all trade union forces and with which employees in private-law employment relationship are represented; that is, employees in the private and the wider public sector, in the state and public entities, provided, however, they are not civil servants. GSEE's pan-Hellenic scope and the recognition of its representativeness have made it the exclusive representative of employees against the government's power and employers' organizations (Koukiadis, 1997).

Each federation organizes at a second degree level first degree associations, whose most members come from certain professional sector; that is, they represent the employees of an industry sector or services or profession, whereas there is no restriction in the geographic scope of federations (Koukiadis, 1997); they only consist of associations, and their members are only legal entities. Federations can be only industry-based or similar occupation-based; that is, they are divided into in industry-based and similar occupation–based; they are pan-Hellenic from their statute, while the number of second degree federations that

26 ADEDY (Supreme Administration of Greek Civil Servants Trade Unions or Greek Civil Servants' Union (Reuters)), which has a membership of 45 federations and associations succeeded in 1945 the Confederation of Public Employees (SD) as a leading trade union official.

belongs to the Greek General Confederation of Labour (GSEE) is too excessive. Their most important work is the conclusion of industry-based or similar occupation-based collective agreements (Katsanevas, 1994). Working centres, as local organizations, are the product of certain financial data that prevailed during the initial period of the trade union formation; that is, in the beginning of the 20th century (Katsanevas, 1994). Thus, today their main mission is the employees' representation at a local level in the various bodies of employees' participation, such as in local councils, the representation of employees' interests in the local authorities, the facilitation of communication and the co-ordination of action of local trade union organizations and the promotion of social activities whose recipients are the employees, such as seminars (Koukiadis, 1997). Working centres that were the base of the second degree trade unionism at the first stages of trade union movement were undermined after 1950 for the benefit of federations, whereas today their role is exceptionally limited.

Business associations – which organize their members with criterion the enterprise they are employed in independently from employees' specialities or categories – developed in Greece in big delay, due to restrictions imposed by Law 3239 of 1955 up to 1990; this law excluded the conduct of bargaining and negotiations and the conclusion of collective agreement at an enterprise level. Business or factory associations consist exclusively of employees of the same enterprise independently from the nature of labour. They organize all wages of financial utilization, independently from professional category. Their objective is to overcome employees' opposition to the enterprise and to substitute their multiple organizations with out-of-enterprise associations. However, the creation of such associations with small number of employees in enterprises is impossible, since the Law requires the participation of at least twenty members. The advantage of these associations is the direct and daily communication with the employees. Moreover, collective labour agreement that they sign with the employer is applicable to all employees in the business, independently from whether they are its members or not (Katsanevas, 1995).

The industry-based associations represent employees with criterion the sector of economic activity independently from the enterprise, the place of employment, profession or specialization. It should be noted that many times an extended form of the same professional associations is concealed under the form of industry-based association either by organizing separately employees and employees of a sector in a region or by including same professional categories from other sectors. Thus, practically there is not always a dividing line between the same professional sector and industry-based associations. A lot of industry-based associations function in the wider public sector, while they constitute the mainstream organizational form that prevails in public common utility enterprises and in transportation means (Katsanevas, 1994). Compared to enterprise-based associations, industry-based associations have the advantage that they gather all employees of a sector, something that facilitates bargaining with employers.

The same professional associations represent employees with the criterion of the particular profession, independently from sector, employer or enterprise, and are the traditional, at least, up to recently the most important in figures form of organization of trade union movement in Greece. The associations of this type have the disadvantage that their members are dispersed in a lot of enterprises that have different economic dynamism and, consequently, different problems regarding production, their operation and their employees, thus impending in the operation of collective bargaining that today require universal approaches. Their disadvantage is also the fact that they cause competition among organizations of relative professions, and that they are mainly a projection of anachronistic corporate economic and social structures, leading eventually to breaking into pieces of employees' forces of a sector or an enterprise, where trade union is considered more powerful and more effective regarding the forms of working mobilization. For example, if all respective employees go on strike within the context of mobilization of an enterprise-based trade union, this puts a much more powerful pressure on the employer than if a same professional trade union went on strike, and, hence, only certain employees of specialities that belong to the particular trade union. Moreover, nowadays that the associated universal address of economic and social problems is quintessential, that is, the problems of the enterprise, production and those of employees, these problems should be dealt in the source where they are born, which is nothing else but the level of the sector and the enterprise and not that of profession. For all these reasons, the same professional organization has already shrunk, and is getting downgraded substantially today (Fakiolas, 1978).

Based on the nature of working and professional activity, beyond trade union organizations of employees and public servants, there are also trade union organizations of self-employed professionals, while employers' organizations are an independent category (Koukiadis, 1997). Employers' organizations represent employers' interests independently, on the one hand, and in juxtaposition with employees, on the other hand. The most important leading employers' organizations are: the Association of Greek Industrialists (SEB in Greek), the National Confederation of Hellenic Commerce (ESEE in Greek) and the General Confederation of Professional Graftsmen and Traders in Greece (GSEBEE in Greek), which also represent the employer's side during bargaining and negotiation and during the conclusion of the National General Collective Labour Agreement. The Association of Greek Industrialists (SEB), which is a corporatist organization, has as its members enterprises that are legal entities and are engaged in manufacturing or related business and industry-based, regional or local employer's enterprises organizations. Respectively, members of the National Confederation of Hellenic Commerce (ESEE), which is the leading organization in commerce, are the second degree commercial organizations of commerce. Another leading employers' organization is the General Confederation of Professional Graftsmen and Traders in Greece (GSEBEE).

The governmental interventionism that had been practised in the system of collective bargaining through Law 3239 of 1955 and, more specifically through the system of obligatory governmental arbitration and the Minister's of Labour control of legality of the conclusions of collective labour agreements had been cancelling in practice the autonomy of the trade union movement for decades. At the same time, the system of bargaining of that law, favouring the same professional bargaining and contracts, condemned the trade union movement in multiple split based on the same professional trade unionism, deterring its industry-based development and "drowning" the enterprise trade unionism, which, however, presented special development in the mid of 1970s. Governmental intervention and the cancellation of the autonomy of the trade union movement was completed through governmental and juridical interventions in the internal processes of the appointment of the bodies of trade union organizations, which continued in the post-dictatorship era (1974 onwards) and to a great degree were covered institutionally by Law 330. The control of the trade union movement to a great degree went through the ODEPES (Special Resources Management Agency of Labour Unions)[27], an organization that was established to monitor the flow of funding to the trade union organizations during dictatorship.

After 1982 with Law 1964 on the "Democratization of the Trade Union Movement", the conditions of democratic organization and operation were restored – without any interventions – in the interior of the trade union movement. Furthermore, the ODEPES (Special Resources Management Agency of Labour Unions) had already been suppressed, and the financing of trade union organizations have gone through the Employees' Housing Organization (OEK in Greek) ([28] – to which social resources are attributed, that is, employers' and employees'

27 The ODEPES was an organization founded by the then government of the dictatorship in 1971 (Katsanevas, 1994).

28 Koukoules, G., (in Greek), Greek Unions: Financial Self-Reliance and Dependence, Odysseus Publications.

contributions (being members of the trade union or not) – and which has been managed by tripartite administration for the last few years in which there is participation of the GSEE representatives and those of employers' organizations. Nevertheless, there is critique that even the current way of financing of trade union organizations leads to their dependence on governmental wills and, hence, on governmental control. However, the employees' organizations under private law are characterized from a mixed system of financing. They collect subscriptions from their members, registration fees from new members; they accept donations and many are strengthened by political or other organizations. The bigger, however, percentage of their income comes from contributions of employees and employers to the Employees' Housing Organization (OEK).

The new spirit that undeniably prevailed in the treatment of the trade union movement from the beginning of the 1980s was not powerful enough to deter governmental interventions, such as Article 4 of Law 1365 of 1983 on "socialization of public enterprises", which – under the pretext of the described objective in the title of law as well as of the protection of a wider public of consumers which the produced goods or the provided services from "socialised public enterprises" – imposed restrictions to employees' right to go on strike in them, causing very intense reactions at the time.

Same reactions, however, were also caused by the practised – with special legislative procedure, that is, with an action of legislative content – governmental interference in collective bargaining, with which, in 1985 – after Article 106 of the Constitution was referred to, namely to protect the national economy – restrictions to wage increases were imposed in a way that was criticised as unconstitutional. However, similar interventions occurred in 1992, when a new state intervention in collective bargaining and wage increases was made, whereas with Law 1915 of 1990 excessive restrictions to the exercise of the right to go on strike were imposed.

Among lasting structural problems of the trade union movement, beyond the history of state interventionism and the lack of economic self-reliance, there could be included: the organizational multiple fragmentation and the breaking into pieces, resulting in the phenomenon of multiple bargaining and the intense involvement of political parties in the operation of trade unions (Kouzis, 2005) during collective bargaining.

Of two and a half roughly millions of employees in Greece, according to estimates, 27% of the unionised employees are members of three thousand seven hundred (3,700) first degree associations and of hundred and eighty (180) second degree organizations. This great and lasting issue of which trade unions are aware, and they have attempted to address it through a series of conferences, aiming to create a "Labour Centre" at the level of every prefecture, only one federation at a sector level, only one trade union in the enterprise, while trying to limit the number of the "same occupation" organizations. However, from 1989 – that the target of creating twenty-one (21) industry-based organizations within the GSEE context, and, more generally, the need for restructuring the structure of the trade union movement came strong and urgent – to 2003 and 2005 Conferences, although this issue came up and tried to be dealt with, no significant progress was made.

There has also been a similar problem of distribution and multiple fragmentation of trade union powers in the trade union movement of civil servants. It is characteristic that there are sixty (60) second degree trade unions in sixteen (16) ministries.

Regarding the phenomenon of the close relation between political parties and trade union blocks – which has resulted in the latter's politicization, it should be noted that the characteristic is not a simple ideological affinity or identification between trade union blocks and party-political bodies, but a development of close organizational links which are reflected in the operation of trade union blocks and representatives. Implications of this situation are: the vertical organizational structure of the parties, their close identification with party reports and the testimony of different party ballots in elections. These data often function in a way that they either contribute to bureaucratizing its structure or repelling employees.

In the case of the Greek trade union movement, practices that were adopted and operated historically, as the state embrace, cliental relations and intra-union, intra-party and inter-party conflicts became factors that contributed to deteriorating and marginalizing the trade union movement (Koukoules and Tzanetakos, 1986). The relation between the state and trade unions as well as between parties and trade unions riveted and made elliptical the relation between trade unions and employees, deterring the possibility of the trade union organizations to get transformed into autonomous dynamic entities within the context of civil society (Ioannou, 1998, pp. 63–64).

According to the International Labour Organization (ILO), the trade union density[29] between 1985 and 1995 showed a strong decline[30] in Greece, as it did in most European countries, thus reaching hardly 24.3%. With the most favourable estimates, that is, both public and private sector included and, since the trade

29 It is the percentage of unionized employees out of the total.

30 It was decreased by 33.8%; see Kotsaridas, 1999, pp. 6–9, esp. pp. 6–7.

union density in ADEDY and public enterprises is very high, the trade union density for the total of employees was calculated to be 35.8%, according to 1997 data, and 27%, according to 2005 data[31]. This constant trend of trade unions' demass has resulted in the fact that the trade union density in the purely private sector does not exceed 15%. It should also be pointed out that, on the one hand, the distance that employees have kept from the trade union movement has increased in foreign enterprises and decreased in mobilizations. Yet, employees' participation in associations has increased compared with that of other employees in the private sector.

Generally, a higher degree of trade unionization and participation in trade union activities have been shown by civil servants, employees of public enterprises and employees in public services with a private law employment relationship for a fixed or indefinite period. The two last categories are unionised under the GSEE, while civil servants under the ADEDY. Main differentiating element that determines the features of trade unionism and employees' attitudes towards any trade union action of all aforementioned categories is basically the fact that the employer is – in one form or the other – the state itself and, thus, it will take a political, bargaining or cliental position, something that removes the possibility of dismissal or other sanctions for trade union action.

More particularly, key role for civil servants and employees in public enterprises plays the issue of permanence that eliminates completely the fear of dismissal. More specifically, in the case of civil servants, the constitutional consolidation of permanence makes things totally different for this category of employees, whereas the provided by the Law or labour regulations permanence for the employees of public enterprises is being shaken nowadays, in view of the policies of privatization, de-publication and flexibility. Nevertheless, overwhelming rates of trade union density are still observed in public enterprises, which in many cases exceed 90%. In addition, however, the power of trade union organizations in public enterprises and banks (Prontzas, 2003) is supported because of their economic independence, since industry-based federations in the specific areas – beyond the subsidies provided by Employees' Housing Organization – have their members' contributions as independent economic resources.

On the one hand, the development and the decline of trade union organizations have been interpreted through three different approaches (Ioannou, 1998, p. 62), and, more specifically, through the theory of structural changes, the institutional theory and the circular theory. Within the context of the theory of

31 In Kathimerini, an Athenean Newspaper 05.10.2005.

structural changes, trends in trade unionization are attempted to be connected with long-term structural changes and changes in the social structure and to be interpreted through these. Thus, as in the old days, the following phenomena have played key role: industrialization, the creation of working class, the development and nourishment of solidarity, class orientation among employees and the presence of big industrial units during mass production and Fordism. In a similar way the trends in trade unionization in the last decades have been interpreted based on the new model of accumulation, new technologies and the new production model, the shrinkage of industry and the expansion of the service sector, the reduction of unskilled labour, the feminization of employment and the prevalence of individualistic values, attitudes and behaviours against the collectiveness that characterized the labour world before.

On the other hand, within the context of the institutional theory, the trends in trade unionization have been interpreted based on national, historical, social and institutional particularities, such as the centralized or decentralised character of the system of collective bargaining, the presence and the effectiveness of trade unions in work places, the operations of trade unions themselves as institutions of collective representation of employees as well as institutions of promotion of social policy and employers' strategies. Finally, within the context of circular theory, the trends in trade unionization have been interpreted through the logic of the operation of the economic and political circle respectively. More specifically, both the upward or downward trends in unemployment and inflation – resulting in the movement and development of the economic circle, the prevalence of the development of the political circle of political forces and correlations that are sometimes "pro-labour-progressive" and promote Keynesian policies and are sometimes "anti-labour-conservative", that promote liberal policies – are the parameters that determine and interpret the upward and downward trends in trade unionization, according to this particular approach.

3.6 Challenges of the Modern Environment: New Technologies, Globalization, European Dimension and Changes in the Structure of the Labour Market

Labour relations are considered more than any other social institution to be affected by political, social and economic circumstances. It is argued that these are indeed influenced by the changes in the business cycle in such a way that processes, content and perspectives can be determined as a whole (ILO, 1977, p. 91). During the last past two decades, labour relations have been moving in an environment whose components, such as: economic, technological, social, have been changing rapidly and radically, producing new original combinations of conditions. All European countries have faced a new economic, technological and social reality. The new data have had a significant socioeconomic impact and have exerted significant influence on labour relations. The economic circumstances of the last twenty years have been represented mainly by the effects of the delay of economic growth or economic recession and inflation, combined with high levels of unemployment and underemployment as well as with an increased international competition.

All these developments have imposed a different approach to the problems of labour, employment and labour relations (Spyropoulos, 1992, p. 8) and, consequently, they have led to a theoretical and practical search for the prospect of labour relations in the conditions of this global economic crisis, which has recently got a new dimension.

As the experience of this period confirmed, trade unions in European countries have been invited to address through collective bargaining two great issues: the large and complex issue of inflation and even the larger problem of unemployment. The data has been inconclusive. There has been no room to choose between unemployment and inflation. There has been a need for a parallel dealing with both issues through medium- and long-term solutions. Within this environment, the reflection in the role of collective bargaining in the battle to address these two aspects of recession emerged (ILO, 1977, p. 51); a reflection that has been maintained in recent years, despite the improvement in annual growth rates and the decrease in inflation, resulting from the restrictive economic and income policies that have been in many states and from the restrictions imposed directly or indirectly on those in collective autonomy. However, the key issue continues to be both in theory and in practice too, nowadays. Collective bargaining is primarily a means of defending social interests rather than being an instrument of economic policy (ILO, 1977). Consequently, it is a difficult in practice to hold that delicate social and political balance which will allow collective bargaining to contribute to exercising a developmental and deflationary policy without, however, altering its fundamental aim, that is, the collective autonomy and the defence of employees' wages and social interests which serve as an institution (ILO, 1977, 91).

At the same time, the exacerbation of the economic crisis and competition has got one more very serious repercussion. It has revealed the modern employers' demand (Christoforatos, 1989, p. 385) of labour flexibility in labour relations and in the labour market, aiming to achieve a lower cost labour factor. This is a development that has determined modern labour relations, and, more particularly, collective bargaining, since it has led to policies from which legislative but mainly conventional regulations have resulted, regulations which have been more flexible in utilizing labour and, especially in hiring, laying off and, generally, in employing and managing human resources (Koukiadis, 1991a, pp. 2–3). Regulations, resulting mainly from bargaining on a decentralised base, are more adapted to the needs of production and economic efficiency. Moreover, they result in the development of an entire theoretical discussion about how much this phenomenon involves minimization of social protection and deregulation of labour relations[32] or a simple transformation and reorganization of Labour Law, not on the basis of the principle of social protection, as it happened traditionally, but mainly on the basis of organizational (Koukiadis, 1991a., p. 2) principle and with primary goal business profitability.

Another important issue that objectively affected industrial relations and by extension the trade unions was the "invasion" of new technologies, which with the great changes it made in production structures determined the labour phenomenon and employment. The various modern types of machines, which have been used henceforth both in industry and the services sector and are operationally connected with modern telecommunications, have led to a change of the organization of labour process (Gill, ny; Thompson, 1982, esp. pp. 67–121), have created dramatic changes in the required professional qualifications (Burgess, 1985, p. 397) and differentiations at employment levels (Rowe, 1986, pp. 29–46). More specifically, in the services sector technological changes have led to a pyramid-shape polarization at the level of professional qualifications that is made by few, creative, highly specialised, secure and with content jobs at the top, while the rest categories of jobs remain in the base and in the periphery, which do not require particular professional qualifications and are downgraded and precarious compared with the former (Rowe, 1986, pp. 58–59 &. 103–107). Generally, the traditional form of labour, based on full-time employment and on a specific career pattern during one's life, employment contracts as well as the location and time of its supply have started being corroded. This leads to the conclusion that the form and structure of labour has now started being de-formalized (Castells, 2000).

More specifically, there are four dimensions (Kouzis, 2001) to the trend of de-formalization and configuration of flexible employment. The first refers to the "working time", the second to the "job stability", the third to the "location", and the fourth refers to "the social contract between employer and employee." Furthermore, within the context of the traditional employment contract there was

32 Romagnoli, 1989, pp. 1041–1056, esp. p. 1042. For the concept of deregulation, see also Papaioannou, 1991, pp. 162–163 & pp. 163–170.

mutual commitment between employee and employer (Castells, 2000; Kouzis, 2001). From the employer's point of view, there was commitment for the employee's certain rights, such as compensation, training, professional development and career. This commitment concerned certain social benefits and defined a career pattern that the employee would have, whereas on behalf of the employee there was mainly "moral commitment", "devotion to the enterprise", "consistency in the work" as well as there was "availability to work". On the contrary, within the context of atypical forms of employment, labour can be granted even in the form of independent services provision, and there is much less legal and moral commitment between the parties of the relationship.

The extension of the use of new technologies has brought about significant changes in economy and production sectors, decreasing the importance of processing and increasing the extent and importance of services sector, with corresponding repercussions for employment. It has brought about serious changes in the market of products, the structure and the size of enterprises, labour market, the extent of unemployment, the structure of employment (Bessant, 1989, pp. 26–60) with repercussions both for the composition (ETUI 1982, pp. 19–20) of labour force and for the trade union density as well as for the composition of trade unionism. It led to job losses in traditional industrial sectors (Gill, 1985, p. 162), the increase of structural unemployment, the creation of new job opportunities in office positions, distribution services and sales, Information Technology (IT), banking, insurance, financial and brokerage services, telecommunications and to public sector (Gill, 1985, pp. 96–114). It provided initiatives so that both the need of continuous professional training and employees' training whose priority is over operational qualitative flexibilities can be implemented, whereas at the same time the "special weight" of other issues is inflated, such as the working time, the content and the organization of labour, the quality of labour life and hygiene as well as safety issues in the working place.

Undoubtedly, new technologies have changed the whole economic and social variables and parameters, especially the environment, institutions and the entire system of labour relations. However, they have not only influenced directly or indirectly the trade unions (Bessant, 1989, pp. 56–57), concerning their composition, density and structure, but they have also opened a new "agenda" of issues for them, which are new challenges for modern trade unions and the institution of collective bargaining the content of which is redefined and enriched (ETUI, 1982, pp. 6–31).

The economic crisis and technological innovations have led to profound changes in the structures of production; more specifically, in industrial restructuring, decentralization of the production system and development of technologically advanced colossal or small businesses that contributed to the internationalization of economy, thus, resulting in various transformations in labour relations (Travlos-Tzanetatos, 1990, p. 88 ff & p. 130 ff; Travlos-Tzanetatos, 1991, p. 18 ff). The phenomenon of economic globalization was accompanied *inter alia* with the centralization of capital in modern, complex transnational companies and business formations and with the creation of international or regional economic integration systems (Spyropoulos, 1977, pp. 15–21). The first case concerns a variety of multinational business formations, covered by numerous terms[33]. The second case concerns supranational politico-economic formations such as the European Union. Both phenomena, however, raise the question of trends in the internationalization of labour relations and collective bargaining and its conduct at the supranational level, which will help restore a balance – at a supranational level – in the relations of capital and labour (Spyropoulos, 1987–1988, p. 25 ff). Within this context, there is need for development and coordination of the trade union action at a European and transnational level in general. The multinational corporation is a group of companies linked with a relation of domination or control, extending to more than one states, and is a transnational entity that requires a common strategy (Lixouriotis, 1992, p. 60). The complexity of shapes, types, activities, the expansion and structure of these groups, the fact that each one of them develops beyond the borders of modern states and, finally, the existence of an independent legal personality in each production unit at a national level of this transnational group highlight major issues and challenges for modern trade unions (Marginson, 1992, p. 529 ff). It creates legal and real problems in relation to the trade union representation and employer, a fact that strongly inhibits the growth trend of bargaining at a supranational level[34]. In this way, their apparent reluctance simply marks the real weakness to conduct effective bargaining at a supranational level, due to lack of clearly distinguished and qualified representation of both sides. For trade unions the key question is whether bargaining takes place not at the level of the subsidiary company but which trade union formation will undertake this representation in the transnational group.

New challenges, however, for the unions are created in view of the institutional capacity that the collective autonomy acquires within the context of the European Union, especially in view of being able to conduct European collective bargaining and collective agreements. The issue of conducting collective

33 For example, groups of companies, multinationals, holdings, joint ventures, cartels and trusts. More specifically, see Lixouriotis, 1992, p. 58.

34 For an analytical approach to the problems involved, see Lixouriotis, 1992, pp. 58–70.

bargaining at a supranational level has been raised as part of the reflection in the operation of social dialogue and institutions in the European Union (Spyropoulos, 1977, pp. 34–35). The post-Maastricht era, according to the protocol and the corresponding agreement on social policy, should not be a period of deregulation but rather that of collective regulation of labour relations with emphasis on collective bargaining. This is a period that – during acute crisis and intense politico-ideological debates at the European level – brings new challenges for the role of trade unions if: (a) the negotiation of the institutions are legalized at European level before the decisions of European Union institutions are made; (b) the production of directives becomes possible through collective bargaining by replacing the European Council; (c) the way for establishment of European (mainly industry-based) collective bargaining agreements is to be opened; and (d) even the joint-consultative (through bargaining) role of the parties becomes more meaningful at an EU level (Blanpain and Koukiadis, 1993, pp. 189–258).

These issues are being currently addressed only at a theoretical or a research level so that there would be initially the formulation not of proposals but rather of simple questions that would outline the context of the problem (ETUI 1992, pp. 41–53 and 83–108). The first, however, issues raised by a prospect of development of collective bargaining – at European or otherwise supranational level – is that how to determine the level of bargaining, how to determine formations that can be genuine representation of social interests involved, and how to determine the applicability of Law if any disputes or doubts may arise. All these, of course, are concerns which touch the current reality only on the part of the development of bargaining in European countries (Lixouriotis, 1992, pp. 52–53), given that existing hesitations currently inhibit the prospect of conducting collective bargaining at the level of transnational corporations Sisson, 1993).

One more factor that affects the physiognomy of trade unions is the change in the structure of labour market, the situation map of the labour market which accepts major influences and is shown significantly differentiated in relation to the past, thus affecting employment and the composition of the labour force, which has been changing rapidly. The increase of rates of structural mainly unemployment, the decline in employment of "blue collar" employees – that is, mainly industrial employees, the increase in demand for technicians and office employees, the feminization of employment – that is, the mass entry of women and various special categories in the labour market, the de-formalization of the work and the development of atypical forms of employment, demographic changes which are due to the long process of immigration, the labour of male and female immigrants (Psimmenos and Skamnakis, 2008, pp. 86–97) have created a kind of regional market of labour force that operates at the same time with the formal and organized labour market making substantial transformations in the labour force and, eventually, in the trade union movement and labour relations (Spyropoulos, 1992, p. 8).

The first issue that seems to be of particular importance is the downturn of the industrial sector, the expansion of service sector (Lytras, 2007, pp. 30–36) and the shrinkage of the rural sector that have caused – as the relevant data show – respective changes in the size of employment per sector and category of employees. The industrial sector has been affected twice. On the one hand, deindustrialization and disinvestment occur as capital for investment is shifted in the stock and financial markets, that is, where yields are fast and high, and, on the other hand, the shrinkage of employment in this sector results from the technological modernization of infrastructure and replacement of human hands from industrial robots. This shift seems to be of particular interest from both the perspective of trade unions and collective bargaining for two reasons: First, it introduces new issues or gives a new dimension to already known issues, such as investment, creating new jobs, lay-offs, the role of training and the reorganization of working time. And, second – and perhaps more importantly – it leads to a change in the number of employees in manual labour; it overturns the today's existing balance between "blue collar" employees and "white collar" employees with multiple effects among which the effect on the dynamism the trade union movement, – both from a qualitative and quantitative point of view – seems to be very important. Structural unemployment has been steadily occurring at high levels and with ever-increasing trends in recent years (ETUI, 1990c, p. 10). The halting of unemployment trends that occurred during the relatively recent past (ETUI, 1990c) has been succeeded by the current period during which unemployment is likely to be ejected. In each case since the 1980s, with successive periods of fluctuations, it does seem to have been essentially dealt with (Kioulafas, 1992, p. 47).

Another important development has been the expansion of the forms of employment that are flexible and deviate from the standard model of employment. In recent years, the increasing trend shown in three basic forms of informal employment, such as: part-time, fixed-term contracts and various types of self-employment, has been very revealing. More particularly, the rates of part-time employment on the total active working population have increased (ETUI, 1990c, p. 52). Moreover, employees with employment contracts of limited duration (or fixed-term employment) have fluctuated in high percentages of total active labour population (ETUI, 1990c, p. 53). Finally, despite the little attention that is often paid to self-employment, it should be noted that there has been an increase in this category of employees, which, to a certain degree, is related to the increase both in the service sector and in part-time employees (Cordova, 1986, pp. 645–646). In Greece the percentage of wage labour represents 60% of total employment, compared to 85% which is the EU average.

The extension of flexible forms of employment, such as part-time, seasonal, occasional, intermittent, work at home, work contracts or fixed-term employment, various forms of self-employment, subcontracting and provision of independent services, "black labour" and, generally, forms of employment that deviate from the standard model of the normal labour relationship (Cordova, 1985, p. 67) have contributed to the influx and growth rates in the labour market of categories of employees, such as women, minors, the elderly, the disabled, former farm employees, immigrants and foreigners being employed illegally. The employment of these categories of people in atypical forms of employment contributes to the increase in regional employment (ETUI, 1985a, pp. 99–117, esp. p. 102), that is, the employment of regional employees in precarious and low-skilled jobs (Lixouriotis, 1992, pp. 42–43) and to the substantial change of the composition of the employed labour force. Moreover, the unprecedented by Greek standards feminization of employment, the rapid entry of a great number of women in labour force – often in positions which provide flexible forms of labour – the employment of a number of young employees often without employment security and low wages, the massive turnout and the employment of a great number of foreign employees or illegal immigrants has resulted in the phenomenon of "poor employees" – either full- or part-time employees, which in its Greek version is called as the "700-euro generation"", if it hasn't already been in many cases less than this amount of money.

The implications of this radical change in the structure of employment are numerous and significant. From the main problems that arise is that of representing special interests, special categories, since these are either not represented at all or not represented adequately by the structure and politics of contemporary official trade union (Bolin, 1985, p. 30) movement, and, consequently, by the official collective bargaining system. It is known that today the official representation system is not covering effectively the employee in one of the flexible forms of employment, the part-time employee, the seasonal or casual employee, the self-employed, the employee at home, the small-subcontractor, the tradesman, the young employee, the young unemployed, the "poor employee", the employee with a contract or a fixed-term contract, the woman, the child, the aged, the disabled person or the immigrant. The limited presence of official demands made by the trade union movement for all these categories of employees – much more for the unemployed, who – although they are potential employees, are usually beyond the political perspective and the protective umbrella of the trade union movement and the system of collective bargaining – suggests that several points in the organization, operation and strategy of the trade unionism have to be reviewed, so that trade unionism can meet the new needs (Dunlop, 1958, p. 151).

Within the modern globalized post-industrial context, changes have been observed that raise important issues and questions about the class structure of contemporary developed societies (Lytras, 2000, esp. Ch. 4–7). Issues and questions that have come out of the research and have been placed in theoretical discussion among sociologists; within the context of this discussion a number of many arguments and counterarguments and counter-proposals have been put forward. First, regarding the upper class, who had the ownership of capital and thus was considered dominant, within the modern context where giant corporations (Giddens, 1989, pp. 72–74) dominate, which as limited liability companies have a wide spread of shares, one wonders whether the ownership of capital is a more critical factor than getting the highest management positions in these enterprises and particularly in certain sectors, such as in Stock Exchange and financial services. Moreover, within the context of the modern "new economy", basically of an intangible economy that is based on innovation, it is argued that the acquisition of knowledge and information is acclaimed as a much more critical element than the simple possession of capital (Giddens, 1989, p. 86). Moreover, as in the modern post-production and post-capitalist economy, the service sector has shown great development and, eventually, "white collar" employees and clerks (Giddens, 1989, p. 82) and the number of employees in the services sector have increased, whereas the employment in manufacturing and industry has decreased, many were quick to argue that this "employability" of employees has resulted in their approaching middle class as they have generally adopted its principles, values and standards. However, it hasn't been considered that such an employment of this kind today –when new technologies are used – is accompanied by trends of labour degradation and de-specialization, something that others call into question, talking about labour re-specialization.

Furthermore, no consideration has been given to job content, the relationship with which this is provided, job security, career prospects and salary, which is extremely low, depressed and insecure for the so-called "pink collar" employees who are largely women, after their massive entry in the labour market and the "feminization" largely in the labour force in the recent decades. It is exactly this category of regional employees in positions of the secondary labour market that A. Giddens categorizes – along with others, such as unemployed, benefit receivers or homeless – as "underclass" (Giddens, 1989, p. 84), who lack any other distinctive features, cohesion and awareness.

The dividing lines and the existence of disparities have not only been a phenomenon of recent years or even of last decades. During the period of great development of industrialism, with extremely low unemployment and strong welfare state (Daskalakis, 2000, pp. 277–321), there was a significant number of socially excluded. Simply, at the time things were much more different than nowadays. Even the existence of full-time employment, strong working class and culture of solidarity were forming a broader social context and a climate of social cohesion, which was restraining social marginalization, but this context doesn't seem to exist now. On the contrary, nowadays if it happens that any individual or group of people, due to social disadvantage, is ostracized in the newly-established and fluid category of underclass (Giddens, 1989, pp. 82–91; Giddens, 1979, p. 288), as it is conceptualised by A. Giddens, weakness in self-identification lurks in society, weakness in identity formation and the risk of cultural exclusion, as within the modern post-industrial context not only the full-time and stable employment is affected by job flexibility and insecurity (Daskalakis, 2004a, pp. 19–22, 97–105, 124–139; Daskalakis, 1995b), not only culture of solidarity has been replaced by culture of competition at all levels, but it is this culture of competition that has declared a key element, as was dramatically confirmed by the phenomenon of working poor, not being an employee but a consumer (Bauman, 2002), since the emerging – in the working class and among social classes – stratification has ended up depending not only on differences in employment but also in consumption and lifestyle (Giddens, 2002, p. 363). The method of delimitation of the concept of social substrate – which, on the one hand, does not seem to have clear boundaries and, on the other hand, internalizes a holistic approach that seeks practically simulate different groups of people without common elements, problems, feelings and without a similar treatment by society – reasonably raises the question whether the new *panopticon* category of social exclusion has been implicitly attempted to be matched and integrated into this concept of social substrate, under which many different groups in society and many different social situations are to be incorporated.

The decline of Fordism (Daskalakis, 2000) and the welfare state, the weakening of the welfare state and the rising levels of structural unemployment (Daskalakis, 2004a., pp. 37–70 & 97–105) coincide with the re-appearance of poverty in developed societies. Nowadays, although the increasing poverty trends, which occurred in the 1990s, have slowed down, their size does not seem to fall; instead, it is crystallized in approximately 20% of the population of Europe and, according to recent data of the Eurostat[35], only around 21% for the entire population

---

35 http://epp.eurostat.ee.europa.eu/portal/page?pageid-073.46870091&_dad=portal&_scheina=PORTAL&p product_code=ILC_LI02

in Greece. In fact, basic feature of modern poverty is its persistence; that is, its appearance is neither random nor transient, but rather a growing number of individuals or households trapped in it, due to various social and economic factors – of which over-lending is a very characteristic feature – and they are getting drown ever increasingly into poverty. As a pervasive climate of competition has been dominating modern society and there prevail conditions that prevent the poor from forming an identity, the poor remain – within the context of underclass of non-employees (Gorz, 1982, p. 67; Giddens, 1989, p. 89–90) – politically, socially and culturally a heterogeneous mixture (Bauman, 2002, pp. 254–255) of children, elderly people, disabled, single parents (Babalis, 2005), migrants, particularly minority groups, unemployed and working poor who have no other common feature than the fact that all of them are poor and, most importantly, all, as poor, become targets: targets of social discrimination and target groups of policies, which, moving within such contexts, are at least partially inadequate and thus ineffective.

At this point it should be noted that the "triptych: poverty, employment, exclusion" has been a key feature both of such studies and relevant policy responses up to now. However, this occurs, although neither poverty nor employment seems to have a stable relationship with social exclusion. And this can, of course, be explained by the fact that there are many people (Ministry of Labour and Social Protection, 2006, p. 15) who believe that social inclusion (Levitas, 2004, p. 214) and dealing with poverty would result from employment, whereas poverty is not related to employment. And while this, on the one hand, has a large dose of truth, on the other hand – and without the contribution of employment policies to address poverty or social exclusion being underestimated – it should be noted that these are certainly not a panacea, especially at a time when the phenomenon of precarious employment and working poor is a central problem in Europe, while the demand for quality jobs, which will generate income sufficient to ensure decent living, has become an issue of need and priority. It is conspicuous that, if tackling poverty and social exclusion is pursued by addressing unemployment, it should be pursued through the promotion of employment, creating new – not the existing – employment with redistribution policies, that is, redistribution policies of wealth and income.

A key factor influencing the developments in the trade union movement and labour relations are the changes being made and the data recorded in culture that permeates the system (Spyropoulos, 1985, pp. 40–41). In the field, significant changes are taking place nowadays. First, within the modern context of acute economic crisis, destabilization of traditional values, overturning of traditional beliefs and the trend of flexibilization or even of deregulation of labour relations and social protection, there is a parallel trend in decline in collective consciousness and solidarity, something that, from a historical perspective, was one of founding pillars of traditional trade unionism (Commission of the European Communities, 1992, pp. 14–18). These cultural data are now being replaced by "individual attitudes" that seek to enhance living standards and employment conditions, not through collective trade union struggle but rather through the personal, professional and social development and individual success "career wise". The extremely important development has undoubtedly serious implications for trade unionization, collective labour relations and collective bargaining.

On the other hand, however, powerful and of opposite direction trends are also observed. In a milieu, in which pressure on personalization in labour relations has been put in the last years, they are getting multiplied all those who insist on a pluralistic approach to the collective aspect of labour relations, the value of dialogue and the need for greater cooperation between representatives of key social interests, aiming to address the encounter of economic and social issues and the balanced control of necessary structural changes in an effort to maintain the social contract and the balance in the social system, getting as background modern relentless changes.

The total of these economic, technological and social changes that are described in this section have had significant repercussions for the trade union movement of employees that is now facing significant challenges against which it must respond decisively.

Chapter 4: Power, Conflict and Mechanisms of how to Achieve Consensus in Industrial Relations: Postfordism, State and Versions of Neocorporatism in Europe

4.1 Introduction

The system of industrial relations in Belgium, Germany, France, Italy, Great Britain, the Netherlands, Spain and Greece are essential components of the European social model. A key feature of these European systems is the common historical, sociopolitical and cultural traditions, which have led them to develop systems that are almost uniform in the mechanisms of solidarity and social protection of employees, procedures and institutions of representation and participation. These data have formed the tradition of the welfare state with a flagship set of social relationships on social dialogue and collective bargaining. The structural changes that have occurred in recent decades in industrialized societies have had a significant impact on national industrial relations systems, which were completed in a dominant economic crisis and an uncertain geopolitical environment. The interaction among national systems of industrial relations and the changing economic and technological environment have shown low growth rates and high unemployment rates as major trends at an economic level. At an infrastructure level, there have been technological and socioeconomic variations that have occurred because of the use of new technologies, trends of internationalization of economy, the integration of new socio-political and economic formations, the change in size and structure of enterprises and diversification of the employment map.

A key feature of modern national industrial relations systems of the aforementioned European nations is that up to date the state that, in various forms and to different degrees, has provided protection, created a minimum level of social rules to combat or curb inequality, and has encountered the size of modern economic and social problems, has been gradually receding, giving a growing regulatory field to the agencies representing social interests, a development that conceals prospects of civic character, too. To this end, legislators of the European states, whenever national legislation was insufficient or inflexible, have changed it so that the current institutional framework could allow the emergence of collective bargaining and its harmonization with modern extended role. In this way, collective bargaining, from a historical point of view, has been given another opportunity to demonstrate that it is an extremely flexible and versatile mechanism that can operate efficiently even in an environment characterized by rising unemployment, underemployment, problems with representation of industrial relations agencies, the changing face of the trade union movement and by decrease in their propensity for strikes (Commission of the European Communities, 1992, p. 29) compared with previous years. Collective bargaining confirms its strategic importance and vitality in a period where all important variables of labour world have changed – at a historical phase during which the developments in industrial relations have been sealed by the change in composition of the labour force, the diversified forms of employment and ways of payment as well as by the adoption of a multifaceted and diverse flexibility. Within all these upheavals, collective bargaining seems to recover its vitality. Through the levels in which it has dovetailed (that is, national, industry, professional, enterprise), collective bargaining is becoming the mechanism through which universal and related management of social and economic issues and the balanced control of change – through the convergence of agencies – that is, the social interests – are achieved. Furthermore, from a historical point of view, this objective is fulfilled despite the turmoil that has been brought about by a propensity to make a new compromise, based on strict income policies, a modest rise in wages and unilaterally imposed measures which, depending on individual national cases, contribute to making flexible or even to individualizing industrial relations.

Industrial relations are considered to be that institution that more than any other social one is affected by political, social and economic circumstances. It is argued that these relations are indeed influenced by changes in the business cycle so that processes, content and perspectives are comprehensively determined. In recent decades, industrial relations have been moving in an environment whose economic, technological, social characteristics have been changing rapidly, producing new combinations of conditions and terms. All European countries have thus been facing a new reality and data that have had a significant impact on industrial relations.

During this period, trade unions in European countries have been called on to address, through collective bargaining, the two great problems of inflation and unemployment that contribute to a developmental and anti-inflationary policy, thus taking the risk of deteriorating their own role in gaining collective autonomy and defending the interests of employees whom they represent and serve as an institution.

At the same time, the deepening economic crisis and competition has highlighted the modern employer's request (Christoforatos, 1989, p. 385) of flexibility in industrial relations and labour market in order to achieve lower costs in labour. It has been a development that has determined modern industrial relations, and, more particularly, collective bargaining, since this request has led to policies that have produced arrangements – legal but mostly conventional – more flexible to utilize labour and, in particular, recruitment, dismissals and, generally, employment and human resource management (Koukiadis, 1991a, pp. 2–3). Regulations, mainly coming out of bargaining on a decentralized basis, are more adapted to the needs of production and economic efficiency, having as their primary objective business profitability and getting more and more distance from the principle of social solidarity, which has been the core of regulations that the social welfare state has been serving since World War II.

Modern developments are related to the "invasion" of new technologies, which – by inducing great changes in production structures – has determined the labour phenomenon and employment. The various modern types of machinery – which are now being used both in industry and the services sector and which are interconnected functionally with modern telecommunications – have led to a change in the organization of labour process (Gill, C., ny; Thompson, 1982, esp. pp. 67–121), created dramatic changes in the required qualifications (Burgess, 1985, p. 397 ff) and have diversified employment levels (Rowe, 1986, pp. 29–46). More specifically, in services sector technological changes have led to the creation of a pyramid polarization at the level of professional qualifications established by few creative, highly skilled, secure jobs at the top, while at the base other types of jobs are maintained, that is, jobs requiring no special professional qualifications are degraded and insecure compared with those at the top of the pyramid (Rowe, 1986, pp. pp. 58–59 & 103–107). Generally, the traditional form of labour, based on full-time employment in a specific career pattern over the individual's life is being eroded. Labour is getting de-formalized (Castells, 2000) in form and structure. Four dimensions of the trend of de-formalization and flexible employment are referred to (Kouzis, 2001): "working time", "job stability", "location" and "social contract between the employer and the employee"

The expansion of the use of new technologies has brought about significant changes in economy and production, reducing, on the one hand, the importance of processing, leading to shrinkage of the agricultural sector, and increasing, on the other hand, the extent and importance of the services sector, with similar effects on employment. The use of new technologies has also induced a serious change in the product market, the structure and size of enterprises, labour market, the extent and character of unemployment and in the structure of employment (Bessant, 1989, pp. 26–60), effecting both the composition (ETUI, 1982) of the labour force and the trade union density as well as the composition of trade unionism. It has resulted in reducing jobs in traditional industrial sectors (Gill, 1985, p. 162), increasing structural unemployment and creating new employment opportunities in office jobs, distribution services and sales, the field of Information Technology (IT), banking, insurance, financial and brokerage services, telecommunications and in public sectors (Gill, 1985). The use of new technologies has also given motives so that the need for employees' continuous training and retraining as well as for giving priority to functional flexibility. At the same time, this use has inflated the "special weight" of other issues, such as working time, content and organization of labour, quality of labour life and issues such as health and safety at work.

The expansion of flexible forms of employment – such as part-time, seasonal, occasional, intermittent, work at home, work contracts or fixed-term work, the various forms of self-employment, subcontractors and independent providers of services, "black labour" and generally employment forms that deviate from typical model of normal industrial relationship (Cordova, 1985, p. 67) – have contributed to the influx and growth rates of categories of employees in the labour market, such as women, minors, aged, disadvantaged people, former farm employees, immigrants and illegal foreign employees. Within the context of atypical forms of employment, these categories of employment contribute to the increase of regional employment (ETUI, 1985a, pp. 99–117 and, esp., p. 102), that is, the employment of regional employees in precarious and low-skilled jobs (Lixouriotis, 1992, pp. 42–43) and actually to the change in the composition of the employed labour force. Moreover, the unprecedented feminization of employment, the rapid entry of women as a working crowd, often in jobs which provide flexible labour, the employment of a number of new employees often without social insurance and with low wages, the massive crowd influx and employment of foreign employees or illegal immigrants have resulted in the phenomenon of "working poor", full- or part- employed people. The implications of this radical change in the employment structure are numerous and significant. Of the main problems that have been caused is that of representation of special interests, special categories, since these either are not represented at all or are not adequately represented by the structure and politics of the contemporary official trade union movement (Bolin, 1987), and thus by the formal system of collective bargaining.

Within the modern globalized post-industrial context, changes that raise important issues and questions about the class structure of contemporary developed societies are being observed (Lytras, 2000, esp. Ch. 4–7). Regarding the ruling class, first, the question asked is whether – within the modern context that is dominated by giant companies (Giddens, 1989, pp. 72–74) which, as corporations have a wide dispersion of shares – the ownership of capital is more critical factor than getting the highest management positions in these companies, and, more particularly, in certain sectors, such as brokerage and financial services. It is further argued that – within the context of contemporary "new economy", an intangible economy based on innovation – the possession of knowledge and information becomes a more critical element than the mere possession of capital (Giddens, 1989, p. 86). To the extent also that, within the context of contemporary post-production, the services sector develops resulting in sharp increase of "white collar" employees and clerks (Giddens, 1989, p. 82), while employees in manufacturing and industry are being decreased, it is viewed that such an "employability" of employees leads them to middle class, as they generally adopt principles, values and standards of this class. At this point, of course, we should claim that it has not been properly considered that jobs of this kind nowadays, within the context of the use of new technologies, are accompanied by trends of degradation of labour and de-specialization.

Finally, a basic parameter that affects developments in the trade union movement and industrial relations is that changes made in culture permeating the system (Spyropoulos, 1985, pp. 40–41), to the extent that a trend of retreat of collective consciousness and solidarity mode has been recorded, which supported historically the structure of traditional trade unionism (Commission of the European Communities, 1992, pp. 14–18). The improvement of living standards and employment conditions is now being sought not through the collective trade union struggle but through the personal, professional and social development and individual "career" success.

4.2 State Intervention: Historical and Theoretical Framework

The questions of the existence of the state and the objectives of government activity (Jellinek, 1976, p. 230 ff), although they are in principle related to a questioning that moves in the field of social theory, can only be explored within the study of industrial relations, since the early 20th century and, especially in recent decades, the state – creating new types of activities (Tzevelekakis, 1974, p. 26 ff; Daskalakis, 1993) – has increased in an impressive way its intervention in industrial relations and, more specifically, in collective bargaining. These new state practices appeared after World War II (Petrinioti, 1985, p. 36), and reached their peak especially after the second oil crisis (Spyropoulos, 1988, p. 537), when the strongest state intervention in industrial relations was recorded in peace time.

The concept of the state has been addressed by two major theoretical traditions: the Marxist and the Pluralist. The differences between these two traditions have been shown more clearly in how each of them views society itself, the relationship between economy and society and the subject's position in society. For Marx and the orthodox Marxists, society, as a formation, has a dynamic character, which is largely determined by the specific mode of production and capital accumulation. For Marxists, the state and its mechanisms, as an expression of an authoritarian phenomenon, is based on relations of production that create class exploitation. The state, as part of the superstructure, is determined by the economic basis of society, and, in this sense, capital determines the operation of the state that works to promote capitalists' interests. The institutional separation between politics and economy, resulting in an apparent distancing of the state from economic factors, is for Marx a necessary prerequisite for building the reproduction of capitalist societies. For Marxists, the state is a mechanism which, with its operation, serves the interests of the ruling class, the growth of the power of capital and the exploitation of the working class, and ensures the process of capital accumulation and social reproduction (Petrinioti, 1985). In this sense, the state is a form of social relations that characterizes the specific class capitalist society. In this society, the individual, as a social subject, is overall suppressed by social structures and thus s/he is in a constant conflict with them. During Industrialization, the appearance of wage labour and state regulation and regularization of contract labour – that is, the contract of sale of labour force as an extension of the individual right of freedom of economic action – is, for Marxists, the state's fundamental legitimacy of exploitation that produces class society and domination of the capital, whose interests are ultimately served by the state with its operation (Hyman, 1975).

Neo-Marxists (Giddens, 1989) – distancing themselves from this instrumental view of the state, that this is a tool of the ruling class – recognize that, within the context of relative autonomy of the political sphere, the state may make decisions that are not directly dictated by the interests of capital but by the special interests of bureaucracy that is part of it, which, however, does not deviate from the strategic interests of the ruling class. Moreover, the state may sometimes make decisions or exercise policies that seem or actually affect interests of individual sections of capital. Typical cases may be the exercise of antimonopoly, taxation and social policies. However, despite the fact that these policies may affect in short- or medium-term interests of individual sections of capital, finally, its long-term interests as a whole are secured, provided that the continuation of the status of capital accumulation and social reproduction is also secured.

Unlike the Marxist tradition, for Pluralist tradition, which adopts a completely different perspective, society is considered as a social system, civil society is a universal form of social organization, and the phenomena occurring in it are treated as being permanent and of universal character. As a social system, society consists of interrelated subsystems, but none of them plays a key economic or decisive role in the outcome of social phenomena. For pluralist theorists – and those neoclassical economists who agree with them from a socio-philosophical point of view – society is a group of people acting on the basis of their individual interests, maximize social welfare, with result that the public interest is promoted only when people act selfishly. The individual is free to compete in society and economy to promote his/her individual benefit, and this individual's ability is ensured in society provided that human rights, meritocracy and social contract work. In such a society, the role of the state is neutral and external; it is restricted to neutral and coordinated actions to provide the regulatory framework that ensures the freedom of the individual's action, the operation of social contract and the balance of power players

The state, as recognized by modern pluralist theories, is a key component of the political system, which – as a social subsystem – makes so sovereign decisions on general social system and its subsystems (Petrinioti, 1985, p. 37). The origins of these approaches are to be found in the traditional absolute theories (Leventis, 1981, pp. 56–57) of the state (Petrinioti, 1985, p. 37) of the 17th and 18th centuries. Of these, some grant to the state absolute freedom of action, to the extent that the individual is sacrificed for the sake of the "common good" (Svolos, 1958, p. 102), while others restrict the state's activity so that citizens' safety, liberty and property are safeguarded (Leventis, 1981, p. 57). According to T. Hobbes, the state is the sovereign political power that enforces compliance with the terms of the "social contract", which people comply with their own free will to form a society, whereas, according to J. Locke, the state is the sovereign political power that expresses the collective interest of the parties of the "social contract" and ensures the protection of urban (Petrinioti, 1985, pp. 37 38) and "natural and inalienable rights of the man" (Manesis, 1980, pp. 39–400. These views were succeeded by relative theories (Leventis, 1981, pp. 57–58), according to which, people mingle in communities to meet their needs. The cornerstone of social formation is interdependence and solidarity of interests among the members of a society and the existence of a "watchdog" state, which is a fundamental element of these theories (Duguit, 1991, pp. 16–17). Within the context of this approach, the power of the state – with regard to the adoption, compliance with laws and penalty clauses – is not uncontrolled (Manesis, 1980, pp. 17–18), since "social contract" restricts the activity not only of each individual but also of the very same state (Petrinioti, 1985, p. 38; Kassimatis, 1980, pp. 18–19 and, particularly, note 31). In any case, however, all three thinkers who first made successive theories of "social contract" recognize, as a source of positive law and the state, the individual's free will to be in contact with other people's free will in order to coexist together peacefully (Manesis, 1980, p. 39).

The origins of modern pluralistic theories can be found in these theories, among which of particular importance is the theory treating the state as the resolution center of major conflicts (Petrinioti, 1985, pp. 30–40). This theory adopts the position that in modern societies there are many centres of power around which various interest groups are clustered. While power centres of various mechanisms are competing, state mechanisms are first prevailing. However, on the one hand, interest groups exercise their power in order to influence political decisions to their benefit. On the other hand, governments in their effort to preserve their power respond to the demands of these pressure groups and meet the specific interests of different allied interests. In this way, decision-making, policy options and, generally, the design and pursuit of policy ends being essentially a process of bargaining. The political system is permeated by this process of bargaining which flourishes in an essentially common cultural foundation and background, ensuring the legitimacy of the interests of various pressure groups, their full adoption, satisfaction and integration in government policies and thus reaching consensus on political power. This operation of the state and the political system in general produces decisions related to and affecting the other subsystems of the overall social system, among which is the system of industrial relations. The experience of the operation of many national systems of industrial relations in Europe – especially that of the "tripartite cooperation" (Spyropoulos, 1987, p. 6–7) and "negotiated legislation" [Italy] / "negotiated regulations (reg/neg)" [USA] (Giugni, 1987, pp. 230–231) – corresponds to the positions of modern pluralistic theory on the political system and the view of modern democracy as "bargaining democracy" (Hayek, 1979, p. 99).

The state within an organized society includes all regulatory, administrative and governmental institutions which are controlled politically (Salamon, 1987, p. 219). Through these institutions, the state exercised the policy that aimed to ban the trade union and the free play of economic freedom and market in the last century. During the last decades of the 19th century, the state recognized trade unions and, by legislation, repealed the regulations that prevented the exercise of collective labour rights (ILO, 1975. pp. 19–25; Abentrot, 1976, pp. 45–54). Since the beginning of the 20th century, there have been distinct legislative interventions on regulating substantial and procedural issues of collective bargaining, imposing obligations to the parties on collective bargaining and on providing resolution and regulation mechanisms of collective differences. During the interwar years, the operation of collective industrial relations seemed to be mainly borne by the parties, while the state – avoiding the direct interventions – became discretely active to facilitate the operation of collective bargaining, safeguard the exercise of trade union action and to enforce the power of collective bargaining agreements (Windmuller, 1987, pp. 121–122). At the same time, the premise that economic freedom and rights of economic content may be restricted for the sake of the general interest (Leventis, 1981, pp. 86–87) was gradually accepted. This position has been historically the background on which both specific measures to reduce and control the market and the acute in the years to come state involvement in the production and supply of goods and services of major importance for society have been based and developed (Daskalakis, 1993).

The answer to the question of the causes of state intervention has its origin, first, in the acceptance by societies of the era of unrestrained liberalism that economic freedom may be restricted in favour of the general interest of all and, second, in the thought that state cannot be indifferent to what happens in such an important social group, as is the group of employees and employers. More specifically, the state's political will was widely believed that it had to rectify market imperfections, private and collective autonomy and to adopt rules that would have an evaluative and moral orientation, ultimately towards the public interest (Leventis, 1981). This thought has been the foundation upon which both specific measures to reduce and control the market and, more generally state interventionism, that is, the state involvement in the production and supply of goods and services of major importance for society were based and developed. In other words, this is the context within which state interventionism was developed historically, aiming to protect society by taking measures and making policies such as free public health, the establishment of maximum and minimum of wages, social benefits, provisions for health and safety at work etc., or protecting economy by making economic policies of how to regulate economy and markets (Daskalakis, 1995a).

Out of this synthesis between the need for economic freedom and the necessary restriction of "socio-political nature" the financial system of "social market economy" has emerged, a system that most Western countries are now following. It makes sense that the emphasis the state would have put on social and economic policies could affect at a large scale and the full range of industrial relations. However, it is argued that an additional cause of state interventionism is, on the one hand, the need for the reproduction of labour power, which was necessary for the continuation of the operation of the production model during the period of Fordism, being safeguarded by state interventionism and, on the other hand, the need of the state, with its policies, to enhance its image as a player who has the will and is concerned about citizens' welfare without making any discriminations. This reference is mainly related to state social policies affecting industrial relations and, more particularly, to the welfare state (Petrinioti, 1985). On this basis, state interventionism was developed historically aiming to protect society, economy and public health; provide free education; establish insurance against illness, old age and unemployment; form minimum or maximum wages and to safeguard various social and welfare benefits. The period of World War II was stigmatized by severe intervention to control markets and by a rapid law-making activity aiming to throw off the constraints imposed on collective bargaining (Windmuller, 1987, p. 124). In the decades that followed, collective bargaining and collective autonomy reached their natural dimension, whereas the first examples of state interventionism and legislative restrictions of collective autonomy recovered after the second oil crisis (Spyropoulos, 1987, p. 4).

Today, the pluralistic approach and systems theory recognize the state as one of the three actors and protagonists in the system of industrial relations. Nevertheless, its role remains largely external since the actors of collective interests of employees and employers seem to bear the burden of conflict, the pursuit of mutually beneficial solutions, the operation of collective bargaining as a form of collaborative basic contrast and thus the main burden of keeping the balance of the system (Petrinioti, 1985, p. 87). While at the same time state interventionism in industrial relations seems to be externally implemented either in favour of the public interest or other specific social interests, with legislative initiatives, or in favour of other policies which are the result of specific social and political associations formed by institutions of a democratic parliamentary regime (Salamon, 1987, p. 221). In any case, however, it is clear that the government sets the guidelines and policies of the state apparatus. The priorities it chooses how to balance economic and social demands and objectives and its specific approach to industrial relations are elements that characterize the general political and ideological orientation of a political power (Salamon, 1987, pp. 219–220).

Within the context of the pluralist theoretical model, the state plays a coordinating, regulatory and helping role for the competing interest groups. Its intervention in industrial relations (Petrinioti, 1985, p. 88) may take the form of forming the regulatory framework for the parties' conduct, repressing unlawful acts, supporting dialogue and conflict resolution or determining the minimum individual employment rights. In any case, nevertheless, the character of interventions is primarily technical aiming to streamline and facilitate the operation of social pluralism and political and economic competition.

4.3 Forms of State Intervention in Industrial Relations

Traditionally, from a social point of view, one of the most important fields of state intervention in industrial relations is how to determine minimum conditions of labour or minimum individual employment rights. Within this framework, very important issues for the employee are determined, such as the maximum allowable working hours, the legal minimum age for work, hygiene and safety as well as various related issues. Moreover, the state establishes a regulatory framework of "behaviour" of the parties in industrial relations. Among other regulations, there are those that regulate collective industrial relations, including trade union law, the right to strike, rules of collective bargaining, whereas the norms that regulate and protect the individual employment relationship and the employment contract are of special value because they are traditionally involved in a protective manner for the "presumed" weak side of this relationship.

On the other hand, the protective labour legislation established by the state's initiative was more than necessary to allow the reproduction of labour force at the time when the working class was working under appalling employment conditions. The legislative activity of the 19th century cannot be argued that it was the result of state initiatives; it was rather a consequence of hard struggles of the first trade unions not only for better payment and employment conditions but also for protective legislation that would prohibit or at least restrict the labour of vulnerable groups of population, such as children. The first attempts were made in England, which was preceeded in industrialization, while in Greece the first legislation on employment conditions passed between 1911 and 1914. The employment contract is a kind of contract that regulates the exchange of labour power over salary between two parties who act under their own will. The state – in its attempt to "serve" the public interest and because the employment contract has certain properties that distinguish it from the joint contract between two parties who conduct other transactions, in this case because of the increased bargaining power of one of the two parties, that is, of the employer – tries to help so that the existing protective regulations can be made used the best way. It achieves this by providing minimum levels of protection of individual rights at work as well as resolution services and dispute settlement, which may arise after the contract is concluded, such as courts, common or civil courts and special labour courts that are provided by some countries, and, more specifically, specific extrajudicial mechanisms providing reconciliation, mediation or arbitration services for resolution and settlement of individual labour disputes (Petrinioti, 1985).

Another component of the creation of the welfare state is linked with the questioning of state interventionism in industrial relations. The first phase of development of social care or welfare is called charity, and is essentially characterized by the absence of state intervention. During that phase, private and religious charities and local authorities provided some rudimentary welfare, which was neither institutionalized nor provided with predefined criteria. The welfare organization (Daskalakis, 2000) was largely based on church, community, union, solidarity, mutual aid and charity, but not as it is known in the 20th-century organized institutional forms (Daskalakis, 2000). The importance of social protection of labour and, especially, of social insurance was consistently an important issue for the aspirations of the trade union movement, as its cost has proven to be of such magnitude so that neither employees were able to handle it nor individual employers were willing to undergo through it. Within this context, the state – seeking to replicate the necessary for the operation of the labour force's production system and at the same time to legitimize the socio-economical system in the social conscience in order to achieve social and industrial peace for the uninterrupted continuation of the production model (Daskalakis, 2000) – was "forced" to intervene and move up to institutions that would deal exclusively with these issues, while taking up the partial funding of social insurance and labour protection. The welfare state – particularly in the form of the welfare state, as this now in most European countries was also resulted from a clear constitutional mandate – consists of a set of institutions that provide insurance against risks of old age, sickness, unemployment, accident, disability, and financial aid and services to certain parts of the population, according to some bureaucratic rules governing the distribution of available resources. During Fordism, when there was massive employment, there were respectively generalized, universal coverage benefits, unlike nowadays when the selectivity of benefits and covered groups has been promoted. More particularly, there were extensive and universal insurance programmes accidents, old age or disability pension, inability to work, sickness, maternity leave and unemployment, and a plethora of various family benefits programmes. At the same time, however, the states took economic and business activities (Daskalakis, 1993) in areas where the phenomenon of "market failure" emerged or wherever it was necessary for reasons of the general interest to produce affordable goods and services of major importance for society, such as the area of the so-called utility or critical care. Those policies led to the formation of public enterprises and extensive policies of "nationalization" or "nationalization" of private enterprises that worked in areas such as the aforementioned ones, a phenomenon that first appeared even to a great extent in the USA in the 1920s and later in European countries.

In the last two decades of the 20th century in most Western European countries[36] it was observed an increased state interventionism to tackle the economic crisis and major structural changes in the field of production, such as, for example, the efforts made that the Fordist model of production would be overcome through the use of new technologies. Thus, governments were forced to take drastic measures to stabilize their national economies, notably by adopting policies of economic austerity. As a result of these situations, the state legislates and now explicitly sets the regulatory framework for the function of industrial relations (Petrinioti, X., 1985). Thus, within this context, the temporary restriction to the freedom of collective bargaining is recorded, too. When all possible conventional responses to government positions and proposals were exhausted, then governments were forced to take action by taking restrictive policies of collective autonomy. As far as the state intervention in relation to the institution of collective bargaining is concerned, it may take the following forms (Spyropoulos, 1992, pp. 9–10):

a) The form that comes out of the role of the state as an employer to the expanded public sector in the recent decades;
b) The form of the unilateral imposition by the state or co-decided restrictions on collective bargaining for certain restrictive fiscal policy;
c) The form that regulates legislatively the procedural framework of collective bargaining and the establishment of principles of their operation as well as those resolution and regulation mechanisms of collective labour disputes;
d) The form of an effective legislative intervention either to cover legislatively the subject of collective bargaining or to impose an obligation or prohibition of contractual arrangement of some issues to the parties; and
e) The form of formation of state or independent or tripartite structures to provide technical support and assist the parties with information, research, studies, statistics, information, training and documentation.

According to the pluralist tradition, a legitimate field of action for the state is the engagement of its mechanisms in the procedures of collective bargaining when reaching a final impasse. In other words, the state, with its actions, tries to support the dialogue among the parties so that a consensus and a resolution of the dispute is achieved or even – with its intervention services that the very same state has predicted – to regulate the collective dispute so that a loophole ceases to exist and, thus, source of social tension disappears. The main forms that the

36 Except for Germany and Switzerland.

state involvement takes in disputes among the parties are: "mediation", which is of a more voluntary character, and "arbitration", which is of a more binding character. Arbitration is no longer optional and becomes absolutely mandatory when in the whole procedure there is an element of coercion, either in the way of the arbitration proceedings or in the composition of the arbitral body or in the binding decision (Leventis, 1981). The purpose of this compulsory arbitration could be considered to ensure social peace, the resolution of collective dispute with a new collective agreement or to enforce the decision of the arbitral body on the parties and, finally, to harmonize the policy of salaries of trade unions with the economic policy of the state (Leventis, 1981). This is especially true whenever the arbitration system is not independent but state-controlled, as it was the system that was prevailing in Greece from 1955 to 1990.

4.4 Fordism and the Welfare State

As it is known, the 1929 economic crisis revealed the need for the development of the working class as a potential consumer power, which consumes what the working class itself has produced at an earlier stage. The negative consequences of the extreme exploitation of the working class by capital, which led to the great financial crash, created the need for the development of a mechanism through which the halt of such procedures could be achieved in the future. So, for the sake of economic stability and functional reproduction of the system, the Keynesian welfare state was launched, attempting to become the guarantor and regulator of the relations between employers and trade unions. Through various social benefits in kind (insurance) and money (allowances), the welfare state is involved in the reproduction of labour power (Leventis, 1981, p. 131), assuming a part of the cost of labour cost, while reducing corporate profits and capital, on the one hand, but ensuring the survival of the system, on the other hand. Since its birth, the Keynesian state has aimed to consolidate social peace in industrialized societies of the West, by promoting and ensuring, nevertheless, the deepest needs of capitalist accumulation and reproduction.

After World War II, the welfare state – without affecting the form of the big corporation, which also elevated and protected – undertook to intervene in economy (Ferner, 1979, pp. 179–203). It got a proactive role and directly involved in economic activity (Vlahos, 1979, pp. 82 and 118), creating public enterprises and undertaking public investments to cover in this way social problems. The crystallization of state intervention in labour issues is the institutionalization of class struggle and the creation of collective agreements. Through these, the relation between capital and working class has taken a more predictable and controllable character, ultimately offering a balance and serenity, which is a necessary condition for the expansion of reproduction and running without problems market growth (Papadimitriou, 1996, p. 132). At the political level, expression of all these processes, which take place in the organization of production, is the establishment of all-inclusive parties that replace the open class struggle, cushion class conflicts and transfer class confrontation to the parliament (Papadimitriou, 1996, pp. 149–154; Voulgaris, 1994).

In this context, every European country has developed its own model of industrial relations and collective bargaining with its particular characteristics, which reflect its character, values and tradition (Windmuller, 1987, p. 81). Depending on the role played by the state and the system of collective bargaining at a national industrial relations system, four different models can be distinguished, which reflect the political philosophy and approach adopted by each government on industrial relations (Salamon, 1987, pp. 222–224; Crouch, 1982, pp. 141–148; Strinati, 1982).

On the one hand, if the unions are weak and the mainstream political ideology recognizes and even gives emphasis on state interventionism, then the model of state interventionism dominates, a version of corporatism in which – due to the failure of collective industrial relations and regulation through these employment conditions – the traditional state regulation with intense protectionism dominates. Since the position of the trade-unions power is weak, collective industrial relations are unstructured and the mainstream political ideology is that of liberalism, then the model of full market liberalization and individualization of industrial relations (Jessop, et al, 1984) dominates, being characterized by strong government intervention or abstention the aim of which is to deregulate industrial relations.

On the other hand, if unions are in a position of power and liberal political ideology prevails, then the model of voluntarism, collective liberalism and free negotiation is mainstreaming (Flanders, 1984, pp. 352–370; Fox, 1985, esp. Ch. 9). The pluralist ideology of this model acknowledges the existence of different or even conflicting political, economic and social references, which, nevertheless, can often prove synthetic and functional for the system. In contrast, however, with the previous model that considers the forms of collective action as destructured for the operation of competition and the market, the model of voluntarism acknowledges the autonomous operation of powerful trade unions and employers so that differences of interests are settled through collective bargaining. This assumption does not exclude, of course, that the state can intervene to ensure individual and collective labour rights or institutional constraints of the intensity of collective struggles so that a balance in the industrial relations system is achieved and the harmonization and reconciliation of social interests are facilitated.

Finally, if trade unions are in a position of power that ensures their autonomy of action, and the mainstream political ideology is such that accepts the state interventionism, especially in the form of state participation as a social partner in a tripartite cooperation, then the model of bargained corporatism (Salamon, 1987, p. 224) prevails, which characterizes the efforts of governments that adopt it so that institutions of collective interests and, especially, trade unions are convinced, through the tripartite social dialogue, to restrict – often in return – the demands and the special interest of their members for the sake of national economic growth policy of the country and the general good of the society.

Nevertheless, despite any individual national particularities, national industrial relations systems of Europe have some common features (Spyropoulos, 1992, p. 15). Since every system of industrial relations is influenced not only by its milieu, technology, balance of forces in the wider society but also by its connection with the political system and dialogue mechanisms and collective bargaining, it is conspicuous that the formation of a typology of national systems should take into account criteria such as: the degree of economic growth and technological development, the degree of organization and autonomy of the parties, the extent of state intervention in sovereign or equivalent way to production decisions through dialogue and consensus, the existence of conflicts as well as the quality and the culture of industrial relations. The difficulty, however, that has such a comprehensive and systematic comparative approach has led to the formulation and acknowledgment – rather schematic – of a typology which, nevertheless, seems to respond to things (Spyropoulos, 1987, p. 3). A first category comprises the countries of central and northern Europe, including Germany and the Netherlands. These countries – having over decades consolidated as features the presence of strong trade unions and employers, the operation of bilateral and trilateral cooperation and collective bargaining with the central role indeed, and the effective operation of a welfare state – can be considered to respond to the model of bargained corporatism or democratic neocorporatism.

A second category of countries is France and Italy, which – having autonomous and powerful trade unions fully integrated in national life for several decades, despite the increase in state intervention in recent years – have achieved in practice the respect of the effective function of social dialogue within the context of their advanced industrial societies; it is towards this category of countries that Spain seems to approximate rapidly. A third category is Greece in which statism had prevailed until recently, and collective bargaining had had a much more limited role (Leventis, 1981, esp. Ch A, C, D, E; Koukoules, 1985, p. 18 ff;

Spyropoulos, 1987, p. 6). Nowadays, it seems, however, that trends approaching to models of voluntarism or bargained corporatism are being developed. A fourth category is Great Britain, whose industrial relations system, which started from the model of a complete freedom of the market over the last century, went on that of voluntarism between 1960 and 1970 (when the Labour and Conservative Parties were in power), went to that of bargained corporatism, while in recent years it seems to have been adopting a model with strong elements of neoliberalism (Salamon, 1987, p. 224).

Within the context of this model, government intervention or abstention from regulation of industrial relations aims to individualize industrial relations and protect the unimpeded operation of the market from "negative and destructured" phenomena of it (Lewis, p. 361). The goal is to protect the market system (Crouch, 1982, p. 143) that is considered as the only tool able to lead to rationalization. Considering these views, politics in Britain in recent years has been seeking to destabilize the legislative employment protection and reduce the power and the activity of trade unions by being based on monetarist economic policies and assumptions in a formal acknowledgement of high unemployment in order to maintain the competitiveness of the UK economy (Aaronovitch, 1981, Ch. 7 and 10). At an international level, the expansion of the Fordist model was accompanied by a series of economic measures and activities, such as: foreign aid and debt of less developed economies, balanced trade relations with the creation of international financial institutions, etc. These changes ensured the development of Fordism as a global model of economic growth and organization of production, which as a system of capital accumulation, was expanded and dominated worldwide. Moving in a globalized environment (Ruccio, 1989, pp. 33–53), the Fordist model gets released from any spatio-temporal constraints and commitments, creating an internationalized model which is based on a new international division of labour and promotes the exploitation of raw materials and labour force of dependent underdeveloped societies by industrialized developed economies, monopolies, multinational corporations, cosmopolitan capital (Papadimitriou, 1996, pp. 129–130). Fordism acquires international connotation; it becomes an internationalized system of the organization of a globalized world economy and society, which reproduces the relation of capital-wage labour in a transnational dimension.

Within this context, a Fordist organizational model of production – which was based on and promoted by the large company – turned into looking at and regulating economy worldwide. As at a national and local level, so the global dimension of Fordism requires, if it is to operate, a stable and readily controlled market. The necessary condition was ensured through international cooperation which worked with the consolidation of an appropriate institutional framework (national and supranational arrangements for the support of a big corporation, etc.). The big corporation was a form of organization of production, which was protected and screened. In addition to the big corporation, the small business was maintained, which was usually limited to the production of specialized products, produced according to the demand of large enterprises. Within this protective, even at the institutional level, context and climate, the big corporation was operating worldwide, and nowadays its operation is further strengthened because there is a big investment in the use of high technology and automation of production.

4.5 The Issue of the Conflict

Central issue in industrial relations is industrial or labour conflict, which seems to be endemic in the relations between capital and labour but obviously is in dynamic equilibrium with institutions and processes of participation, consultation, social dialogue and social consensus in cooperation, which in practice may prove necessary since they work more and more in modern economies and societies. The stakes of the conflict of interest or, in any case, the dynamics of a balance between employees and employers that lead to an informal bargaining process, that is, to a "political" process of "correlation of forces" in regulating and managing industrial relations, defining employment conditions and labour payment, that is, in a situation that eventually leads to the creation of collective industrial disputes.

The question is why industrial conflict rarely happens. There are twofold interpretations. The first is linked with the sense of authority and the other with the institutionalization of conflict. The first interpretation has been discussed extensively by Bendix (1963) and Fox (1971). According to these authors, authority is a legitimate power and so the person who receives an order, accepting the legitimacy of the person who offers it and performs it with no further reactions. In contrast, the second interpretation is linked with the functional role of conflict in a business. More specifically, although some consider conflict as dangerous and deconstructive action, some others believe that this phenomenon can be studied from its positive side. Power and authority are two key areas of interest in social and sociological theory. There are two main problems with these concepts. The first concerns the fact that individuals are assigned the right to practise effectively power upon some people, while the second problem concerns the different and uneven distribution of power and authority. The starting position of this is that the differentiated and uneven distribution of power and authority systematically create social conflict or that similar to class conflict as described by Marx (Lukes, 1974). Power is defined as the probability in which the person in a social relationship is able to impose his/her will without finding any resistance from others, regardless of the basis from which s/he derives his/her power. Power may derive from a reward, the exercise of oppression, from legalization or some specialization. Instead, authority is defined as the probability of a particular group of people to obey a command of specific content. The question that arises here is whether authority requires power to be in existence. The difference, finally, between power and authority lies in the fact that, while power is essentially linked with the individual's personality, authority is always combined with the individual's social positions and his/her social status.

It is characteristic that Dahrendorf (1959) is preoccupied only with the question of authority, because, whereas power allows personal conflict, only authority, as part of social structure, allows social conflicts among groups. Authority is a concept and a theme that is studied together with the conflict, because it always produces conflict as power relations can only be either relations of supremacy relations or relations of submission. Both conflict and the expected results of authority and power are related to social relations and social status rather than to the individual's character. Power relations specify and determine the people who are subject to control as well as the areas within which the control is allowed. In voluntary social relations arises spontaneously a socially and morally legalized duty of obedience. Instead, the case of authority includes legitimized threats of negative sanctions for failure to comply with what is required. Within this context, the legal system also operates in order to support the exercise of legitimate political and legal power.

A social relationship actually involves coordinating roles. Collective social relationships are formed among those who are in a relationship of supremacy and those in subordination. The main task in this case is the effort to coordinate the group members. The conflict analysis explores the genesis of conflicting groups that are generated by power relations due to the imposition of the coordination of them from the above. In any case, the unit of analysis is the specific category of relations, while a dichotomous approach to power relations is being adopted. The dichotomous view expressed by the duality of "group in relation of supremacy – group in relation of submission" concerns all types of relationships and interconnectedness. Everyone takes part in a large number of diverse interconnectedness with a coordination imposed from the above, sometimes being in a position of supremacy, whereas some other time s/he is in a position of submission. One wonders, therefore, if power and authority in this analysis are concepts of "zero sum". Because everyone in every relationship and interconnectedness has some power, which to the extent is not evenly distributed, it is doubtful whether authority can ever be a concept of "zero-sum game." Instead, power is a concept of "zero sum", which, regardless of how fairly it is distributed, always draws a dividing line between those who have little power and those who have none.

In his work, Wright Mills (1948, and 1956, esp. p. 269–324) argues that in modern times the basic problem with power is decision-making. Today, power is associated with the management of condescension and consensus and is used without the logic and sense of who is in the relation of submission. Three are the main types of this power. First, power is what is justified by the beliefs of the person who submits himself/herself willingly. Second, manipulation, that is, power that operates without the weaker being aware of it; and third, coercion and oppression, that is, power that operates through the use of threats and creates fear of punishment for non-compliance.

The origins of the theoretical discussion about conflict are detected in the oeuvre of Marx and Weber and in the concept of coercion rather than in consensus as a pre-condition, which safeguards social order (Filias, 1980 and 1988). Marx points to the existence of a bipolar system in social structure: the proletariat and capitalists who compete for control over the means of economic production. Although he agrees on the importance of wealth, Weber argues that power and social status are equivalent in terms of importance. However, both theorists essentially argue that different groups are in conflict due to the scarcity of social goods.

Functionalist theories that prevailed after World War II treated conflict as a phenomenon of an important social character the nature of which is extraordinary; they were criticized mainly by Marxist sociologists that their frameworks are not strong theoretical interpretative ones, thus they are unable to make people understand the phenomenon of conflict (Clegg, and Sewell, 2001, pp. 2554–2559, esp. p. 2555). For Parsons, "analysis of conflict and change is of minor importance compared to the crucial question which is to analyze the factors of maintaining a system in balance despite the existence of social conflict and social conflict areas" (Filias, 1980, p. 150). Nevertheless, Parsons (1964) himself was obviously aware of the fact that conflict does not outflank social relations, so the primary objective of the theoretical scheme he established was to make it rare and exceptional as a phenomenon. Functionalism treats social institutions as overlapping, interlinked and dovetailed with the mechanisms of social integration. However, "social integration, even if it is unfeasible, is the mainstream objective in every social system. Social conflicts and social tension – which are forms of "deviation" and operate in a deregulatory and deconstructive way – have an inherent tendency to get integrated and institutionalized in the system."

(Filias, 1988, p. 22) Nevertheless, despite the fact that there is no conflict for most of the time, social relations remain very vulnerable. This situation is a sign that something is dysfunctional, that something abnormal is happening, that great social dislocation is occurring, which may lead to a change (Cohen, 1986). This social change, however, even if it occurs, is of a sorted character, "which is due to the fact that social balance is not upset by any 'dysfunctionalities', since there is enormous regulatory power of 'common assumptions' that remain steadfast and support the existing order" (Filias, 1988).

On the one hand, Parsons' functionalism does not see Marxists' perception of society. More particularly, Parsons does not include the concept of power struggle in his approach to society; instead, he envisions a utopian society of consensus and harmony. Thus, what can reasonably be asked is how Functionalists interpret conflict, imbalance and disharmony that occur daily in society. According to functionalist theory, every society is a relatively stable structure of components dovetailed harmoniously together, each of which performs a function, which helps maintain the social system. But every function in the social structure is based on consensus among members of society on the value system.

On the other hand, the Marxist theory of conflict argues that every society is in a state of constant change at every moment. Every society displays disintegration and conflict at every point. For Marxists, conflict is to be found in all important social relationships because these incorporate class relations in a number of ways, relations which are fundamental to social life and are based on conflicting interests (Clegg, and Sewell, 2001). Conflict is everywhere and every component of society contributes to disruption and change in society that is based on oppression that some members impose on others. So Marxists do not agree theoretically with the approaches to conflict that believe that this occurs only when it is expressed openly. For them, as for other sociologists, such approaches simply cover conflict, which is apparently inherent in conflicts of interest, since the weakest part of this conflict is usually quite frightened, if not alienated, so it is reluctant to express and support its interests (Clegg, and Sewell, 2001).

Being convinced, therefore, these theorists that conflict is endemic in wider social relations look for and explore primarily the most subtle and hidden manifestations of it (Lukes, 1974). Obviously, Functionalism and Marxism are opposites. However, in reality it seems that they agree on the dimension, the importance and universality of the conflict as a phenomenon. For Marxist and Functionalist sociologists, conflict may be extremely important in its consequences and its effects, since it causes widespread and indeterminate social disruption before social change follows (Clegg and Sewell, 2001). As they claim, capitalist economic organization requires a class system based on the relation of capital and wage labour. Capitalist class relations are relations of exploitation and promote lasting forms of conflict and class struggle (Giddens, 1989, p. 61). Social conflict, therefore, comes from the fact that there is scarcity and uneven distribution of economic power in society, and some are owners of the means of production, while others simply sell their labour power to the former. Social and political conflict in any form is only one form of manifestation of underlying economic conflict in the society (Salamon, 1987, p. 31). For Marxists, without social conflict, which is the source of social change, society would stagnate. It is thus a constant of the way how underlying contradictions of social relations are conclusively, even catastrophically, resolved, upon which social order is based. For this reason, unlike the initial view they create, both Structural Functionalism and Marxism do not seem to be diametrically opposite, in the way they treat the collision and conflict. This comment refers to the particular way in which Marxists face the existing social order, which sometimes seems to lead to adoption of functionalist assumptions. For example, for Marxists, the nature of social and political institutions reinforces the position of ruling class (Salamon, 1987). Thus, in both approaches, all social institutions are interrelated and, to the degree that, for Marxists, class domination operates effectively, all institutions tend to maintain the stability of the existing social order. This inherent and latent in Marxist theory functionalism became particularly conspicuous in structural Marxism, which was developed in France in the 1970s – with the characteristic example of Althusser (Filias, 1988, pp. 28–50; Poulantzas, 1968), who outlined the total of capitalist domination in such a way that social conflict may seem almost impossible (Clegg, and Sewell, 2001, p. 2556). The modern theory of conflict reopened the debate about social conflict in the 1960s. The functionalist theory focused on the role of "dominant", harmony and integration of the social system, whereas the Marxist theory of conflict focused on the role of oppression of the dominated. In this way, society is constantly changing, that is, the change results from social conflict.

An important, though, development in the study of social conflict arose the 1950s with the idea of institutionalization of conflict (Harbison, 1954). Dahrendorf's theory (Pazarzi, 2001, pp. 105–106), using the theory of confrontational approach, attempts to demonstrate how power relations produce conflicts of roles (Filias, 1980) and of interest, and how, under certain conditions, they lead to formation of organized competing groups within limited social organizations and societies (Clegg, and Sewell, 2001). Class differences and frictions, which were intense when the industrial society emerged, have largely disappeared "since the establishment of acceptable ways 'industrial bargaining' in conjunction with the extension of the right to vote and form political parties in the general population"

(Giddens, 1989, pp. 52–53; Lipset, 1960)and, of course, of the total of all political and civil rights, which were the background of legitimization of both the private business activity and the contract wage labour on contractual basis contributing to the formation of capitalism (Giddens, 1989, pp. 53 and 78–79).

At this point, the theory known as "institutionalization of 'class conflict'" was formulated (Giddens, 1989, p. 52). This view was based on the assumption that if there were mechanisms that could distinguish among different institutional areas, then conflict that occurs in one area would effectively be prevented without being dispersed to other institutional areas, something that would reduce conflict. Because this component was considered critical of the success of the communist regimes at the time, there was then a great theoretical interest in those mechanisms that can separate politics from industrial conflict (Clegg and Sewell, 2001, p. 2557). Dahrendorf (Lytras, 2008, pp. 180–184) argues that the exercise of power in society does not aim to annihilate the other side. The world is not completely divided; there are simply "winners and losers." Power dominates and controls the weakest, whereas the strongest establish a social structure through which they seek to keep control of things. Within this context, positions of power are widely distributed, while individuals have always got partial power. And it is a fact that social interests were expressed organizationally through a large wave of institutionalization developed already in the first half of the 20th century (Clegg and Sewell, 2001, p. 2557).

Theories of institutionalization of conflict often overlap with the functionalist approach. First, representatives of both approaches disagree with basic Marxist assumptions. Moreover, the idea that institutional areas can be isolated from each other was quite compatible with the functionalist approach, which argues that such mechanisms exist between the formations through which social integration is achieved (Clegg and Sewell, 2001). Functionalism, however, and T. Parsons insisted on aspects related to stability, balance and consensus in the wider social system, whereas Dahrendorf pointed to two aspects of society. Considering that Functionalists are utopians, Dahrendorf argued that there can be no society in which there are no power struggle and conflict. In real societies intensity and alternating phases of stagnation and change are maintained, while consensus and coercion as well as functionality of conflict coexist. According to Dahrendorf, the industrial society is a diverse society in which there is "complexity of cross-conflicts and alliances " (Giddens, 1989, p. 58). The fact that he generally adopts an optimistic view is because he considers that existing conflicts are channeled into the structures of institutionalized political and economic world order. He considers that multiple political parties play a critical role through which converge or get synthesized divergent class interests and industrial arbitration that allows the "consensus" of different interests only in the "industrial sector", "averting the activated bomb called 'class struggle'" (Giddens, 1989, p. 58). At the same time, social mobility, being a mechanism for providing "opportunities to individuals for social advancement", mitigates the devastating consequences of conflicts, preventing "the collapse of industrial societies" (Dahrendorf, 1959). Moreover, the emphasis of the approach to the institutionalization on institutional separation could lead theorists away from focusing on the overall interconnectivity of social institutions, which was the distinctive feature of structural functionalism (Clegg and Sewell, 2001, p. 2557).

Central questions of entire social thought have been how societies manage issues related to social structure, interest and conflict groups since the beginning of societies. As responses to these questions, two basic positions have been formulated and consolidated traditionally in theory. On the one hand, the functionalist theory, that is, the theory of integration which is represented by those considered as utopians, and, on the other hand, the contentious theory, that is, the theory of repression which is represented by those considered as rationalists. The conflict between utopians and rationalists, that is, the conflict between the two approaches is old and strong and can be traced back to Aristotle and Plato, Hobbs and Rousseau or in Kant and Hegel, and highlights the fundamentally different philosophical, cognitive, moral and political orientations of the two approaches. The two positions in all sectors seem to be mutually exclusive. But in the field of sociology it is shown that they can creatively synthesize a third new position.

Marxists argued that "at the economic level, class struggle gets the typical strong pressure exerted by firms and the state so that the so-called 'industrial relations' can be kept away from political contests" (Giddens, 1989, p. 66). For theorists of industrial society and, of course, for Dahrendorf, "the institutionalization of class struggle", which succeeded historically the open and aggressive class struggle, which, in their view, is confined only to first stages of the development of capitalism, that is, "the appearance accepted or regulated modes of industrial arbitration served to mitigate class struggle and turn it into 'industrial conflict'" (Giddens, 1989, p. 76).

The differences to the degree that conflict could be considered as a quite everyday phenomenon can be seen from the approaches to the study of industrial conflict. As far as the issue of conflict and cooperation in industrial relations is concerned, three approaches of different orientation have been developed: the unitary, the pluralist and the radical approach.

According to the unitary approach (Salamon, 1987, pp. 26–28), conflict is considered as an irrational activity, which – being manifested in the workplace – is a temporary de-structure, resulting either from failure of management or from the trade union activity or from behaviors of employees who do not adapt to the organization culture. While trade unions are considered as key competitors of dedication and cooperation of employers/employees. A fundamental premise of this approach is the promotion of harmony and common interests from which all members of the organization benefit. Thus, various types of conflicts such as strikes are considered not only as unnecessary but also as de-structural.

The unitary approach is based on the central assumption that there is a common purpose and common objectives rather than a fundamental conflict of interests between capital and labour. The conflict, therefore, is a deviation, resulting from communication problems and power management, whereas trade unions are treated as an unwelcome intruder. Addressing and resolving conflict is a matter that is exclusively handled by the administration, an issue of good communication, so the role of administration is very critical.

Unlike the unitary approach, the pluralist approach (Salamon, 1987, pp. 28–30) treats organizations as coalitions of competing interests, whereby the role of government and trade unions are purely intermediary, whereas the stability of the system of industrial relations is a product of concessions and consent between management and trade unions. The pluralist approach is based on a number of key assumptions. According to this approach, society and the workplace are composed of different groups, each of which is entitled to exist, and are legitimate to the extent that represent the interests of one social group.

There are five features of industrial labour, which are important as they determine conflict as industrial. In particular, industrial labour "is a collective activity," "co-exists with the division of labour", "is controlled by management rather than by employees", "is conducted under conditions of job uncertainty" and "is done so the owner of means of production gets profit", who recruits employers / employees for this very purpose and thus can also exploit them.

More specifically, it is pointed out that there are three main areas of work conflict. First, there is organic and institutional conflict, stemming from the settlement of the labour effort control, a field in which the rivalry between the two sides is strongly manifested, that is, between employers and employees (Jackson, 1985). Further on, there is conomic conflict, if employees demand higher wages, while employers greater profit. Economic conflict may be due to relative lack of payment, when there are unmet expectations and needs created in a specific way of life and a specific consumption pattern with the salary, the comparative lack of salary, that is, compared to other employees lower payment or even a total lack of payment, namely, poverty and the inability to meet even basic needs (Jackson, 1985). In this form of conflict, the main problems of the employee are income distribution, wage dissatisfaction and employment insecurity, whereas the main causes are to be found in resources distribution between labour earnings and business profits. However, as technology changes lead to the creation of new skilled labour positions and the elimination of the old ones, they often become major sources of employment insecurity (Jackson, 1985) and thus of conflict. Furthermore, research has shown that monotony and dehumanization of the work on the assembly line (Chinoy, 1955) have been a major source of labour conflict, whereas higher wages have rarely been able to balance the intense resentment caused by employees' faster pace, bigger noise or the "sense of achievement" that continuously decreased (Walker and Guest, 1957).

Within the context of the traditional pluralist approach, it is considered that these interest groups are equivalent in terms of power. They compete among themselves, but none ultimately dominates over the other for a long period, because they almost have equal power. This competition may lead to conflict, which is not easy to avoid in the context of competing interest groups. But as it remains "within the context", it is a "normal" and acceptable phenomenon. Within the context of this approach, trade unions are a legalized employees' representative, who mediates their interests and resolves conflicts. The administration, of course, may disagree with their employees but in no way it should obey blindly to them or to their oppression. The administration's aim should not be to eliminate the views that are contrary to its own but to achieve a compromise between views and preserve conflict within an acceptable framework, so that the enterprise is not done any harm. Whereas the state is almost a neutral guardian of the "general welfare", that is, of the "public interest", used as a tool by the majority to pursue its interests over the interests of the "few", so its role – under certain conditions – as a welfare state lies in protecting the weak and in limiting the power of the powerful.

The pluralistic approach has two basic versions ("Industrial Conflict in the Contemporary Business World", 2009), expressed, on the one hand, through pluralist theorists of industrial relations and, on the other hand, through pluralist theorists of political transaction. The theorists of both trends agree on some central assumptions, accepting as a basis of conflict the allocation among organized interests and as causes of an open conflict collective labour disputes, differences of interests, rights and legal differences. For pluralist theorists of industrial relations, pivotal points of research and their theoretical interest are: collective bargaining, institutions of consultation and labour participation as well as mechanisms for resolving collective labour disputes, which are paid special attention to and which are considered institutional arrangements that mediate between trade unions and employers, resulting in conflict being kept within acceptable limits. On the one hand, through these institutions, and especially through collective bargaining, which form the core of the analysis of this approach, conflict is attempted to get settled, before it is expressed with the last resort which is to go on strike (Koukiadis, 1999, pp. 246 ff). On the other hand, some pluralist theorists have argued that conflict is channeled into political transaction, mechanisms of social dialogue and social contract, that is, into mechanisms essentially of social negotiation, proclaiming strong corporatism as the core of the analysis the center of the political system and as a means of minimizing conflict and tension.

The pluralistic approach has been criticized manifold (Salamon, 1987, p. 30). First, it has been criticized that it is unclear due to the fact that several interrelated theories but quite diverse among themselves have been formulated within its context. Moreover, the implicit assumption that both sides: employees and employers have equal power is contested and decried, as various economic, social, political and legal reasons differentiate the balance of power in favour of the employers' side. Finally, the pluralistic approach is criticized that it downplays and impairs conflict in collective labour disputes, that is, it makes something standard that can be resolved or settled through relevant institutional mechanisms and procedures.

The radical approach (Salamon, 1987, pp. 31–33), like the pluralist one, treats conflict between employers and management and between employers and employees as inevitable. However, whereas the pluralist approach takes for granted the role that conflict and competing interests play in organizations, the radical approach, which is rooted in Marx, views conflict as a product of capitalist society and associates it with relations of production that takes the form of conflict of class interests. Conflictual relations in the workplace are just one aspect of class conflict. For this reason, the radical approach considers that what is important is society itself where an organization operates. The basic premise of the radical approach is the view that there is a fundamental and inherited conflict of interests between employers and employees, a conflict that arises from the uneven distribution of income, wealth and power in capitalist society. Those who own the means of production dominate over those who sell their labour power for a salary. Thus, there is not simply a conflict between competing interests, between employees and employers, but rather a clash of class interests between capital and labour.

An analysis of all three aforementioned approaches shows that the common underpinning assumption of all three is that conflict is inevitable. The difference among the three approaches lays not so much in the existence of conflict itself, but rather in how employers and management respond to this phenomenon (Salamon, 1987).

According to Dahrendorf (Lytras, 2008, pp. 180–184), conflict could not only be functional, but also social order that in fact could be supported by conflict. Since the individual conflict zones could be mutually separated, as it has been specifically provided for this concept, the open expression and functionality of differences, difficulties and contradictions are essentially the way in which people are renewed, develop institutions and in reality support social relationships. If conflict were restricted, it would have no chances to perform these functions, relations would fail to be open and honest and innovations would not occur.

In contrast with the radical approach, structural functionalism claims that the endemic and daily nature of conflict is that ensures social order (Clegg and Sewell, 200, p. 2557). Dahrendorf introduces another dimension of conflict by comparing labour conflict in post-capitalist and capitalist societies (1968, pp. 241–248). He claims that conflict in capitalist societies has been particularly pronounced as "lines of labour and political conflict were imposed from above." In contrast, in post-capitalist societies industry and society have been separated so industrial conflict has been isolated institutionally and thus has yet to influence other aspects of society.

Dahrendorf (1957; 1972) wrote having in mind the tragic history of his homeland, Germany, during the first half of the 20th century (Dahrendorf, 1966). In this sense, his work can be seen as part of a broader trend in postwar German sociology to focus on issues of dialogue and communication, which should be necessary for handling conflicts (Habermas, 1981). Thus, in order for conflict to get institutionalized, all interested parties should first recognize its existence. Given that, even today many representatives of employers and business management do not accept conflict as an inevitable fact, it becomes obvious how important is Dahrendorf's claim. Conflicts got further canonized with the developments that occurred during the 1960s and 1970s, which are based on Max Weber's authority.

4.6 Crisis, Post-Fordism and the Welfare State

However, since the 1970s and in response to the oil crisis of 1973, the Fordist production model – due to its "stiffness" (Lyberaki and Mouriki, 1993, p. 36) – led to the emergence of a new way of organizing production based on new economic and theoretical concepts and proposals. Flexibility – both in production and the labour process – was an answer to the problems that led the Fordist model in crisis. The persistence of Fordism in standardized mass production made it unable to successfully respond to new developments. Its inflexible nature led to stagnation, an increase in unemployment and saturation of the plethora of standardized products. Its inability to integrate developments made it overthrow more flexible models of production and organization. Both the massive use of high technology and globalization of the economy have contributed to the process of its overturning. Global competition and production for a global purchasing public, combined with the inability of Fordism to predict demand and, much more, to get modified according to this demand have led to the adoption of new more flexible models.

The production for a global market (Giannitsis, 1993, pp. 510–521) and the consequent fierce competition require a new way of doing business. The aim is not just to reduce costs per unit of output, but to survive and get developed in a rapidly changing world full of competitors. The most important in this uncertain environment is to ensure that consumers will choose the product of the given company against its competitors. For this reason particularly important for new businesses are research and development departments of innovation, which process how products will become more competitive in the market.

4.6.1 The quiet revolution

Under the crisis of Fordism, the business model that survives tends to be the small business that employs multi-specialist employees, makes extensive use of new technologies (microelectronics, computers, internet, email, satellites, and modern forms of communication) and gets specialized in the production of specialty products for demanding markets, with immediate and swift service. In the business of this form flexible specialization and new forms of flexible employment are attempts made by capital to reduce production costs by producing goods that are of quality, diverse and available in quantities which are determined by the current demand at any time. The use of new technologies by these small companies is their structural component, since technology enables them to overcome the disadvantage of their small size. With the increased use of automation is possible for these small in size and personnel companies to oversee the production process with the appropriate, of course, multi-specialised personnel. Small and flexible companies can more effectively cope with international competition. One particular form of this model is outsourcing, in which small production units produce specialized products for a larger enterprise (Georgakopoulou, 1996a, pp. 61–74).

Theories about Post-Fordism refer to a set of trends and changes taking place in the economic and social fields. They refer to the transition from mass production to flexible manufacturing, where -with new methods and with the help of technology innovations -specialty goods are produced to satisfy every consumer's need at the time s/he wants. Within this context, there are increasingly adopted new methods of management systems, such as quality control in production and working groups as well as new non-bureaucratic organizational models that are characterized with horizontal hierarchies, group management, performance measurement of customer satisfaction, payments based on group performance, maximization of contacts with suppliers and customers and employees' retraining at all levels (Georgakopoulou, 1996a, pp. 61–74). It should also be noted that the main source of productivity is knowledge in new economy. The importance of advanced knowledge and expertise will continuously increase, and economic activity will shift more intensely than the production of goods to services. The main objection to the theories of postindustrial society relates to how these theories deal with knowledge and information. Since knowledge and information were also central during the industrial era for production and productivity, it is argued that rather the real revolution of information technology and, especially, technological innovations differentiate "new economy" that was forming during the second half of the 20th century from that of the first half of the century; a "new economy" the main features of which are: information, globalization and networking.

Finally, the objection to the main positions of post-industrial era theories is formulated, that is, that there is not only an increase in professions requiring high specificity but also a corresponding increase in occupations requiring a low level of competence and skills. What seems that comes out is a creation of a pyramidal polarization between highly specialized professions, on the one side "at the top of the pyramid", and low or no specialized occupations, on the other side "at the bottom" of it.

The prevalence of the new model of organizing production has had chain effects both on the relationship that is being established between the state and society under these new conditions. The disorganization of the welfare state in the new conditions of Post-Fordism associated with the strategic use of flexible forms of selective work (Papadimitriou, 1996, p. 135). The emergence of the new model of organization of production and employment has gradually led to the weakening of both the industrial mode of production, which is the embodiment of Fordism and the welfare state, which was its functional articulation. Rapid changes – arising from the introduction of new high technologies in the production process (qualitative change technologies, decentralization of production into small flexible enterprises, substitution of the standardized repetitive human labour by machines, the weakening of national markets and the creation of supranational markets, the strengthening of capital when required for the renewal of new technologies, reduction in the value of human labour and, finally, rapid development of new forms of communication and dissemination of information and data) – have been modifying not only the organization of production and industrial relations but also the very structure of the new emerging society.

Under these circumstances, the state is necessarily modified and formulated as a decentralized and flexible mechanism. The modern state – as a result of the decentralization of production and fragmentation of the production process in small flexible companies, which operate on a transnational global market – shows limited potential, since the old mechanisms of intervention and control in the national/domestic market is limited vis-à-vis globalization. The welfare state abandons many of the functions that had during the Fordist period of mass production to ensure mass consumption (Papadimitriou, 1996, p. 128). Its protective character is expressed at this stage mainly with a shift from the reproduction of society as a whole to the selective support of private initiative and highly skilled labour force. The former protective for the working class character of the state, which was expressed by the institution of the welfare state, is being abandoned under the pressure of economic globalization and globalized capital. Labour protection and social character are surviving only to the extent that they are not in conflict with the conditions created by the global market now. Thus, in Post-Fordism, a mutation of the classic welfare state with a shift towards a fordist state is being made, which – in any of its versions (Jessop, 1994, pp. 266–268; Lyberaki, and Mouriki, 1993, pp. 40–43) – is characterized by its weakening as a national state. The new state tends to depend heavily on external factors, gradually delegating powers to supranational institutions and mechanisms.

In his analysis, Jessop believes that the post-Fordist state can consecutively take various forms, getting flexibility and customization to any power relations and questioning arises. Adaptability under post-Fordism is so successful that can adapt to different systems. This questioning distinguishes three basic types of models: the liberal, the neocorporatist and the neo-statist one. In the first model (i.e. the liberal), the market is the driving force for the transition to the new economic system. This transition is based on the privatization of public enterprises (public sector) and the establishment of a cosmopolitan, liberated spirit (private sector), which promotes internationalization of the financial system (even at the expense of domestic businesses) and the abolition of mandatory procedures (social dialogue, consensus). In the second model (the neocorporatist), the post-Fordist state has a centralized role, grouping individual private interests and aiming at innovation. Finally, the model of neo-Statism aims to strengthen the state, which operates independently from the market and individual economic interests. The state in this proposal assumes a dominant role in shaping the national economy, by intervening actively in pursuit of transformations and changes in various sectors of economy, promoting flexible functional form and by designing specific development strategies.

4.7 Power and Achievement of Consensus

The rationale of the welfare state – as it was after World War II, and social balances that emerged from the struggles of the working class and welfare policies adopted by the Fordist model of mass production – was expressed theoretically at the level of industrial relations by H. Clegg who, essentially equating industrial democracy to collective bargaining, focuses on encouraging and expanding the role of the latter. His theoretical effort, which is in full correspondence with a pluralistic approach to industrial democracy and industrial relations, includes as its key component strong, well-organized unions who represent the genuine interests of employees and operate independently from the state and employers, thus essentially performing the role of "opposition" in a proportion which the writer inserts between the enterprise and the system of political democracy. The aim is to develop both collective bargaining and a strong labour unionism, as both elements are key factors for employees' participation in decision-making related to working life.

In analogy to this perception, there have been developed formations of "bilateral or trilateral" participation in "social bargaining" of local or regional "pacts for development and employment", national institutions and processes of 'social dialogue' of bipartite or tripartite composition for "development, competitiveness and employment", and corporatist mechanisms of social contract for "social bargaining of modernization" and the consensual adoption of restrictive macroeconomic and income policies (Trebilcock, 1994, pp. 7–28). Such permanent institutions at national level not only in the form of Economic and Social Councils but also in the form of *ad hoc* procedures are currently operating in most countries of the European Union.

The criticism that has been exercised in these participatory institutions argues that these institutions were developed in the context of social and humanitarian policy and literature and met some rudimentary demands of employees who were progressive. However, granting such rights and introducing these participatory institutional innovations have been directly linked with operating problems in reproduction of the model of accumulation during the 1950s and 1960s, when the Keynesian welfare state, until the crisis of Fordism in the mid-1970s with the interventionist role in economy and society (Bonefeld and Holloway, 1991, p. 29), had taken both the reproduction for continuing the operation of the production model, the accumulation of labour power and the ideological legitimacy in social consciousness (Fox, 1985). The ultimate aim, therefore, to implement participatory schemes was not to democratize production, enterprise and labour but to manipulate and integrate employees in political adaptation and modernization of enterprises, that is, to change those conditions for utilization and profitability capital (Daskalakis, 1995a), when required. "The implementation of the institution in social-democratic European countries took place in cooperation with trade unions that had connections with political leaders (Nicholaou-Smokovitis, 1987, p. 29)". What followed was the rationale that prevailed corporatism, seeking essentially to obtain consensus. In the same train of thought, the operation of the institution of collective bargaining was extended and encouraged, while policies of social contract were being promoted either through *ad hoc* meetings and bargaining or through institutional mechanisms and procedures for conducting bilateral or tripartite social dialogue at national level so that consensus (Daskalakis, 1995a) would be achieved, with the ultimate goal to share the political cost of imposing restrictive economic and income policies (Daskalakis, 1995a).

Further on, the criticism focuses on that the particular version of employee participation which, without affecting property relations, does not contest the mainstream power, (Mitropoulos, 1985, p. 26) but it concerns arrangements within the context in which employees operate. Consequently, the development of employee participation and industrial democracy are exhausted in collective bargaining "and generally in the system of collective autonomy that exists and operates in capitalism" (Mitropoulos, 1985), without the relations of power and property being fundamentally altered.

The last, however, decades, the creation of international organizations, which are involved in issues of social policy and industrial relations, including the European Union (EU) and the International Labour Organization (ILO), and institutions of financial interest or restrictions that arise within the context of international cooperation, such as the Economic and Monetary Union (EMU) in the European Union, the World Bank, the International Monetary Fund (IMF), the World Trade Organization (WTO), are data indicative of modern economic and political globalization. This new reality – coupled with extremely high competition that the conditions of economic globalization generate as well as the change of the production model and the new economic growth model – has created new standards that affect policies that states make for industrial relations and the forms of state intervention in these industrial relations. Given that nowadays most centres of decision-making are being shifted to a supranational, European or international level, beyond the borders of the nation state, the key question is whether and to what extent each nation state can actually take initiatives and perform policies according to its will. It is a fact that within the modern politico-economic context, a revision of the traditional role of the state is essentially being made in practice, and important responsibilities concerning economics and society are gradually being displaced either "downwards", towards the regional and local level and sometimes to the level of the enterprise, or, on the contrary, "upwards", towards supranational, European or international level (Spyropoulos, 1987).

However, it is true that today, under the pressure of a globalized economy, the state is 'forced', by its acts or omissions, to a "policy of abstention" from the regulation and control of markets and enterprises. This concerns primarily sectors and markets where scale economies develop, so states employ various patterns and practices in order to regulate them. Such a version is the most flexible "privatized" construct of independent administrative authorities, which do not intervene as does the state traditionally, with "regulations of sovereign character", but in a regulatory way through "soft regulatory rules", such as "codes of conduct", which are not based so much on obligatoriness and imposition but mainly on the concepts of ethics and social responsibility. A similar rationale characterizes the downward trend of the state, on the one hand, from the control and supervision of industrial relations in colossal multinational companies, where the role of "Labour Inspection" is performed by the same group of companies or their subsidiaries and their subcontractors companies and, on the other hand, by regulating individual and collective industrial relations on the grounds that consensual solutions are of priority and that there is a general trend of contractualization of regulations, which at this juncture means their flexibilization (Koukiadis, 1991a). Today, the process of European integration is affected with neoliberal options that are adopted by the leaders of the European Union and several leaders of national member states. Degradation of work and deregulation of industrial relations (Kouzis, 2001) are manifested primarily in and by policies aiming to fulfill the requirements of the Stability Pact.

Within the context of the developments described above, it should be noted that the last three decades in most European countries[37] an increased state intervention has been observed so that the financial crisis and major structural changes in the area of production – such as efforts to overcome the Fordist production model through the use of new technologies – are to be tackled. Thus, governments have been forced to take drastic measures to stabilize their national economies, notably by adopting policies of economic austerity. As a result of these

37 Except for Germany and Switzerland.

conditions, the state more explicitly legislates and sets the regulatory framework for the operation of industrial relations (Petrinioti, 1985). Thus, it is within this context that the temporary restriction of freedom of collective bargaining has been recorded as well. When all possibilities of conventional responses to government positions and proposals are exhausted, then governments are forced to take action with policies that limit collective autonomy.

4.8 Substantive and Procedural Legislative Interventions over the Past Decades

Another form of state intervention occurs within the context of legislative competence and initiative of the state to regulate substantive and procedural requirements of collective bargaining.

Procedural legislative interventions – such as those brought by the enactment of relevant laws in Belgium in 1968, in France in 1982, in Spain in 1980 and in Greece in 1990 – aimed to define the basic rules governing collective bargaining (Spyropoulos, 1988, p. 537). Based on up to day experience (ILO, 1977, p. 86; Bamber and Cordova, Ch. 16, p. 362, par. 31 ad 32), it can be argued that -contrary to the data of the U.S.A. and Canada, where the state seeks legislatively to develop a detailed framework for the mechanism structure of collective bargaining – in European countries there is a trend towards procedural legislative interventions that are limited only to formulate certain general principles regarding modernization (Petrinioti, 1985, p. 41) processes of collective bargaining. Usually, these interventions refer to the scope of collective bargaining, the recognition of the right to collective bargaining, the imposition of an obligation on the parties to negotiate in good faith and commitment, the employer's obligation to inform his/her employees (ILO 1977, p. 11; Spyropoulos, 1992). Finally, special care is taken by the modern European states – and this concerns all advanced societies – of establishing legal mechanisms to support, encourage and facilitate collective bargaining, to create special services and independent dispute resolution and regulation mechanisms of collective labour disputes, as well as to develop and operate organizations for technical support of the parties by providing documentation, statistics and financial information, carrying out research as well as by organizing training programmes of business managers and trade unions of both employees and employers (Spyropoulos, 1988, p. 538).

Such formations are the Advisory Conciliation and Arbitration Service (ACAS) in Great Britain, which – in addition to the role it plays in conciliation and arbitration procedures (Advisory Conciliation and Arbitration Service (ACAS), 1979, pp. 5–17 and 19–28; Dickens, 1991, pp. 248 ff) for resolving or settling labour disputes – provides advisory services to the parties' activity[38], by informing employees and employers individually or collectively about all employment matters.

At the same time, and in this role, in addition to significant advisory activity engaged in a large number of special editions, ACAS has essentially "scientific laboratories" that can provide counseling to parties and complete scientifically valid proposals and policies on specialized issues. In recent years there has been an attempt in Greece so that a network of institutions will be developed and be able to provide support to the parties. A characteristic example is the Organization for Mediation and Arbitration (OMED in Greek)[39], which – in addition to its role in resolving collective labour disputes – after its Board of Directors' relevant decisions, can develop advisory services in issues of industrial relations, provide assistance to improve collective bargaining, conduct research on industrial relations as well as to prepare and publish a printed "Code of Practice" in order to indicate to the parties ethical issues and practical solutions to issues of industrial relations[40]. However, the intention of the Greek legislator to ensure support to the parties was manifested by the establishment of the tripartite National Labour Institute (EIE in Greek)[41] among the aims of which is to study and research the labour market, create a data bank for issues of industrial relations, classify systematically labour legislation and to promote measures for consolidating and developing social dialogue between employees and employers[42].

A second form of legislative intervention is the legislative regulation of substantial terms in collective bargaining that can be either a ban on certain terms, as it has happened with indexation in recent years, that is, legislative commitment of the parties not to include in collective bargaining agreements such clauses or not to impose legal obligations on the parties, to include some issues in the

---

38 For the advisory role of ACAS, see paragraphs: "Information and Advice" and "Promoting Good Practice" in informative edition "Promoting the Improvement of Industrial Relations", Advisory Conciliation and Arbitration Service (ACAS), 1993; see also, Kahn-Freund, 1983, pp. 142 ff.

39 Articles 14–18, Law 1876/1990 "On Free Collective Bargaining" in the book, "The New Ways of Solving Collection Labour Disputes", Edition of the Legal Society of Northern Greece, Nr 14, Thessaloniki, 1992, pp. 105–111.

40 See Section 1.2., Article 3 "Rules of Organization and Operation of the Organization for Mediation and Arbitration" in Papadimitriou, 1992, p. 193.

41 See Articles 1–11, Law 2150/1993 "National Labour Institute and other provisions" FEK/98 / issue A′ of 16th June 1993.

42 See the first six paragraphs of Article 2, Law 2150/1993.

collective bargaining agreement and, therefore, to settle them on contract basis, regardless of the content of this arrangemen (Spyropoulos, 1988, p. 538).

There have been such typical legislative interventions in many countries. In the Netherlands, the 1927 law on collective labour agreements considers inadmissible any contractual arrangement under which the employer discriminates against employees based on their membership in a particular trade union or their religious and political beliefs. In Germany, the provisions that regulate the freedom of association restrict substantially the ability of the parties to arrange more favourably conventional regulations of trade unionized employees. In Great Britain, the relevant legislation imposes restrictions on dismissal of employees because they are not members of a particular trade union, whereas in France the previous institutional framework for collective bargaining stipulated that in order for the validity of certain collective labour agreement to be extended this should necessarily regulate certain employment conditions.

A more indirect form of intervention in regulating substantive terms of collective bargaining is that which either has taken the form of the "negotiated legislation" [Italy] / "negotiated regulations (reg/neg)" [USA] (Lixouriotis, 1992, p. 9, ft. 21) or concerns the regulation of employment conditions that could have been configured with collective bargaining agreements. By "negotiated legislation" [Italy] / "negotiated regulations (reg/neg)" [USA], we refer to following phenomenon: the content of certain laws might have been designed and decided either upon collective bargaining or upon the basis of extensive consultation with the interested parties. It may take two forms: first, the form of "negotiated legislation" [Italy] / "negotiated regulations (reg/neg)" [USA], that is, the law that came out after bargaining, negotiations and consultations. In France (Caire, 1987, p. 203) as negotiated laws can be considered the 27 December 1968 Law on "Branches of Trade Unions" and 13 July 1971 Law on "Collective Bargaining"; and, in Italy (Giugni, 1987, pp. 230–231), Law 675 of 1977 on "Industrial Recovery", Law 91 of 1977 on "Lowering Labour Costs" and Law 297 of 1982 on "Restriction of Compensation." In Greece, as a negotiated law can be considered Law 1876–1990 on "Free Collective Bargaining", since it came out after a long and painstaking preparation by a committee comprising of representatives of all political parties. It was voted for by the Greek Parliament, after all political parties had agreed upon, and, most importantly, after the leading trade unions of employees and employers had agreed upon it, as well (Koukiadis, 1992, p. 18; Lixouriotis, 1992, pp. 168–176).

A second form of bargained legislation is the case of a law, which essentially reproduces partly or in the whole the provision of specific collective labour agreement, usually national. Under this category there can be placed, in France

(Caire, 1987, p., 203), the 19 January 1978 Law, which gave legal effect to multi-sectoral collective labour agreement of 10 December 1977 on the status of the wage of manual employees. In Italy (Giugni, 1987, pp. 230–231), Law 164 of 1975 on the "Protection of Wages" and Legislative Acts No. 17 of 1983 and No. 10 and 12, 1984 "On the Implementation of the Tripartite Pact." A similar case in Greece[43] are the provisions of Articles 14 and 15 of Law 2224 of 1994, which adopted two special accounts, one for employment issues and the other for tackling upon unemployment, which had been predicted by clauses of the previous National General Collective Agreements (EGSSE in Greek) and the provision of Article 9 of Law 2224 of 1994, which acquired the force of law regulating the previous EGSSE for maternity leave.

Another form of indirect intervention in collective bargaining is the legislation on employment that could have been settled with collective bargaining, such as issues of form of employment and labour relations, as well as issues of working time, health and safety and any kind of payment (Windmuller, 1987, p. 130). Of particular importance is the fact that legislative interventions that regulate such issues followed the trend of flexibilization (Spyropoulos, 1987, p. 5) of management rules of human resources during recruitment, giving emphasis on flexible forms of employment during and at the end of employment, especially with an emphasis on mass dismissals. In this way, these regulations were aligned with the principle of weakening the stability of employment, contributing ultimately to restructuring Labour Law (Koukiadis, 1991a, p. 1), and its development was based not on the principle of social protection, which was traditionally in effect, but rather on an organizational principle the aim of which was to achieve efficiency and competitive operation of the production mechanism. Despite the fact that the trend in flexibilization of Labour Law coexisted with a parallel trend in their contractualization, there were state regulations in national legal orders that complied with this adjustment (Papaioannou, 1991, pp. 165–166). Typically,

43 More specifically, see Article 14 of the Law 2224/1994 which has established the Special Account for Vocational Training and Education (ELPEKE), ratifying the provision of Article 4 of National General Collective Agreement (EGSSE) the years 1991–1992 (Submission Act to the Ministry of Labour 10/4-4-1991) and Article 4 of the N.G.C.A. of the year 1993 (Submission Act to the Ministry of Labour 37/11-6-1993). Article 15 has established the Special Joint Account for Unemployment (S.J.A.U.) by ratifying Article 3 of the N.G.C.A. of the year 1993 (Submission Act to the Ministry of Labour 37/11/-6-I993). See also, Article 9 of Law 2224/1994 on maternity leave, ratifying the provision of Article 7 of the NGCA of 06.09.1993 (Submission Act to the Ministry of Labour 37/11-6-1993), which became law.

in Belgium, on the one hand, the warning notice given to the employee by the employer in case of termination of the contract got shortened, on the other hand, the employer was provided with the right to put off the payment of compensation to the dismissed employees, since the enterprise is in financial difficulties.

In France, when the relevant decrees were issued, on the one hand, the use of fixed-term contracts was facilitated and their duration was increased from six to twenty months, on the other hand, the requirement that dismissals be approved by the labour inspector was repealed and the obligation to merely inform the public authority was introduced; and this was valid only for companies employing more than ten employees. In Germany, on the one hand, the use of fixed-term contracts was also facilitated and their maximum duration was increased to eighteen months, whereas, on the other hand, the scope of protective legislation on collective dismissals got restricted. Similar trends were crystallized in regulations in Italy too, which, in the case of this country, were of conventional origin. In Greece, flexibilities have been regulated with a series of Laws up to date, starting with Law 1982 of 1990. An issue of a particularly regulatory interest has been the flexible forms of employment and working time. A special case was Great Britain, which, in the 1980s, the State – innovating historically and subverting the tradition of non-intervention – brought a series of legislative interventions that aimed not simply to flexibilize but to deregulate and de-collectivize industrial relations (Papaioannou, 1991, p. 168).

4.9 Economic Policy, Incomes Policy and Consensus Forming Mechanisms

The state attempts to achieve its economic goals through a variety of policies and interventions. More specifically, there are three basic economic functions of the modern interventionist state (Karagiorgas, 1981). First, the operation of distribution of production means. Here, the society is supplied with public goods, regulation of foreign economics and charges and correction of monopoly deviations. Second, the operation of distribution where all actions are incorporated, aiming to correct how distribution is provided. Finally, there is the operation of both stabilization and the development of economy, which are part of how to deal with depression, fight inflation and how to take measures so a socially desirable pace is developed. This latter function is directly related to the operation of distribution. It is reasonable and expected that many of these actions will affect labour relationships. The first conscious exercise of economic policy had to do with industrial relations was the employment policy aiming to eradicate unemployment that was plaguing the U.S. economy since the Great Depression of 1929.

After World War II the conditions for development and prosperity that were created in the upstanding postwar economies of many European countries enabled the construction of the welfare state and a quite often provision of very satisfactory increases in wages and salaries by employers to their employees (Leventis, 1981, p. 286). At that time, Keynes' contribution was important. This economist suggested that the level of nominal wages is an exogenous variable that might be intervened by the state. Keynes' thought was that the state could subsidize investments and boost the private sector that would benefit the unemployed. Based on this thought, the birth of fiscal policy occurred where manipulation of government spending and money supply are supposed to ensure the output of periodic crises that take the form of inflation and unemployment (Petrinioti, 1985). This development was spurred to confirm the view of orthodox economists according to which nominal wages are a key element of the birth and maintenance of inflation (Petrinioti, 1985, p. 136). The provision of increases in wages and salaries generated income growth, which led to higher demand and therefore inflation rate, that is, inflation. The increase in wages and salaries was shifted to higher prices. This naturally creates further demands for wage increases, the satisfaction of which would result in a further increase in prices and therefore the function of the phenomenon of spiral movement of wages and prices (Leventis, 1981, p. 286). But because the causes of inflation are many, inflation cannot fully take the "blame" for wage increases (Leventis, 1981, p. 285).

Decisive factor in the developments occurred both in macroeconomic data and industrial relations were the two oil crises in the mid-1970s. The first resulted in the decline of traditional industries and increased inflationary trends. The solution to these problems was sought in policies aiming to reduce aggregate demand and declining real wages. The second crisis led to the need for measures to combat unemployment, inflation control and achieve competitiveness. These developments brought about significant changes in the macroeconomic data of the developed countries. In addition to the increase in the price of oil, oil crises were characterized by recession and unemployment, the decline in growth rates, the balance of payments difficulties, the decline of traditional industries in which there was a structured and strong trade unionism, and the increase in international competition that was intensified due to rapid technological changes that occurred at the time (Windmuller, 1987, p. 140). During such a severe crisis the problem of inflation was becoming more and more acute. Its treatment was sought on policies aiming to reduce aggregate demand and real wages (Petrinioti, 1985, p. 136). The policies pursued and the measures taken aimed at organizational restructuring and modernization of economy by using new management techniques in the labour market (Daskalakis, D., (1995a). In other words, countries had to adjust their labour legislation to the problems of crisis at the time. Thus, it could be argued that the conditions that allowed the formation of national economic policy with its individual parts – that is, monetary, fiscal and income policy – were now unable to restore balance in the labour market through the mechanism of prices and level of nominal wages.

After a slight downturn in macroeconomic problems, these phenomena recurred more intensely in early 1980 with the second oil crisis (Spyropoulos, 1987, p. 3). To tackle the Great Depression, most states took measures to stabilize their finances (Spyropoulos, 1988, p. 536). Economic austerity policies were intensified, aiming primarily to combat unemployment, inflation control and foster competitiveness in the national economy of each country (Spyropoulos, 1987, pp. 3–4). More specifically, those policies were seeking to use financial and monetary measures, incentives for productivity, encourage investment and to create new jobs, by reducing government spending, public investments and social programmes and, in general, by restructuring the organization of modernization of economy, using new management techniques of markets and, more particularly, of the labour market (Windmuller, 1987, p. 141). These policies included mostly control prices, wages and incomes (Spyropoulos, 1987, p. 4) that were manifested to a different degree – by country and time – by state intervention in collective bargaining (Windmuller, 1987, p. 141), which in fact restricted the freedom of collective bargaining (Spyropoulos, 1988, p. 536).

From the aforementioned it is conspicuous that fiscal policy is a direct intervention in industrial relations from the moment when the state intervenes in the distribution relation between capital and labour or wage setting or taxation. The importance of this intervention lies mainly in the interdependence of the size of wages with the progress of national economy. For this reason, since the early 1980s it was for the first time perhaps in peacetime that European states played such an active role in collective bargaining (Windmuller, 1987, p. 140). Of course, there are differences among countries. However, the common feature in the countries of Western Europe in the last two decades (Spyropoulos, 1988, p. 536) has been the increased role of the state in collective bargaining and, more particularly, in wage formation, which was manifested by cutting wages in the public sector, with a variety of legal restrictions to wage increases and frostings and, finally, with the effective abolition of automatic indexation mechanisms (Clarke, 1984, p. 19).

The main conclusion, therefore, from the European experience of the last two-three decades has been that, due to the fear of the impact of wage increases on the society, labour payment, the determination of which undoubtedly belongs to the regulatory power of collective bargaining, has been the cause and object of widespread state intervention (Leventis, 1981, p. 283), a fact that pulled to the surface the old debate and reflection on the relationship of the state and collective autonomy and bargaining (Spyropoulos, 1988, p. 536). This experience suggests that state intervention in collective bargaining in order to influence the level of wage increases was brought in European countries through practice of: (a) persuasion; (b) the direct or indirect participation; and (c) controls and restrictions (Windmuller, 1987, p. 141).

Given the assumption that deflationary measures are more successful, when arising through the close cooperation between the state, employees and enterprises (Zolotas, 1978, p. 21 ff), European governments often choose consensus and solutions in connection with determining the amount of payments (Spyropoulos, 1988, p. 537). Usual government practice was the formulation of estimates of and prompts for social partners in an effort to convince them, in their mutual negotiations, to take into account the government's economic policy and, more particularly, its macroeconomic goals (Windmuller, 1987, p. 141). Governments often support leading labour organizations in different ways so that the direction of the central players at national-level negotiations becomes a pilot for bargaining at industry- and enterprise-level (Windmuller, 1987, p. 141). A more direct form of intervention has been the state's participation in tripartite bargaining at national level, which in some cases has resulted in tripartite pacts or social contracts (Spyropoulos, 1988, p. 537), as used in Belgium and the Netherlands earlier and in Italy and Spain later.

The main conclusion from this experience has been that the *ad hoc* and non-institutionalized intercourse and cooperation between the state, employers and employees have been effective but have had neither duration nor continuity over time that would ensure greater functionality. This finding has led many European states to adopt stable and permanent structures of trilateral cooperation. The degree of understanding among the state, employees and employers either in the form of bilateral or trilateral national (statutory or otherwise) bargaining or in the form of negotiated legislation or tripartite pacts and social contracts arising within the context of national institutions for economic and social cooperation among different countries and time spans (Spyropoulos, 1987, p. 6). Wherever meaningful participation of representatives of social interests and consensus on economic and social policy was achieved, the results were satisfactory. The restrictions on collective bargaining agreements to combat inflation and stabilize economy are easily accepted by society if the institutional structure of the formal industrial relations system respects collective autonomy and gives priority to consensual solutions against unilateral decisions (Spyropoulos, 1988, p. 537).

The special institutions of economic and social cooperation, the state and trade unions of employees and employers seem to have come out to fight inflation (Leventis, 1981, p. 290). In the process, however, beyond the role they played in building consensus and acceptance of restrictive income policies, they focused on dealing with other, major economic and social issues; such instruments were created in many countries after World War II.

Nevertheless, social partnership may be established in a less institutionalized or non-institutionalized basis (Windmuller, 1987, p. 142). National general collective agreements may fall under this category, and have played a major role, for example, in the case of Italy, Spain and France (Spyropoulos, 1987, p. 6). In such types of bargaining, governments often have decisive influence without, however, being formally one of the parties. On the contrary, in other cases, the tripartite cooperation is very evident and clear, with direct state participation as one of the parties engaged in the formation of an agreement (Windmuller, 1987, p. 143). Such cases were the 1983 and 1984 tripartite collective agreements in Italy (Giugni, 1987, pp. 231–232), which marked a qualitative change of state intervention in industrial relations and, for the first time, launched a practice for the Italian data that continued later. With these two agreements – which were broad in scope and included tax issues, cost, benefits, employment measures for the labour market and labour flexibility – the state sought and obtained as a party to form tripartite agreements that linked collective bargaining agreements with the potentials of the economy and led to limiting wage increases to the limits determined by the objective so that inflation would be reduced. In Italy, however, social cooperation has recently been manifested in the form of negotiated legislation (Giugni, 1987). Law No 164 of 1975 on the "Protection of Payments" and Acts No 17 of 1983 and No 10 and No 12 of 1984 on the "Implementation of the Tripartite Pact" are examples of legislation that were reproduced partly or in whole by national general collective bargaining agreements. Moreover, Laws of 1977 No 91 "On the reduction of labour costs" and No 297 of 1982 "On Restriction of Compensation", which had a decisive influence on collective bargaining and, more particularly, the level of wage increases, became a second type of negotiated legislation, which was designed in consultation with the parties.

In Spain, events of social cooperation and consensus approach have also been the "Agreement Package" because it addressed the associated economic policy objectives and aspirations of social partners (Windmuller, 1987, p. 143). In Great Britain, formerly the "New Social Contract" with the Federation of Trade Unions (TUCs) – was established under the policy of the British Government between 1974 and 1977 to provide tax relief to employees, while explicit commitment of trade unions to limit their demands for the level of wage increases (Jekinis, 1984,

p. 75). A case of social contract in the Netherlands is the Social Contract of 1972 (Albeda, 1987, p. 254) and some subsequent efforts of recent years towards this direction (de Nneubourg, 1990, pp. 133–137).

On the other hand, failure of voluntary solutions and the persistence of high inflation in recent years have often led many Western European states to take action directly to control and limit the increase in wages and salaries (Leventis, 1981, p. 292). The policies pursue their goals by imposing legislative or administrative prohibitions, restrictions or controls not only on economic activity of individuals but also on trade union activities of trade unions of employees and employers in collective bargaining, especially, on the levels of pay increases (Leventis, 1981).

Such measures are often imposed after bilateral or tripartite national collective bargaining has failed, as it happened in Belgium and France and after governments have exhausted every alternative (Spyropoulos, 1992, p. 10). When voluntary solutions fail, either by persuasion that the state seeks to bring to social partners, or through tripartite institutions and processes of consultation and cooperation with the participation of the state, then state intervention is directed to control wages and payments (Windmuller, 1987, p. 14). Such phenomena have occurred in Belgium, France, the Netherlands, in Great Britain and in Greece for several years. Direct government intervention – which is a blend of state in the distribution relations of capital and labour (Petrinioti, 1985, p. 136), and, more particularly, intervention in the labour market so to determine nominal wages, with the unilateral determination of the amount of wages – may be exercised (Leventis, 1981, p. 293) in three ways: (a) referral to arbitration, if there is an institution of compulsory and state controlled arbitration in this country; (b) administrative intervention[44], which can amend or refuse to approve a particular collective bargaining agreement by invoking the public interest; and (c) the adoption of laws or ordinances that prohibit or control wages and salaries for some time.

In the Netherlands (Albeda, 1987, p. 256), key law was the law on "Wages Determination" of 1970, which gave the opportunity to the Government to intervene in collective bargaining in favour of public interest and impose "wage freeze" in case of national emergency. There were similar laws in subsequent

44 Oldest in Greece under Paragraph 2, Article 20 of Law 3239/55 Ministers of Labour and Co-ordination could amend or could not approve Collective Labour Agreements or Arbitration Awards. Moreover, in Belgium the King Ordinance Nr 179/December 30/1982 provided that under certain conditions the Collective Labour Agreements should be approved and countersigned by the Minister of Labour.

years. Law "on Income Policy and Protection of Employment Opportunities" in 1974 was a result of the oil crisis and imposed a wage freeze. In 1978, although there was a similar law, it was not applied so that a consensus on the issue of increases would be achieved. However, the policy of legislative intervention and the wage freeze came back the following years. In France (Delamotte, (1987, p. 549), after a year of reinvigoration of the economy, an austerity policy followed which, among other measures, was manifested with the imposition of "the freeze" of prices and wages for the period July-November 1982, whereas the following year the government intervention was of milder form and was manifested in recommendations by government officials so that during wages bargaining the social partners should adapt to the model for staggered increases and deindexation.

In Belgium (Blanpain, 1987, p. 180) there were also legislative measures that imposed restrictions on wage increases. More specifically, a law of 1982 provided that restrictions on wages would be imposed unilaterally by the state, if the parties failed to conclude a national general collective agreement. Then, the 2 February 1982 Law was passed, whereby seeking to tackle the crisis of the Belgian economy the legislator gave special extraordinary legislative powers to the government which was to control wages for several years. Based on this Law, Decree No 11 of 15 February 1982 was issued and banned the pay increase from 1 March 1982, whereas at the same time it provided partial adjustment of wages by paying a lump sum for all employees for the period from 1 June to 31 December 1982. Decree No 180 of 31 December followed, which extended the restrictive measures of Decree No 11 of 15 February 1982, and any increase in cash or in kind, provided by an individual or collective agreement or provided by a unilateral decision of the employer was banned until 31 December 1984.

In Greece, legislative restrictions on wage increases were imposed for many times over the last fifteen years. Such regulations were provided for by Article 27 of Law 1320 of 1983 (Government Gazette-FEK 6/A711-1-1983) and Article 49 of Law 1947 of 1991. There were also other cases of regulations which became known since various criticisms and comments were made on them. The Ordinance (PNP) (Government Gazette-FEK 179/A718-10-1985) of 18.10.1985, issued under the special legislative procedure of Article 44 § 1 of Constitution 1975/86, imposed a ban of stipulation, administration or pay increases in every kind of employees' payments in the public and private sectors of the economy until 12/31/1987, if they were not within the scope of the government's fiscal policy (Article only, Paragraphs 1 and 2), whereas, at the same time, it provided penalties and fines to companies and employers for any violation of these prohibitions (Article only, Paragraph 3; Pararas, 1981, p. 227; and the speech by Manitakis, 1987, pp. 201–218).

A characteristic case was also Law 2025 of 1992 which imposed a ban on any increases to employees in any capacity in the public sector[45]; that income policy also received strong criticism. For its implementation it was not employed a grid of penalties (Article only, Paragraph 6) for the governing bodies and the managers of legal entities and public sector services in case of breaching prohibitions, which included immediate termination of the term of the employment contract or employment relationship and a fine of salaries of twelve months of the offender. At the same time, the Law included authorization (Article only, Paragraph 5) under which it was possible for the Minister of National Economy to determine the threshold of each type of expenditures for the staff of every agency or public enterprises, a fact that resulted in the imposition of specific restrictions on employees' payments. The validity of this authorization (Paragraph 10, Article 38, Law 2065/1992/FEK 113/A730-6-1992) was extended for the years 1993–1994, too.

There was also a phenomenon of enforcement – unilaterally by the state – of restrictive income policy in Great Britain over the last two years of the 1960s, but it was limited to public servants (Petrinioti, 1985, p. 141). This is rather an exception to the data of the country, as Great Britain has been following another model over the last years. Instead of imposing restrictions on wage increases, the state imposed institutionally financial and monetary controls, deregulated individual and collective industrial relations and weakened trade unions, while it recognized that there were high unemployment rates. In this way, instead of wages being directly controlled and be cut down, they were adjusted to low levels through the market mechanism (Windmuller, 1987, p. 144).

In conclusion, it can be argued that social cooperation and consensus built on fiscal policy is the only socially acceptable way of economic recovery in modern democratic pluralistic societies (Spyropoulos, 1988, p. 537). However, whichever model – providing instructions and directions, imposing legislatively a fiscal policy, concluding bilateral or tripartite contracts and agreements, through either collective bargaining or social dialogue institutions or through informal consultation – may be chosen for the implementation of an income policy, questions that arise in each case revolve around the same axes (ILO, 1977, p. 91). How is it possible to fix prices and wages without collective bargaining and party autonomy being affected? To what extent can an income policy be successfully implemented without being accepted by key organizations that represent social

45 As this concept was clearly defined by the provisions of Paragraph 6, Article I, Law 1256/1982 (FEK 65A') and Paragraph 5, Article 19, Law 1586/1986 (FEK 37A').

interests? And, most importantly, how much are employees and employers able to participate in formulating the economic and social policy of the state?

Today, in view of the expanded role that collective bargaining is called for to play, the issues are becoming more and more complex. They do not concern just the traditional questioning of the relationship between state and self-regulatory power of the parties, the relationship of law and collective bargaining or between the delimitation of powers of the Parliament and collective bargaining, respectively. Instead, nowadays these questions are being extended to a new type of political systems. It is common knowledge that trade unions both of employees and employers – although, according to modern European constitutions, they are not included in the responsibility for the formulation of economic and social policy of state institutions – participate *de facto* in the exercise of political power. Therefore, it is reasonably expressed the major question of the role of collective autonomy, professional organizations and tripartite cooperation in the formation of the state's will (Leventis, 1981, p. 81) within the context of modern parliamentary democracy.

4.10 The Corporatist Model of Cooperation

On the one hand, the changes that were made in the economy of the 20th century had as a result – due to a more centralized economic power – the strengthening of the position of private capital against labour. On the other hand, the labour movement, both as a response to the capital and as a result of the complexity of modern economy, has become "more centralized, more bureaucratic and more professional" (Held, 1995). Thus, powerful organizations of capital and labour compete against from each other to hinder the one the plans of the other.

Moreover, after World War II, the state got into a very difficult position, as capital and labour were given the power to influence economic growth and political stability in a disruptive way: capital, by abstaining from investment, and employees, by declaring strikes. More particularly, the trade union movement between 1965 and 1975 is characterized with a period of "development and progress" (Therborn, 1984, p. 50), as a "revival of class struggle in Western Europe" was being observed, leaving stunned scientists and politicians (Deppe, 1996). Thus, the state attempted to overcome the problems they were borne with an "imaginative integration policy strategy" (Held, 1995), on which theorists of corporatism have been focusing.

Thus, corporatism is "an individual political subsystem of mediation and resolution of social conflicts, incorporating competing interest groups in institutional and intra-agreed frameworks of permanent interaction among them and among them and the State, through organizational structures and negotiating behaviours which, with the establishment of new or diverse interests already crystallized, are oriented towards consensus formation and implementation of public policies in areas of intervention critical to governance and control of global economy (Psimitis, 1999). Therefore, organizations in a corporatist system, which have state recognition or authorization, intentionally are awarded with a "representative monopoly" (Held, (1995), exchanging restrictions with selection of leadership, formulating demands and internal governance as well as providing support from organization leaders in the agreed policy, thus ensuring members' agreement and discipline (Schmitter, 1979, pp. 85–131). More particularly, four dimensions of development of corporatism are quite distinct (Offe, 1981, pp. 123–158), depending on the extent to which the State, in relation to professional organizations: (a) provides resources; (b) determines the scope of their representation; (c) regulates their internal operation (relations between members and leadership); and (d) issues formal permission, official recognition, institutional role or the right to self-government. A prerequisite for the transition of a society to social corporatism or neocorporatism is a liberal pluralist past (Schmitter, 1997).

So, corporatist arrangements usually refer to the tripartite relationship between the State and organizations of employers and employees, where the state is the one who formulates the framework for economic and social affairs. These are political strategies, with which the state attempts to secure support from business associations and labour unions. In this way, the mainstream organized interest groups are engaged effectively in policy (Schmitter, 1979, pp. 85–131) and, based on social relationships established, seek to promote their own interests in maintaining social and political stability (Robolis and Kollias, 1998, pp. 171–175). Thus, the tripartite cooperation is a means for the parties to achieve acceptable compromises, which are more likely to be implemented effectively, thus promoting social harmony.

Corporatism has received negative criticism as a survival strategy of capitalism, as the aforementioned institutionalized tripartite collabouration skillfully and effectively masks the class unbalanced and uneven effects of corporatism. The only people who are truly committed are employees, while capital – getting power from its discretion to invest – is not bound by the statements of professional organizations (Mavrogordatos, 1988). The challenge, then, is to provide, either directly or indirectly, the consensus of the working class to adjustments to and, ultimately, to the survival of capitalism. Indeed, as decisions are made through extra-parliamentary political procedures, the role of parliament is considered to be eroded. Furthermore, trimerization favours strong or mainstream groups, while marginalizing or excluding others (Held, 1995). Unlike corporatism, pluralism is argued to allow greater freedom of movement and self-determination of organizations of lower classes, and, especially, to that of working class, since they are not limited to permanent cooperation schemes and do not receive any State intervention in their operation (Mavrogordatos, 1988).

It should be noted, however, that the prospects for the development of tripartite relations were very favourable during the period of economic growth (that is, sn the 1960s and early 1970s), which showed that it would be possible for common ground of maneuvers and a common base of satisfaction to be found, as employers responded positively to trade unions' requests (OMED, 1993), in contrast with the period of economic difficulties (since the mid-1970s), when governments faced serious budget problems and prospects begin to narrow. Therefore, it is argued that corporatism, as a system of cooperation of the state with strong economic institutions, has facilitated the crisis of capitalist democracies (Kioukias, 1994).

Thus, social pacts and tripartite agreements made in the context of neo-corporatist systems prevailed in the countries of Central and Northern Europe (Germany, Austria, Scandinavia, etc.) during the 1960s and 1970s, while during the last three decades they have been expanded in southern Europe (Italy, Spain, Portugal, Greece) (Spyropoulos, 1998b, pp. 1–13). However, it should be noted that one of the main consequences of the aforementioned changes of the last twenty years has been the decline of neo-corporatist procedures and their replacement by other forms of social cooperation (Spyropoulos, 1998b; Kioukias, 1994).

4.11 The Development of Social Dialogue in Europe

Social dialogue may, at first, take many forms and can be deployed at many levels. Depending on the content and outcome of the procedure, it may take the following forms (Spyropoulos, 1998b) of: simple information or information about social partners, consulting or advisory process that result in the expression of opinions or proposals, without necessarily achieving an agreement or collective bargaining (that is, bilateral or trilateral agreement, which may result in signing binding texts) and the procedure of co-decision; this procedure consists of joint decision-making and is considered the most restrictive and rarest form of dialogue to be used when international conventions of the ILO are to be adopted.

Depending on the composition of the parties involved (Kouzis – Robolis, 2000), the participation of representatives of employers and employees can be either bilateral or tripartite with participation of representatives of employers, employees and the State or a third group representing social interests (such as self-employed, farmers, etc.) or multilateral with the participation of a large number of lobbyists and organizations.

In particular, tripartite negotiations are divided into formal and institutionalized or informal and *ad hoc*. It should be noted that the existence of formally established institutions does not negate the need for informal agreements. Indeed, *ad hoc* negotiations have often been proven to be the most effective expression of trilateral cooperation (Trebilcock, 1994). This can take place within institutions (Kouzis – Robolis, 2000) whose nature and character depend on its development, since their task is: first, to establish a direct social dialogue (e.g. Economic and Social committees [ESCs] or OKE in Greek); second, to develop social bargaining through participatory institutions, especially at enterprise level (e.g. employees councils); and, third, to seek mutually acceptable solutions – on a bilateral or trilateral basis – through procedures of dialogue and negotiations (e.g. collective bargaining).

It should be noted that the main difference between the pre-eminent institutions of social dialogue in relation to the institutions of employee participation and collective bargaining lies in that the former move within frameworks without legal commitments and the outcome of procedures produce political consequences and moral character. Moreover, social dialogue can take place at all levels: enterprise, regional, industry, multi-industry, national inter-occupational, European and international, and refers to issues of economic and social interest. The most important, however, forms of social dialogue are those developed at national level, that is, social consultation and social cooperation.

In Europe, social dialogue has developed first at national level, where it has shown a great diversity. It works in all European countries, where its structure and results reflect the main features of industrial relations in each country, the degree of state intervention, the degree of autonomy of the social partners and the existence or lack of social consensus and social cooperation institutions (Spyropoulos, 1998b).

More particularly, forms of social dialogue in European countries are related to the mainstream system of industrial relations system in each country:

- consensual systems (Austria, Germany, Scandinavian countries) where there are strong representative organizations, a full legislative framework and a long tradition of social consensus;
- competing systems (Mediterranean countries, France), where there can be observed multiplicity and relative weakness of institutions, mechanisms and professional organizations, as well as reluctance of social organizations for the development of institutions of social dialogue; and

- mixed or intermediate systems (Belgium, Switzerland, the Netherlands), where features of the two previous categories are combined.

Whereas social integration was of secondary importance to European policy until the early 1980s (Addison and Siebert, 1994, pp. 5–27), in recent years the institution of social dialogue in European countries has been strengthened – due to the deterioration of economic and social problems – either through legislative intervention or through agreements between the parties, which has often led to nationwide agreements (Robolis and Kollias, 1998). Two basic forms of social dialogue, which were developed at national central level, constitute social consultation and social cooperation. Since social consultation is defined as "the institutionalized participation of representatives of various social and professional classes in processing bills or other government decisions, which takes place through specifically for this purpose institutionalized bodies which are called Economic and Social Councils (ESCs) or Committees" (Giannakourou, 2001).

The initial attempts to create these Committees received the support and protection of the International Labour Organization (ILO) (OMED, 1993). There were harbingers of the institution of the Committee (the Economic Council under Article 165 of the Weimar Constitution of 1919 / National Economic Council, France, in 1925), but the establishment of relevant councils was made after World War II in Europe. The ESC (or Committee) institution is an institution born during the postwar period and component of the European social model (1950–1970). It began to develop in the 1950s, at a national level, and then it was adopted by the Treaty of Rome that established the European Community. The Committee was established by the Treaty of Rome (1957), its position, as an institution body, was consolidated on the Single European Act of 1986, was equated with other institutions by the Treaty of Maastricht (1992), and its scope was broadened significantly by the Treaty of Amsterdam (1997). It is an advisory body of a general character of the Council, the Commission and the European Parliament, in which economic and social forces of the member states are represented. It advises on all areas during the EU legislative procedure or prepares opinions on its own initiative. The existence of such Councils (ESCs) in European countries or the lack in others (Germany, Denmark, Sweden, the United Kingdom), and the model of social dialogue that has been developing in them is due to the different European national traditions, regarding the pluralistic or corporatist form of organization of interests, the degree and intensity of articulation with the state (Kioukias, 1994).

The ESCs recommend institutional meeting space and expression of mainstream organized interests, where information is exchanged and dialogue is conducted, and there is an institutionalized channel of access to and participation in major economic interests in political decision-making in specific areas (Giannakourou, 1996, pp. 102–108).

The main responsibilities of the Committee / ESCs are as follows:

1. Advisory: is the most important responsibility and provides advice and opinions to the Government on socio-economic issues in the form of opinions – which are not binding, are political in nature and are formed with technocratic and scientific support. In some cases, their advice is binding for the Government with respect to economic issues, social security and Labour Law (OMED, 1993);
2. Preparation of reports, studies and research on socio-economic issues (at the request of the government or on their own initiative), which is a parallel and complementary responsibility; and
3. An annual report on the economic and social situation of the country (it is a responsibility of most ESC).

Some ESCs, indeed, have been assigned special powers, such as to monitor law enforcement (ESC Netherlands) and evaluate positions and policies (ESC Portugal) and others. Furthermore, the National Labour Council of Belgium (CNT) has been able to decide on collective bargaining for employees in all sectors (OMED, 1993). Moreover, the enlargement of their responsibilities (e.g. ESC Italy) should be noted. National ESCs differ in their composition, organization and operation. The membership ranges from 15 subjects (Portugal – CRCS) up to 230 people (France – CES), while the term varies from 2 to 6 years, and, in some cases, goes indefinitely.

The institutional involvement of the government is the norm in their composition, with the exception of Belgium, Austria and Greece. Their composition consists of representatives of employers and employees, and the third part includes representatives of other social groups or members of the government or experts appointed by it. The President of the Council is appointed by the Government (in 2/3 of cases), or elected by the Council (in 1/3 of them).

The difference in the composition of relevant boards is typical in European countries. In France, for example, the composition of the Economic and Social Council (ESC) is very bold, since all social and professional organizations playing an important role in economic, social and cultural fields are involved (OMED, 1993). In the Netherlands, a number of independent experts participate in the board, apart from employers and employees (OMED, 1993). Councils are financed by the state, except the Netherlands, where the activities and actions of the council are funded by employers. Evaluation of the ESCs work should be made in relation to the scope and extent of their responsibilities. The main indicators of evaluation is often addressed by Government Bills or other documents in question, the degree of acceptance of their Opinions by the Government, Parliament and the public, and, finally, whether the pursuit of and achievement in political and social agreements occur substantially within councils. These councils, in countries that work, "served the idea of providing opinions and advice as well as bargaining with institutionalized rules, mechanisms and priorities" (OMED, 1993).

The second basic form of social dialogue at a national level is social cooperation and refers to tripartite negotiations among the state, employers and employees as "*extra legem* practice, whose main feature is the signature of social pacts" (Giannakourou, 2001). Since the 1980s the ESCs have been facing the dilemma of overcoming their institutional role – that is, social consultation – and engagement in the process of social cooperation, which – in its micro-economic form – has a long tradition in Europe. In the 1990s, social collaboration was revived in order for the programme of convergence with the EU to be implemented, and issues being objects of the income policy are: flexibilization / deregulation of employment, reduction of non-wage labour costs, taxation and consolidation. Thus, in some European countries (e.g. Italy), there was a legislative restatement of the ESCs' powers / responsibilities. Furthermore, they undertake supportive action in the process social cooperation, that is, they intervene during the preparatory phase, providing supporting tools (strategic studies and reports and distribution information for the preparation of the ground of social dialogue), without direct and active participation in bargaining of tripartite social pacts, with the exception of institutional consolidation of the ESC Portugal, as an instrument of social understanding.

Fruits of the procedure of social cooperation are social agreements that involve political commitments of the parties but no legal commitment. More particularly, social arrangements involve: first, self-commitment in aligning with the content of the bargaining with the agreed and, second, control of centrifugal trends at decentralized levels. There have been notable examples of such agreements in Portugal, Ireland and Italy.

Succinctly, as far as promoting dialogue at a European level is concerned, it should be noted that, according to Article 3 of the Agreement on Social Policy, the European Commission has the task to promote the consultation of social partners, take all necessary measures in order to facilitate dialogue and to ensure that its support is provided to all parts in a balanced way. According to some scholars, "the method of dialogue has been proven as one of the most dynamic in social harmonization at Community level" (Spyropoulos, 2000, pp. 1–18). However, it has gradually been conspicuous that the official institutionalized tripartite advisory bodies with multi-composition, whose work is highly publicized, are not sufficient to meet new and urgent needs. Along with their operation, an additional step for a closer contact and cooperation is required, away from the spotlight. Thus, casual informal gatherings of a small number of authorized representatives of the parties to confidential discussions, meetings type Val Duchesse, which have no agenda, do not result in binding documents, press releases for the media are not issued – they might have facilitated the procedures of social dialogue (Grote, 1985). Community experience, as it is the wider political environment of the development of the dialogue is of particular importance for European countries. As the legislation of the last decades in our country has been of Community origin and Community decisions in turn have been a product of multi-layered dialogue, consequently, a country should: (1) assimilate and implement the EU appropriate dialogue procedures; and (2) make proposals to the European Union that should be characterized by greater legitimacy to influence community options (Koukiadis, 1996).

4.12 The Development of Social Dialogue in Greece

The Greek reality shows peculiarities in relation to social dialogue. And this happens because the idea of social dialogue, bargaining and genuine participatory culture has not been cultivated in Greece. It should be noted that during the Greek Civil War and until the late 1980s, the National dialogue at central level was at "an embryonic stage" (Papaioannou, 1997, pp. 913–921). There has been such a situation due to uneven political developments that dominated until 1974, the paternalistic nature of the state, resulting in strong state intervention in the pursuit of economic and social policy, the guardianship of the trade unions by governments and political parties (Roussis, 1985) and the presence of strong clientele relationships (Robolis and Kollias 1998), employers' earlier intransigence of employers, and, of course, the intense atmosphere of trade unions' confrontation against the state interventionism and employers' intransigence.

More particularly, the state of the trade unions is described as follows (Fakiolas, 1985): most of them were merely extensions of political parties and their number was too large to allow coordination and discipline of their members, whereas their organizational structure was highly decentralized. Their policy in broader political and social issues had no consistency; it was aggressive and extreme opposite to any new technological challenges and almost indifferent in the need to create employment opportunities for new entrants in the labour sector. More specifically, the existence of two categories of trade unions was a major impediment to the development of social dialogue (Papaioannou, 1997).

On the one hand, in the first category there were those unions that came under the full control of the government, often without real democratic legitimacy, whereas, in the second category, there were trade unions operating out of the GSEE, which, regardless of the degree of internal democratic legitimacy, were unable to play the role of the official interlocutor with employers at a national level. On the other hand, the political leadership viewed social dialogue negatively (Koukiadis, 1996) since it considered it as a front to undermine its authority, a time-consuming procedure that would slowdown rapid decision-making and as lack of will to take decisions.

The result of the aforementioned situation is that Greece has a long but not a positive experience in participatory institutions at national level, in employment and social policy issues. The image of the above is completed, if it is considered that the participatory institutions in businesses developed only in the 1980s, and until 1990 there were no substantial and free collective bargaining. Therefore, whereas the first advisory body on issues at national level, the Labour Council, was founded in 1930, and while after World War II the establishment of several advisory bodies followed – including representatives of professional organizations of employers and employees – their operation was incomplete, their duration ephemeral, and they generally failed in their mission. Indicatively, it should be mentioned that relevant advisory bodies were established after the fall of the dictatorship (i.e. after 1974), such as the Council of Social and Economic Policy (SKOP in Greek) in 1978, and the National Council of Development and Productivity (ESAP in Greek) in 1980.

Additional reasons contributing to the failure of the tripartite advisory bodies in Greece have been that these bodies are off-handed in their composition and operation, they lack clearly defined objectives or lack political will for genuine dialogue and cooperation; they also lack irrefutable scientific secretariat to prepare issues (Spyropoulos, 1998a). As, however, the economic crisis and the worsening of social problems cannot be tackled upon through more customer relations, institutions of social dialogue have been developing to enhance the role of the social partners and interlocutors (Robolis and Kollias, 1998).

So, according to the model of the Economic and Social Committee (ESC) of the European Union, its Greek counterpart (OKE in Greek) was founded by Law 2232/1994 in 1994; its composition is tripartite. More specifically, an equal number of three groups of social actors participate in its 48-member Plenary, which are: (1) employers-business people (SEV, GSEVE, ESEE, etc.); (2) employees in the private and public sector (GSEE, ADEDY); and (3) other productive and professional classes: farmers (PASEGES, GESASE), professionals (doctors, lawyers, etc.), Local Authorities, Chambers and consumers.

The Greek Economic and Social Committee (OKE) began operating in 1995, and have been managed by an Executive Committee, a President and three Vice-Presidents, one from each group. For the first time in Greece there is a body operating without the active participation of the State. This feature, with its solely advisory competence, makes it differ from other European Economic and Social Committees (ESCs). First, its task is to express reasoned Opinion on draft laws at the request of the Government, on issues of special importance related to industrial relations, social security, tax measures, as well as on the general socio-economic policy, with the exception of the budget; its intervention is mandatory before respective formal laws are voted. Second, it is to intervene voluntarily in issues of social and economic policy so that Initiative Opinion can be issued.

Since January 1996 the OKE has issued 38 Opinions, of which eight (8) are Initiative Opinions. It is a mechanism of "expression, synthesis and normalization of all socio-occupational interests that comprise the Greek society" (Giannakourou, 2001), without being identified with the organizations that are represented in it (organizations that are tertiary and represent of the sector they express) and without expressing, in the strict sense, their occupational corporate interests. So, the institutionalization of the dialogue at this level is an important innovation for the following reasons (Papaioannou, 1997):

- The scope of dialogue has been extended, since dialogue has no longer been concerned exclusively with traditional issues of industrial relations, and a clearly political role is recognized to the bodies, as the OKE ought to advise on any bill of social or economic policy. The disclosure of its opinion, which is not binding on the government, is an aspect of political pressure;
- Dialogue has acquired a permanent character, as meetings of the agencies are held on a permanent basis, and, for the first time, without the participation of the State, the partners' base is broadened, as representatives of social groups or occupations are included, representatives who up to now they were chosen only by political power; and
- The non-binding nature of the opinion, either on the Government or on participating social organizations, reflects a different philosophy of the concept of social dialogue, compared to that was governing the process of collective bargaining.

Two main factors hindered the operation of the Committee (i.e. of the OKE) and dialogue (Koukiadis, 1996): first, indifference or detachment – latent or otherwise- of some government members, and, second, the lack of culture in social dialogue – in the third group of partners – that has had as a result the failure in participating actively in preparing proposals.

Social dialogue in Greece – in the form of tripartite bargaining: the State, employers and employees – took place for the first time in 1997. In the spring of 1997, the government took the initiative of *ad hoc* tripartite consultations in a social dialogue on the triangle "Development – Competitiveness – Employment." The organization of dialogue was undertaken by an *ad hoc* coordinating secretariat (by order of the government), in which the government, the party in power, as well as organizations of employers and employees participated. The Committee (OKE) was excluded from that unusual experience of Greece, which resulted in signing the "Confidence Pact between government and social partners towards 2000." The OKE was restricted to the role of the observer of the procedures and its advisory role, and its request to play a supportive role – that is, administrative and scientific – was denied.

The proposals that were put forward, based on the government's initiative, involved three themes: structural policies for development, competitiveness, employment and tax reform, and industrial relations. From the proposals submitted to that social dialogue it was shown just from the outset that there was a significant differentiation in participants' strategies. On the one hand, the trade unions supported the strategy to enhance production, income and employment. More specifically, they claimed an increase in investments, better wages and enhancement of the Welfare State as well as the reduction of working hours without pays being reduced. On the other hand, the government and employers supported consolidation, development and improvement of competitiveness, by monitoring fiscal policy and the implementation of flexible labour market arrangements, proposals that were not included in the pact of trust, as not universally accepted (Robolis and Kollias, 1998). It should be noted that, despite the title given to the Pact, there was no agreement upon the most important issues, as there was no general acceptance by the social partners. Its content is a framework of guidelines, with limited references to specific decisions and proposals. It is true that in Greece there is a lack of important tripartite agreements upon policy at a macroeconomic level, which are required for the development of a country.

4.13 Criticism of Social Dialogue

Social dialogue, as a concept, philosophy and practice, has received positive and negative criticism. Its adherents believe that social interests are different, but not conflicting, and that social dialogue is an effective instrument to achieve social consensus. Moreover, the starting point of its theoretical conception is that social consensus is necessary if solutions to pressing economic and social issues are to be found. Social dialogue at national level has positive effects as it contributes to: building a constructive exchange of views, drawing useful conclusions and developing evidence-based arguments (Mousouris, 1996, pp. 32–37), going away from arbitrary state and employer's choices, developing a broader reflection of the society – regarding burning socioeconomic issues – raising the awareness of the society and mobilizing it, discouraging efforts to create social upheaval and rupture, and, finally, it contributes to making more consensual proposals (Papaioannou, 1997) to improve the quality of policy-making, a culture of tolerance and anti-authoritarianism, anti-paternalism and strengthening democracy, by involving social partners in policy-making and decision-making on socio-economic issues.

Those who oppose to the idea of social dialogue argue that the interests of social groups are opposed to each other and that its practice is not possible to help alleviate inequality. Instead, they believe that it helps integrate the logic of employees' representatives with that of capital, something that is a threat to traditional vested rights of employees and contribute to eliminating or dehydrating the class struggle (Rousis, 1985); it reproduces and expands social injustice, especially with the employees' consent, it is used by the state as a tool to seize the consent of trade unions, to promote measures at the lowest possible political and economic cost; its economic efficiency is questioned at national level, while decentralization of industrial relations is supported, something that is disputed by other scholars (Spyropoulos, 1998a), and it becomes a monopoly of employers' and employees' representatives, while it excludes other representatives of civil society. According to the last criticism, it is sought institutions reflecting the organized civil society – such as institutions and associations of all types – can build and take part in political management. More specifically, it is considered as necessary organizations working in the third sector – that is, in non-governmental and non-economic organizations, such as women's organizations, environmentalists, consumers, the unemployed, people with disabilities, minorities, etc., which are sources of influence of public opinion at national and European level – to work with social partners.

A third, synthetic, view (Kouzis, 1993) claims that the competitive relationship between capital and labour is not incompatible with the existence of social agreements, which are temporary solutions to mutual benefits, and that the balance of power is reflected in the agreements achieved in given periods. As the risk of absolutizing the need for social consensus (Papaioannou, 1997) on economic or social policy is highlighted, it is argued that social dialogue is not an end in itself, does not necessarily lead to an agreement; any social consensus is rather the result of processes of social conflict and contributes to dwindling the margins of tolerance so that solutions are found in order for more dynamic mobilizations to be followed.

It should be noted that social representation must be substantial, that is, there shouldn't be a distance between top and down; the briefing of the represented basis about the course of the dialogue should be essential, and the participants should have honest intentions of seeking mutually acceptable solutions. However, it is recognized that trade unions are called for dialogue under the pressure of difficult times for them (Kouzis, 2000). They are required to adapt to the needs of businesses and work flexibilization, which is a key feature of the EU policy and is imposed by the global correlation of economic, social and political forces.

The correlation of forces is extremely adverse to employment, as employees usually are those who bear "social solidarity", assuming pressure to limit the scope of their social conquests. The state sometimes operates as "a supporter of employees' institutional demands" and some other times as "a breakwater of their claims", while trade unions juxtapose enhancement and adaptation of industrial relations to new data of production and technology.

4.14 Challenge for the Future

Forms and methods of exercising state intervention are historically associated largely with particularities and needs of each community. In particular, they are related to needs and demands of employees and capital and as to whether these specific needs can be reconciled with the broader needs of society for economic and social development and modernization. In another sense, state intervention and the forms it assumes are related to how every time the political system and the mainstream ideology believe that they can meet the needs of the wider society. State intervention in industrial relations in Greece and, generally, in Europe, has assumed various forms over time. The study of how state intervention has been exercised in industrial relations leads to the conclusion that over time, as changes occur in the socio-economic environment and the needs of communities, respective changes occur in the role the state plays in industrial relations and the forms by which the respective state activity is surrounded each time. So, whereas in the past some social and economic needs demanded the intense, immediate and direct state intervention in industrial relations, today it seems that the state rather evades the intrusive and hence the protective role, which in fact extends in practice to the regulatory role of either the market or, in the best case, of collective bargaining.

An effort to record and assess the situation in national industrial relations systems of most European countries would lead to the conclusion that most prevalent models are those of voluntarism and corporatism, between which policies of most European governments "have oscillated" in recent years, "shaded" by individual national, ideological and political particularities of each government. It is an issue of special scientific and political and societal interest of how the landscape of industrial relations is going to be shaped and what the role of both the nation state and supranational organizations would be. It is expected that during the next few years the impact of the global economic crisis would lead the social field to dramatic changes. The phenomenon of poverty in the developed world, long-term unemployment, poor employees and various forms of employment flexibility have been producing a binary model of labour, projecting as a background a binary model of society that entrenches social fragmentation, and serious social pressures for exercising social policies are foreshadowed.

However, a wider context that is characterized by cancellation of the given national market, economic globalization, centralization of capital, colossal enterprises, as well as by geopolitical concentrations – that is, constructs such as the European Union – as the potential of state intervention appears restricted and decision makers seem to shift to local or supranational level, it is of special scientific and socio-political interest, an interest prominent both in social theory and in terms of political practice to determine the role that individual nation states and supranational organizations would play in designing and executing necessary social policies – that is, in making policies in general or in showing regulatory abstinence, letting trade unions and employees cope without adequate support for the consequences of the global economic crisis of globalization and neo-liberal policies, which now seem are the most dominant.

The new orientation in industrial relations is the management of change through collaboration. The issue is to set the boundaries of change and to secure guarantees for bidirectional diffusion effects. Social dialogue is a method of action in this direction, "with distinct rules and principles that define decision-making process, how to contact social agencies and the content of the public interest"; it is "the foundation and prerequisite for the implementation of social policy" (Spyropoulos, 1998a). Besides, the degree of development of dialogue in a country is a "law-abiding element of democracy and expression of cultural sensitivity" (Koukiadis, 1996). Then, as the new that the interested parties have to deal with is the extent and the rapid changes brought about by technological development in all areas – an unprecedented fact in history (Hinterscheid, 1985), a new perspective is opened before them, that is, an exit from the crisis can be achieved within the context of consultation and cooperation (Bolin, 1985). This will help in the revision of the traditional role and problem solving, in an atmosphere of cooperation, support, trust and respect by all and to every direction.

Thus, with regard to trade unions, they can follow two ways: either to rest on what has been conquered or to renew their frameworks and practices and employ new strategies to meet the challenges of the times so to keep up with developments (Hinterscheid, 1985). As far as their action is concerned, it can be more effective internationally, if trade unions increase their effectiveness at national level by addressing problems that are international in essence (Bolin, 1985), and if they take heed that their tactics and influence in the past was not always beneficial and constructive for the broader society and economy and even for their very same members (Fakiolas, 1985). Employers should revise their practices and strategies, if they are to meet the demands of the times.

Regarding the state, realizing that new challenges require high levels of organization, discipline and experience to solve problems that arise, it should must recognize the important role played by the social partners, in terms of influence in the community, show sincere intentions, accept them as equal partners and collaborators in shaping policy, and be committed to the decisions taken within such a framework. As far as all three main partners are concerned, they should realize that their responsibilities at all levels are "interrelated, interdependent and complementary" (Spyropoulos, 1998a; Spyropoulos, 1998b). Important issues such as unemployment, social security, taxation, regional development, imply – through dialogue – that sacrifices, responsibilities and expectations of each one should be delineated in order to pave the way for development in the long term.

Ensuring the symmetrical distribution of power between the dominant organized interests and the interested parties' participation in decision-making, non-favouritism towards some powerful groups, the exclusion or marginalization of others and decisions not taken in advance by the state favour the successful conduct of social dialogue. In this way, the sense of political efficacy is strengthened, the sense of alienation from the centres of power is reduced, and an interest in collective problems is nurtured. The essential role of dialogue and cooperation should be primarily how to harmonize the imperatives of social justice with those of economic development.

New technologies have led to reversals and upheavals everywhere: in ideas, values, way of thinking, the way of life, knowledge, international relations, economy, trade, production and labour. Benchmarks were changed and have been changed radically. New global balances and new social realities are being formed. Globalization of the economy, characterized mainly by opening the market to international competition, is the big change that poses relentless questions to every country, society, business and citizens, to which sociological thought is required to respond effectively. It is obvious that nowadays humanity is in the midst of a great evolutionary overturn. Labour, which was the cradle of world civilization from antiquity to the present, has been systematically eliminated from the production process and has been increasingly replaced by "smart" machines. The industrial age is ending and a new era, the Information Age or the Computer Age is being established. However, this new era is calling into question full and massive employment. At the same time, along with new technologies, productivity of economy is growing indefinitely. The produced social product is expected to multiply in an inverse direction of declining employment, thereby increasing the potential of humanity to meet its needs (Spyropoulos, 1998a, p. 70).

Within today's globalized economy, it is conspicuous that collective bargaining and collective agreements which were mechanisms for consensus building and maintaining balance within the national context can no longer be effective in the form they have got so far. In the new environment, the collectivities of the past are getting weakened and must be replaced by new ones. The labour movement and the formations of its political and social representation need to develop and pursue new strategies of convergence of social forces of labour, taking into serious consideration that modern conditions of globalization call for industrial action not only at local but also at international level, in cooperation with trade unions in other countries, with particular emphasis on European dimension (Spyropoulos, 1985, pp. 175–178). They should realize that the persistence in demands and institutions that modern social and productive structures have gone over and beyond do not strengthen social justice and protection. The new welfare state – being an aspect of a modern development strategy, the core of which are new technologies – should succeed in incorporating new principles of social solidarity and protection and be able to cope with the new type of social inequalities and exclusion of large sections of population.

Chapter 5: Collective Bargaining

5.1 The Significance and the Role of Collective Bargaining: Introductory Remarks

The term "collective bargaining" has two meanings worldwide[46]. In its broad sense, it refers to any form of communication between employees and employers, whereas in its narrow sense it refers to collective bargaining, resulting in binding texts mutually acceptable, that is, collective bargaining agreements. According to the definition adopted by International Labour Convention 154: "for the promotion of collective bargaining"[47], the term "collective bargaining" refers to all negotiations that take place, between an employer, on the one hand, and a group of employers or one or more employers' organizations, on the other hand, in order to (a) determine the terms and conditions of employment (or employment conditions); and / or (b) to regulate relations between employers or professional organizations and one or more unions. Collective bargaining is one of the oldest and most important institutions in industrial relations that emerged in the 19th century (Koukoules, 1985, p. 414)and followed the course of the development of mass trade union movement, especially during the first and second industrial revolution. It is the expression of the right to collective autonomy (Daskalakis, 1993, pp. 209–211), and is connected with the right to form unions, which is usually safeguarded with the constitutions of the European Nation-States.[48] The importance of collective bargaining is determined by the fact that the institution that developed in free economy and in the countries of the former socialism – with, of course, different features (ILO, 1977, p. 7.) – with the regulations it produces, it covers very significant

46 The dual notion – broader and narrower – of the term collective bargaining is adopted by Bamber and Cordova in Blanpain and Engels (eds.) (1993), vol. 2, Ch. 22, p. 151.

47 Article 2; see the translation of an extract of International Labour Convention 154 that is listed by Spyropoulos, G., (1992). This International Convention was not ratified by Greece until 1995.

48 See the First Report on the Implementation of the Community Charter of Fundamental Social Rights of Employees, Commission of the European Communities, COM (91) 511 final, Brussels, 1991, in which there is a reference to the issue of the constitutional safeguard of this right in France p. 62, in Greece p. 109, in Ireland p. 145, in Spain p. 164–165, in Italy p. 187, in Luxembourg p. 214, in Portugal p. 267, and in the Netherlands p. 239.

percentages of the total workforce in all countries it operates[49], mainly in industry and commerce and less in small businesses and the agricultural sector (Spyropoulos, 1992, and ILO, 1977).

Today, the economic crisis (ILO, 1977, pp. 41–46), the introduction of new technologies, production and technological restructuring (Rowe, 1986, pp. 47–68 and 69–89), significant changes in qualifications (Bessant, 1989, pp. 41–51), the composition of the workforce (Braverman, 1974, pp. 377–402) and unions, destabilization of employment and unemployment (Gill, 1985, pp. 80–116 and mainly pp. 90–91), the introduction and widespread use of flexible forms of employment and working time (ILO, 1986, pp. 7–19; ETUI, 1985, pp. 119–149), downward trends in trade union density[50] and bargaining power of trade unions as well as personalization, to a large extent, of employees' behaviour[51] certainly affect and influence the development and dynamics of collective bargaining. Nevertheless, it can be said without hesitation that collective bargaining is a very important form of participation[52] with resilience and adaptability to changing environmental conditions in the system of industrial relations (ILO, 1977, pp. 50–52). It is a highly flexible mechanism for conducting social dialogue, co-deciding upon modernization and flexibility and for searching on behalf of the interested parties for mutually acceptable solutions and arrangements for reasonable but often conflicting economic and social objectives and demands (ILO, 1977, p. 7). It is perhaps

---

49 See Commission of the European Communities, (1992), Annual Report of the European Industrial Relations Observatory in Europe, Directorate-General, V/1466/92, p. 29, where the coverage of industries from collective agreements on percentage of active employed population is as follows: Belgium 80%, Denmark 83%, Germany 100%, Spain 61%, France 80%, Ireland 57%, Italy 100%, the Netherlands 70%, Portugal 80%, the United Kingdom 55%; there are no data for Greece and Luxembourg.

50 Salamon, 1987, pp. 62–63, esp. Index 4.2. and pp. 559–560, Appendix Nr 1, which clearly show that since the end of the 1970s there has been a decline in unions' density. See also: (a) the results of research carried out by the company DIMEL on behalf of GCGL (: General Confederation of Greek Labour, GSEE in Greek), "The Modern Greek Employee", December 1989 – January 1990, pp. 83–84 and 88; and (b) Commission of the European Communities, (1992), op cit., p. 22, according to which the average trade unionism in private sector in OECD countries does not exceed 8% of the employees. See the results of research carried out by the company DIMEL on behalf of GCGL, "The Modern Greek Employee", pp. 87–89 and 117–132.

51 Ibid.

52 Salamon, 1987, p. 301, index Nr 14.1; see also ETUI (1990), in which collective bargaining is considered one of the most participatory institutions and processes.

the only socially acceptable mechanism for promoting modernization[53] in economy and businesses as well as for promoting social justice and stability of employment.

In recent decades, collective bargaining has experienced great development in the systems of industrial relations of all developed countries[54], and that's why since 1960 the industrial relations research seems to have been focused increasingly on this institution (Daskalakis, 1989a, p. 71). While the first studies on collective bargaining were more fragmented, the relevant research in recent decades has got methodological unity and cohesion, a fact that is due to the formation and use, from some time and beyond, of special theories of the institution, in addition to the general theory of industrial relations which has been developing gradually (Bain and Clegg, 1974, Vol XII, No I, pp., 92–93).

In recent years – in view of new technologies[55] the financial difficulties that businesses face[56] and of the new "demand" for flexibility in industrial relations[57] – collective bargaining has been broadening its scope, acquiring new content and has been developing new trends[58]. These new standard forms of

53 For the role of collective bargaining in modernization and formulation of labour market policy, see the report of the French former Minister for Employment and Training, Soissons, 1990, in "Fighting Unemployment and Managing Structural Change, Report of an International Trade Union Seminar, held by the OECD, Paris, 29-31 January, pp. 15–23, and, especially, pp. 17 and 21.

54 Koukiadis, 1981, where the author makes reference to the development of collective bargaining in Germany pp. 75–80, Italy pp. 95–100 and France pp. 113–121.

55 A revealing record of the impact of new technologies on collective labour agreements was presented by Gill (1985, pp. 121–139), where extensive reference is made to new technologies, based on the experience of Britain pp. 121–132, France pp. 132–133, West Germany pp. 133–134, Italy pp. 135–137, USA pp. 137–138, and Norway, Sweden, Denmark pp. 141–160.

56 For the economic difficulties of the enterprises and their impact on conditions of employment see XIII International Conference of Labour Law and Social Security, Athens, 1991, 1st Topic, Rapports National. Especially for the Greek experience, see Agallopoulos and Travlos-Tzanetatos (1991, pp. 286–338).

57 Flexibility refers to the modern "employer's request". Christoforatos (1989, p. 385, in particular footnotes 1-4); see also Deligianni-Dimitrakou (1989, p. 145, and, in particular, footnotes 1 & 2).

58 Spyropoulos, (1988, pp. 529–541, and, particularly, pp. 532–533), where the writer refers to new trends and the new wider content, within which collective bargaining has been acquired in the developed countries in recent years.

collective agreements confirm this fact[59]. They confirm the view that collective bargaining is a flexible mechanism for participating in[60] and conducting social dialogue, aiming to address global and related social and economic demands and objectives (Daskalakis, 1991a, f. (1914), 10.01.91, pp. 37–38), balancing interests, co-deciding upon important mutually acceptable flexibility[61] – as well as training and implementing effective strategies of social contract (de Neubourg, 1990, pp. 133–136) that have been implemented by many European countries in recent years.

Nowadays, the institution of collective bargaining is constitutionally patented and / or regulated in most developed and developing countries. Its development in practice is now no longer a fundamental feature of industrial relations systems of modern states, marking the trend of contractualization and flexibilization of industrial relations law[62]. Furthermore, it also confirms the fact that collective bargaining as a mechanism for promoting social dialogue is a component of any modern, pluralist, social and political democracy that collective bargaining has gained in developed countries in recent years.

In Greece, the need to match the institutional framework of collective bargaining with the new needs has been met through the implementation of Law 1876/90 "On Free Collective Bargaining" (Koukiadis, 1992, pp. 15–25, and, in particular, pp. 18–19). However, the utilization of an adapted to current conditions modern and flexible mechanism for collective bargaining (Daskalakis, 1992, pp. 28–34, and, in particular, pp. 28–29) in Greece requires departure from traditional beliefs and practices, change of attitudes and mentality of every side, consolidation of a new culture and a culture of dialogue of the parties about industrial relations so that new roles may be undertaken by them and, more particularly, a training policy for the representatives of the parties may be established as well as a network of institutions for scientific and technical support for collective bargaining should be developed.

---

59 See Gill, (1985, pp. 121 -139), where reference is made to new technology contracts; see also, Delamotte, (1987, pp. 552–553), where reference is made to original agreements including the case of the original agreements "hand in hand".

60 ETUI (1990b), where collective bargaining is considered one of the most participatory institutions and processes.

61 For the need "to codetermine the flexibility", see ETUI (1998), pp. 113–188.

62 Contractualization is a key feature of the labour relations law that has already been developed. More particularly, see: Koukiadis, 1991, pp. 1–6, in particular p. 2.

5.2 Meaning and Nature of Collective Bargaining

Collective bargaining[63] and collective agreements are institutions (Leventis, 1981, pp. 20–25) through which procedural or substantial rules for the regulation of industrial relations can be generated (Leventis, 1981, pp. 28 & 31–32). According to the definition adopted by the International Labour Organization (ILO) in Convention 154 (Article 2), the term "***collective bargaining*** extends to all negotiations which take place between an employer, a group of employers or one or more employers' organizations, on the one hand, and one or more employees' organizations, on the other, for –

(a) determining conditions of employment and terms of employment; and/or
(b) regulating relations between employers and employees; and/or
(c) regulating relations between employers or their organizations and a employees' organization or employees' organizations" (Spyropoulos, 1992, p. 2).

At times various texts and authors or researchers have adopted a variety of positions, approaches, definitions and characterizations for the phenomenon. More particularly, collective bargaining has been described as:

(a) a method of co-decision – co-regulation and determination of conditions of employment (Flanders, 1968, pp. 11–26);
(b) a large social invention that has institutionalized industrial conflict (Dubin, 1954, p. 44); and
(c) a right that is or would still be the fundamental right of every employee in a democratic society (Donovan Commission, 1965–68, p. 54).

The term "collective bargaining" was initially used by the pioneers of industrial relations, the Webbs, who, as writers, dealt with the activities of trade unions in the late 19th century. The study of these authors' texts reveals that the term refers to all collective bargaining negotiations between the union, on the one hand, and an employer's or employers' association, on the other hand, in relation to pays and conditions of employment (Jackson, 1985, p. 114). In other words, it concerns a process through which unions can maintain and improve terms and conditions of employment for their members (Webbs, S. and B., 1902, p. 155). According to these authors, employees through unions eliminate

63 For collective bargaining and the nature of the institution as freedom of exercising the right that involves an obligation, see Aliprantis, 1979, pp. 523–524.

the disadvantageous position they are in when negotiating with the employer (Webbs, S. and B., 1902, p. 178) as individuals.

As it is typically argued, unions are primarily a kind of employees' coalition who achieve collectively "a mutual coverage and security" as well as bargaining and settlement of their terms and conditions of employment directly with employers. Through the process of collective bargaining, the individual employees "are turned into a union of employees", which negotiates expressing the collective will of its members (Webbs, S. and B., 1902, p. 172). Within the context of collective bargaining, employees, since they act collectively, are expressed through representatives. In this way, their position varies substantially. Instead of signing a series of agreements with individual employees, the employer has now come to face with the collective will of employees (Webbs, S. and B., 1902, p. 172). As a matter of fact at this point, as the Webbs' claim, the real power of unions lies exactly in that: that is, they replace the individual with collective bargaining, through which employees can obtain better conditions of employment, since the employer can no longer take advantage of the cyclical weaknesses or needs of each individual employee (Webbs, S. and B., 1902, p. 174).

Moreover, employees with their collective organization and the conduct of collective bargaining manage to reduce the number of negotiators, thus the number of competitors (Webb, S. and B., 1902, p. 561), and, therefore, competition among employees as individual units in the labour market (Petrou, 1988, p. 340). At the same time, the conduct of collective bargaining leads to shaping uniform rules and regulations (Petrou, 1988, p. 340) on conditions of employment for all employees, which means that the pay and conditions of employment are left neither in competition nor in individual bargaining of each individual employee – bargaining which is based on the uneven economic and bargaining power of the employee and the employer (Webbs, S. and B., 1902, p. 560). In this way, unions are considered as an agent seeking to establish a new balance in the existing imbalance in the labour market (Jackson, 1985, p. 114).

Younger writers, such as Flanders and Fox, agree that collective bargaining, especially if it regulates other issues other than purely economic, may be viewed as a political process through which power is exercised and rules are generated (Salamon, 1987, p. 271). This view is supported by Flanders after he had made an extensive effort to compare features, commonalities and differences of individual and collective bargaining (Jackson, 1985, p. 114). As he argues, in particular, collective bargaining – unlike the individual one which is a market activity – is essentially a political process, even though – for reasons of tactics – it passes through conflict or strike, it does not ultimately aim at the definitive and complete rupture of the relation (Flanders, 1968, p. 7) but at the conclusion of an agreement and signing of a collective agreement. Furthermore, collective bargaining – contrary to the individual one – does not concern just financial issues but includes issues of participation, rights and distribution of power to institutions of industrial relations. Finally, while collective bargaining regulates minimum terms and conditions of employment, the individual bargaining regulates in more detail the conditions under which the transaction is made: "job offer by the employee vis-à-vis wage offer from the employer." In other words, selling or hiring labour is not an active part of the bargaining process but rather remains a matter to be determined on an individual basis between the employer and the employee.

For these reasons, Flanders concludes that the collective bargaining process is in fact an activity of a "pressure group", aiming at a compromising settlement between the opposing forces, implying the absence of any possibility to identify this process as any other process and procedure of market bargaining (Flanders, 1968, pp. 4–6). Collective bargaining is thus a process of production of rules, regulating rather than substituting individual bargaining (Flanders, 1968, pp. 1–26) and, therefore, the use of the word "bargaining" in the term "collective bargaining" is – it could be argued – misleading (Flanders, 1968, pp. 1–26).

Flanders' views and, in particular his comments on the Webbs, was much criticized by Fox (1975, pp. 151–174), who described his approach as false and, more particularly, his distinction and comparison between individual and collective bargaining, based on where it was attempted. More particularly, Fox considered that individual and collective bargaining are wrong to be considered different, given that the former results in a contract and the latter in the generation of rules and regulations. However, none of the two ends up necessarily in agreement. It is conspicuous that collective bargaining does not always result in a transaction and therefore in a contract (Jackson, 1985, p. 117). Regarding Flanders's view that collective bargaining is a political process that includes a "diplomatic use of force", Fox notes that the same phenomenon occurs in the individual bargaining with the difference that here the inequality of power is blatant (Fox, 1975, p. 156). The extent, that is, the size of the parties is clearly greater in individual bargaining than the collective one – and, of course, more power is clearly in favour of the employer (Fox, 1975, p. 156). Finally, citing empirical data, Fox (1975, p. 170) suggested that they do not support Flanders' theory that collective bargaining performs a political rather than economic operation.

At this point, it is appropriate to mention Chamberlain and Kuhn's views (1965) who argued that collective bargaining performs a number of different operations, each of which emphasizes a different theoretical concept of process and refers to a different stage of development of the institution (Flanders, 1968, pp. 18–19). These authors saw collective bargaining from three different angles:

a) As a market – economic operation of selling labour (marketing theory). Under this approach, collective bargaining is a process that determines under which essential terms and conditions employees are employed (Chamberlain and Kuhn, 1965, p. 113).
b) As a political process grounded in "mutual dependence of the parties," it aims to produce rules, both procedural that concern the distribution of power and substance that is relevant to the allocation of financial resources so that a mechanism for management of labour and regulation of industrial relations of production can be developed (governmental theory) (Chamberlain and Kuhn, 1965, p. 121); and
c) As a management method based on a functional relationship between employers and employees.

Through collective bargaining, both parties are able to co-decide upon which they will mutually benefit. More specifically, employees have the opportunity – through their union representatives – to participate in determining choices that regulate life of employment (Chamberlain and Kuhn, 1965, p. 130).

Nowadays, the following view seems to be gaining more ground: that collective bargaining with the diversity and differentiation showing in modern industrial relations usually contains components of all three aforementioned operations, which certainly are not incompatible with each other. At the same time, certain assumptions are getting more and more accepted (Chamberlain and Kuhn, 1965, p. 135). Complex problems are created in modern industrial pluralistic societies. The exercise of power, namely sovereignty over citizens and employees, requires acceptance, acquiescence, consent, participation in decision making, solutions and regulations commonly accepted. In addition, both parties – employers and employees (Chamberlain and Kuhn, 1965, pp. 428–429) – are always interested in reaching an agreement or finding a solution to their differences, in any case. An agreement may not be reached only if both parties have a viable alternative solution. If only one of the parties has such an alternative solution, then an agreement can be reached, since the other party will eventually be forced to give in. However, it is argued that neither of the parties has such viable alternatives in modern societies

Finally, it is now accepted (Bamber and Cordova, 1993, Vol. 2, Ch. 22, p. 151) that the term "collective bargaining" has essentially two meanings (Blanpain and Koukiadis, 1993, p. 247): In its narrow sense, it refers to discussions between employees and employers in general terms and the processes that lead to written agreements containing binding rules on the parties, whereas, in its broad sense, it refers to any bilateral or trilateral discussions, consultations, bargaining and, generally, to any processes in which representatives of employees, employers and the state participate, through which they approach issues of common interest and process shared solutions for them.

As it is understood, in its narrow sense the term refers to collective bargaining that leads to familiar collective labour agreements, whereas, in its broad sense, it refers broadly to collective bargaining processes of general importance, through which social partners – employees, employers and the state – can conduct social dialogue at every level, something that is a strategic choice in contemporary societies (Blanpain and Koukiadis, 1993, Ch. 1st, III, pp. 205–211 and 247–262; ETUI, 1990a and 1990b) and promote the achievement of convergence in economic and social issues of "major importance".

In each case, a pluralistic approach (Daskalakis, 1989c, pp. 25–26; Pool, M., (1975), Ch. 4; Maclanes, 1985; and Fox, 1971, Ch. II) cannot but recognize that collective bargaining is – in fact – a form of participation (ETUI (1990b), through which wages and employment conditions can be determined, disputes and conflicts of interest can be settled, conflicting economic and social demands (Ross, 1958, p. 121) can often be harmonized, and, generally, parties' relations acting in any industrial relations system can be regulated at a collective level.

Collective bargaining is one of the most important institutions in industrial relations. In the course of research – from a historical point of view, while researchers' interest has been accumulated, collective bargaining is often in the heart of industrial relations research and has been identified with their concept (Daskalakis, 1989b, p. 8; Goutos, 1985, pp. 196 ff) or with industrial democracy (Daskalakis, 1989c, p. 25). The great variety of and differences in opinions (Koukiadis, 1981, p. 26, in particular ft 2) on the scope, purpose, and epistemological texture of industrial relations (Dunlop, 1958, pp. 5–6; Gill, 1969, Vol. VII, Nr 2, pp. 265–267) dictates that the approach to collective bargaining can primarily take place only if the concept of industrial relations is detected and delineated (Behrend, 1963, p. 383; Spyropoulos, 1977, p. 10).

5.3 The European Experience of Collective Bargaining

A major issue in the study of collective bargaining, as the experience of many European countries reveals, is the relation between state and collective autonomy, state self-regulation, on the one hand, and collective self-regulation, on the other hand (Leventis, 1981, pp. 37–38). There is another concern as to whether the interventionist role of government regulations can help industrial relations, above and beyond negotiations and the market can operate. A special issue in the study of collective bargaining is the issue of fiscal policy – which, as shown by the experience of a number of European countries in recent decades – has been regulated by one of the following two models (ILO, 1977, pp. 42–44): either (a) by imposing – through legislation or by providing guidance from relevant government agents – incomes policy (ILO, 1977, pp. 29–32 and 52 par. 20; Commission of the European Communities, 1992, p. 28) that put a ceiling on wages and increases; or (b) through its policy of social contracts and co-decision upon income policy, tactics often followed by governments (ILO, 1977, p. 33). The really rich experience of a number of European countries in at least the last two decades confirms that the institution of collective bargaining in its progress – particularly in terms of business and industry, without compromising the significance of bargaining at national level – has been the main mechanism of conducting social dialogue and adjusting issues of modernization and industrial relations (ILO, 1977, pp. 29 and 31–32).

Technological and productive restructuring, problems of finances and businesses, the issue of productivity and competitiveness, income, terms and conditions of employment, the issue of unemployment, social security issues, the issue of flexible forms of employment and the reorganization of working time, and more recently business investment policy, training, and the impact on the environment have been the "modern problems" whose nature has imposed de *facto* global and universal treatment (ILO, 1977, pp. 33–52) by the same partners, that is, employers and employees. The developments at a European level – after the Treaty on European Union as well as the Protocol and the Agreement on social policy were signed – shaped the parties in collective bargaining. The way for European collective agreements has now been opened (Blanpain and Koukiadis, 1993, pp. 187–189 and 247–262). It is possible to generate instructions through collective bargaining (Blanpain and Koukiadis, 1993, p. 261) too. The role of the parties is becoming increasingly vital. Their power is increased, since they now acquire a decisive role in the incorporation of EU directives into national law of each member state (Blanpain and Koukiadis, 1993, pp. 34–35, par. 50). In this sense, despite many technical problems and the reasonable caution that is expressed by many sides, the use of collective bargaining in practice form a new dynamic balance between conventional and governmental regulations and among national regulations, on the one hand, and community regulations on the other hand, which will answer to key questions and concerns of all agents of power – employers, employees, governments – in the European Union and each state separately.

The institutional framework of collective bargaining varies greatly from country to country when being determined by the social and economic structure, customs and the tradition of industrial relations (ILO, (1977), p. 11). In the recent decades, efforts have been made in many European countries to strengthen the institutional and procedural framework of collective bargaining so that it can cover all aspects of contemporary operation of the institution, something that does not mean that loopholes are not covered by rules formulated by case law, custom, practice or the common intention of the parties. Institutional regulations are seeking to form the basis – always taking into account the specificities of each country – for an elementary and streamlined regulation of the framework of development of collective bargaining with predefined – often mandatory for the parties – procedures and rules defined in advance for all preliminary and procedural aspects of bargaining.

Until recently, the international practice of collective bargaining has enabled the delineation of two (2) basic models (Bamber and Cordova, 1993, pp. 362–363, par. 31 and 32) of the institutional framework that regulates them. On the one hand, the first has been modeled on the European model, placing great emphasis on the mechanism of collective bargaining, and often leads to the establishment of bilateral or tripartite permanent bodies for their conduct; and, on the other hand, it has been modeled on the American model, which – giving emphasis on the processes – includes detailed regulations for the recognition of trade unions, the establishment of bargaining units and for the imposition of reciprocal commitments and obligations between the parties, such as the obligation to bargain in good faith and the prohibition of unacceptable labour practices.

Nevertheless, in recent years elements from both models have been integrated in new institutional regulations for collective bargaining resulting in new intermediate mixed models (ILO, 1977, p. 86) being detected and delineated, which regulate in some detail preliminary and prejudicial *issues*, the issue of representation and recognition of parties, and seek to clarify, record and broaden the scope and content of collective bargaining, coordinate and construct the structure and the levels of their conduct in a rather decentralized way, and, finally, to introduce institutions and processes that contribute to rationalizing collective bargaining. However, additional mechanisms and technical support, resolution of collective disputes as well as management of collective bargaining agreements and arbitration awards are most often provided for their more effective functions.

Two key provisions, adopted by many national legislators, are those related to the establishment of a procedure for the recognition of trade unions so that social interests are genuinely represented and the parties are obliged to negotiate in order for a smooth functioning of collective bargaining is achieved. Until recently, there had been two models based on the practice followed by national legislators. The first model included legislative or administrative regulations for union recognition and bargaining obligation and implemented in countries where industrial bargaining has traditionally dominated. Whereas the second model, based on each party's voluntary willingness to recognize the other party and the acceptance of the bargaining, responded more to the tradition of voluntarism and implemented in countries dominated by bargaining at industry level (BELGIUM) (Stergiou, 1988, p. 109, ft 40; Windmuller el al, 1987, p. 51).

The set of institutional regulations mentioned above and the principles they adopted and internalized has allowed and encouraged the development of some new trends (Daskalakis, 1984, p. 356) in collective bargaining, and in particular: (a) expanding the scope of their implementation in sectors or fields of economic and business activities and categories of employees where there were no collective bargaining in the past (ILO, 1977, p. 8); (b) widening the scope of collective bargaining and the content of collective agreements so that the interested parties, employees and employers, have full authority in dealing with and regulating universally all important social and economic issues that affect them (Spyropoulos, 1992, pp. 31–32); and (c) developing a flexible structure of interlocked levels of collective bargaining, which–by internalizing elements of centralization and decentralization trends – both utilizes national inter-professional collective bargaining and emphasizes their "downwards" (Spyropoulos, 1988, p. 532), towards the areas where economic activities and the primary promotion of economic, social and labour problems occur, that is the industry, the company and the individual production unit.

5.4 The Greek Experience of Collective Bargaining in the Past

Until recently, collective bargaining was regulated by Law 3239/1955. While that Law was in effect, there was a system of industrial relations characterized by complete distrust in collective bargaining (Koukiadis, 1981, p. 165), centralization (Koukiadis, 1981, p. 168) the strong presence of government intervention and regulations (Lixouriotis, 1992, p. 161), and conflict situations (Ioannou, 1988), dominance of a confrontational culture and negative attitude of the parties towards accountability, mutual commitments and conduct of dialogue with substance (Daskalakis, 1991a, p. 7).

Main features of the Law were the scarcity of the content of collective bargaining (Ntasios, 1991b, p. 37, par. 5), which in practice they were only regulating pays. The Law led to the development of centralized collective bargaining and settlements (Daskalakis, 1992, p. 28) and contributed to maintaining the fragmentation of the trade union movement with its emphasis on the occupational-level bargaining (Article 21 par. 2, 7 par. 1 subpar. b′, subpar. c′ & subpar. d′ of Law 3239/1955). Furthermore, it did not provide for conducting collective bargaining and concluding collective labour agreements at an enterprise level, excluding those of utilities (Paragraph 1, subpar. d′ & Paragraph 5, Article 7, Law 3239/1955). The whole system of Law 3239 of 1955 was accompanied by provisions of suspending strikes (Leventis, 1986, pp. 376–381) and regulating collective labour disputes through State compulsory arbitration (Mitsou, 1971, p. 21). The specific point is what had been criticized by social partners for many years. The primary and secondary administrative arbitration tribunals, which were set up by a decision of the Minister of Labour (Ntasios, 1991b, p. 58, par. 7) – the state nature of the mechanism that was providing arbitration services – was the fact that could not secure a system of resolution and settlement of collective disputes, a function without interventions by the state. At the same time, a critical issue was obligingness (Koukiadis, 1981, pp. 210–220) of arbitration, namely that any collective labour dispute would lead to arbitration anyway. However, the problem with Law 3239 of 1955 did not concern its individual points but rather its whole underlying philosophy, since – as it was illustrated by its title – the legislator knew only the existence of collective disputes and dealt collective bargaining simply as a means to solve them[64]; indicative of this philosophy is the very title of this Law (i.e. Law 3239/1955) which is "Regulating Collective Labour Disputes".

5.5 The Recent Greek Experience drawn upon the Model of "Free Collective Bargaining"

The new Law on collective bargaining passed while there was a Universal Government in March 1990, since only then the right balance (Daskalakis, 1992, p. 28) for amending the institutional framework of collective bargaining occurred. The new Law introduced a completely new concept for collective bargaining and collective labour disputes. With the title that s/he gave to the Law "On free collective bargaining," the legislator shows that s/he is no aware primarily of collective disputes but the dialogue between the parties through collective bargaining so that economic interests are settled and disputes are prevented (Koukiadis, 1992, p. 18). The Law introduced a number of important innovations. First, it broadened the scope of collective bargaining to include not only those employees working under a legal relation of salaried employment but also those who are employed under contracts that underlie dependence from an employer and

64 See the title of Law 3239/1955 which is: "Regulating Collective Labour Disputes".

salaried employment (as often happens with various types of contracts, farmers etc) (Travlos-Tzanetatos, 1990, pp. 95–96 and 134–135).

The Law expanded the scope of collective bargaining so that the parties can have universal surveillance in their relations. Today, there can be the subject of collective bargaining and collective bargaining issues such as: wages, benefits, leave, how to pay overtime working, conditions for recruitment and dismissals, the expansion of union rights, social security matters – except for pension, issues of competence of employees' councils – such as the internal regulation of the company, health and safety regulation, employees' training and retraining – improving terms and conditions of employment, productivity issues, enterprise policy that has a direct influence on industrial relations, such as the reorganization of production, the introduction of new technologies, the introduction of flexible forms of employment and working time – as well as the interpretation of regulatory requirements for collective bargaining agreements (Article 2, Law 1876/1990). Of particular importance is the fact that, although the Law provides procedures for dispute resolution and settlement of collective labour disputes, it also allows the parties to settle, if they wish, these issues differently through collective bargaining and collective agreements (Articles 2 & 14, Paragraph 2, Law 1876/1990).

Meanwhile, the new Law – along the lines of corresponding Laws of other European countries – introduced a series of rights and obligations for the parties, aiming to rationalize (Koukiadis, 1992, p. 18, par. 4.1), make effective the dialogue and alter strike into the last resort. More particularly, it made the employer accountable to employees so that dialogue could be meaningful (Koukiadis, 1993, p. 16). It introduced the principle of bargaining in good faith, the violation of which was referred to as the basic criterion for the judgment of the courts for the legality of strikes. It empowered the role of representative organizations (Lixouriotis, 1992, pp. 127–160) so that the represented interests would be empowered too. It provided for the establishment of institutions and processes that supported and facilitated the dialogue between the parties (mediation and reconciliation), if bargaining failed. It also provided, through sensitive institutional balance (Daskalakis, 1992, pp. 30–31), the potential of purely supplementary use of the institution of arbitration (Koukiadis, 1992, p. 21, par. 5.1) so that situations of unregulated industrial relations and conflict could be prevented. The Law was giving very clear priority to the sovereign will of the parties concerned in matters both substantive and procedural (Vagias, 1991, p. 898).

A major innovation of the Law – leading the institutional framework of collective bargaining in Greece in line with the needs, trends, and data that the modern European experience indicated – was, through Law provisions, the possibility to develop a disaggregated system of collective bargaining which, without undermining the importance of the National General Collective Agreements (EGSSE), will put emphasis on industry collective agreements (Ioannou, 1992) introduced for the first time (Paragraph 1, subpar. C, and Paragraph 5, Article 3, Law 1876/1990). Law 1876 of 1990 provides for four types of contracts: national, general, industry, occupational agreements (at national or local level) and enterprise-level agreements (Paragraph 1, subpar. a', b', c', d', e', Article 3, Law 1876/1990). With these regulations, however, especially those concerning the confluence of collective regulations, it degrades the contracts of occupational-level bargaining against industry-level and enterprise-level bargaining[65], with many positive effects. In this way, problems are tackled upon when surging, that is, that of economy as a whole, industry or enterprise, while corporatism is being weakened and the overthrow of the segmentation and fragmentation of the trade union movement is routed.

Finally, of great importance is the novelty of the Law, that is, the introduction of a new model of mediation and arbitration so that collective labour disputes could be resolved and settled (see Chapter I (Articles 14-18) of Law 1876/1990). With this new Law, the NPID (or PEL – Private Entity Law) was established, which is funded mainly by social resources[66]; it is independent and managed by the Board (of Directors), where the social partners have the primary saying (Koukiadis, 1991b, p. 37). In this Organization, a special body of mediators and arbitrators was established (Gladstone, 1984, p. 17; Zack, 1980, pp. 7 ff; Zack, 1985, pp. 189–192), especially by specialists in labour issues, who were to provide mediation and arbitration services so that collective disputes could be resolved and settled (Jacobs, 1993). The emphasis and priority were put on mediation process (Papadimitriou, 1992, p. 25; Daskalakis, 1991a, pp. 30–3), aiming not to replace but rather to assist the direct dialogue between the parties. Moreover, there is arbitration, which is of an auxiliary character and which – without meaning that it is strictly necessary for the outcome of any collective dispute – is to ensure that conflicts are avoided in borderline cases of minimum collective settlements.

65 See Paragraph. 2, Article 10, Law 1876/1990 that shows that collective labour agreement at industry- or enterprise-level prevails in the case cited.

66 Although the OMED is entitled to subsidies from the State budget (Paragraph 1, subpar. b', Article 18, Law 1876/1990), it has been financed so far solely by the "Organization of Labour House", so the used funds are only contributions made by employees and employers.

5.6 Collective Bargaining after and under the Memorandum with the E.U. and the I.M.F.: Law 3845/2010 that Verified Memorandum, the Updated Memorandum and Law 3899/2010 which Introduced the "Special Enterprise-Level Collective Agreements"

By force of the Memorandum, which was ratified by Law 3845/2010, significant changes have been made in Law 1876/1990 "*on free collective bargaining.*" More specifically, in the same text of the Memorandum, namely Law 3845/2010, "*Measures for the implementation of the support mechanism for the Greek economy by the Member States of the euro and the International Monetary Fund*", there is a provision with which the system hierarchy of collective bargaining agreements, which Law 1876/19990 had provided, has substantially been altered. This is the provision of Paragraph 7, Article 2, which states that "*The terms of occupation-level and enterprise-level agreements may diverge from their respective terms of industry agreements and national general collective agreements and the terms of industry agreements may depart to their respective terms of national general collective agreements may diverge from the respective terms of national general collective agreements and with the Minister's decision every necessary detail can be adjusted to implement the provisions of this paragraph.*" That Ministerial Decree was never issued. Instead, the Ministry of Labour undertook legislative initiative that promoted the institutionalization of special enterprise-level collective agreements (SELCAs or EESSE in Greek).

At the same time, the initial Memorandum included "*a clause for a three-year wage freeze*" beyond the public and private sector, which however, as it will be discussed later, was only partially implemented. In addition to all this information, the "Updated Memorandum" of August 2010 stated that: "*The government must ensure that the enterprise-level agreements override industry agreements*" and that "*the Government should withdraw the provisions of Law 1876/1990 which allows the Ministry of Labour to extend all industry agreements also to those who are not represented in the bargaining.*"

Following those developments, extensive, continuous and repeated, tough bargaining between the Ministry of Labour and representatives of the *Troika* were conducted, the results of which were: (a) With the stated, active and written support of all social partners, the abolition of the institution of the expansion of industry agreements should finally be prevented. (b) The amendment of Article 10 of Law 1876/1990 on the confluence of collective agreements should be prevented, an issue which, however, had been additionally raised with emphasis on the course of bargaining; and (c) Never was the Ministerial Decree provided by Paragraph 7, Article 2 of Law 3845/2010 issued; but, at the same time, a new provision of Article 13 of Law 3899/2010 was issued, a provision which limited to special enterprise-level collective agreements. If these bargaining they had not been relatively successful, not only would enterprise-level collective bargaining agreements be generalized and unconditionally under those of industry ones, but both these and their industry ones could move below the thresholds of the National General Collective Agreements (EGSSE), that is, without a safety threshold being for how much wages would drop.

In this way, industry collective agreements were preserved, and the government kept the right to extend their general validity for all companies in an industry. At the same time, the necessary flexibility was given to a company that faces financial problems to reach special enterprise-level collective agreement, in agreement with both the employer and employees. Terms were placed to ensure that a limit both to the divergence in wages from the industry collective agreement and to potential dismissals. The direct involvement of social partners in the whole process was sought for, because social partners are those who are familiar with the needs of businesses, whereas the institution of Arbitration was rescued. The aim of all settlements, which were the subject of tough negotiations between the Greek side and representatives of the EC, the ECB and the IMF (the so-called *Troika*), on the one hand, and of the national tripartite dialogue-negotiation, on the other hand, was the survival of enterprises and the preservation and creation of jobs in this critical period of our country.

Thus, Law 3899/2010 introduced "*Urgent measures for the implementation of the support programme of the Greek economy*" to the Collective Labour Law. In the system of collective bargaining, which is basically determined by Law 1876/1990, a new form of collective agreement, the "Special Enterprise-Level Collective Agreement" (SELCAs or EESSE in Greek), whose main purpose is to create and preserve jobs as well as to improve the competitiveness of enterprises. The terms and conditions of the SELCAs are determined by the social partners at the enterprise level on an annual basis, as it happens in collective agreements. More specifically, even with Article 13[67] of this Law, it was decided that, with the special enterprise-level collective agreement – which is a new kind of collective agreement – wages and conditions of employment may diverge from those of the respective industry collective agreement; yet, it shouldn't be below the level of the National General Collective Agreement (EGSSE). In other words, within the context of those SELCAs wages may diverge from the respective industry

67 Article 5A is added to Article 3 of Law 1876/1990.

collective agreement, up to the level of National General Collective Agreement (EGSSE), which is the threshold, whereas, at the same time the number of jobs and other terms and conditions are specified, such as part-time, job rotation, availability, duration of implementation, including any terms and conditions for the return process in the implementation of the normal terms and conditions of employment provided by industry collective agreements. With the special enterprise-level collective agreement, the number of jobs, terms and part-time conditions of employment, job rotation, and availability, as well as any other term of implementation, including their duration, can be regulated.

In the case of "special enterprise-level collective agreement", this may be renewed. About the new provision[68], however, the Scientific Committee of the Greek Parliament, during the processing of the Bill, raised important questions. More specifically, the Committee asks: "It could, however, be questioned whether this regulatory power has limitations and to what extent, if, for example, the duration of availability can be increased and enforced not only up to three months, but for longer, or if half pay may not be paid to the employees on an inactive status etc. In short, the question arises whether such a regulatory ability may involve deregulation of the Law, by amending indefinitely for worse for those who fall within its scope. Furthermore, the question arises as to the scope of regulation of the number of jobs, if, a ban may include reducing the number of jobs or elimination of these positions, notwithstanding the provisions on mass redundancies."

Special enterprise-level collective agreements (SELCAs) take into account the companies' need to adapt to market conditions in order to create or preserve jobs and improve their productivity and competitiveness. The special enterprise-level collective agreement[69] can be drawn up by an employer who employs fewer than fifty (50) employees, with the respective enterprise association, and if there isn't such an association, with the respective industry association or their respective federation. Consequently, SELCAs can be concluded in businesses with fewer than 50 employees, where if there is not an enterprise union, employees are represented by their industry association or their respective federation. Under the new provision, a "special enterprise-level collective agreement" can also be made up in enterprises with fewer than fifty employees. Furthermore, it is provided that, in terms of employees, the special enterprise-level collective agreement is

68 The second subparagraph of Paragraph 1, Article 14, Law 3899/2010.

69 A Special Enterprise-Level Collective Agreement (SELCA) starts from its conclusion and is valid in accordance with the existing provisions in Article 5 of this Law.

signed by "the respective enterprise union and, if there is none, it is signed by the industry union or their respective federation." For these special enterprise-level collective agreements to be awarded, neither particular conditions nor special terms for their implementation are required, other than those agreed upon and defined specifically and concretely in the text of this agreement. Therefore, an "enterprise-level collective agreement" may be renewed annually, without the number of these renewals being restricted. The only proviso is that the writing of an "Explanatory Report" to the Council for Social Control of Labour Inspection (SKEEE in Greek) about the reasons justifying the conclusion of this agreement.

For a SELCA to be concluded, interested parties submit a joint reasoned report to the Council for Social Control of Labour Inspection (SKEEE), which makes simple opinion on the advisability of this. With a view to concluding a special enterprise-level collective agreement (SELCA), the parties shall jointly submit explanatory statement of the reasons justifying their intention to draft a special enterprise-level collective agreement for the Council for Social Control of Labour Inspection (SKEEE), which give an opinion on the appropriateness of its drawing up, through an exclusive period of twenty (20) days after the end of which it is granted. By the same procedure any extension of it is agreed upon. This Council just gives an opinion, but its consent is not required. In case of breach of these terms and conditions, the special enterprise-level collective agreement is invalid, and in case of termination of this agreement, the compensation is calculated based on the earnings of the respective industry collective agreement. Any reduction in employees' pay violating the agreed under the special enterprise-level collective agreement is considered a failure to pay legal wages, to which what is valid is applied[70]. Furthermore, other law[71] provides that "the central office of the Ministry of Labour and Social Security holds a general register, in which all collective agreements are recorded by type, and these documents are posted as such on the website of the Ministry of Labour and Social Security."

The applicability of the SELCAs to wages, employment, productivity and competitiveness will depend on the maturity and the active participation of the interested parties. Working together to tackle upon problems in a spirit of dialogue in good faith, objective information and shared responsibility are prerequisites for achieving their goals. According to the Circular of Labour Inspection Authority (SEPE in Greek) for this purpose, a Special Register Book is kept in SEPE for the

70 The exceptionally mandatory Law 690/1945, as amended by Paragraph 1, Article 8, Law 2336/1995.

71 The provision of Article 12 of Law 3846/2010: "Guarantees on labour safety and other provisions" is replaced by Paragraph 6, Article 5, Law 1876/1990.

joint (by employers and employees) submission of explanatory statements. This Register should contain the following:

(1) Column with "Serial Number"; (2) Column with "Submission Date"; (3) Column with "Sector of Economic Activity"; (4) Column with the "Name of Company"; (5) Column with the "Name of Business Association" or if there is the "Name of the relevant Industry Association or Federation"; (6) Column with "Date Sent to SKEEE"; (7) Column with "Date of Opinion – Positive or Negative – by SKEEE"; and (8) Column with the "Submission Date" of the "special enterprise-level collective agreement". Furthermore, upon the submission of the Explanatory Report, a checking is conducted as to whether the submitted Explanatory Report has been concluded and signed by both parties in accordance with the provisions of Article 13 of Law 3899/2010. Finally, the document with the Explanatory Report should be submitted by email to the Secretariat of the SKEEE within twenty-four (24) hours from the date it was submitted to the Department of Social Inspection (TKE in Greek.). If awarded a "Special enterprise-level Collective Agreement", after the opinion of the SKEEE, and submitted to the local Department of Social Inspection, as provided in Law 1876/1990, monthly statistics of submitted a "Special enterprise-level Collective Agreement", should be sent to the relevant Department of Planning and Coordination Directorate of Social Inspection[72].

Special enterprise-level collective agreements (SELCAs) override their respective industry collective agreements, without restrictions. Because of their special nature, the SELCAs are neither covered by the principle of the most favourable settlement of industry collective agreements nor are any expanded industry collective agreements applied to them. Provisions of Law 1876/90 on the confluence[73] to extend collective labour agreements (sse) do not apply to these collective agreements. The Scientific Committee of the Parliament was, however, preoccupied particularly in its Report with the issue of confluence of collective agreements – while processing the Bill "Urgent measures for the implementation of the support programme of the Greek economy" – claiming: "The provision of Article 14 of Law 3899/2010 provides for a "special enterprise-level collective agreement" as a new category of collective agreement, which is added to those already provided for in Article 3 of Law 1876/1990, and the wording of Article 10 Law 1876/1990 is amended which regulates issues of confluence collective

72 A model form is attached to the relevant official Ministerial document, which is an official part of it.

73 See the provisions of Article 10, and those of Paragraphs 2, 3 and 4, Article 11 of Law 1876/1990.

agreements." Confluence occurs when the employment relation covers more collective labour agreements. Article 10 of Law 1876/1990 resolves the issue of confluence by stating that if the employment relation is regulated by most existing collective agreements, then the most favourable to the employee is implemented. Thus, the principle of the most favourable settlement is that it leads to the selection of the applicable collective agreement (except for the case of confluence of the occupational agreement with the enterprise-level or industry-wide collective agreement). The provision of Paragraph 7, Article 2, of Law 3845/2010 defines, then, that the term "enterprise-level collective agreements" may diverge from their respective terms of Industry Collective Agreements and the National General Collective Agreements (EGSSEs)."

It was also specified that the terms of Industry Collective Labour Agreements may diverge from their counterparts of the National General Collective Agreements (EGSSEs)." The provision of Article 14 of Law 3899/2010 provides that special enterprise-level collective labour agreements (SELCAs) "prevail over their respective industry collective agreements without limitations." Therefore, any kind of terms of special enterprise-level collective agreements (SELCAs) are applicable, even if they are unfavourable to those of industry collective agreements, having as limit the levels of the national general collective agreement (EGSSE). Accordingly, it is stated that the provisions of Article 10 of Law 1876/1990 do not apply, as the provisions of Article 11 of the same Law aren't applicable to the extended application of collective agreements, that is, they have been declared as universally applicable to all subordinate employees, regardless of their membership of the union. Nevertheless, in the present cases, the question of the importance of such a reference to the provisions related to the extension of application is raised. Provided that the provision of Article 14 of Law 3899/2010 provides that rules of confluence do not apply, and that the special enterprise-level collective agreement is applicable anyway, according to the provision of Paragraph 3, Article 8 of Law 1876/1990, even to all employees in the business, thus there is neither question of extension of the application of certain collective agreements, nor question of the results of such an extension".

The regulated divergence of enterprise-level collective agreements from those of industry ones is a choice that takes into account the experience of countries and industrial relations systems as well as economies that preserve jobs, maintain competitiveness and stand effectively in crisis. In principle, the international practice concerns the long German experience, which extends more than ten years. Austria and Ireland have implemented similar practices over the past years. Since 2009 there have been such settlements in Ireland, whereby employers who could demonstrate "inability to pay wages" have been entitled to avoid granting increases, which were agreed upon at national – industry level. The court may grant a business that is financial hardship single exception – up to one year – from the mandatory industry minimum wages. The employer must have the consent of the employees' majority. Austria has implemented respective practices in recent years. Similar provisions, possibility of divergence of enterprise-level collective agreements from those of industry ones were included in the reform of system of collective bargaining discussions between the government, unions and employers in Italy in 2009, although the labour confederation CGIL disagreed with the special settlements for the exclusion of enterprise-level collective agreements from those of industry that were adopted.

The most characteristic, however, case is Germany, whose long experience is useful and instructive. Germany's more than ten-year experience has been proven an important tool for processing the unification of Western and Eastern Germany, facing the effects of globalization, and, especially, of preserving jobs during the present recession and crisis. In Germany it is assumed that there is agreement between employers and employees upon the industry level so that a divergence may be possible. Here, a potential divergence is legislated but in order for its implementation to be economically and socially efficient the necessary role is attributed to social partners by strengthening their role in tripartite institutions of social control, as in Greece, the SKEEE (Council for Social Control of Labour Inspection). Basically, it is about mechanisms of exceptions of enterprise-level collective agreements from those of industry ones, which are the rule of the regulation of wages and labour relations. According to German Law (*Betriebsverfassungsgesetz*), the management and the representatives of employees have no right to regulate at enterprise-level issues that are regulated by industry collective agreements. On the contrary, mechanisms of exceptions apply to enterprise-level collective agreements. Enterprise-level collective agreements may diverge from the provisions of the existing industry collective agreement, if there is an opt-out right, under certain conditions, in the industry collective agreement. The conditions, scope, content and standard procedures of the enterprise-level collective agreement, which may be diverging, are defined generally by the industry unions of employers and employees. The legislator in Greece, avoiding bureaucratic solutions, enables parties, employees and employers proceed to exceptions in order to support jobs and competitiveness of the business and exercise this right by regulating it in an organized manner.

After the new regulations of Law 3899/2010, concerning the special enterprise-level collective agreements (SELCAs), industry collective agreements continue to apply to all businesses that do not conclude this kind of agreements (i.e. SELCAs), and even in case of the conclusion of an SELCA, the National General

Collective Agreement (EGSSE) remains intact as the threshold of wages and statutory rights. Furthermore, not only are the industry collective agreements kept but collective bargaining is also strengthened at an enterprise-level, with the introduction of a new form of collective agreement, the Special Enterprise-Level Collective Agreement (SELCA) to the Greek Collective Labour Law. Otherwise, a trend of deregulation of the system of collective bargaining and individualization of industrial relations would have prevailed. In contrast, by preserving the principle of "confluence" and the principle of the most favourable for the employee settlement, employees' rights and industry collective agreements are protected, the abolition of their capacity to expand would create fragmentation of the workforce – that is, it will create not only "two- or multi-speed" employees but also conditions of a fierce "wild" and unfair commercial and economic competition between businesses.

Law 3899/2010 "*Urgent measures for the implementation of the support programme for the Greek economy*" was not mainly designed to reduce wage costs, as it has been argued, but primarily aimed to protect jobs at a very critical juncture for the country. Moreover, the state cannot and should not foresee what will be the result of free collective bargaining, whether this occurs at national or industry or enterprise level. Free collective bargaining itself is an institutional achievement, which was passed unanimously by the National Assembly in 1990. What the state and, so a government, has an obligation to do is to ensure, as far as it is possible, terms of equal bargaining between the two parties, as it is known that many times there is asymmetric bargaining power between the parties especially at the operational level. It is also an obligation of the State to ensure that there are not only equitable bargaining terms but also a safety net for minimum wages. For this reason Law 3899/2010 requires collective bargaining with the presence of the same union or federation of the employees and an agreement between the social partners so that a special enterprise-level collective agreement (SELCA) is signed, whereas the National General Collective Agreement (EGSSE) is set as safety threshold for all, meanwhile the institution of the possibility of expanding industry collective agreements, by which employees who work in businesses but are not subject to provisions of a SELCA may be covered.

At the same time, in the new Law all boundaries and limitations, and hence redundancies are put on the table and are agreed upon jointly. Thus, the employer does not select arbitrarily, but the union must rather agree upon the number of dismissals that may be done as long as the special enterprise-level collective agreement lasts. The employer ought to observe the agreement. In contrast, with no agreement the employer could make use of the existing legislation and dismiss five percent (5%) of staff per month without quantitative restrictions.

Regarding particularly SMEs (small and medium-sized enterprises), adverse effects on industrial relations are rather avoided with new regulations. More specifically, the employees' bargaining power is rather ensured in SMEs, as well as in these cases where fewer than fifty employees are employed, they are represented by their union, or if there is none, as in the case of businesses with fewer than twenty people – by their respective industry union or federation, whose bargaining power carries its own weight. Article 13 of Law 3899/2010 prevents the widespread and without reasoning implementation of enterprise-level collective agreements and their preponderance over industry-level collective agreements. With the provisions of this Law, there is divergence only after employers and employees have agreed upon it and, moreover, the decision on inclusion in the SELCA must be justified in writing and the Council for Social Control of Labour Inspection (SKEEE) should be informed about it so that there is transparency for every employee and every citizen as to where there is a problem in the enterprise and what this problem is about.

In conclusion, important issues that have affected decisively the model of collective bargaining in our country have been: (a) Law 3845/2010 "*Measures for the implementation of the support mechanism for the Greek economy by the Member States of the euro zone and the International Monetary Fund*", in Paragraph 7, Article 2 of which a provision is included that essentially refutes the system of collective bargaining and the hierarchy of collective agreements in the country, which were provided by the "universally" accepted Law 1876/19990 "On Free Collective Bargaining". More specifically, this Law provided that: "*The terms and conditions of occupation-level and enterprise-level collective agreements may diverge from the respective terms of the industry collective agreements and national general collective agreements and the terms of the industry agreements may diverge from the respective terms of national general collective ones and with the Minister's decision every detail necessary for the implementation of this paragraph can be regulated*". But the aforementioned Ministerial Decision was never issued. Instead, the Ministry of Labour has undertaken legislative initiative (Law 3899/2010) which promoted the institutionalization of special enterprise-level collective agreements (SELCAs). However, there is not straight abolition of the provision in question – that is, that of Paragraph 7, Article 2 of Law 3899/2010 – anywhere in subsequent legislation. For this reason, although even today in practice of industrial relations there have been no problems that the Greek justice system will be called to finally resolve, from the phase of the first process of the Bill for the SELCAs the Scientific Committee of the Parliament wonders: "Finally, the question is whether the provision of Paragraph 7, Article 2 of Law 3845/2010 is abolished as a whole with the proposed measures (that is, the provisions of Article 14 of Law 3899/2010)[74] a provision that provides generally that the terms of "Enterprise-Level Collective Agreements" may diverge from their respective terms of the Industry Collective Agreements and the "National General Collective Agreements", and that the terms of the Industry Collective Agreements may diverge from the respective terms of the "National General Collective Agreements".

Finally, Law 4024/2011 (see Government Gazette 226, vol. A' 27/10/2011) – which passed very recently by the Parliament (October 20, 2011) and, in particular, Article 37 – has raised major political issue concerning the institution of collective bargaining and introduced significant changes. More specifically, enterprise-level collective agreements are concluded in order of precedence by enterprise unions that cover employees or, if there is no trade union in the enterprise, by association, and, regardless of the category, position or specialty of the employees in the enterprise and, if these are absent, by their respective primary industry associations and employer. The association is composed of at least three-fifths (3/5) of the employees in the enterprise, regardless of the total number of employees in it, and without its duration being subject to time limits. If, after any composition of the association for that purpose, the term of the participation of three fifths (3/5) of the employees ceases to exist in the enterprise, which is required for its formation, this association is dissolved, without further formality.

Most importantly, however, is that industry collective agreements are suspended for four (4) years. Thus, employers are facilitated to sign business contracts, leading to large reductions in wages. More specifically, the measures are included in the new multi-faceted Bill are the following: (a) Suspension of the extension of business and industry collective agreements at least until the end of 2014. The aim of this measure is to give more flexibility to businesses and their employees to come to an agreement on wage levels at the enterprise level. As it was argued characteristically, there are indications that wages agreed with settlements at industry level are becoming more and more restrictive for small businesses and result in substantial job losses. (b) Abolition of the clause of a more favourable settlement in case of confluence. The goal of this settlement is to decentralize collective bargaining by enlarging the scope of business contracts; and (c) An extension of the enterprise-level collective agreements to businesses of all sizes. According to this argument, or what was employed for regulating, in some cases, particularly for small businesses, a key obstacle to sign an enterprise-level collective agreement is the absence of an institutionally regulated partner

74 The parentheses and their content are by the author.

with the employer. This role will now be played the Associations and Unions in the Law passed.

All this denotes that the principle of the most favourable to the employee agreement (that is, provisions for confluence) is abolished, paving the way for re-bargaining of all pay terms and conditions and their redefining by signing enterprise-level collective agreements that will take precedence over industry and occupational agreements. Enterprise-level collective agreements could prevail apart from those of occupational and industry ones, but they will not be able to provide more unfavourable terms and conditions than the EGSSE (National General Collective Agreement). The abolition of the principle of the most favourable settlement in collective agreements, leading to a predominance of an enterprise-level collective agreement over that of industry or that of occupational collective agreement in case of confluence – combined with the ability to conclude enterprise-level collective agreements not only by the representatives of trade unions, but also by associations – signals the potential for uncontrolled and steep wage cuts in the private sector. The GSSE (or GCGL: Greek General Confederation of Labour or General Confederation of Greek Labour) considers that the reduction can be from 25% up to 35%.

However, it should be noted that the question of the minimum wage in Greece is still open, as in the European Commission's report – which is the harbinger of lenders' report – is explicitly stated that the Greek government will promote discussions with the social partners so all parameters of labour market that affect the competitiveness of businesses and economy as a whole will be considered. According to representatives of the EU, the aim is for a national tripartite agreement to be singed, an agreement that addresses challenges to support competitiveness, development and employment. Indeed, it should be understood that the discussion should be put all the parameters that have an impact on labour costs, wages, including minimum wage and the National General Collective Agreement, as well as parameters of non-wage labour costs, such as insurance contributions.

5.7 Regulations of the New Memorandum for Collective Bargaining

With the new Memorandum, the imposition of reductions and other measures with legislative acts has been provided until the end of February, if social partners themselves have not agreed to impose the Memorandum. Among the measures decided upon, some were of special importance. More specifically, there is provision for the reduction of minimum wage in the National General Collective

Agreement (EGSSE) by 22% compared with what was in force on 1 January 2012, and for young people under 25 years the reduction was provided to be 32%. Furthermore, it was provided that wage increases would be frozen for as long as the programme runs, and maturities until unemployment falls below 10%.

Additionally, those collective agreements have been running over 24 months, they end no later than in a year. The current collective agreements expire one year after the programme has been legislated. The duration of the "aftereffect" is reduced from six to three months, while the maximum duration of collective agreements will now be three years. If there is no new collective agreement within three months, basis is considered the basic salary of the National General Collective Agreement. As benefits are maintained those of position, children, education, risk. The configured salary is maintained until a new collective or individual agreement is concluded. By "aftereffect" until now it has been designated a regime under which the terms of collective agreements continue being in direct and binding force, that is, the force of law for six months after the expiration of collective agreements. Upon the expiration of this semester, these terms were incorporated in the individual employment contracts and were their content, which could be amended only with the consent of each employee. With the new measures, those employees who are paid based on industry collective agreements – three months after their term is expired or terminated by the employers' organizations – will lose the minimum level of protection of industry conditions and, as a new "threshold" of employment conditions will be the National General Collective Agreement, as long as it is valid. Those employees that are hired after the quarter will receive the minimum basic salary of the National General Collective Agreement, provided that this will continue to exist.

At the same time, however, a clear timetable for the review of the National General Collective Agreement was made at the end of July 2012 so the EGSSE is aligned with the competing countries. The painful reduction (22%) of the minimum wage with the new Memorandum has admittedly overshadowed another very important provision that overthrows the status of collective bargaining and cancels the National General Collective Agreement itself. In the law of the new Memorandum, it is stated that as of July the 2012 "*minimum wages will be determined by bargaining between the social partners, but will be enacted by the government in consultation with social partners.*" In this way, any government, that is, the state is not required to reduce by law minimum wages, which were formed together by employers and employees, as it will "shape" from scratch itself (i.e. the state). The existing status of the 1950s and, mope specifically that of Law 3239 of 1955, which provided that: "*National General Collective Agreements are concluded and signed by employers (SEV [Association of Greek Industrialists] and GSEVEE [General Confederation of Professional Graftsmen and Traders in Greece] and on behalf of employees by the GSEE [Greek General Confederation of Labour or General Confederation of Greek Labour].*" It was even improved by Law 1876 of 1990, which is considered as one of the most progressive laws on collective bargaining in Europe. It was voted by all parties in the Parliament when there was a universal government in power. What is happening is that a regulation in a law introduced by the government provides that the minimum wage essentially repeals the National General Collective Agreement. Although it is only the minimum wage that it is repealed, nevertheless the constitutionally guaranteed collective autonomy suffers, since the constitutionally delegated regulatory power of social partners is lifted legislatively.

By the end of the aftereffect, pays will be reduced automatically, that, the individual employment contract will be modified without the employee's consent. This would cause dramatic wage cuts in the private sector. The Memorandum states that the reduced wages will be implemented until there in a new contract, collective or individual. However, it is clear that employees will be forced to agree, at an individual level, on lower wages under the direct or indirect threat of dismissal. The inability of labour unions to sign an agreement is given within this new regime. This also becomes absolutely impossible due to another additional fact: that the recourse to arbitration is no longer feasible, since it requires the consent of both employers and employees.

The reduction in the minimum wage – the effectiveness of which is to stimulate competitiveness of the economy is now openly questioned even by the most extreme neoliberal economists – has gripped a series of benefits and those people who are paid more than the minimum wage, and even unemployment benefits, which are calculated based on the minimum wage, something that has been forcing a large part of society in utter misery and ultimately social exclusion. Moreover, the reduction in the minimum wage raises a serious constitutional issue, as the key core of Paragraph 2, Article 22 and Paragraph 1, Article 23 of the Constitution gets along with International Labour Conventions 98 and 154 and the European Social Charter that fortify collective autonomy.

Even those who were in favour of these measures, they recognize that in medium term structural reforms will create favourable conditions for employment. Nevertheless, they – together with the European Commission – in their interim report acknowledge that the decision of the specific government to proceed to a reduction in the minimum wage, bringing an overall impact on wages in order to improve competitiveness and increase employment of the young and unskilled employees, is expected to be an obstacle to domestic demand, which in short term will affect employment negatively.

Repeated legislative changes to the system of collective bargaining, starting from the initial Memorandum, the updated Memorandum up to the latest Memorandum have led to a complete restructuring of the system of collective bargaining. Up to the latest Memorandum, the system of collective bargaining was operational, since it had been making use, at a central level, of national bargaining to guarantee the minimum levels of protection and payment, while leaving flexibility so that the system of collective bargaining can be decentralized at enterprise level, but within a structured framework of industrial relationships that had ensured primarily decentralization at industry level. Collective bargaining labour agreements at industry level functioned as an "Umbrella" and underneath them there could be further decentralization and flexibility at the company level, while the regulations for confluence were providing the employee with adequate protection.

With repeated legislative changes that have occurred as a result of Memoranda first decentralization at industry level is removed. The abolition of the institution of expansion of collective agreements has led to multi-segmentation in regulating industrial relations by sector. It cancels the value and role of sectoral regulation. It creates conditions for wild and extreme competition. And as it is framed by the new institution of special enterprise-level collective agreements (SELCAs) and the abolition of previous regime of the confluence of collective bargaining labour agreements, there have been formed institutional and potentially real conditions of further exacerbation of competition, multi-fragmentation of industrial relations per enterprise and/or decollectivization and individualization of industrial relations, meaning deregulation of industrial relations and labour protection framework. These data are exacerbated by an additional fact; there is not just the dramatic shrinkage of the minimum wage but the intervention of transnational legal abolition of the minimum wage as an institutional product of the constitutional recognition of collective autonomy.

5.8 Epilogue

The rich experience of the practice of collective bargaining in European countries in recent years along with all new statutory provisions, both at national and European level, have undoubtedly created new challenges and new opportunities for both the institution of collective bargaining and settlement mechanisms and regulation of collective disputes. They have created new prospects for cooperation between the parties, collective bargaining and social dialogue, which have been selected as alternative mechanisms able not only to detect solutions commonly accepted by the (interested) parties but also to move away from rigid, unproductive, bureaucratic or obsolete regulations and structures, by generating new, more socially acceptable reliable, flexible and competitive ones.

Finally, critical conditions and terms for the use in practice of the capabilities of the new institutional framework of collective bargaining are: First, the development of a network of reliable and socially acceptable institutions fostering the dialogue between employees and employers, such as the Organization for Mediation and Arbitration (OMED), the National Institute of Labour (EIE or NIL in English), the Greek Institute for Health and Safety at Work. Second, and most importantly, the change of attitudes and mentality of each side, the interested parties' departure – despite the fact that there may be a conflict of interest between them – from traditional practices and the consolidation of a new concept and culture of dialogue and cooperation in order to create socially acceptable settlements.

Chapter 6: Settlement and regulation mechanisms of Collective Labour Disputes in Greece

6.1 Introduction

A further innovation in the new bargaining model – perhaps the most important – is that the state mandatory arbitration is now abolished (Daskalakis, 1994, p. 356). The literature indicates that there are two kinds of arbitration disputes: disputes of "substance or interests" and "legal" differences. Legal differences are those that are relevant to the interpretation of existing regulations. For example, a labour regulation dictates that a break should be done four hours after an employee has started his/her work, while employees in practice do it earlier. This is a legal difference. Collective bargaining, mediation and arbitration systems may resolve such legal disputes; that is, what is not clear. There are, however, differences of interest or substance, as mentioned above. These relate to the essence of things, fees, increases, employment conditions, etc. In order for both these categories of collective disputes to be resolved and regulated specific institutions and mechanisms are employed nowadays (Daskalakis, 1994, pp. 30–31). There are systems in Europe where one intervenes with one form of mediation or reconciliation, something that was first introduced in Greece in 1990, but, in addition to these systems, there are various systems and arbitration (de Roo and Jagtenberg, 1993, pp. 28–39; Koukiadis, 1991).

There are systems of compulsory arbitration and voluntary arbitration. When employees and employers do not end up with the collective agreement or collective bargaining agreement (CBA), the case goes to mandatory (*ex officio*) arbitration. This is a mandatory arbitration. But there are systems of voluntary arbitration. These are used more in Anglo-Saxon countries. And here again, there are two types of systems: one type requires the agreement of both parties so the case goes to arbitration and the outcome of the arbitration is mandatory, while the other type states that the case can go from one or the other party or by agreement of both parties to arbitration, but what the arbitrator decides upon must be accepted by both to operate. These are two different types of voluntary arbitration systems (Petrinioti, 1985; Koukiadis, 1991).

To resolve collective labour disputes, the Greek new system provides two separate processes: mediation and reconciliation. These two are about the same but they also compete with each other. Reconciliation process is provided by the

Ministry of Labour, whereas mediation process is provided by the independent system that provides arbitration as well. It is a new organization that employees and employers govern and the state participates in its board with only one of the eleven members. So, there is a balance system between employees and employers, and mediation and arbitration services are provided by mediators and arbitrators who are very highly qualified people, of university education. They have comprehensive education on a wide range of issues concerning employees and businesses. They operate independently during their term and are assigned either by agreement of the parties or by the clergy. The result is that, in view of this new model of collective disputes and the new system of negotiations in general, the situation has reversed; that is, most cases "close" with a collective labour agreement. Yet, even those that will reach arbitration, they will reach a collective bargaining agreement before the ultimate point of an arbitration decision. Thus, the institution of collective bargaining in Greece started being in operation for the first time in 1990 (Daskalakis, 1995), and it has been operating ever since.

Arbitration entrusts to a third party of the crisis to resolve the dispute of the interested parties, which they have failed to resolve on their own (Koukiadis, 1991). In this way, at least in cases of differences in interests, self-help and enforcement of the fittest are avoided. The third party, with the guarantees that must accompany his/her choice, is considered to offer a correct and fair solution. As an institution and a way of termination of disputes, arbitration applies to many fields of legal relations. The rule of law has a reasonable interest in such disputes being resolved with "peaceful" means and does not consider the collective labour struggles as the only solution. Employees' struggles are internationally considered as the last resort to solve collective disputes. At this specific point it is arbitration, as a special dispute resolution institution, that intervenes and acts. Furthermore, it is worth mentioning that the arbitral award is binding in the original form of arbitration, and that is exactly its difference from other forms of actions of third parties, such as mediation or attempt to negotiate, to resolve disputes.

Arbitration in collective labour disputes appears in mandatory or voluntary form, in each of which there are several variations. There is voluntary arbitration wherever the interested parties get into this process voluntarily, by agreement between them. Arbitrators are specified primarily by the interested parties either lump sum or as appropriate, without the establishment of a permanent arbitral institution being excluded. In contrast, compulsory arbitration in principle can include a combination of mandatory and voluntary components. For example, it can include voluntary inclusion of collective dispute to compulsory and binding arbitration, while another possible combination provides that arbitration, as a process, is mandatory, but the parties are free to formulate it in a joint agreement. Finally, arbitration is possible to be provided entirely as mandatory as well, as in the case in which it is specified by legislation that, if bargaining fail, then the dispute would lead to compulsory arbitration with binding effect, even if the interested parties are concerned or any of them does not wish so (Karakatsanis, 1992).

The system of arbitration to resolve collective labour disputes is set out in Law 1876 of 1990 (in Articles 14-16), where the legislator gives, in order of precedence, to the parties of the collective dispute the discretion that they may agree and, according to the case, may resort to mediation and arbitration processes. Alternatively, if there are no such agreements, mediation moves and arbitration moves in a completely alternative manner, again with the initiative of one of the parties of a collective dispute. During mediation and arbitration there are arbitrated those collective differences that could be subject to the regulatory part of collective agreements. Moreover, during mediation and arbitration there can be submitted such differences of interests, even if the relevant issues are regulated by the applicable collective bargaining agreement, if there is significant change in circumstances and conditions under which it was agreed, a subject which, if there is a dispute, is arbitrated with the same process. Moreover, disputes related to the interpretation of terms of a collective agreement or arbitration award are settled.

The Greek new arbitration system is neither voluntary nor mandatory arbitration system. Instead, it is a mixed system, which, whereas it gives great emphasis on joint agreements and consensuses, retains some components of obligatoriness but only for borderline cases of weak unions that cannot negotiate seriously and want to avoid situations arising from unregulated labour relations; it maintains components of obligatoriness (de Roo and Jagtenberg) in the arbitration system it establishes.

6.2 Reconciliation

Before the main stage of mediation (Article 13, Law 1876/1990) has commenced, the institution of reconciliation is provided for any matter related to the employment relationship, being irrelevant whether it is or is not the subject of collective agreement. The trade union or the employer may request services of a conciliator. An employee of the Department of the Ministry of Employment is assigned as a conciliator, who is appointed by the Minister or an authorized officer. If the conciliator's efforts thrive and the subject belongs to the issues of a collective agreement, a collective agreement is signed. However, a protocol is composed at the end of the reconciliation process, where the agreement or disagreement of the parties is confirmed. Therefore, reconciliation is provided as a smoothing and reception mechanism for all disputes between employment and capital (Article 13, Law 1876/1990). This is an autonomous institution differentiated regarding the purpose and function of mediation despite the close affinities between them. More specifically, it is provided that any matter of dispute triggered by the employment relationship, even if it is not the subject of collective agreement, may be required to be settled by the unions or the employer individually or with a conciliatory intervention (Paragraph 1, Article 13, Law 1876/1990). This is intervention comes as an employee of the Ministry of Labour or Labour Inspection[75]. But the Minister himself/herself may exercise tasks of a conciliator, too. The purpose of reconciliation is to make the views of the parties get close together, so that the conflict ends as soon as possible.

Based on the above, the Greek model of reconciliation can be defined as the provision of good services by a representative of the Ministry of Labour so that there is reconciliation in a conflict situation between employees and employers generated due to the employment relation. The subject of reconciliation is specified in a way wider than the subject of mediation and arbitration. More particularly, this can be either subject to a legitimate content of collective bargaining agreement, as it happens during mediation and any other conflict whose cause is an employment relation.

Reconciliation is a third party's provision of good services to the parties in a labour dispute so to be settled. This is a method of dispute resolution that is traditionally used in international political conflicts, where it was initially utilized. But later, the institution has experienced major implementation in labour differences for domestic social conflicts. It is a means of their mitigation or prevention, without being considered whether the cause is difference of interest or legal dispute or both. In reconciliation, the reconciler is limited to approach both parties, whereas in mediation the mediator's right to submit a proposal is displayed. Basically, the conciliator should avoid taking a position, especially if it is not requested by both parties. Reconciler is the Minister of Labour or an employee of the Ministry of Labour appointed by him/her. There are reconcilers in all local labour inspectorates[76]. It is characteristic that reconciliation remains the work of public administration, whereas mediation and arbitration have been detached from reconciliation and have been entrusted to an autonomous body.

---

75 According to Paragraph 3, Article 13, Law 1876/90.
76 See Decision of Ministry of Labour 12584/27.3.1990.

They are two systems with different approaches that operate at the same time. Nevertheless, expressed views by the conciliator serve as a simple recommendation. Regarding the whole process, reconciliation lasts as long as the parties assess that there can be a solution and ends with a protocol where the agreement or disagreement of the parties is stated. Technically, the role of the conciliator coincides with that of the mediator. In both cases, special techniques are required involving personal style, how to ask questions, persuasiveness, independence and impartiality. According to studies carried out by the International Labour Organization (ILO), there are different stages that conflicts have gone through, such as intolerance, recognizing the need for regulation, presenting alternatives, which the conciliator must know in order to adapt his/her role.

Reconciliation moves after trade unions of employees and employers have submitted a request to the respective inspection. Employees are not entitled to move reconciliation as individuals. Respective right has only the employer to initiate and move reconciliation process, without the number of employees being taken into consideration, because the employer is generally empowered to participate in collective disputes. Law refers to the relevant organizations, meaning organizations in which there is dispute among their members. There are no limitations on representation, unless a collective agreement is sought to be signed. The application is not notified to the other party, but the invitation is addressed to the conciliator. The attendance of the opposing party is optional. Additionally, it should be noted that reconciliation is provided after a court order in some countries. The protocol confirms the agreement or disagreement. If there is an agreement, there is a commitment on behalf of the parties depending on the type of dispute and the persons referred to. Agreement on matters that can be subject to a collective agreement results in the composition of a collective agreement, according to the conditions ascribed by law. The possibility that, despite the agreement, the other party may not sign the collective agreement has not been provided. The most practical solution is to move the mediation and arbitration process with retrospective effect from the time of reconciliation (Koukiadis, 1997).

6.3 Organization of Mediation and Arbitration (OMED)

By Law 1876 of 1990, the mediation process is conducted within the Organization for Mediation and Arbitration (OMED in Greek). More particularly, "it is established a private entity under the name of Organization of Mediation and Arbitration, based in Athens. This organization is an independent entity and operates under the provisions of this Act and the regulations issued under its authority notwithstanding the provisions related to the public sector" (Paragraph 1, Article 17, Law 1876/1990).

With the wording of the text of the specific Law, it is stated that the mediation and arbitration award to a private entity is a major indication of independence and disengagement of the work of resolving collective disputes from state control. Furthermore, the economic autonomy of the Organization is also guaranteed (Kazakos, 1998, pp. 68 and 80). It is noteworthy that the Organization for Mediation and Arbitration (OMED) has been operating since January 1992, and is financed by both the Organization of Employees' Housing and the regular budget of the Ministry of Labour. In particular, the resources of the organization is 3% of annual revenues of the Organization of Employees' Housing, which can increase with the decision of the Minister of Labour, regular subsidy from the budget of the Ministry of Labour, amounts received from the interested parties who use the services of the organization and revenue from donations, publications, events, publications, etc.

Furthermore, it is useful to make a reference to the composition of the Board of Directors of the Organization. According to the relevant Law, the Board of Directors consists of three representatives of employers and three representatives of trade unions, a representative of the Company Law of Labour and Social Security, a representative of the Ministry of Labour, two university professors (a Labour Law Professor and a Professor either of Labour relations or economic courses recommended by the Senates of the Universities of Athens and Thessaloniki) and a representative of wider acceptance who is elected by the ten aforementioned representatives (Paragraph 1, Article 17, Law 1876/1990).

The Board of Directors of the Organization is responsible solely for issues of governance, whereas the services as such, mediation and arbitration, are provided by the Body of Mediators-Arbitrators, who exercise a public service and are independent during the performance of their duties; for this reason, they have a number of incompatibilities, are guaranteed with three-year tenure, and enjoy stability in their relation with the Organization, so they can remain unaffected in their work. More specifically, "mediators-arbitrators perform a public service without being a civil servant and enjoy complete independence in the course of their duties". Mediators-arbitrators have relevant education and training as well as practical experience of workplace issues, sign three-year contracts to provide independent services, receive ongoing training and participate in workshops with the participation of social partners, where various discussions on labour issues are presented and develop. Moreover, the Organization for Mediation and Arbitration (OMED), among others, advises on labour issues and conducts investigations. Briefly, the Organization for Mediation and Arbitration is an independent body that operates in labour relations issues and provides plenty of useful advice to employers and employees' unions (Koukoules, 1998, p. 11).

There are general principles underlying mediation and arbitration processes. In particular, there are some general principles which are designed to ensure confidence in the system of mediation and arbitration (Kazakos, 1998, pp. 82–90). These are: the principle of equality of the parties to litigation,[77] the principle of optionality of procedures, the priority principle of contractual arrangements of the parties,[78] the principle of the previous hearing of the parties,[79] the principle of flexibility of the process,[80] the principle of orality and immediacy of the process[81] and the principle according to which neither the mediator nor the arbitrator may propose benefits that go beyond those that are claimed by the negotiating parties.

6.4 Mediation

Mediator's services can be asked by any of the interested parties of the collective dispute, or both together. Mediation[82] is the process through which the parties attempt to reach an agreement on matters that were the subject of negotiation failure; normally, a proposal is submitted by a third party, the mediator. For the success of mediation, it is not all negligible the pedagogical function of the culture of dialogue between the parties exercised by the mediator.

The application of mediation is only possible from the representative group and not from other unions, which by Law do not have the capacity to conclude collective agreements but only to sign the mediation proposal as they can do

77 This principle should be implemented at all stages and acts of the process and is based on the constitutional principle of equality (Paragraph 1, Article 4 of the Constitution).

78 This principle refers to the fact that the interested parties, that is, trade unions and employers, have the first word on the regulation of the terms in how mediation and arbitration are conducted, within the framework of mediation and arbitration process provided by Law 1876 /90; the consents and agreements between the parties take the precedence.

79 This is the right that the parties in bargaining can support their positions and interests, having ensured active listening of the mediator or arbitrator.

80 The whole process, as conducted, allows the development of the themes of collective disputes in a freestyle manner, without any special conversation schedule being followed.

81 The two processes do not prohibit the parties using documents for completion of their requests and views. Since, however, the procedures should be governed by immediacy; the dialogue is the principal means of communication and exchange of views.

82 What is related to mediation is defined in Article 15, Law 1876/90.

for collective agreements. If not co-submitted, the application is notified to the other party, which is entitled to refuse the mediation process. The application shall contain, in addition to the information about the parties and their representatives, requests, and, accordingly, the reasons justifying them or, if it renders impossible their satisfaction, any alternative suggestions or whatever else that can facilitate the resolution of the dispute.

It is shown from previous data of the OMED[83] that recourse to mediation was a request from the employees' side in 88.6% of the cases, at the request of the employer's side in 11.4% of the cases, whereas a joint request of both sides in 0.0% of the cases. By contrast, in arbitration, except for a recourse made by mutual agreement between employees' and employer's side, the other recourses were made unilaterally by the employees' side.

6.4.1 Multilateral Negotiation

The first phase of the new collective bargaining model and the new model of mediation and arbitration highlighted between the problems not only that of the fragmentation of the parties' representation but also that of multipartite negotiation during collective bargaining and, by extension, during mediation and arbitration processes before the OMED mediators-arbitrators. More particularly, as the national labour relations system, so the total number of cases handled by the Body of Mediators-Arbitrators is characterized by the phenomenon of multilateral negotiation, where one union negotiates and concludes on a collective labour agreement. It is not surprising that 36.4% of the first 44 cases that had come to the Organization[84] concerned only seven unions. This phenomenon mainly concerns occupational collective agreements. The phenomenon of negotiation on the employer's side is shown with the presence of numerous and fragmented representation. Without collective agreements for the public sector being considered, where typically the employer's side is represented by the Ministry of Finances and the other parent Ministries, it is concluded that one of the important issues that have been causing dysfunction in collective bargaining and mediation is the plethora of employers' unions that are invited to bargain and conclude collective agreement. In national and local occupational agreements,

83 The data mentioned comes from the study conducted by the Mediator Chr. Ioannou, on behalf of the OMED.

84 A sample of only 44 cases in the early phase of the operation of the OMED; it is a study that was conducted by the Mediator Chr. Ioannou, on behalf of the OMED.

the employer's representation consists of two to six different unions, whereas in industry agreements it ranged from four to ten unions[85].

The parties choose the mediator from a special list of mediators, and, unless they do not agree on his/her person, there is a draw 48 hours after the request. The mediator invites the parties in discussions, hearings, s/he examines persons, s/he carries out research, s/he can use the experts of his/her choice to determine employment conditions, the financial condition of the company, etc. The employer's side has the obligation under Article 4 to provide him/her with information. The same obligation applies to relevant divisions. If the parties do not reach an agreement with his/her help within 20 days, the mediator submits his/her own proposal, which s/he has the right to publish in the press. If in five days, the parties in dispute do not notify their acceptance of the proposal, it is concluded that they have rejected it. The acceptance of the proposal from one party is notified to another. If the proposal is accepted by both parties, then they sign it, and this proposal is equated to a collective agreement.

From the aforementioned, the substantial conditions for mediation can be discerned, which are: (a) specific subject; (b) failure of direct negotiations on the above subjects; (c) intervention of a third party, the mediator, coming from the body of mediators, who offers his/her services to bring the parties together, s/he makes informal solicitations for sse (: collective agreements), and, at the end, s/he may submit and typically a specific proposal with which the Law binds certain consequences.

The opening act of the mediation process is the submission of a relevant application (Paragraph 2, Article 15, Law 1876/90). More specifically, the requirements are as follows: (a) an application is made by the interested parties; (b) an application is submitted jointly or separately by the interested parties; (c) an application with certain content that its framework is determined by Law; and (d) an application is submitted to certain agency, which is the Organization for Mediation and Arbitration (OMED)[86], and it is the Organization that manages mediation and arbitration services[87]. The application will also be notified to the other party, without the legal enforcement of the notification by a bailiff.

85 The data mentioned comes from the study conducted by the Mediator Chr. Ioannou, on behalf of the OMED.

86 It is provided by Article 17, Law 1876/1990.

87 Articles 3 and 17 of the Regulation of the Organization and Operation of the OMED, and Article 6 of the Regulation of Mediators and Arbitrators of the Organization (i.e. the OMED).

From the description of the content that must have the application, it is concluded that the application, in order to be accepted, should contain all the elements that will allow the mediator to continue negotiations. The selection of the mediator is made with the aid of the relevant departments of the OMED, within 48 hours from the time of application (Paragraph 3, Article 15, Law 1876/90). Within this period, all parties of the collective dispute are called upon, as mentioned in the application, to come to the offices of the OMED to suggest the mediator, who will assume the mediation. The designation must be made between those who constitute the body of mediators. The originality of the Law lies in the fact that the mediator is not appointed by an agency, but s/he is indicated by the interested parties. The innovation has been successful and has contributed substantially to the adoption of the principles of impartiality and neutrality, which should govern the mediator's work. The appointment of the mediator can be made by mutual agreement or by lot, when the parties cannot reach an agreement. The agreement may relate to the selection of one mediator, which is the norm, or even three. Therefore, the mediator is a one-person or a three-person agent. The right to *veto* is another objective term to reduce ambiguity as to the mediator's person. In each case, a replacement is also indicated. Then, proceedings of selection are composed and the mediator is invited to take office conforming to that of the corresponding minutes of the appointment[88]. Here ends the selection process.

Mediation process is inspired by the principles of fast processing and sincere discussion during its conduct, in proportion to bargain in good faith, and the priority of the conclusion of the parties to an agreement. In this respect, the rules governing it are an extension of the rules governing free bargaining. The whole process should be completed in twenty days, unless the parties mutually agree to extend it. The mediator's task is to persuade the parties to reach an agreement. This is a provision of good services based on persuasion. For this purpose, s/he has broad capabilities such as: to call upon the parties together to hear their opinions in an individual hearing of the parties concerned, to examine people, to get an expert offer his/her expertise, the right to request information from the employer and the relevant agencies[89], the right to investigate the financial situation of the company, to conduct in-depth discussions with the parties and to submit alternative proposals.

---

88 Paragraph 3, Article 15, passage c, Law 1876/90 and Paragraph 2, passage d, Article 6 and Paragraph 7, Article 7 of the Regulation of Mediators and Arbitrators of the Organization (OMED).

89 According to what is defined in Paragraph 4, Article 4, Law 1876/1990.

The Greek legislator did not want to standardize the mediation processes, but s/he provides a broad framework of freedom to the mediator. It is a process that is not strictly governed by strict legal and procedural rules, but its key feature is flexibility. In the relevant Law, the mediator's job description is general and provides only a framework of action. Furthermore, it empowers the interested parties themselves to adopt the process to be followed during the mediation, which demonstrates the elasticity governing mediation. To date, however, there has been no comprehensive process around this issue (Koutsibou, 2000, p. 5).

When starting the mediation process, the mediator is mainly interested in understanding the essence of the dispute and its underlying deep causes. During the process, the mediator is required to establish the basic and essential aspects of bargaining. In particular, s/he should determine whether there are financial issues behind the institutional and legal differences, find a common ground for the benefit of both parties and to determine the actual bargaining area (Staboulis, 2000, p. 2). After the mediator has received and studied the dispute case, s/he invites interested parties to meetings.

There are two types of meetings, the joint and personal ones. Regarding personal meetings, when there is too much tension, the mediator may decide that it is necessary to meet each party separately, and the Law gives him/her the right to do so. Separate meetings allow the mediator to understand each side's position, to discuss any opportunity to resolve the dispute without the pressure of the other party. In this way, on the one hand, there can be the right climate for subsequent joint meetings of the parties. On the other hand, joint meetings take place where the interested parties discuss with the mediator. Timing and sequence of talk, the agenda of discussion etc. are not defined in advance.

All aforementioned issues vary depending on the subject of negotiation. What is required is the availability of the parties and the mediator, as well as the available time to defuse the tension (Koutsibou, 2000 p. 7). Most times repeated meetings are necessary to take place, aiming to restate the parties' positions so that their opinions may gradually converge. During these meetings the mediator calls upon the two parties involved in the dispute to submit rather specific positions and arguments than general views and attitudes. A prerequisite is the parties' goodwill and their sincere attitude in good faith (Staboulis, 2000, p. 7).

Regarding the duration of the meeting, the practice followed within the framework of the Greek Organization of Mediation (i.e. the OMED) is to provide as much time as needed. This duration can cover even a continuous clock. Moreover, it may take the parties a long time to express their initial positions. Many times it has been observed the interruption of the process for unrelated to negotiation reasons. In these cases, the approach work must be repeated, something that costs time. Nevertheless, there have been uninterrupted negotiations that have resulted in very significant agreements (Koutsibou, 2000, p. 8).

Another important issue for the success of mediation is the collection and processing of data relevant to negotiation. Providing the necessary information is crucial for bargaining. Many times, however, this process is not as simple as the negotiators are charged by collective difference. Furthermore, the mediator may ask for the help of experts for research related to employment conditions or the financial position of the company. Indeed, "the mediator may claim from the employer's side to provide all information that is required and refers to the financial situation, economic policy and the operation of the personnel so that negotiations are facilitated" (Paragraph 4, Article 4, Law 1876/1990). As it is readily apparent, it is about the evidence that the employer's side is sometimes reluctant to provide.

The mediator's task ends: either when both parties sign an agreement or when the failure of mediation is simply stated, or when the failure is found and a proposal for making collective bargaining agreement is submitted. The submission of a final proposal, in the literal sense of the word, is not the mediator's obligation but his/her right (Paragraph 6, passage a, Article 15, Law 1876/1990). This provision is a key, because the recourse to arbitration depends on the use or not of this right. It is the central connection point between negotiation, mediation and arbitration, and, therefore, the main element of balance of the whole system of resolving collective disputes. A specificity of the collective bargaining system introduced by Law 1876/90 is both the mediator's right to submit a proposal to the parties and the necessity of the proposal as a requirement for the referral of the case to arbitration.

The situation with the submission of the proposal shall be as follows: the parties are invited to accept it, within five days of its notification to them. Acceptance may just be explicit, because it is only this that is expressed with its notification to the mediator[90]. If the parties accept it, they are invited to sign it. The signature by both parties changes the proposal into collective labour agreement[91]. This is

90 Paragraph 6, passage b, Article 15, Law 1876/1990 and Paragraph 3, Article 7 of the Regulation of Mediators-Arbitrators of the OMED.

91 During the first phase of the operation of the OMED, a key finding was that collective labour agreements signed with the help of a mediator or arbitration awards issued by the Arbitrator of the OMED moved slightly above the increases provided by the biennial National General Collective Labour Agreement of 1991–92. A characteristic "model" regarding the content of collective labour agreements for increases in basic

an unusual way to draw up a collective labour agreement, to which are applicable all the rest; that is, everything that is valid for the joint collective labour agreements. The collective agreement is signed based on the mediator's proposal, whereas modifications are possible only if agreed by both parties. As it is valid for acceptance so it is valid for refusal, there is no partial rejection. More particularly, when the proposal is rejected by the employers' side and is accepted by the employees' side, the law entitles the employees' side to unilaterally resort to arbitration, an issue that will be discussed below. This right is entitled to the employer in the same terms, but only for Collective Agreements (Paragraph 1, passage d, Article 16, Law 1876/1990). The procedure of submission of the application is completed with the notification of the proposal to the parties. Another type of publicity is not enforced. However, the mediator is given the opportunity to publish the proposal in the daily and periodical press (Paragraph 6, passage b, Article 15, Law 1876/1990). This optional publicity is left to the mediator's discretion. Obviously, such posts will generally involve disputes with wider societal implications and raise the awareness of public opinion, which is the ultimate evaluator of major social conflicts (Koukiadis, 1997). It should be noted that during the mediation process there is no obligation to terminate or suspend the right to strike. In this way, the employers' side cannot recourse to mediation to obstruct the right to strike. It can, however, hope and seek to find a solution that will lead the working side so to cancel the strike (Staboulis, 2000, p. 12).

The available data from the first cases[92] handled by the OMED and the body of arbitrators-mediators show that there was a tendency for a model for proposals to be formed. However, an attempt was made so the establishment of a model of a proposal – within whose context the proposal would be taken for granted as a way of referral of cases to arbitration – would be avoided. Nevertheless, the conclusions drawn from the first data of the OMED are that the proposal used

---

salaries was shown by the submitted proposals of the mediators of the same period. The suggestions ranged in higher rates of increase of 1.5% – 2.5% of the level of the National General Collective Labour Agreement of 1991–92. Basic conclusion, therefore, is that perhaps because of economic conditions both concluded collective labour agreements and the mediators' proposals were moving based on the National General Collective Labour Agreement of 1991–92 for the increases in basic salary in two installments 5.4% + 4.0% (plus 0.8% correction amount), whereas the issue of benefits during this period was marginally adjusted. (The data mentioned comes from the study conducted by the Mediator Chr. Ioannou, on behalf of the OMED).

92 The data mentioned comes from the study conducted by the Mediator Chr. Ioannou, on behalf of the OMED.

to function primarily as a method of case referral to arbitration rather than as a final effort to achieve convergence and an agreement between the parties[93].

6.5 Arbitration

So the conceptual elements of the regulated form of arbitration arise as those of mediation provided by Law 1876 of 1990 "On Free Collective Bargaining". Some of these are common. Arbitration is the way to solve a collective dispute, which is applied to the event of failure of negotiations or mediation to conclude a collective agreement, which is carried out with the intervention of third parties and is set in motion by agreement or unilateral action by the parties so that its final resolution is achieved with a an arbitration award of regulatory texture (Paragraph 1, Article 14, Paragraph 1, Article 16). The commonalities between arbitration and mediation are in principle their subject and the qualified persons for the motion of the corresponding processes, which are the parties of collective bargaining. Arbitration is, therefore, another way to resolve the dispute coming out of the failure of bargaining. Exceptionally, there is no reference to arbitration of disputes arising in connection with security personnel and certain other issues that are the content of only agreed solutions to collective bargaining agreement and, thus, they may be the subject only of mediation or at least of arbitration agreed. Nevertheless, whereas mediation is a mechanism to assist the continuation of direct bargaining between the parties, arbitration is a last resort mechanism substituting these so that a regulatory vacuum is avoided. More specifically, "mediation is a mechanism of overcoming deadlock and restoring the social partners in the 'table of negotiations', arbitration is not longer to reinstall a climate of understanding between the parties, but, given the weakness of the agreed regulation of employment

93 More specifically, the data were as follows:

- Submission of proposals of total cases: 29.5%;
- Conclusion of collective labour agreement with a proposal on the total of collective labour agreements: 13.3%;
- Conclusion of collective labour agreement with a proposal on the total of the proposals: 15.4%;
- Recourse to arbitration with a unilateral acceptance by the employees' side on the total of the proposals: 69.2%; and
- Rejection of proposals by the employees' side: 15.4%.

The data mentioned comes from the study conducted by the Mediator Chr. Ioannou, on behalf of the OMED.

conditions, it acts as a mechanism of overcoming the impasse of not reaching a common agreement, so that some working relationships are prevented from being unregulated. In this case, the parties are replaced by a third party, the mediator, who takes up their role to resolve the collective dispute" (Lixouriotis, 1995, pp. 2–3; Lixouriotis, 1996, pp. 2–3), thus, imposing a collective settlement with the arbitration award.

It should be emphasized that the exclusion of the state from arbitration, even from collective disputes affecting the broader society, is of particular importance, because the state's intervention in a process leads to a binding decision and essentially cancels collective autonomy. The state's exclusion from arbitration award is of more importance than that from mediation, because arbitration is the final solution that, with the state's exclusion from it, remains exclusively an issue of the interested parties. So, government's intervention to impose its income policy is, in very exceptional cases, the only way to release a special law and under certain conditions, which have been analyzed earlier. However, the apparent weakening of the state power is relative, because the state has alternatives to pass its policy in the final decisions.

The process can be initiated by mutual agreement or at the request of either party. Given that the process concludes, as it will be shown, in a decision which is binding on both parties, the agreed or the unilateral action is of major importance, that's why each case is considered separately. There are several forms: The first and the most orthodox form is the conventional recourse, which is the agreed recourse, that's exactly why the Law puts it in front (Paragraph 1, passage a, Article 16), providing that this can be done at any stage of the bargaining. Second form is the recourse initiated only by a single party. In this case a process of unilateral recourse is provided that moves only on the initiative of trade unions, and there are cases of unilateral recourse initiated by any of the parties, either because the other side has refused the mediation process or because it is a bargaining at an enterprise level.

In each case there is the attempt to compel the other party to participate in arbitration and be bound by its results, but in the last two the right is given equally to both parties, whereas in the first the right is given only to one party. More specifically, the cases of recourse to arbitration are:

- Recourse from one party due to the refusal by the other party of mediation (Paragraph 1, passage b, Article 16). The recognition of this right to a party, when the other refuses mediation, is part of the whole system of strengthening the institution of mediation as a natural extension of free bargaining, and leads to their enhancement.

- Recourse from any party while the enterprise-level collective agreement is being prepared (Paragraph 1, passage d, Article 16). In the explicit wording of the Law, especially for enterprise-level collective agreements in which there are agreements of businesses and organizations of common utilities, right of recourse to arbitration is the party that accepts the proposal of the mediator, which the other party rejects.
- Recourse is initiated only by trade unions (Paragraph 1, passage c, Article 16). Thereby, it is recognized that trade unions have the right to unilaterally resort to arbitration, if they accept the mediator's proposal of the mediator, which was rejected by the employer.

The selection rules of an arbitrator are the same as those of a mediator[94]. The only difference is that the arbitrator ought to assume office within five days from the drafting of the minutes of selection[95], whereas the mediator ought to do that once commanded[96]. Like other respective deadlines, its failure to comply does not affect the validity of the process. This can only lead to disciplinary sanctions (Koukiadis, 1997). Arbitration and mediation proposals, when signed, solve the collective labour dispute by imposing regulations on issues.

Mediators–arbitrators judge freely, and with their decision they regulate, amend or readjust collective labour relations. The mediator's proposal and the arbitration award must be justified not only for those requests that parties have accepted but also for those they have rejected. When signed, the mediation proposal and the arbitral award are acts of Private Law. After signed, the mediator's proposal and the arbitration award are treated as a collective agreement, and, by analogy, all provisions on collective agreements are applied to them. In addition, we should mention that each one has its own local, professional and personal scope. The mediation proposal and the arbitral award by their nature do not have any guilty part, such as collective agreements do, but only regulatory one. More particularly, the effect of the arbitration award in labour relations is immediate and enforced. Agreement contrary to regulations is invalid, unless it is favourable to the employee.

During bargaining and mediation and arbitration processes, employees can exercise their right to strike (Paragraph 4, Article 4, Law 1876/1990), unless a

94 Article 6 of the Regulation of Mediators and Arbitrators of the Organization (OMED).

95 Article 16, passage d, A.N. 1875/1990, and Paragraph 1, Article 8 of the Regulation of Mediators and Arbitrators of the Organization (OMED).

96 Paragraph 1, Article 7 of the Regulation of Mediators and Arbitrators of the Organization (OMED).

previous collective agreement provides the contrary. There is an exception for those employees whose unions have applied for arbitration after they have accepted the mediation proposal which, however, has been rejected by the employer's side, when the right to strike is suspended for ten days after the recourse (Paragraph 6, Article 16, Law 1876/1990). The suspension of the right to strike is generally reasonable, as it serves the real meaning of the right of unilateral recourse (Kazakos, 1998, p. 285).

6.6 Mediation for the Conduct of "Public Dialogue"

"Public dialogue" is the consultation between trade unions and the employer of an enterprise in the presence of a mediator and probably before third trade union or other agencies, and seeks to resolve both differences, which have led the parties to a labour conflict, and collective labour disputes" (Lixouriotis, 1996, pp. 2–3). This process was initially provided (Law 1915/1990) for the cases when a strike was planned in public, the public entity (Private Entity Law) and businesses of major importance for the society as a whole, but it has never been implemented. So, this process has been readjusted with a more recent Law (Law 2224/1994) in a way that applies to all businesses in both the public and private sector. Whereas the recourse to the use of the process of public dialogue in the case of private firms is discretion, in the case of utilities[97], the sustained peculiarity is that the process of public dialogue is an obligation of the relevant trade unions, which are required to observe this process, since this process will judge the legitimacy of their strike. In this case, the recourse to the use of the process of public dialogue can be carried out both before and after the decision to get on strike, whereas the employer may resort to recourse anytime. The appointment of a mediator is made in accordance with the existing at the OMED procedures – that is, with a joint selection of the parties or by public lottery. Within a 48-hour indicative time limit a public dialogue is conducted, and after this time has been exhausted, the mediator has the right to submit a report to the parties (Lixouriotis, 1996). This mediation process is associated neither with the common mediation process of Law 1876 of 1990 nor with the conditions and terms of referral of a collective labour dispute to Arbitration Law 1876 of 1990.

97 More precisely, the obligation concerns the enterprises of Paragraph 2, Article 19, Law 1264/1982.

6.7 Assessment of the Institutional Reform in Greece

The first observation on Law of 1876 of 1990 is that it was one of the last pieces of legislation of the Universal Government launched with the agreement of all political parties in the Greek Parliament and the interested parties[98]. What it should be emphasized is that a series of painful and perennial pressures and efforts were made to adjust or "readjust" both critical issues that were ultimately regulated by Law 1876 of 1990; they were able to succeed only under the "special" conditions and "balance" that emerged at that time – that is, the legislation that was launched during the Universal Government (Daskalakis, 1991, p. 1). All this does demonstrate the complexity of the matter, that is, how difficult the task is to be carried out by Law 1876. The new Law with its provisions regulated in a pioneering manner a number of critical issues which had been treated by the legislator with reservation or hesitation for many years. Despite the various critiques that may have been made, eventually Law 1876 is the necessary and sufficient legal framework to modernize the entire system of labour relations[99]. More specifically, the provisions of the new Law create a nexus of complementary among them modern mechanisms for balancing different social interests and harmonizing the often delegated economic and social demands and objectives.

In particular, regarding issues of mediation and arbitration, it should be noted that during the period of validity of Law 3239 of 1955, for various historical, political, cultural and institutional reasons, there was a system of industrial relations whose features were: (a) centralization, which was achieved either by government interventions and regulations or by central collective bargaining and contracts (Koukiadis, 1981), p. 165; Ioannou, 1989, pp. 69–85); (b) government intervention to control collective autonomy; and (c) the shrunk compared to today's field and scope of collective bargaining (Paragraphs 1 and 2, Article 1, Paragraphs 1 and 2, Article 2; Goutos – Leventis, 1988 pp. 423–36). There was also skepticism, on the one hand, between the state and agencies, and, on the other hand, a strong presence of conflicting situations among agencies themselves (Ioannou, 1988, pp. 92–99). Furthermore, both a confrontational culture

98 Inauguration Address by the President of the OMED, Professor Koukiadis, I., (1992), in the first meeting of Mediators and representatives of agencies held in November 1991. See Corps of Mediators – Arbitrators of the OMED, publication of the Organization for Mediation and Arbitration, Athens, p. 12

99 About the concept of the system in the theory of industrial relations, see: (a) Daskalakis, 1989, pp. 71–76; (b) Koukiadis, 1981, Chapter 1st; (c) Kochan, Mckersie, and Capelli, 1984, a; and (d) Blain and Gennard, 1970.

dominated and a negative attitude of the parties that they refused assuming responsibilities, making mutual commitments and conducting dialogue of substance (Daskalakis, 1991, p. 37).

This whole system of industrial relations was framed by compulsory state arbitration exercised by administrative bodies and was based on the logic of enforcement[100]; that is, under this model, arbitration was an "unswerving" and "mandatory" bond of any collective dispute. What should be noted is that Law 3239 of 1955 should have been changed earlier, before this Law had been in an obvious mismatch with social conditions that prevailed later (Nikolouzos, 1991). Nevertheless, the power of this Law has made until recently this Law operate as a reproduction mechanism for the parties' negative attitude towards the person in charge for dialogue; it has deterred parties from assuming their responsibilities and becoming "adults"; it has promoted, at times, many and, of course, unacceptable state interventions[101], and most importantly, perhaps, it has operated as a mechanism to provide the necessary excuse for perpetuating this situation, that is, everybody being responsible for it.

During the years that followed, the presence of deep economic crisis and recession, the increased competition, particularly in the integrated European market, the need for specialization and modernization, production and technology, the imperative to secure a desired flexibility in production and labour relations (ETUI, 1985, esp. pp. 113–199; Evans and Bell, 1986, pp. 1–26) and the emergence of parallel sharpened social problems created new conditions for labour relations of the involved parties.

Within this context, there has been a need to deal with a series of objectively reasonable economic and social demands and objectives, which, however, may be objectively and reasonably at odds with each other (Daskalakis, 1991b p. 37). In this reality, two issues have emerged: First, the overthrow of until today existing negative roots of the past which hamper the dialogue and cooperation between parties – all three parties, the joint search for mutually acceptable solutions to problems of employees, businesses and economy; and, second, there was the necessity to form a new institutional framework, which – by

100 Article 9, Law 3239/55, as amended with Paragraph 1, Article 7, Legislative Decree/Statute 3755/57, and, finally, it was replaced with Article 7, Legislative Decree/Statute 186/69. It should be noted, however, that constitutionality of that specified in the aforementioned provisions of arbitration model has been questioned in theory. More specifically, see: Koukiadis, 1981, p. 538; and Leventis, 1981, p. 335.

101 Greeting of the Chairman of the GSEE, (1992), Formal Opening Conference of the OMED, held on 15th November, Royal Olympic Hotel, Athens.

modernizing institutionally labour relations, would make up of a nexus of mechanisms for harmonizing and balancing social and economic demands, objectives and interests[102].

Law 1876 of 1990 came to fulfill the last gap. More specifically, this Law has given the opportunity for free collective bargaining and collective and enterprise agreements to be conducted (Article 3, Law 1876/90). It broadened the scope and purpose of collective bargaining (Article 2, Law 1876/90); it created the framework of decentralized collective bargaining system that could utilize mainly industry and enterprise bargaining agreements (Ioannou, 1992), and, finally, it institutionalized modern and reliable Mediation and Arbitration processes, according to the successful models in other developed countries (Articles 14, 15 and 16, Law 1876/90; Koukiadis, 1992). In particular, the system of resolving collective labour disputes – while under the old Law 3239 of 1955 was based on the state and complaisance, enforcement and state control (Leventis, 1981, pp. 310–338) – under Law 1876 of 1990, is based primarily on the dominant role of party will (Papadimitriou, 1991, pp. 270–274), reliability and social acceptance of the mediator and operates autonomously, using persuasion, responsible attitude, cooperation and agreements between the social partners[103].

The main point that should be noted in relation to the model is that the Mediator–Arbitrator is considered as an independent, reliable, socially accepted[104] "Third Party" intervening primarily conciliatorily to achieve rapprochement between the parties and only alternative arbitrarily imposing a solution to the dispute between them (Articles 14, 15 and 16, Law 1876/90). To this end, within the Law and the relevant regulations, there are institutional safeguards designed to ensure the Mediator-Arbitrator's Independence and ensure his/her Reliability and Social Acceptance. Such predictions are those referred to: Mediators-Arbitrators'

102 About the trends in the development of collective bargaining and the content of collective labour agreements, see: (a) ACAS, 1980; (b) Harbison, 1954; (c) Deaton and Beaumont, 1980: (d) Salamon, 1987, pp. 266–295; and (e) U.S. Labor Law and the future of Labor – Management Cooperation, (1986), U.S. Department of Labor, Bureau of Labor Management Relations and Cooperative Programmes, BLMR 104.

103 For the difference and the relation between the Mediation and Arbitration processes, see: Conciliation in Industrial Disputes, A Practical Guide, International Labour Office, Geneva, (Trans. in Greek by the OMED), Chapters 1 and 2. Furthermore, Zack, 1985, pp. 1–12.

104 Law 1876/90 provided that Mediators-Arbitrators would constitute an independent, special body (Paragraph 2, Article 17), which will operate within the framework of the new Organization for Mediation and Arbitration (OMED) (Paragraph 1, Article 17).

Incompatibility[105] during their recruitment and their term of office, the Code of Ethics[106], to flexible and reliable processes and procedures for the selection and appointment of arbitrators and mediators[107] and, more specifically: First, to the free, joint selection of one up to three mediators-arbitrators by the parties[108]. Second, to the reliable procedure of draw in case the parties disagree[109], and, third, to possible exceptions, during the draw, up to a total of two Mediators-Arbitrators at the parties' will[110].

At the same time, the focus and priority of mediation process compared to that of arbitration is attempted to be given by institutional safeguards, which are expected to operate as an incentive or means for this process. As such safeguards there could be considered today, first the provision for allowance of a successful mediation to the mediator, if the parties reach an agreement with his/her intervention[111], and second, the terms of recourse to arbitration as such. More specifically, this issue is something that should be noted: that, that is, as the conditions for recourse to arbitration are drafted, it cannot be ruled out that a difference may not be referred to arbitration (Paragraph 1, Article 16, Law 1876/90). Therefore, in this case there are a pending and a potential gap that are expected to serve as a means of pressure on the parties to reach a solution by common consent. What is thus desirable is that conditions and terms of recourse to arbitration and pending issues that they may form may not eventually become a problem, but they may actually operate in practice as a means of pressure on the parties to produce consensual solutions. Finally, a prerequisite for the success of

105 Article 4 of the Regulation of the Situation of Mediators-Arbitrators of the OMED.

106 The Qualifications and Incompatibilities of Mediators-Arbitrators of the OMED in Law 1876/90 which are mentioned in Article 4 of the Regulation of the Situation of Mediators-Arbitrators of the OMED (hereinafter, they will briefly be referred to as KKM-d)., and the elements that constitute the Code of Ethics (Article 5 in KKM-d), fully meet the standards set by the publications of the International Labour Office (ILO). More particularly, see: (a) ILO, 1973, pp. 23–30; (b) Gladstone, 1984, pp. 15–20; and (c) Zack, 1985, pp. 22–31.

107 Article 5 of the Regulation of the Situation of Mediators-Arbitrators of the OMED.

108 Paragraph 1, Article 6 of the Regulation of the Situation of Mediators-Arbitrators of the OMED.

109 Paragraph 2, Article 6 of the Regulation of the Situation of Mediators-Arbitrators of the OMED.

110 Paragraph 2, passage C, Article of the Regulation of the Situation of Mediators-Arbitrators of the OMED.

111 Paragraph 2, passage a, Article 9 of the Regulation of the Situation of Mediators-Arbitrators of the OMED.

the institution of mediation and arbitration of Law 1876 of 1990 is the exhaustion of all provided institutional capacities. This report covers original or sensitive institutions provided and which are key institutions for the Organization's success (i.e. the OMED's success).

First, the exhaustion of all institutional capacities is required so that mutual agreement procedures and terms of mediation and arbitration are defined (Paragraph 8, Article 2). Meanwhile, the mediator-arbitrator Regulation states that "parties withdrawn can select up to three mediators or arbitrators to handle a case"[112]. Based on these institutional information, a basic question arises: Given the existence of a specific provision (Paragraph 1, Article 16, Law 1876/90) that defines the conditions and terms for recourse to arbitration and the "gap" in the Regulation of Situation of Mediators and Arbitrators of the OMED, which contains no explicit provision or prohibition, reasonably the question arises as whether the parties can determine by mutual agreement the relationship of the two processes, that is, that of mediation and arbitration, and the conditions and terms for recourse to arbitration.

Second, the exhaustion of institutional capacity is required so that credibility and acceptance of mediators-arbitrators are ensured. This observation concerns particularly institutions, first, the application of self-exemption of the mediator arbitrator[113], and, second, exceptions of mediators-arbitrators from the parties during the draw. In this regard, it should be clarified that these institutions were provided to ensure the credibility and acceptance of the mediator-arbitrator. Therefore, they should be used to serve the purpose for which they were created, and, at the same time, their use is to be made responsibly and sparingly. An essential issue is the use of institutional capabilities so that mediators-arbitrators do not become only units and a special body[114]. The special body should meet

---

112 Paragraph 1 passage A′, Article 6 of the Regulation of the Situation of Mediators-Arbitrators of the OMED. This process refers to this mediation and arbitration model for resolving collective labour disputes within whose framework the relevant adjustments can come out of the parties' agreement. A special reference, especially of comparative content, is made to this model in: ILO, (1980), Conciliation and Arbitration Procedures in Labour Disputes, A Comparative Study, Chapter 4: Bipartite arrangements for preventing and setting disputes, pp. 53–84.

113 Paragraph 2 passage F (Στ′), Article 5 of the Regulation of the Situation of Mediators-Arbitrators of the OMED.

114 Paragraph 2, Article 17, Law 1876/90, Paragraph 4, Article 20 of the Regulation of the Organization and Operation and Paragraph 5, Article 2 of the Regulation of the Situation of Mediators-Arbitrators of the OMED.

on matters relevant to the exercise of the office of its members and to submit its opinions to the Board of Directors of the Organization (i.e. the OMED). Finally, another term and condition for the effective operation of the new institution is the use by the mediator the right to submit proposals to the parties[115]. More specifically, it is stated: "If the parties do not reach agreement within twenty days, the mediator has the right to submit to them his/her own proposal" (Paragraph 6, Article 15, Law 1876/90). Based on the wording of this provision, it is clear that "the proposal is not an obligation but only the mediator's right".

The adoption of this view on the issue of the mediator's proposal affects how conditions and the terms of recourse to arbitration operate in practice, if the terms are determined by the existence and acceptance or otherwise of the mediator's proposal[116] in two of the four statutory cases of recourse to Arbitration. Therefore, the failure to submit a proposal on the part of the Mediator can increase those cases during which the collective dispute will not be led to arbitration, thus, increasing the chances to maintain "regulatory backlog" around a collective dispute. When, however, the presence of "regulatory backlog" is desirable and acceptable to the legislator's whole philosophy – that is, they operate in favour of mediation and consensus solutions – then, the interpretation that wants the "Proposal" a right and not an obligation of the mediator supports this spirit (i.e. it supports the spirit of the law).

First, every factor – the state, agencies and institutions of industrial relations, every officer could in any way, directly or indirectly – can affect the course and development of the new institution; s/he should understand and accept the view that the Organization for Mediation and Arbitration (OMED) is necessary to continue to operate as precisely it was inspired and designed by the legislator from the very outset. More specifically, it should be understood and irrevocably accepted that the legislator, having made use of the possibilities of the constitution, ruled that the public interest in this case[117] is met more effectively with the provision of Mediation and Arbitration services through an independent, non-public legal private entity (Private Entity Law) (Paragraph 1, Article 17, Law 1876/90), which is free from state intervention, will create trust and social acceptance.

---

115 For the role of the Mediator's Proposal, see: Zack, 1985, p. 175.

116 It is about the cases of passage (c), Paragraph 1, Article 16, Law 1876/90.

117 It should be noted that there are views according to which the provisions of Law 1876/90 that the non-state arbitration is unconstitutional. More specifically, see: Tz. Kontrarou, 1991, p. D2, Economy. Moreover, see the view of the minority in the decision 2620/91 of the Fourth Division of the Council of State.

At the same time, each of the parties involved in industrial relations agencies or agents should be aware of the need and actively take action to restructure and modernize the system of industrial relations so that the system (Analytis, 199, pp. 12–13; Argyros, 1991) will free itself from the negative "legacy" of the past; it will consolidate a new culture of cooperation and understanding of the parties in industrial relations (Daskalakis, 1991b, p. 37) it will build relations of parity, reciprocity and trust between the parties; it will utilize all the existing institutional safeguards for the emergence of new potential role of collective bargaining; and, it will make state intervention retreat, thus giving birth to social dialogue (Soisson, 1990, pp. 15–23, and esp. pp. 17 and 21).

Nowadays, the new mediation and arbitration model has already become a new reality. As shown in practice by the flow and development of mediation and arbitration cases, the new Organization is beginning to consolidate an impartial and transparent operation that ensures reliability and acceptance. The parties "greeted" with a particularly favourable mood and attitude the new Organization. They have included people representing it with confidence. Within this context, they have made efforts to conduct a dialogue of substance. Even though in some cases the parties had never done before, they "have now sat at the same table" and discussed; and indeed had they often agreed.

The new settlement system and regulation of collective labour disputes appears to have delivered and this is confirmed by the statistics associated with the operation of the Organization (i.e. the OMED). During the period 1992–2001, a total of 1,825 requests for services, mediation and arbitration were submitted to the Organization, of which 1,652 applications and cases under Law 1876 of 1990 and 173 mediation cases so that security personnel and public dialogue were determined under Law 2224 of 1994[118]. From the analysis of the aggregated data on collective arrangements[119], the following important conclusions can be observed: First, there is a significant reduction in the number of arbitration awards since the enactment of Law 1876 of 1990; second, the operational arrangements cover the majority of collective agreements signed by year; and, third, industry and operational (enterprise) agreements have been firmly in the lead against occupational agreements since 1992, something that was also the target of the new model of collective bargaining of:aw 1876 of 1990. More specifically, the data are as follows:

118 Assessment of the Work of the OMED 1992–2001 and Planning of Action 2002, (January 2002), Organization of Mediation and Arbitration – OMED, Athens, p. 3.

119 See ibid., Table 4, p. 4–5.

The distribution of the cases at national, local and operational level for all of 1825 cases, which evolved in the OMED in the period 1992–2001, is as follows: (a) at National level (industry and enterprise): 989 cases – 54%; (b) at local level (industry and enterprise): 380 cases – 21%; (c) at an enterprise level: 456 cases – of 25 %; that is, Grand Total: 1,825 cases – 100%[120]. The distribution of cases by category of collective settlement in the period 1992–2001 is as follows[121]: (a) industry: 630 cases – 34.5%; (b) occupational (at national and local level): 739 cases – rate of 40.5%; (c) Enterprise: 456 cases – 25%; that is, Total: 1,825 cases – 100%. In particular, 1,117 cases involve mediation of Law 1876/90, 535 cases involve arbitration of Law 1876/90, 93 cases involve mediation of Law 2224/94 for security personnel, and 80 cases involve public dialogue of Law 2224/94[122]. Most cases of the OMED are about the private sector. In particular, of a total of 1,825 cases[123], the private sector accounts for 70% and the public and the broader public sector accounts for 30%.

Moreover, the available data[124] indicate that three regions of the country, namely Attica (393), Crete (220) and Northern Greece (144) account for 91% of collective arrangements at local and operational level. It should be noted that the large number of cases in the Prefecture of Attica is due mainly to enterprise-level

120 Ibid., p. 5.

121 The data of the first phase of the Organization (i.e. of the OMED) show a disproportionately high percentage of occupational collective agreements in relation to "share" with the national industrial relations system come to the OMED. To an extent, this is linked to the fact that, as a rule, occupational collective agreements concern the least developed areas of the national industrial relations system, where the employees have relatively low bargaining power, and the employers are characterized by fragmented representations, by many uncoordinated employer organizations. Of the total number of cases of the first phase of the OMED, the majority concerned occupational collective agreements. More specifically, any issues of collective bargaining or collective arrangements are divided as follows: 38.6% occupational agreements at national level, 11.4% occupational agreements at local level, 29.6% industry agreements, 20.4%, enterprise agreements. (The data mentioned come from the study conducted by the Mediator Chr. Ioannou, on behalf of the OMED).

122 Ibid., p. 3.

123 In 1994 the Branch of the OMED was established in Thessaloniki. During 1994 -2001, there were submitted: 88 mediation cases, 40 arbitration cases, 18 personnel security cases και 12 cases of public dialogue. Furthermore, there were signed: 43 collective labour agreements at mediation stage and 3 collective labour agreements at arbitration stage. Finally, 6 cases closed positively for establishing security personnel and 1 for public dialogue, ibid., p. 5.

124 Ibid., p. 3.

collective bargaining since this Law covers 68% of the total enterprise arrangements at the OMED level, whereas in Crete the vast majority of cases concern sectoral or occupation arrangements for employees who work in the public sector but they are under private law[125].

Of 1,117 mediation cases that came to the Organization to conclude a collective labour agreement in the period 1992 to 2001, the rate of the successful outcome of mediation efforts amounted to 46%. It is worth noting that this figure stands at 81% with respect to cases at enterprise level. More specifically, of the applications submitted to the OMED for conclusion of such collective bargaining agreement pursuant to Law 1876/90 in the period from 1992 to 2001, and, of a total of 283, 230 cases ended successfully, that is, a collective bargaining agreement was signed. It should be noted that the number of 574 collective agreements signed in total with the OMED – of which 512 were signed at the mediation stage and 62 at the arbitration stage – accounted for 21.4% of all collective bargaining agreements, that is, for 2,763 collective agreements were signed at national level during the period 1992–2001. It is also observed that the volume of cases of the OMED concerns mainly sectoral and occupational / of the same occupation, and, sideline enterprise, which, however, are constantly growing. These enterprise cases include requests for drawing up labour regulations[126].

Between 1992 and 2001 the Organization handled 535 arbitration cases, of which 464 cases were issued arbitration awards and 62 were signed collective bargaining stage of arbitration[127]. According to the aforementioned, the arbitration awards represent 41% of requests for mediation services of Law 1876/90 handled by the Organization. It should be noted that arbitral awards rendered in full by the O.ME.D. (464) represent only 14.8% of all collective regulations, collective agreements or arbitral awards; that is, of 3.139 arrangements made nationwide between 1992 and 2001[128].

Of the 93 mediation cases of security personnel handled by the Organization since Law 2224 of 1994 came into force, 43 cases ended successfully and the minutes of the agreement between the parties were signed, thus bringing the rate of successful outcome at 46%. It should be noted that cases of this category

125 Ibid., p. 6.

126 Ibid., p. 4.

127 Ibid. It should be noted that in other five cases arbitration awards collective bargaining agreements were issued and signed and in three cases the (arbitration) process was suspended at the parties' request.

128 See ibid., Table 4, pp. 4–5.

concern mainly utilities and large private enterprises in sensitive sectors[129]. Of the 80 cases of public dialogue handled by the OMED since Law 2224 of 1994 came into force, 39 cases had positive results and the strike either stopped or did not take place finally (the percentage of the successful outcome is 49%). It should also be noted that cases of public dialogue concern mainly the public and broader public sector[130].

The new institution has now been able to balance in really fragile environment that creates, surrounds and supports it. Nowadays, review of progress so far and the problems of implementing the new law can be extremely helpful to draw conclusions, make the necessary complementary and corrective adjustments and movements, be more mature and settled institutional and operational options, capitalize on the experience so far so that infrastructure, support structures, statistical and research data can be created, as well as to develop even with special emphasis appropriate training activities in the coming period. These new data leave room for developing a policy that will not actually limit the role of the OMED to provide just mediation and arbitration services, primarily to determine pays, but it will set a chain of initiatives that will contribute to the development of a new potential role of collective bargaining as a dominant component of the tripartite dialogue that should operate in a modern social and political democracy.

6.8 Regulations for Mediation, Arbitration and the OMED after the Memorandum

6.8.1 Legislative Confirmation of the Intention to Change the Institutional Framework

In Law 3863/2010 *"New insurance system and relevant provisions, regulations on industrial relations"*, and, more specifically, in Article 73 there are provisions on the organization of mediation and arbitration system. In particular, the following are stated: "1. If the bargaining between employers and employees to resolve collective disputes interests fail, the interested parties may request mediation or arbitration services. 2. The legal entity of private law (Private Entity Law) known

129 DEH (Electricity Power Company), OTE (Telecommunications), OSE (Railway Company), EKO (Greek Oil Company), O.A. (Olympic Airways), B.P., MOBIL etc, ibid, p. 4.

130 Olympic Airways, OSE (Railway Company), EKO (Greek Oil Company), Ministry of Agriculture, IKA (Institution of Social Security), etc, ibid.

as "Organization for Mediation and Arbitration" (OMED), set up by Article 17 of Law 1876/1990 (Government Gazette 27 A), continues to operate under the terms and conditions of this Article. 3. By presidential decree, issued within three (3) months from the publication of this Law, after the proposal of the Ministers of Finances and Labour and Social Security and the consent of the International Labour Organization, in particular the International Labour Office, some issues are settled; these issues concern: (a) the manner of resolving collective disputes between employers and employees, based on the principles of good judgment, objectivity and impartiality; (b) the possibility, the way and the cases of recourse of the interested parties to mediation and arbitration, based on the principle of equal treatment of the parties; (c) the establishment of separate bodies of mediators and arbitrators with the unanimous opinion of the presidents of the GSEE, SEV GSEVEE and ESEE or of their legal replacements defined by them; (d) specifying the qualifications of mediators and arbitrators, the manner of their appointment and of any renewal of their office; (e) the way of selection of arbitrators in case the agreement or disagreement of the parties concerned; (f) cases where the arbitration award issued will be challenged before competent civil courts; (g) the purpose, organization, administration, operation, management and property of the OMED, any question related to its operation, and any other relevant matter of technical or detailed character. 4. Until the Presidential Decree of Paragraph 3 of this Article, and the latest by 31.12.2010 Articles 14, 15, 16 and 17 of Law 1876/1990 (Government Gazette 27 A) continues to apply, and which will subsequently be repealed". The essence of the above provision had primarily a political objective and lies in the fact that after the Memorandum and the "pressure" for changes in the mediation and arbitration system as well as the "creeping whispers for repealing arbitration" that had caused social reactions, it is, on the one hand, reaffirmed that the OMED will continue to operate, but, on the other hand, there will be legislative initiative within a specific timetable, which will bring improvements in its operation, removing primarily existing asymmetries in mediation and arbitration processes, in dealing with the parties.

6.8.2 Legislative Restrictions on the Increases Granted by the OMED

Provisions for the content of arbitral awards issued by the Organization for Mediation and Arbitration (OMED) were also included in Article 51 of Law 3871/2010 "Financial management and accountability, which has subsequently been adopted. These provisions aimed to impose restrictions on granted increases and, therefore, refer to the issue raised between "state intervention and collective autonomy", which is of the most central issues in the theory and practice of industrial relations and collective bargaining in particular. It should be noted that the Annex to the Memorandum included a clause which provided three-year "freeze" of pays, that is, until 2012. Because, following informal bargaining, both at a tripartite national level and informal bilateral talks between the Greek side and Troika – instead of applying the above clause, which was socially burdensome and would be met with reactions – upon informal agreement – it was decided simply to impose restrictions in principle on Arbitration Awards and, consequently, on those of collective labour agreements would be concluded by the OMED. The argument that imposing legal restrictions on arbitration decisions, that is, on decisions of a third party that do not constitute an agreement between the social partners but are imposed to them externally, as it could have happened in a court decision does not breach the collective autonomy, certainly could not proportionally supported and appropriate expansion of regulated and prescribed restrictions on collective bargaining agreements, even if they were concluded with the assistance of mediation of the OMED. Only one argument, concerning the protection of the national economy in view of the dire economic situation of the country, could be viewed and certainly evaluated in social, political and constitutional terms. As restriction the limit of the national general collective labour agreement was provided, which was 0% for 2010 and the European inflation for 2011 and 2012.

Article 51 of Law 3871/2010 specifically provides that: "(1) The publicized by the publication of the present with the process of the Organization for Mediation and Arbitration (OMED) arbitration awards, for resolving collective disputes, do not apply and do not have any legal effect, if pay increases are given in any way for 2010 and the first half of 2011. Moreover, they do not apply and do not have any legal effect if they give wage increases in any way for the period from 1.7.2011 to 31.12.2012, in addition to the following: (a) Since 1 July 2011, increase in threshold wages, that have been configured on 31.12.2009 based on the EGSSE for the years 2008–2009, at a rate equal to the rate of annual change in European inflation for the year 2010; (b) Since July 1, 2012, increase in thresholds wages that have been configured on July 1, 2011 based on case (a) at a rate equal to the rate of annual change in European inflation for the year 2011.For the purposes of this paragraph, "European inflation" is considered the average annual percentage change over the previous year of the HICP (Harmonised index of consumer prices) of the Euro area as announced by Eurostat. The amounts resulting from the calculation increases are written with two (2) decimal digits and rounded to the next centimeter, if the millimeter is equal to or greater than five (5). (2) Arbitration awards issued after the effective date of Law 3845/2010 (Government Gazette 65 A) and give in any way wage increases beyond those provided in the preceding paragraph, are subject to recourse within fifteen (15) days from the publication hereof by the parties involved in the relevant collective dispute or by the Minister of Labour and Social Security, in front of the arbitrators of the OMED with three Judges, raised under the provisions of Law 1876/1990. (3) Mediation agreements may not exceed the specified in paragraph 1 limits for the three years of 2010–2011–2012".

This regulation eventually applied. But it did not take, on the one hand, arbitration awards and "mediation agreements" (an inappropriate term of the legislator to refer to the collective labour agreement concluded by the OMED) that were issued before 18 August 2010 when Law 3871/2010 was published and applied, and on the other hand, collective labour agreements that were concluded normally without the intervention of the OMED. Moreover, throughout the year 2010, "in pending" of a regulation by which the institution of the extension of industry collective agreements would be abolished, which was rumored, in reality all processes of the extension of collective agreements were implicitly suspended, resulting in the pending of the extension of thirty-seven collective agreements and arbitration awards at the end of the year. The total of these data led, as it is easily understood, in forming companies and employees at different speeds, at least as regards pay and employment conditions, and, of course, labour costs.

6.8.3 From Arbitration Law 1876/1990 to the System of Law 3899/2010

The most important, however, change in the resolution and settlement system of collective labour disputes occurred with Article 14 of Law 3899/2010, which replaced Articles 14, 15, 16 and 17 of Law 1876/1990, where the referred to the process of resolving collective labour disputes and the OMED provisions were amended. The system for resolving collective disputes through mediation and arbitration, which was initially provided in Law 1876/1990, is being altered by the 18-year experience of the institution. With the legislative initiative of Law 3899/2010, the 18-year experience of the resolution and settlement system of collective labour disputes was utilized to amend the relevant legislation (Articles 15, 16 και 17 amend Law 1876/1990) in order to enhance it. It is conspicuous that the existence of a voluntary-optional system, a compulsory or a mixed system of arbitration affects the parties' behaviour during the course of the bargaining, determining their outcome and the result, and, therefore, largely the possibility that after the process has been completed there may be regulated or unregulated labour relations. Thus, it is reasonable for it to be at issue between the factors of labour relations and the people involved with the design and implementation policy or the wording on general legal and scientific views on the issue. The issue of amending the institutional framework of arbitration derives largely from the origin of this problem.

For this reason, Article 15, Law 3899/2010 – which followed and amended the legislative regime of the recourse to arbitration (which is one of the main ways to resolve collective labour disputes) – has also been a disputed object and of particular concern not only among experts but also within the Scientific Committee of the Parliament during the processing of the relevant Bill. Arbitration process is a regulatory mechanism of industrial relations in accordance with the Constitution[131], in which the creation of arbitration bodies is provided (Paragraph 2, Article 22 and Paragraph 1, Article 23 of the (Greek) Constitution) so that the resolution of collective labour disputes is facilitated, provided, however, that arbitration plays only a subsidiary role in relation to collective bargaining or in any case it operates somehow as a penalty, in case that one party does not fulfill its statutory obligation to bargain. According to Law 1876/1990[132], as it was in force before the enactment of Law 3899/2010, recourse to arbitration was possible by mutual agreement of the parties at any stage of the bargaining. It is obvious that this case involved a version of voluntary arbitration. Furthermore, unilateral recourse to arbitration was possible, and under certain conditions related to the behaviour of specific party during the mediation, such as acceptance of the mediation process or the mediator's proposal. With the provision of Law 1876/1990, which was eventually amended, three cases of unilateral recourse to arbitration were provided: (a) Of any side (i.e. employer's or employees'), if the other side refused mediation. In this case, the arbitration is obviously of a character of sanction. (b) Only by trade unions, in the case of collective disputes involving the conclusion of national general, industry, occupational collective agreements, if they accept the mediator's proposal while the employer's side rejects it. (c) In the case of enterprise collective agreements and agreements in organizations of utilities, there can be unilateral recourse to arbitration by either party (either employer or employees), who accepts the mediator's proposal while the other party rejects it.

---

131 In Law, the common legislator is in his/her discretion to choose the arbitration system (AP or Supreme Court-Plenary) 25/2004; Deltion Ergatikis Nomothesias (DEN or Bulletin Of Labour Legislation), 2004, 1399; Council of State 3204/1998; DEN 1999, 13; Council of State 2620/1991; Epitheorisi Ergatikou Dikeou (E.Erg.D. -Revew of Labour Law), 1991, 924).

132 See Article 16, Law 1876/1990, before it was replaced with Law 3899/2010.

The aforementioned provision of Law 1876/1990, which allows the unilateral recourse to arbitration, has been held by the Law to comply with the provisions of the Constitution and International Labour Conventions of the International Labour Organization (ILO)[133], if the recourse occurs after all efforts for an amicable settlement of the dispute have been made and exhausted (Koukiadis, 1981, pp. 376; Leventis, 2007, p. 575; Papadimitriou, 1991, p. 128; Kazakos, 1998, p. 116). On the contrary, according to the Freedom of Association Committee of the ILO (2003), recourse to compulsory arbitration is only allowed in cases of so-called "necessary" services, which serve basic needs of society. Finally, regarding the legislator's ability to form the institution of arbitration, this Law accepts that s/he is first free to formulate the arbitration system that s/he deems appropriate[134].

6.8.4 System Arbitration Law 3899/2010

The key points of amendments made are: essential rules of mediation and arbitration processes are enhanced with straight legislation, rules which were the subject of regulations of the OMED. New arrangements expressly provide: first, the application of the principle of good judgment, objectivity and impartiality of the arbitration and mediation process. Second, during mediation and arbitration, the economic and financial situation and development of the competitiveness of productive activity is taken into account, to which the collective difference refers. Within this framework, the competitiveness of enterprises in relation to the cost of inputs, productivity and their viability is assessed. This approach is an extension of the issues, which mediators and arbitrators had[135] to take account anyway, and which have been of much weight in the current economic crisis.

More sspecifically, with the new regulations[136]: the general rules of the mediation and arbitration process are laid down, with an emphasis on the primacy of

133 (AP or Supreme Court-Plenary) 25/2004; Deltion Ergatikis Nomothesias (DEN or Bulletin Of Labour Legislation), 2004, 1399; Council of State 3204/1998; (in Greek) Deltion Ergatikis Nomothesias (DEN or Bulletin Of Labour Legislation), 1999, 13; Council of State 4555/1996; Deltion Ergatikis Nomothesias (DEN or Bulletin Of Labour Legislation), 1997, 441).

134 (AP or Supreme Court-Plenary) 25/2004; Deltion Ergatikis Nomothesias (DEN or Bulletin of Labour Legislation), 2004, 1399; Council of State 3204/1998; DEN 1999, 13; Council of State 2620/1991; Epitheorisi Ergatikou Dikeou (E.Erg.D.-Revew of Labour Law), 1991, 924).

135 Based on Paragraph 4, Article 15, Law 1876/1990.

136 The aforementioned are provided by Article 15, Law 3899/2010 with which Articles 14, 15, 16 and 17, Law 1876/1990 are replaced.

the parties' agreement, good judgment, objectivity and transparency. The procedural rules concerning mediation provided by the services of the OMED are readjusted. The procedural rules governing the arbitration are readjusted completely, and it is specified that a recourse to arbitration can be made at any stage of bargaining by mutual agreement of the parties or unilaterally in the following cases: either if the other party has refused mediation from and party after the mediation proposal has submitted, or if both parties attended and participated in the mediation process. With the regulation of the new provisions of Law 3899/2010, the employer's ability to unilaterally resort to arbitration is also extended to the case of enterprise-level collective bargaining, an ability that is valid for all the other collective labour disputes.

Therefore, for all collective disputes both parties have the right to resort to arbitration unilaterally. It should be reminded that in the pre-existing system of Law 1876/1990, unilateral recourse to arbitration required the prior acceptance of the mediator's proposal, as a manifestation of good faith and as a means of pressure to both parties to accept the mediator's proposal (Koukiadis, 1981, p. 365; Leventis, 2007, p. 562; Papadimitriou, 1991, p. 113; Kazakos, 1998, p. 278). With the new provision of Law 3899/2010 the acceptance of the mediator's proposal is not provided as a precondition for arbitration. Thus, any party will be able to resort unilaterally to arbitration, even though they have rejected the mediator's proposal. In each case, the pivotal point of collective bargaining is to find mutually acceptable solutions and balance economic and social interests.

Central choice is also the strengthening of the role of collective agreements with arbitration awards, especially at an enterprise level by limiting issues that the arbitration award may regulate at an enterprise level. Asymmetry in the exercise of the right to resort to arbitration is removed, so that both the employees and employers' side have the right to resort to arbitration. In this way the existing basic asymmetry is removed, and the employer now, after the amendments that were made in the process of resolving collective disputes, has the potential, if bargaining fail with employees, as can employees do otherwise, to use mediation and arbitration.

With the new provision of Law 3899/2010, the work of arbitration may be awarded, at the request of any party, to a three-member Arbitration Committee, too. In accordance with the relevant provision of Law 3899/2010, the exercise of the right to strike is suspended for ten days from the day of recourse to arbitration. In contrast, under the force of Law 1876/1990[137], provides the suspension of

137 See Paragraph 8, Article 16, Law 1876/1990.

the right to strike was also suspended, but only for unilateral recourse to arbitration undertaken by the employee, and then only in cases where the Law provides this unilateral recourse as their privilege[138]. With the new provision, the suspension of the right to strike is effective in every case, even when the recourse to arbitration is unilaterally undertaken by the employer's side. In this case, however, while such a provision sounds like an equal, mutually binding on the parties and, in principle, a reasonable provision, it raises, nevertheless, serious concerns as to its compatibility with Article 23 of the Constitution, which guarantees the free exercise of the right to strike. Because it could not be excluded that in some cases the employer's side to unilaterally resort to arbitration, with the main purpose to suspend the exercise of the right to strike by the employees' side.

With the new statuary scheme of Law 3899/2010, the recourse to arbitration is limited to defining basic wages and / or basic salary. On other issues collective bargaining may be pursued whenever so that a collective agreement is concluded. Arbitration can determine by arbitration award the salary or wages, that experience dictates that moves in the middle of those proposed by each side (that of employer and that of employees). It should be reminded that with the new statuary scheme of Law 1876/1990 there was no restriction as to the issues that could be settled by arbitration award. Instead, the provision of new Law[139] 3899/2010 provides that arbitration and arbitration award are restricted to determining the basic wage or salary and cannot be concerned with other issues[140] that are the subject of collective bargaining agreement. However, regarding this issue, questions about the specific issues are raised, that's why the Scientific Committee of the Parliament in its Report[141] on the Bill "Urgent measures for the implementation of the support programme of the Greek economy" noted that: "*... in most current regulations, the basic salary or the basic wage is only part of employees' salaries (more or less where applicable). The question, therefore, arose whether the proposed regulation enables the percentage or absolute number of reported ("drachma") benefits, which are provided for in effective collective arrangements, to be incorporated in the basic salary by an arbitration award. ...... assuming that, for the purposes of the proposed article, this incorporation is not*

138 In this case, the suspension of this strike could be considered to counterbalance employees' choice to unilaterally resort to arbitration. See Papadimitriou (1991, p. 133) and Koukiadis (1981, p. 367) who emphasize that the choice is left to the union.

139 Paragraph 3, Article 16, Law 3899/2010.

140 They refer to Article 2, Law 1876/1990, as content of collective agreements.

141 Report of the Scientific Service of the Parliament on the Bill: "Urgent measures for the implementation of the support programme of the Greek economy".

possible, the termination of an effective Collective Labour Agreement (sse) by either side will result in that these benefits can only be reiterated with the sse, if collective bargaining fail, they cannot be provided by an arbitration award, thus the employees' earnings will be reduced. Furthermore, the question arises whether the preceding restriction concerns the case when the parties have resorted to arbitration by mutual agreement, according to the first paragraph of Article 16 of Law 1876/1990. Finally, it remains unclear whether the proposed regulation amends the provision of Paragraph 4 of Article 12 of Law 1767/1988, as amended by Article 8 of Law 2224/1994, during which, in case of disagreement between the employer and employees' council on issues for which co-decision is provided (e.g. Labour Regulation, Health and Safety Regulation), the dispute is resolved by mediation and arbitration process. ...... There is concern regarding the regulation of these issues on dissent, especially when their regulation is mandatory (e.g. mandatory Labour Regulation in enterprises employing more than 70 people). That is, the issue will be referred to the unilateral regulation on behalf of the employer or, despite this above legal requirement, may it remain unregulated?"

6.8.5 Changes in Law 3899/2010 on Mediation and Arbitration

The role of social partners in the governance of the OMED and the selection and evaluation of mediators-arbitrators is strengthened. The purpose, organization and operation of the Organization of Mediation and Arbitration (OMED) are delineated and determine the composition of the Board of Directors of the Organization is determined, which has now got seven member from eleven that it used to have, and consists of three representatives of the main employers' organizations – that is, a representative of Association of Greek Industrialists (SEV in Greek), one of General Confederation of Professional Graftsmen and Traders in Greece (GSEVEE in Greek) and one representative of National Confederation of Hellenic Commerce (ESEE in Greek), with their deputies – three representatives of General Confederation of Greek Labour (GCGL or GSEE in Greek) with their deputies and the President and his/her alternate, who are selected by unanimous decision of the members and representatives of social partners.

Moreover, a representative of the Ministry of Labour and Social Security participates in the Board of Directors of the Organization of Mediation and Arbitration, as an observer, without voting rights. According to Law 1876/1990 (Paragraph 7, Article 17, Law 1876/1990), the Board of the Organization of Mediation and Arbitration (OMED) consisted of three representatives of employers and three representatives of trade union, one representative of the Ministry of Labour, a representative of the Law Society of Labour and Social insurance, two

University Professors (one of Labour Law and one of Economics or Labour Relationships) and a person of wider acceptance who was elected by the previous ten members.

With the new provision of Paragraph 3 of Article 17 of Law 1876/1990, as amended by Law 3899/2010, the number of Board members is limited from eleven (11) to seven (7). No longer do two University Professors, the representative of the Company of Labour Law and Social Security and the representative of the Ministry of Labour participate as experts, but only representatives of employers and employees' unions, as well as a distinguished person who is selected by the parties. The representative of the Ministry of Labour will nevertheless participate in as an observer (Paragraph 4). Finally, it is possible that representatives of employers and employees' unions are members of their (respective) administration, contrary to this prohibition, which was provided by the previously effective regulation of Law 1876/1990[142]. Moreover, according to the original statutory scheme of Law 1876/1990, mediators – arbitrators are a single body, whereas with the new provision of Paragraph 8, passage a, of the new Paragraph 17 of Law 1876/1990, after it has been recently amended by Law 3899/2010, the creation of two separate bodies is provided, one consisting of mediators and another composed of arbitrators.

All decisions of the Board of Directors are taken with the unanimous decision of all its 7 members. It is also determined that mediators-arbitrators are selected and evaluated by the unanimity of the representatives of the social partners who are members of the Board of Directors. It is also provided[143] that after three (3) years from the date of the enactment of this Law have been expired, the social partners involved in the preparation of national general collective agreement evaluate the effectiveness of the institution of Mediation and Arbitration, and recommend to the Minister of Labour and Social Security to maintain, remove, or modify their regulations; that is, in the relevant provision of new Law 3899/2010[144], whereas it is stated that after the expiration of three years from the enactment of the Law, there will be an evaluation of the new institutional framework for resolving collective labour disputes so that the "social partners" will decide to maintain, repeal or modify the regulations. Nevertheless, it is not clear who will take the initiative to start the process, what the consequences will be if no one takes this initiative and what the consequences will be if the interested

---

142 That of Paragraph, Article 17, Law 1876/1990.

143 According to the provisions of Article 16, Law 3899/2010.

144 Article 16, Law 3899/2010.

parties disagree as with the effectiveness of the institution. The new framework is completed[145] with general provisions as well as with necessary transitional regulations for the immediate operation of the new organization of the OMED.

6.8.6 The Arbitration System in Law 4046/2012 – The New Memorandum and the Establishment of Voluntary Arbitration

Finally, in the new Memorandum (Law 4046/2012), the implementation of which was the Cabinet Act (PYS in Greek) 6/28-2-2012, the arbitration is now available only on a voluntary basis. Thus, the arbitration system loses its mixed character and becomes voluntary, helping decisively overthrow the operational context of collective labour relations in Greece with other regulations. More specifically, this regulation – as it makes disappear any perspective of a framework of collective regulation at the "end of the street" of the bargaining "in any case", under great depression, unemployment and downturn bargaining power of the unions – leads to fatal decollectivization and individualization of industrial relations.

All these measures in the new Memorandum are incorporated in Law 4046/2012 and annexed to this Law as Appendix V, the provisions of which are laws which come into effect immediately (Paragraph 6, Article 1 of Law 4046/2012). At the same time, details for the implementation of these provisions are regulated by the PYS 6 / 28.02.2012 (02.28.2012, Government Gazette [GG] 38, Vol A).

6.9 Instead of an Epilogue

In conclusion, it could be argued that the changes that have been made, especially in collective labour relations, have not only brought individual changes but also led to an overall readjustment of the labour market in Greece, which has brought drastic and immediate results. What should be emphasized is that the new Memorandum is only of horizontal cuts in wages and pensions, which may well be reversed in the future. It deconstructs the whole system of collective bargaining and cancels employees' right of recourse to arbitration. Employment conditions in the private sector cease being the subject of bargaining between social partners; they are regulated either by the employer through individual contracts or by governmental intervention. Even the minimum wage of National General Collective Agreement (EGSSE) is also canceled, since it can be decreased whenever the Troika or the government requires it.

145 See the provisions of Article 17, Law 3899/2010.

A series of individual changes in the structure of the Greek system of collective bargaining will result in their decentralizing at company level rather than at industry level which has been in effect up to date. Such regulations and changes have been both the elimination of overlapping provisions of collective labour agreements (**sse** in Greek) and the ineffective principle of favourable regulation combined with the introduction of the new institution of special enterpris-level collective agreements (SELCAs). Equally important, if not the most important issue, are other measures adopted such as: the abolition of the institution of the extension of **sse**s, a fact that leads to the creation of conditions of fierce competition between companies, fragmentation and competition among employees, multi-fragmentation of the market and to the deregulation of labour relations. This measure, combined with the former – that is, the decentralization at company level – intensifies the competition in the market and the multi-fragmentation in industrial relations.

The previous status of collective bargaining – both maintaining the national collective employment agreement in a prominent position and ensuring the decentralization at industry level – offered, on the one hand, conditions of decentralization and thus of flexibility, and, on the other hand, clauses of necessary social protection through minima. Today, with the emphasis on the decentralization at company level and the abolition of the provisions for concurrence – with the establishment of special employment agreements at company level, decentralization at company level does not simply become flexible; it rather gets fragmented and liquify labour relations. At the same time, the minimum wage and protection, apart from the fact that they have already have been decreased legislatively, are being de-rooted, since collective autonomy is canceled by the Provisions of the new Memorandum and is provided in Annex (p. 801) of Law 4046/2012 that "the government as of July 2012 legislates the minimum wage in consultation with the social partners." This provision combined with that in Paragraph 7, Article 2 of Law 3845/2010 – that is, the ratifying Act of the First Memorandum that provides that the terms of any kind of collective labour agreements (**sse**s) may diverge even from the national general collective agreement (EGSSE) (despite the fact that this executive decree might never have been issued) dislocates and deconstructs completely the collective bargaining system in our country.

With such an institutionally reformed framework of collective bargaining, this institution – when operating in an environment where poverty is about 30% of the general population, the risk of poverty or exclusion in 37% and youth unemployment (18–24 age group) is more than 50%, it is self-evident that as a political mechanism, reflecting the balance of power – will produce very poor results for employees. Ever more, after the repeated partial modifications that took place, eventually with the provisions of the new Memorandum, the previous system of mixed arbitration has been abolished; a system which, in spite of the fact that it featured bold elements of obligation, ensured that there would be no phenomena of unregulated labour relations. But within a context where society and employees are tested and unemployment has exploded to unprecedented heights, it is very doubtful whether and to what extent the institution of collective bargaining will operate; especially, when there is not even the prospect or the "threat" of arbitration "downs the road". According to the data of the new Memorandum, arbitration may be conducted only when both sides agree upon it. So, it is very likely that there may an increase in cases of failure to reach agreements and collective employment agreements, absence of collective arbitration rules (arbitral), thus there will be a transition to decollectivization and individualization of collective labour relations.

Consequently, the new landscape in industrial relations is characterized by an intense multi-fragmentation (decentralization at enterprise level – each enterprise has an individual status – either decollectivization and individualization of labour relations – that is, absence of collective arrangements and conclusion of individual employment agreements or contracts), while the question of whether and how the state will intervene – certainly unconstitutionally – for the formation of a minimum wage will linger.

Chapter 7: Flexibility in Labour Relations

7.1 Labour Flexibility: Concept and Types

Despite the fact that the discussion about flexibility has been developing for about two to three decades at European and international level, only recently has it been developed in Greece. Flexibility (Christoforatos, 1989, p. 385), a multifaceted and multidimensional concept, derived from sciences means in principle the ability to adapt to internal or external changes (Georgakopoulou, 1991, pp. 2–3). As a principle, however, that is implemented in the operation of enterprises, the structure of labour relations and the organization of labour market, flexibility has received strong ideologically charged support or negative criticism, according to the relevant rich literature (Koukiadis, 1991, p. 1; Travlos-Tzanetatos, 1986, pp. 105–111; Mitropoulos, 1991, pp. 9–25). This fact requires so the researcher primarily discharge the concepts so that the diagnosis of the actual parameters and the absolute size of the whole issue can be feasible.

Flexibility is a principle that may assume a variety of forms[146] that refer either to the organization of production or to the structure of labour relations and the labour market. More specifically, two basic categories from all different versions of flexibility (Kouzis, 2001) can be distinguished. On the one hand, the qualitative-operational flexibilities, namely those that are based on qualitative dimensions of operational policy, which enhance human factor, and, on the other hand, the quantitative flexibilities, that is, those that focus on defensive and conjectural choices of reduction in labour costs to deal with crisis. From the current mainstream classification of flexibilities is clear that of these production flexibilities concern the degree of adaptability of production process of enterprises vis-à-vis qualitative and quantitative developments imposed by the rules of the market, with emphasis on adapting the entire operational system and not only adjusting individual factors or variables of the enterprise. In contract, labour flexibilities are meant adaptation policies in business formation, suspension, mobility, use and reproduction of labour force on the needs and conditions of capitalist production and reproduction (Georgakopoulou, 1996a).

As production flexibility is meant the creation of a flexible enterprise with high degree of automation, which, while utilizing an equipment of multitasking capabilities, manages to adapt the product and its volume to consumers' needs

146 Kouzis, 1992, p. 46, where the author lists a distinction of forms of flexibility.

and the changing demand. Flexibility is a key concept in modern technological, production and structural socioeconomic changes, procedures and processes; it refers to the ability to adapt to internal or external changes (Daskalakis, 1995b). Within this framework there is need to find new ways to achieve time savings through a combination of working time and space as well as of the employees' time and that of machines. Flexibility in organizations has a direct impact on working time and space, and, consequently, on employment contracts, schedules, principles of labour organization, internal mobility of labour force, the wage-setting systems and on the forms of correlation in the internal and external labour market (Doukakis, 1988).

The flexibility that is referred to labour force (Boyer, 1987, pp. 107–109; Atkinson, 1986; Poitet, 1987, pp. 27–28) may assume a variety of forms. First, it may assume the form of the employee with multiple qualifications and skills, who, broadly educated and technically or generally specialized, can move to different jobs of one or more production units. Generally, qualitative or operational flexibility of labour falls in this category, aiming to enrich labour, upgrade specialties, develop employees' pluripotency and initiatives, as well as to enhance the quality of labour relations in the enterprise. The consequences of the implementation of new technologies in labour organization and the content of appropriate skills nurture the need for qualitative labour flexibility through complex processes of despecialization and re-specialization.

An equally important factor is the relative shift of competition from price competition to competition that places greater emphasis on diversification, reliability and product quality. The aim of qualitative flexibility is the most comprehensive qualitative utilization of human resources or a part of them that an enterprise has, which should be established and developed within the enterprise (Atkinson, 1986, pp. 11–12). As a rule, different combinations of quantitative and qualitative labour flexibility as well as techno-organizational flexibility of the enterprise are implemented. The qualitative or functional flexibility is a permanent or occasional business strategy adjustment that is based on the development of an internal labour market, internal mobility, restructuring of specialities, and content change with reorganization or job enhancement, in contrast with external quantitative flexibility that has as axis the external labour market, hiring, firing, etc (OECD, 1986). This reorganization may be in use re-specialised redundancy or parallel use of old and new specialties (Atkinson, 1986, pp. 11–12).

Qualitative or functional flexibility is defined as the ability of enterprises to reorganize their working skills within a broader context of tasks. To the extent that it interferes with structural elements of the enterprise and labour, qualitative flexibility requires that certain conditions be met (Atkinson, 1986, pp. 13–14), such as, there should be no corporatist commitments to skills, and there should also be appropriate forms of continuous employee training in operation, both at enterprise level and at the level of the economy in general. In addition, there should be a positive working environment in the enterprise, conducive to motivation, consensus, employee participation, good health and safety conditions, flexible management, mutually accepted goals and flexible scheduling, guarantees for employment and pay, and enhancement of collegiality and representation of employees. And, finally, there should be adequate remuneration schemes and criteria wage developments, which would eliminate the differences in training, contribution and skills among employees, and would encourage continuous quality improvement of human resources, training, and responsible participation in production processes and decision-making processes.

Often qualitative flexibility is associated with the increase in employees' autonomy and with the replacement of rigid hierarchical structures with structures relatively flatter with greater employee involvement. This involvement, if significant, is one of the key conditions for success, every effort of qualitative flexibilization of labour and all factors of the company. This is due to the fact that employee's pluripotency has been designated as a key concept of quality labour flexibility, since it connotes the employee's ability and competency to perform new tasks, more complex tasks, to often change object of work, get re-specialized and get trained, and all these tasks can be achieved without involving insurmountable cost to the company or constant supervision and guidance. In this sense, the qualitative functional flexibility constitutes a serious objection to the degradation of the elements of the employment relationship by some arbitrary and unilateral implementations of quantitative flexibility. This does not mean that the implementation is free of problems and that poses no challenge for the labour movement. This is even more true when qualitative flexibility associated with new technologies applications and flexible organizational, production and administrative practices that can have a positive or negative impact on some or all data of the wage relation and the labour market.

Flexibility that refers to human resources (Boyer, 1987) may, however, assume the form of adjustment of wages and, generally, that of pay in the company's financial situation and labour market conditions. The wages flexibility lies in the possibility to raise it in contexts other than the applicable ones, as they are mainly defined by the system of collective bargaining and labour agreements. Characteristic features of wages flexibility are their destabilization, variation depending on circumstances, company's output, staff performance etc (Kouzis, 2001, p. 53). Wages flexibility is the main expression of the reduction in labour cost, as staff wages concern the core of labour cost. It includes two main aspects: the flexibility of the direct wage labour costs and flexibility of indirect wage labour costs that is related to "mandatory taxes" of the enterprises for the use of paid employment.

On the one hand, "the flexibility of the direct labour costs" unfolds through changes in the way salaries are formed, canceling or modifying the stability that distinguishes it. Main axis of this flexibility is reforms occurring in the system of collective bargaining and the content of commitments that produce collective labour agreements are the main axis of this flexibility. Basic expressions of the flexibility of the direct wage costs are: a "reassessment of the role and the institution of minimum wage"; the "linkage of pay with individual or collective performance of employees"; and the "linkage of pay with the company's output."

On the other hand, the "reduction of indirect labour costs" consists of policies to relieve businesses from financial costs arising from "mandatory social taxes" for employment of paid labour. Specific expressions of this form of flexibility is the "reduction of employers' social contributions" that is manifested primarily in the base of the employee's particular features, as well as in the reduction of employers' contributions and corporation taxes on accidents and insolvency, arguing that these phenomena do not involve all businesses to the same degree (Malinvaud, 1998). Finally, other forms are various savings accruing to the enterprise by elastication of regulations governing labour and industrial relations, as well as "various forms of tax reliefs", which are commonly associated with policies to support employment and business competitiveness.

Finally, the flexibility that refers to human resources can assume the form of an employee mobility that allows adjustment of employment and working time to general and local economic situation, as well as to the conditions of the external and internal labour market. More particularly, the latter category specializes, on the one hand, in internal quantitative or numerical flexibility that consists of adopting individual or group, seasonal, permanent or casual differences in working time of the staff, depending on production needs (flexible or reduced working hours, overtime, and shift work). On the other hand, the external quantitative or numerical flexibility encourages geographic mobility of labour force depending on production needs, and its employment so as human resources management (recruitment-redundancy) and its exploitation in the context of specific forms of employment (part-time, seasonal, casual, intermittent, temporary contracts, procurement, agency work, loaned employee-jobbing work at home, teleworking at home, in telecentres or tele-farmhouses, etc.) become as free as they can be.

The variety of forms of labour flexibility is great, but, according to the literature and in order for a more detailed presentation of basic forms and kinds of flexibility to be facilitated, the following forms are mentioned (Malinvaud, 1998):

First, "Flexibility of wage labour", which is, for example, related to destabilization of earnings, their free variation depending on the outputs of businesses, etc. Second, "Qualitative and functional labour flexibility", which is, for example, associated with the enhancement of labour, upgrading skills, the development of employees' multipotency and initiatives etc. Third, "Internal quantitative or numerical labour flexibility or flexibilization-reorganization of working time", which involves flexible hours, shifts, reduction or settlement of the weekly or annual hours of work etc. Fourth, "External quantitative or numerical labour flexibility", which, for example, concerns the freedom in recruitment-redundancy, geographic labour mobility, the use of special forms of employment, such as part-time work, procurement contracts, fixed-term employment etc.

Despite the necessary separation in categories, flexibilities of labour are shown in practice in various combinations or contrasts between them, coupled or not with the overall strategic restructuring of productive forces of economy. Qualitative labour flexibility is the most difficult but most appropriate way to adapt and modernize. For this reason, it is ranked among the so-called aggressive strategies of flexibility, whereas quantitative flexibility often contradicts the goals of qualitative and belongs to defensive or conjectural strategies (Boyer, 1987, pp. 107–129, especially pp. 109–111; Boyer and Coriat, 1986, p. 63). The last two decades, at European level, main exponents of the two basic models of flexibility is, on the one hand, Sweden that has adopted a rather qualitative model and, on other hand, Great Britain that has adopted a rather quantitative model, aligned with neoliberal spirit. Between these two versions there are countries that get closer to the Swedish model until the mid of the 1980s, as for example Germany, whereas France seemed to show a tendency towards the British model. As far as the Mediterranean countries are concerned and especially southern European countries such as Italy, Spain and Greece, beyond the legal practice of flexibility, which was dealing basically with quantitative flexibility, the phenomenon of illegal labour flexibility causes sensation, which displays size similar to that of the informal economy of these countries (Kouzis, 2001, pp. 33- 39). More specifically in Greece, while a wide range of more flexible forms of employment are operating, illegal flexibility is being developed. This a feature, which is expressed either with a breach of individual provisions of labour and social security laws on behalf of certain enterprises or with the full abuse of labour rights of the unreported, "black", labour (Kouzis, 2002, pp. 257–265). The practice of illegal flexibility is somehow a tradition in the Greek labour market, favoured not only by the extensive growth of informal economy, immigration and, especially, of illegal immigration in recent years but also by serious inadequacies that the control mechanisms of the legislation has always had.

7.2 Internal Quantitative Labour Flexibility-Flexibility of the Working Time: Dimensions of the Problem and Basic Forms

Working time is one of the first issues of employment conditions that were settled in industrial relations by lawmakers of various European countries after industrial revolution. There were laws on this issue known during the last century (Geary, 1988, p. 60; Abendrot, 1976, pp. 20–21 and 32–33; Rojot and Blanpain, 1994, p. 5): In 1802, 1833, 1847 and 1850 in Great Britain, in 1839 in Prussia, in 1848 and 1850 in France, 1873 in Spain, and, in 1889 in Belgium, there were laws that regulated working time and, more especially, they imposed restrictions on hours of daily labour and employment of small ages.

Since the beginning of the 20th century, a multiplicity of laws has followed, of which the most significant have been those that consolidated 8-hour working time, and were introduced in 1919 in Germany and 1921 in Netherlands and France (Blanpain, 1986, p. 193). Legislative activity on working time occurred during the decades that followed in almost all European countries. Nowadays, there is also basic legislation on this issued in all developed countries[147].

Working time – while at first it seems like a completely technical issue, in relation to which restrictions are imposed rather for reasons of hygiene and safety of employees – is in essence a point (Rojot and Blanpain, p. 2) where social interests and opposing views meet, and, of course, it is a key issue for the employees' protection, the competitiveness of enterprises and for each economy as a whole. Since its beginning as an issue, working time has become an issue with political and moral dimension in labour relation since it is connected with the freedom of labour and social protection. It is an issue of religious dimension, considering the holiday of Saturday and Sunday. It is an issue of economic and social dimension, being associated with the profitability of enterprises, with employees' income and leisure, facilitating the general consumer public[148] and, mainly, with the controversial issue of job creation through the redistribution of volume of available jobs[149]. This is an issue which ultimately affects actual human reproduction – see

147 See ILO, (1986), Vol. 5 (2), p. 22, where there is a detailed listing of the modern legal framework in many member states on working time.

148 See statements by the representatives of the business world, who brought the matter to the Athenean newspaper "To VIMA", 11-10-1992, pp. D24-D25.

149 This problem has been largely supported by the measures proposed in the "White Paper on Development, the Competitiveness and Employment. In particular, see Kouzis, 1994, pp. 16–19.

limits on working time to protect motherhood (Rojot and Blanpain, p. 2) – and the whole organization of modern social life.

For all these reasons working time has been a major issue of regulation in Labour Law, labour market and industrial relations (Koukiadis, pp. 1–6). Nowadays, it is also one of the key points that articulates a new equilibrium that is detected in modern relations of capital and labour, as it is also revealed clearly from the whole recent discussion about flexibility (ETUI, 1985A, pp. 99–149).

The interest shown today in flexible forms of employment and working time arrangements is rooted in economic and social reasons (ILO, 1986, p. 1). Fierce competition and rapid technological development with changes that they make in productive structures have pushed entrepreneurs to seek various productive and organizational ways to adapt business operation to changing market fluctuations. One of these ways is the expansion of time operations of the business some hours a day or a week, as well as the adoption of any other changes in seasonal or occasional basis while flexible forms of employment and working time are being utilized so that these new functional needs can be met (Toutziarakis, 1990, pp. 183–193).

At the same time, the modern employee faces many and various opportunities and options for labour and social life. Employees as consumers may prefer certain services being provided for a longer period or for more hours a day. Young employees, employees with family responsibilities and, especially, women, the elderly and retired, although they are social categories with diverse orientations, are likely to have in common a particular interest in some special forms of employment or flexible arrangements of working time (Tzekinis, 1986, pp. 6–7).

7.2.1 Problems and Prospects of Part-time Employment

Another good reason concerns major changes in working time that have occurred in recent decades in many developed countries. More specifically, in recent years in many countries, working hours have conventionally been reduced[150]. Employees and trade unions had focused their interest in claiming the reduction of working time as a means both to improve employment conditions and living standards and for their increased rates of unemployment to be dealt with. This

150 The reduction of working hours resulting from chronological tables particularly included in: (a) The Employment and Training Report of the President, (1979), U.S. Department of Labor, Washington, D.C., p. 322; (b) The Statistical History of the United States from Colonial Times to the Present, Fairfield Publishers Stanford, CN 1965, pp. 92 and 94; and (c) ETUI, 1979, p. 4.

interest of the employees' side in the working time has been utilized by the employer's side for its benefit (ILO, 1986, p. 1). To ensure flexibility in and low cost of the labour so that the needs of the demand were satisfied, the employer's side proceeded and expressed the major modern employer's request (Christoforatos, 1989, pp. 385–386) for flexibility in labour relations and suggested a variety of special forms of employment or reorganization of working time as alternative solutions.

Nowadays, one of the major problems in relation to working time – essentially a methodological one – is what the working time means in relation to which experience dictates that restrictions are imposed or that it is reduced or it is made various changes and flexible arrangements. In most countries there are many different concepts of the term "working time". However, as a rule, the strict sense of the term (Rojot and Blanpain, 1994, pp. 13–15) is accepted by the Member States of the European Union (EU), which is based on a fundamental distinction: On the one hand, between the hours that are really used for employment, and, on the other hand, between the hours during which the employee while s/he is not working formally, either s/he is at his/her employer's disposition to perform a task, or s/he is engaged in tasks that are out of his/her actual working object but they are related to it.

The most important issue today, however, in relation to working time is the provided restrictions of it (Paoli-Pelvey, 1993, pp. 395–421), which are divided into two categories: There is a category of restrictions, which aim to reduce (ETUI, 1980, pp. 1–63) the duration of labour and are related to specific periods or days on which the employee will not work. These restrictions concern specific categories of people, such as youth, women, people with disabilities, pensioners, people who do specific tasks – such as night work, shift work, part-time or casual employment – and are established in most European countries either by legislation or conventionally (Blanpain, 1986, p. 195–196). These restrictions can be considered as "normal restrictions" (Rojot and Blanpain, 1994, p. 18), while at the same time exceptions are often provided today – that is, more flexible arrangements – for exceptional cases, force majeure, technological, productive or organizational restructuring of the business (Rojot, 1991).

Nowadays, working time reduction, and, in particular, its disconnection from the time that the business runs has formed both for the employer and the employee new challenges, new needs but also new opportunities. Nevertheless, it has raised a big issue on the future and the characteristics of employment itself (Cordova, 1986, pp. 641–657, esp. pp. 641–643 and 655–656). Reduction of working time in the form of adopting specific forms of employment and flexible working time arrangements will simply mean an increase in flexibility and in the creation of new employment opportunities to deal with high levels of unemployment in European countries or will mark the extensive and rapid replacement of the traditional model of full-time employment from other shorter employment forms, which will be unstable and insecure; and, with a load of various questions, of course, even when compared to the organization of social life in general.

The new regulations that have been presented internationally in relation to working time and employment are an aspect of the overall trend to search for flexibility. These include in particular a whole series of measures, of which the most important are: facilitation of overtime, reorganization of working time on a weekly, monthly or annual basis, shifts, flexible schedules and placement of a series of flexible forms of employment.

Overtime is a basic, common and convenient form of flexibility in working time. Overtime is considered the time that the employee is employed in addition to the hours s/he works normally under statutory or contractual working hours, for which there are legal or contractual restrictions accordingly (ILO, 1984b, p. 35, par. 68). Since labour pay is tied with the concept of working hours, when this is exceeded creates demands for extra pay. Conventionally or under legislation, regulation of issues of overtime usually focuses on specific points. First, a common element in national regulations of various states concerns the provision of the approval of overtime (Paoli-Pelvey, 1993, pp. 399–400 par. 17 & par. 21) which as arrangement, theoretically at least, aims to diagnose whether there is a need for them. These regulations are usually supplemented with restrictions concerning the extent of overtime on daily, weekly or yearly basis (ILO, 1986, p. 10). The compensation with which the employee is compensated for overtime may take the form of either a payment or a provision of leisure from work, or a combination of these two systems. In any case, however, overtime connotes the employee's reward for the extra fatigue and decrease of his/her family and social life, which is brought about by the longer labour time (ETUI, 1986, pp. 25–26).

Similarly, it should be noted that there are many forms of reorganization – arrangement of working time on daily, weekly, monthly or seasonal basis (ETUI, 1985a, pp. 131–132). This involves, of course, reorganization of the classic form of the 8-hour and 5-day (employment), that is, 40-hour or possibly of fewer-hour employment a week which was consolidated in some countries, companies, industries or sectors (Paoli-Pelvey, 1993, p. 397, Index 1). It should also be noted that most forms of reorganizing working time that have been introduced in recent years are positively or negatively related to the length of time of daily or weekly work – that is, increase or decrease in 5-day and 8-hour employment – as well as the duration of the operation of the enterprise. The same applies to the plethora of forms of shiftwork adopted, which are usually combined (ETUI,

1986, pp. 44–46) with the extension time of running the business and which are usually connected with night work, systems of rotating shifts, work that diverges from the model of full-time employment, or even with employment during Saturday and Sunday on weekend.

Other forms of reorganizing working time are arrangements for flexible schedules (Evans, 1973, pp. 40–42 & pp. 45–48; ETUI, 1985a, p. 122) under which employees have a choice – within a certain time framework – of the time of arrival and departure, without, however, the total of their working time being changed on a daily, weekly or monthly basis. The principal, however, elements of the time schedule that are subject to flexible arrangements are the arrival time, departure time and breaks (Paoli-Pelvey, 1993, p. 411). Flexible arrangements can be made on an individual or a collective basis; that is, a flexible arrangement of working time can concern either an employee or a group of employees or all employees. Moreover, either flexibility can be pre-established in consultation with employees, or the employee can select the hours s/he will work each day, of course, within the limits set.

It should be noted that, regarding these flexible forms of organizing working time, the attitude of trade unions in most European countries has been very cautious, whereas a request for reduction of working time has clearly recorded which will be based primarily on the traditional framework of its organization (5 days x 8 hours) (ETUI, 1980, pp. 12–63 and pp. 89–99). More specifically, regarding overtime, whereas trade unions accept their use in view of contingencies, they reject any thought of their extensive and generalized application, if something like that limits, as they support, the opportunities for new jobs to be created. Trade unions also appear cautious or even negative with the introduction of flexible reorganization of working time on a weekly, monthly, seasonal or yearly basis, while they show a milder attitude towards shifts – additional working groups – either these are combined with extension of time of the operation of the business or not (ETUI, 1986, pp. 32–33, 41–42 and 55–56). Finally, regarding flexible working hours, it should be noted that no strong reactions have been registered by employees' side, as this side considers that such forms have no negative impact on the quality and conditions of working life. At the same time, such forms have a positive aspect that they often lead to reduced absenteeism, increased productivity and creation of multiple labour force qualification without directly affecting negatively the employment.

What, however, seems to concern most trade unions is the fact that especially some forms of flexible working hours lead essentially to individualization of labour relations, thus resulting in the disempowerment of employees' cohesion and have negative impact on the exercise of their collective rights. However, safety valve for this problem seems to be – in the opinion of trade unions – the formation of contractual arrangements for the introduction of flexible working hours (ETUI, 1985a, pp. 124–125 and 155–157).

7.3 Flexibility and Reduction of the Working Time: European and Greek Experience

What characterizes the organization of labour before the appearance of large manufacturing plants that used mechanical energy was the "irregular rhythm." Depending on the overall work of the week or fortnight, the working day was lengthened or shortened (Mamford, 1994, pp. 27 and 69). The nature of that employment did not require the use of the "exact" and financially important time, a fact that allowed humanization of social time and its non-division into working time and non-working time.

The changes in manufacturing techniques that resulted from the use of conventional machines required a greater synchronization of work, a higher accuracy in measuring time experience and a new organization of the social time, adapted to new social and industrial production relations of the model, such as that was supported by Puritanism and Protestant ethics. Getting rid of old habits of people at work and in social life, that is, the change of the pre-industrial framework of labour and social life was dealt with great reactions at first, as it was natural. But in the next step, to the extent a discipline of time was imposed, employees began to struggle not against work but against reducing working time. The factory employees of the first generation "learned" from their employers and supervisors the importance of time. The employees of the second generation organized committees to reduce working time and were mobilized to achieve a 10-hour work. The third generation went on strikes for overtime or hourly earnings. It had accepted the employers' rationale and had learned to use it to its benefit; it has learned the lesson that "time is money" very well (Mamford, 1994, p. 51).

In the industrial model of the Fordist period, working time was characterized by homogeneity, standardization, mechanical rhythms and precise timing, since it presented a strict definition and fixed reference points, that is, steady daily, weekly and annually course, but fixed time point in beginning and end. Exceeding the industrial society, which was based on the typical working time, and the transition to post-industrial production and society makes contemporary human being confront, among other things, a new conflict between the old industrial and the new postindustrial organization of social time. Within the framework of the Fordist production, working time is differentiated and characterized by a variety of exceptional accuracy, absence of any time barrier, whereas the fixed points of reference that defined it in the past were lifted, the working time necessary for the production of the social product is reduced due to new technologies, and the measure of its calculation is altered, since the diverse business needs retain the annual basis compared to the weekly one, as the most probationary period, which used to be traditionally the mainstream (Karantinos, Ketsetzopoulou, and Mouriki, 1997, p. 109).

Following these, only two elements, which are associated with the concept of working time, remain firm today: First, the concern for social management of the non-working part of social time, and, second, the steady downward trend in working time, from a historical point of view, which stresses the previous concern.

The duration of working time, in its historical evolution, presents a downward trend in all countries of the world. In 1837, working time was 80 hours a week and 14 hours a day. In 1890 it fell down to 60 hours a week and 10 hours a day. Since 1919, in France the working day has been 8 hours a day, while in 1936 the annual leave of two weeks was established (Tahar, 1985 pp. 13–25). Today, the usual weekly working time of Europeans is 40.4 hours a week, while the usual weekly working time of the Greeks is at the same level (40.5 hours). Within a century the annual working time was reduced from 3,000 hours significantly (Georgakopoulou, 1998, p. 33). So now the real annual working time for the full-time employed in manufacturing is: for the Japanese 1,957 hours, for the Americans 1,896 hours, for the Portuguese 1,882 hours, for the Greeks 1,832 hours, for Finns 1,790 hours, for the Germans 1,602 hours, for the Austrians 1,657 hours, for the Danes 1,672 hours, for the Swedes 1,154 hours, while the average in the European Union is 1,700 hours (Hunt, 1998; Hoidas, 1997, pp. 19 and 115).

From a historical point of view, however, the reduction of working time is set under a different perspective every time: Sometimes as an important issue for the employee's health. Sometimes as an issue of saving more free time so that the employee's living standards, quality of life and personal development are enhanced. Sometimes, not as a means of redistribution of productivity and the existing workload, which shrinks because of new technologies. Some other times, it is taken as a means of redistribution of productivity and the existing workload, which is shrunk due to new technologies; that is, essentially, as a means of income redistribution and combating unemployment. In recent years, especially during the 1990s, the issue became the subject of intense discussion and relevant studies. Nowadays, it is presented both as a possible solution to the problem of unemployment and as a "like exchange" to employees to accept flexible working time arrangements or other labour flexibility (Gabroglou, 2001, p. 59).

In recent years the number and range of relevant surveys and studies, carried out by governments, international organizations and research centres, have illustrated, on the one hand, the expanded interest, and, on the other hand, the concerns that arise. The difficulty in determining the impact of the reduction of working time on employment lies in the fact that only assumptions can be made on the factors associated with employment, for example, employees' total compensation, technological equipment, labour costs and productivity growth, growth of labour. Certainly, difficulties and divergences in various existing studies proliferate, if other parameters – which are difficult to identify – are considered, such as changes in labour supply, replacement of labour by newer technological infrastructure and the nature of business as "labour intensive" or "capital intensive" (Gabroglou, 2001, p. 117)

The attractive argument that the reduction of working hours contribute to employment growth is difficult to be proven and does not lead to reliable conclusions regarding the specific contribution of the measure to increasing employment, since the combination of many factors, which are not well defined and stable, have positive or negative economic and social impact of the reduction of working time (Gabroglou, 2001, p. 60).

Nevertheless, significant developments have been recorded in Europe in the last twenty years with regard to the issue of reducing working time. In 1981, mobility around this issue began in France, with the result the workweek in metallurgy was formed in 38.5 hours and in chemicals sector in 38 hours.

Nevertheless, due to the fact that this development was considered responsible for the problems of productivity and competitiveness of enterprises, since 1983 there has been prevailed the view that the issue should be subject of bargaining not at industry but rather at enterprise level (Mousouris, 1996, p. 25). Similar developments occurred in Britain. Since the late 1970s there have been decisions first in metallurgy, on reduction of working time. So, in 1981, the weekly working time was reduced from 40 to 39 hours, whereas from the mid 1989 there were enterprises in the mechanical engineering industry that agreed to reduce the working week to 37.5 hours, in return for reduction of breaks and intensification of labour. In Germany, although the issue had been known since 1978, it came back in 1984 with the result that – after seven-week strikes in steel industry and twelve-week strike in typography, there would be an agreement on the reduction of the working week to 35 hours. The large and powerful trade union of industrial employees, the IG Metall, after three agreements were concluded in 1984, 1987 and 1990, applied 35 hours with the commitment not to re-request for further reduction of working time until 1998.

Already in 1984, Volkswagen and IG Metall, aiming to maintain employment, agreed to reduce the working week to 28.5 hours, while reducing earnings (Mousouris, 1996). Their example was followed by another industry of massive size, Siemens, which adopted the reduction of working hours. The German company agreed with IG Metall, which counts 2.7 million members, to reduce the time of working week of the staff over 55 years of age and reduce net earnings to 82%. At the same time, since the beginning of 1999 the employees of a large steel enterprise in Belgium, whereas they had a typical 34-hour working week – instead of 37 hours they had had until then, they actually continued to work 37 hours a week, but got paid for 34 and, in exchange, they got a 17-day additional holidays. Moreover, the recycling system of employees combined with retraining was implemented in Denmark. The alternation of the employed and unemployed in the existing jobs resulted in decreasing unemployment from 12.3% that it was in 1993 to 8% in 1997 and thus, 110,000 new jobs were created, of which 90,000 in the private sector (Hoidas, 1997).

What is conspicuous – not only from the above illustrative cases but also from a thorough and detailed examination of developments in European countries (OMED, 1993, esp. pp. 1–12) – is that generally the reduction in working time was not introduced but conventionally; that this was not implemented across the board and binding, but mainly by collective contracts and agreements at industry or enterprise level, depending even on the specific problems and the dynamism that existed in each case, and that the reduction in working time that was adopted in most cases was combined with various forms of defensive (it is mainly based on low wages and many working hours) or aggressive flexibility (it is combined with the reorganization of working time and the more intensive use of technological equipment) (Karantinos, Ketsetzopoulou and Mouriki, 1997, p. 123), a development that fueled the debate on "deregulation" of labour relations through bargaining (Daskalakis, 1995a, p. 248; Spyropoulos, 1987, p. 10).

The first attempt to regulate labour flexibility in Greece was Law 1892 of 1990. The Third Chapter of this Law – which should be noted that it was the Law for Economic Development of that period and not a Labour Law- included regulations for part-time, introduced the requirement of written agreement between the employee and the employer for its introduction and provided the framework of rights of part-time employees (Daskalakis, 1995b, pp. 42–44). At the same time, this Law offered the applicability of the system of four-group employment to enterprises with continuous operation, with the employees' consent, and introduced the possibility for these enterprises, if their operation requires it, to hire extra staff for the weekend so that this staff is employed in two alternating shifts for twelve hours a day (Daskalakis, 1995b, pp. 45–46). Furthermore, the same Law established the possibility of working time settlement, after enterprise-level collective agreements or agreements for up to three months had been signed, with an increase in employees' working time to 9 hours a day and 48 a week, provided the average daily working time of reference period does not exceed 40 hours (Daskalakis, 1995b, pp. 44–45).

Moreover, the last decade for the first time in Greece there have been developed institutions and social dialogue[151] processes, the institution of employees councils and collective bargaining (Koukiadis, 1992) has been enhanced, new institutions to mitigate conflict and resolution of collective labour disputes and new reliable mediation processes were introduced, as well as a mixed system of arbitration of a completely alternative character, which has replaced the previous state-controlled, mandatory and socially discredited model, and new processes of public dialogue. These new institutional data – combined with the expansion of the implementation and the enlargement of the scope of collective bargaining, as well as the safeguards for the decentralization of their system, by upgrading industry agreements and establishing operational agreements – have reinforced the direct dialogue between employees and employers and indeed about a whole range of issues of mutual interest, including working time. This is of special importance for the issue under discussion, given that it is reasonably supported that the general trend of contractualization of regulations governing industrial relations is in line with that of their flexibilization.

In 1998, after the "Confidence Pact Towards 2000" (Ministry of Labour and Social Security, 1997) was concluded between the Government, employees and employers, the enactment of Law 2639 followed, by which issues of employment flexibility were regulated. More specifically, issues as how to determine social security of special forms of employment such as providing work or independent services, teleworking, the piecework (under contract) were provided. Furthermore, a new institutional framework for part-time employment was created, its definition was broadened since both "rotation" and intermittent employment went under this category, time calculation from daily and weekly to fortnightly and monthly basis was extended, and most importantly, the expansion of the institution of part-time employment in the public sector was also provided.

The same law formulated both the legislative framework for local employment pacts, which, among other things, provided the possibility to set wages below the level of industry collective agreements and up to the level of the general thresholds set by the national general collective labour agreements. Finally, Law 2639 of 1998 expanded the possibility of working time arrangement conventionally,

151 Papaioannou, 1996, esp. pp. 3–7, where reference is made to the innovation economies of the 1990s and particularly to the Organization for Mediation & Arbitration (OMED); Daskalakis, 2004a, pp. 109–112; and Daskalakis, 1995a.

over a three-month application framework which was initially provided by Law 1892 of 1990. More specifically, Law 2639 of 1998 provided that small businesses, of five to twenty people, can – with the employees' consent – engage in excess of the daily employment up to 9 hours daily, for up to two months. In addition, businesses that employ more than twenty people were provided that, with a collective contract or agreement with the employees' council, it was now possible for the business to make an excess of an hour a day and up 9-hour daily employment, the conventional daily working hours for a period of up to three months. Whereas, at the same time, in specific instances associated with objective or technical reasons it is possible for the business to exceed the daily working hours by two hours up to 48 hours a week for a period up to six months (Annual Report, 2000, pp. 138–139).

From the aforementioned regulations that were product of the strategy of social dialogue and the orientation of the state to the strategy of adaptability (Ministry of Labour and Social Security, 2000, pp. 48–49) to industrial relations, it seems that at least those concerning the organization of working time were proven ineffective, since they were exploited by employers and employees, thus, they were soon altered[152]. Two years later, in 2000, Law 2874 was passed; this Law introduced a new regulatory framework, aiming – as Law 2639 of 1998 – to strengthen the competitiveness of Greek businesses and deal with certain lasting problems, which had been inhibiting the creation of new jobs and had been exacerbating the phenomenon of unemployment, especially, that of long-term[153]. The provisions of the new legislation[154] that came into force in April 2001 include significant regulations. More specifically, that part-time employment in the private sector provides surcharge earning of 7.5% if the employee is paid the minimum wage and his/her employment hours are less than four hours daily. This measure – in addition that it acts as an incentive for the employee's employment in part-time position, thus making proportionately "more expensive" the intra-day part-time employment – acts as a disincentive for the employer for both the use of hourly wage jobs or intra-day part-time as well as any replacement of full-time employment by part-time employment. Furthermore, it was

152 The negative sentiment concerns the measure of the arrangement of the working time, because their regulation has resulted 190.311 contracts relating to such forms. See Ministry of Labour and Social Security, 2000, p. 49.

153 The negative sentiment concerns the measure of the arrangement of the working time, because their regulation has resulted 190.311 contracts relating to such forms. See Ministry of Labour and Social Security, 2000, p. 49.

154 Law 2874/2000, FEK (Government Gazette) 286/29.12.2000/ T.A/ 1rst Issue).

for the first time that some categories of long-term unemployed were offered the opportunity to have part-time employment, while augment their income with financial aid, equivalent to one third of the unemployment benefit for a period of twelve months.

Additionally, the overworked employment was abolished, and, more specifically, the employer's managerial prerogative that s/he may require the employee work up to five hours more a week over 43 hours. These five hours for forty-six (5x46) working weeks are 230 hours a year that the employer has no more right to seek the employee's additional employment, who then is obliged to work. Furthermore, the increase in overtime costs discouraged their use. That measure aimed to strengthen the incentives for new recruitment, instead of relying on expensive overtime, mainly to meet the seasonal demand or increase production[155].

At the same time, amendments were made to the regime of working time arrangement, the usability of which was combined now with the reduction of working time. More specifically, on the one hand, employers were offered the opportunity to engage, in agreement with employee representatives, in working time arrangement and, more particularly, in the flexible use of 138 hours a year per employee. On the other hand, the employees of the company where the implementation of working time arrangement is agreed upon are favoured with the reduction of their work by 92 hours a year, that is equivalent to 2 hours a week, that is, a reduction of weekly working hours on average from 40 to 38 hours. This means that employers and employees jointly guarantee that the reduction of working time does not undermine the competitiveness of the company, but rather the way it is implemented – that is, associated with a general review of how businesses run and working hours – essentially offers benefits to all sides, giving the employee the opportunity to earn free time, contributing to the creation of new jobs, while ensuring the competitiveness and the business itself.

These reforms in the institutional system of organization of the labour market seemed, however, to have begun to pay off, since there were some early positive results. The regulation on working time arrangement had already seemed to have started and have been utilized. More specifically, at the first phase that this law was effective, there were agreements in three companies that were employing from 100 to 320 people, for calculating working time on an annual basis for

155 Reply to the Questionnaire of the European Commission, op. cit. This objective serves the fact that the legal working time is dropping from 48 to 43 hours per week and that increased remuneration of overtime, namely the "peculiar" overtime from 125% to 150%, the "regular" overtime from 125% to 175% and the "illegal" overtime from 200% to 250%.

38 hours average weekly work, came into force in July 2001 (Data of "Labour Inspectors", 2001). These businesses are a flour mill, a shoe industry and a paper mills. What this case shows is that it depends on social partners making more legislative framework in order to reap the benefits that the implementation implies for each side. Finally, regarding the measure for overwork and overtime, it should be noted that this seemed to have started to bear fruits, since many businesses as early as in June 2001 had announced that in view of the new provisions were led to an increase in jobs in order to maintain production levels (Data of the Supreme Labour Council, 2001).

Assuming that the "statism" and the intervention of the 1980s resulted, at least at the institutional level, to "close the scales" in favour of the employee's side in the regulation of labour relations, it should also be recognized that the last decade the state with its interventions, which seem to correspond to the model of democratic negotiated neo-corporatism (Daskalakis, 2004a, pp. 104–143, mainly p. 105; Daskalakis, 1995a, pp. 168–173), has brought an institutional balance in industrial relations and, more particularly, in the issue of working time – between state regulation and collective autonomy, an institutional balance that allows the operation of the labour market in Greece to rely on socially protective but also flexible and legal frameworks that cover a large range of most modern needs of both business[156] and labour relations.

The flexibility, however, in the labour market in Greece is not only ensured by the fact that settled some basic quantitative forms of employment flexibility have been regulated legislatively. The existence of "pure rules of the game" – after a large part of the rules governing industrial relations have been modernized the last twenty years – assist enterprises in decision making in relation to the adoption of flexible policies that reduce labour costs. The same result, more or less, comes out of the existence of peaceful employment conditions in the private sector in recent years as well as out of the consolidation of an environment of trust, dialogue and cooperation between the parties. The fact that all these have become reality are confirmed by the operation of the Economic and Social Committee and the new mechanisms of resolving collective labour disputes, National General Collective Labour Agreements that have already been concluded from the 1990s onwards and, generally, by the new major regulatory capacities that

156 According to EUROSTAT 1996, the 1/3 of industrial enterprises and the 86% of all Greek enterprises, compared to 71% which is the weighted average term in the European Union, use the shifts systems introduced by the article 40 of law 1892/1990. See Labour Institute GSEE-AD.E.D.Y., 2000), p. 137.

are utilized by the social partners and are acquired by the institution of collective bargaining after the enactment of Law 1876 of 1990.

The whole framework that facilitates flexibility is further enhanced: First, by the extensive illegal employment, mainly by economic immigrants; second, by the limited effectiveness of control mechanisms of employment; and, third and most importantly, by the network of active labour market policies that have been promoted recent years and have dramatically enhanced the possibilities of increasing the qualitative functional labour flexibility. The combination of data from the entire aforementioned spectrum can help decisively in the development of flexible working time, as it has become evident from the respective European experience (OMED, 1993; Karantinos, Ketsetzopoulou and Mouriki, pp., 109–152).

With the recent Law of 2005 an extensive intervention was accomplished, particularly as regards the status of overwork, overtime, and working time arrangement. More specifically, at first overtime hours increased from 3 – they occurred between the 41st and the 43rd hours- to 5 hours a week – they happened between the 41st and 45th hours. In Business of 6 working days a week, overtime will now be 8 hours a week (between the 41st and the 48th hour). Overtime work, as it is known, the employer under managerial prerogative can demand it and enforce it on employee. Moreover, non-acceptance of overtime work may be a reason to dismiss the employee. With the new law the employer's managerial prerogative is extended concerning overwork, since now the employer can require an overwork not only of three hours but also of 5 or 8 hours, if it is about businesses of six days a week. At the same time, the pay of overwork and overtime is decreased as follows: (a) the hour of overtime used to be paid according to the hourly rate plus 50%, whereas now the increment is reduced to 25%; (b) each hour of illegal overtime was paid according to the hourly rate increased by 150%, whereas the increment is now reduced to 100%.

"Something completely novel," is that the new Law eliminated the concept of illegal overtime. The new Law states that whatever overtime occurred notwithstanding, hereinafter they will be called "exceptionally" overtime. This, in addition to its intricate view of its authors which is echoed in it, will have very significant consequences in practice. Because, despite the fact that administrative fines have been ineffective, the only thing that might be holding employers from circumventing the Law on overtime was the fear of lawsuits by the Labour Inspectorate, which was, however, supported legally by the characterization of overtime as illegal.

It is a fact that the current until the new Law is effective regulating system of overtime (i.e. the system of Labour Law 2000/2001- Giannitsis Law) was quite restrictive and "tight". The restriction on hours of overwork and overtime and their prevention by increasing their cost had created pressures on businesses, which largely offset the system's flexibility of working time settlement. This tight system of overtime, the like of which had never been applied in Greece in the past, aimed to increase employment. Nevertheless, in practice both the system of overtime was circumvented mainly on the pretext of pre-Olympic period and the settlement system of working time was not applied almost at all. Moreover, it seems that employees wanted the overtime system to be more relaxed than cheaper, because in many industries labour income is substantially supplemented by overtime.

The same Law introduced a new system of working time settlement concerning enterprises to which contractual working hours to 40 hours a week is applicable. The same was provided by the until then effective settlement system (of Labour Law 2000/2001- Giannitsis Law), but it also stated that enterprises that make use of the settlement will have an average weekly working time on an annual basis of 38 hours, that is, a reduction in working hours so that employment increases. In contrast, today the new system maintains 40 hours as an annual average of working week, for those companies that introduce a system of working time settlement. The new Law introduced a system of working time settlement of two speeds. First, it provides a 4-month system of working time settlement, where the working day may be increased by two hours for two months and may be decreased by two hours for other two months. Furthermore, it provides an annual reconciliation system of 256 hours of working time from annual working time (whereas until then the current system merely provided 138 hours be settled).

Under the system of working time arrangement introduced by the new Law, the employee may well refuse to provide this extra work; nevertheless, this refusal should not be contrary to the "good faith". It is obvious that it is "too heavy" for an employee to "bear the burden" of this evidence. What isn't truly contrary to good faith? Is the employee's weakness due to fatigue or due to family commitments? His/her desire to spend his/her spare time for personal development or entertainment? During the period of increased employment, daily employment should not exceed 10 hours; this means that in practice the working day will be of 10 hours during periods of increased employment.

In an absolutely original and unusual way, the system of working time arrangement introduced by the new Law is interwoven with a special regulation with the system overtime. More specifically, in addition to the basic rules of overtime made by another Article of the Bill, the Article on the organization of working time provides that overtime can be utilized during periods of reduced employment within the framework of the settlement. For example, employees of 5-day work, who will be working for 30 instead of 40 hours during the period of reduced employment, the employer, with managerial prerogative, may impose five hours overtime a week. Thus, the employee reaches to work 30 + 5 = 35 hours during the period of reduced working time, unless the employer also requests overtime, as this overtime is quite cheap so far, and which – it should be noted – would be too difficult for the employee to refuse in practice. Similarly, an employee of a 6-day employment who will be working, for example, 36 instead of 48 hours during period of reduced employment, the employer, with managerial, prerogative may impose a 8-hour overtime. Thus, this employee works 36 + 8 = 44 hours a week.

Of course, the remuneration of overtime, when combined with an arrangement in this way, is increased by 30% instead of 25%, as provided for joint overtime (that is, when it is not combined with settlement). Moreover, overtime, which can be discussed about in both previous examples, is provided in Law that, on the one hand, legal overtime can collect a salary increment of 75% instead of 50% as provided for joint overtime (that is, when it is not combined with a settlement) and, on the other hand, the illegal ones – "the exceptionally overtime" – can collect a salary increment of 100%, that is, as this overtime is paid even when it is not combined with a settlement. Instead, in the system that was effective until then, the employee had tangible returns, if s/he entered in settlement; for example, s/he had a 15-day leave, which is particularly appreciable.

The system of working time arrangement is introduced at first with an agreement between the enterprise and the most representative trade union at the operational level or between the enterprise and the council of employees. The current hitherto system provided an introduction of settlement by agreement even if there was no trade union in the enterprise, since it provided the intervention of the respective enterprise unions. It also provided that the relevant differences were referred to the independent Organization for Mediation and Arbitration (OMED) of Law 1876 of 1990 "On free collective bargaining", which was passed when the Universal Government was in power. The new Law came to alter Law 1876 of 1990 "On Free Collective Bargaining", which was voted with an agreement between employees, employers and all parliamentary parties when Universal Government was in power. The new Law describes a procedural framework for negotiating settlement agreements on working time and reference of such disputes to a peculiar arbitration regime. In other words, this Law is concerned with issues that are the subject of collective bargaining, which are regulated by Law 1876 of 1990, which was of universal consensus and which was sought today with all diligence not to be harmed by any unilateral political interventions until today.

Within this context, according to the new Law, disputes arising when bargaining about settlement agreements of working time is in process are not referred to the system of independent Mediation and Arbitration of the OMED of Law 1876 of 1990 "On Free Collective Bargaining" (which is probably one of the most important institutional achievements of the past 15 years in the national industrial relations system), but rather to state-controlled (Arbitration) Committees, something that bring he national industrial relations system back "memories" of "state compulsory arbitration". More specifically, the failure of a bargaining for a 4-month settlement for 4 months is referred to a 5-member Prefectural Committee (1 social inspector, 2 employers' representatives and employees' representatives). To the same committee, however, an application is directly submitted by the employer so that the arrangement system is approved, if there is no business association or council of employees in the business, something that indirectly supports the employer's managerial prerogative. Whereas, finally, disputes arising from the implementation of settlement agreements, which should be the subject of the OMED, are resolved by Labour Inspectorates, that is, by the state.

Policies, regulations and settlements for the labour market and especially for flexibility should: (a) be integrated in wider strategies and policies for development, competitiveness, employment and social protection; and (b) should arise in processes of social dialogue and broader social agreements. If they do not fit in such a framework, they are the least fragmented and ineffective, as they result from unilateral and, therefore, authoritarian decisions, resulting in widespread flexible labour relations and often in conflict situations with the only put pressure on labour costs in certain enterprises. This legislation moves in this framework, and, finally, with unilateral procedures and processes, imposes regulations that do not serve an overall development strategy – competitiveness – employment – social protection; they do not aim at flexicurity but just at squeezing labour costs. A feature of the authoritarian character of the regulation is to regulate the issue of working time arrangement by altering substantially the Law on Free Collective Bargaining, since it restores the state compulsory arbitration, something that brings the national industrial relations system back "memories" of "state compulsory arbitration".

Furthermore, you should note the following: (a) the government's intervention in the regulation system of overwork and overtime so that their cost get relaxed and reduced, in addition that it cancels a policy tool for the promotion of employment, squeezes labour costs; and (b) this legislative intervention, aiming to make the 8-hour employment flexible, will result in further squeezing of labour cost. Thus, the combination of such two interventions would greatly squeeze labour costs. In practice, there will be a reduction in income of employees, who will have to work longer hours for a proportionately less pay. It is argued that this should happen for the sake of competitiveness, because in Greece there is low productivity of the labour factor. Nevertheless, at this point two issues should be taken into: First, the competitiveness and development cannot only rely only on labour productivity but also on capital, investments etc., which have also shown low productivity; and, second, labour productivity is low in Greece, but the rate at which it increases – it grow this low-productivity – is one of the highest in Europe.

The discussion about flexibility in Greece is often focused on the organization of working time. The issue of flexible working time is normally shown as a demand of enterprises that productions should be aligned with the volatile market demand. Nevertheless, the flexibility of working time is also an issue concerning employees' needs for harmonization of family and social obligations with employment. The available data[157] show the percentages of employees per country member of the European Union who believe that their working hours are aligned with family and social responsibilities "very well or fairly well" or "little or no good at all". It might be assumed that the distinct displeasure that the Greeks express for their working hours stems from the excessive flexibility of working time imposed by employers. But this assumption is not supported by the available evidence, showing that the Greeks have the least flexible working hours in the European Union[158].

The same data shows that working hours for 85.8% of the employees in Greece does not change at all in a month, when the same is true for 76.2% of the employees in the European Union average[159]. Working hours change 1-5 times a month for 9.3% of the employees in Greece – a much lower percentage of the EU average (15.5%). Working hours change from 6 to 10 times a month for 3.3% of the employees in Greece and 4.4% in the whole EU. Yet, it is interesting that Sweden, despite the fact that it has a strong labour movement and a limited impact of neoliberalism, has the greatest percentage of volatile working time in the European Union: only 54.0% of its employees work on fixed-time; for 32.6 % of the employees working hours change 1-5 times a month, and for about 8.4% of the employees in Sweden their working hours vary from 6 to 10 times a month. These findings reinforce the view that the flexibility of working time may serve the needs not only of enterprises but also of employees.

---

157 Employment Observatory Research-Informatics SA (P.A.E.-P.A.E.), (2003), Flexibility and Work Organization: Empirical Evidence from Greece and the European Union, (2003), Working Papers, No 9, March.

158 It should be noted that these figures cover the total of employment, so they include self-employment as well, which in Greece is much higher than in other countries.

159 Only in Portugal there is recorded higher percentage of employment with certain and established working hours (94.2%).

7.4 The 35-hour Week in Italy and France and Reflections on its Implementation in Greece

The 35-hour work a week, full-time without loss of pay, was expressed as a request from the European trade unions since the mid-1970s. Since then it has often returned to the fore along with other claims, which were aimed either to ensure more free time and better quality of life for employees (for example, additional holidays) or to maintain and increase employment (for example, restricting overtime) (Georgakopoulou, 1996, p. 3). The request to work 35 hours a week has been expressed with a special emphasis for the last years, and it is often a core of public dialogue in many European countries. It is supported by strong argumentation and no longer derives from theoretical analyses of working time, "alienation" and "right to laziness" but from urgent social needs and the increase in unemployment that result from corporate restructuring, extensive use of new technologies and reduction in production needs in human labour.

In view of this reality, who could disagree with the reduction of working time? Who wouldn't increase the demand for labour? Who wouldn't want the young to be employed, to be fewer young people unemployed, to have much more free time? However, it seems that the trend is not straight and unequivocal, as shown by the recent experience in Italy and France, which is indeed very revealing. Despite the fact that working hours were reduced in many countries and in individual sectors of economic activities, issue of generalized and mandatory reduction of working time which is most often combined with other flexibility measures no country has launched until recently. Exception was France, while in Italy an effort was made. In 1998, the government R. Prodi in Italy brought a Law to the Italian Parliament to reduce the working week from 40 hours to 35. Aim of the proposed regulation was that as from 1-1-2001 working hours should be reduced from 40 to 35 hours a week to all enterprises employing more than 15 persons. The legislative provision for higher contributions for labour beyond the 35-hour work a week and overtime compensation for hours worked beyond 40 hours would work as a pressure to reduce working time, whereas the issue of the division of working hours and the impact of the reduction of working hours on pay would be determined by collective bargaining. The opposition to the regulation that was expressed by the employers' side by Confindustria, the concerns of the working side that wanted the reduction of the working time to emerge from bargaining, and the successive changes in government led eventually to the non-implementation of the measure.

Widespread implementation of a 35-hour work a week and without loss of pay occurred only in France. The Aubry Law passed in 1998 provided for the establishment of 130 hours a year as a maximum overtime per employee and the reduction of the working week from 39 to 35 hours (calculated on an annual basis) without loss of pay for enterprises employing more than 20 people starting as from the year 2000, and for all other enterprises (employing fewer than 20 people) starting as from the year 2002. Nevertheless, at the same time it provided greater subsidies for enterprise that would hire people with special needs, young and long-term unemployed as well as state subsidies or significant tax reliefs for enterprises entering into agreements to reduce working time by at least 10% and maintain or increase employment by at least 6% (European Foundation for the Improvement of Líving and Employment conditions, 2002).

Regarding this French project though, some remarks are necessary to be made. As important advantages of the regulations of the new Law were considered, at first, the substantial reduction in working time to 62% of full-time employees, the projection for creation of 265,000 new jobs by the end of 2000, the absence of negative effects on the competitiveness of enterprises, the increase in free time, the enhancement of employees' quality of life and the significant development of the institution of collective bargaining, especially at the operational level (Report of the Commisariat General du Plan, 2001). But, whereas there had been very supportive response of enterprises and a number of agreements covered a large number of employees in the initial implementation of the Law, subsequent evaluations confirmed a large deviation of the achievements of the original government targets (Gavroglou, 2001, p. 104). In addition, an interim evaluation of the implementation of measures for a 35-hour work week[160] by the French government showed that they had negative consequences for employees, such as containment or pay freeze, the marginal decrease in the purchasing power of employees, the restriction of benefits, the imposition of irregular hours and labour intensification (Report of the Commisariat General du Plan, 2001).

"The impact of the measures did not seem to have been positive about employment conditions and quality of life of several categories of employees. Many enterprises adapted the new regulations on working time to their own priorities, thus burdening with additional stress, fatigue and more work their employees. In a poll conducted in May 2001, a third of respondents assured that their employment conditions had been worsened. According to the estimates of inspectors, the 35-hour work had increased the incidence of an increasingly productivist management, in which the quest for effectiveness was going along with the employees' accountability and their nervous tension. According to a poll by the Institute of Dares, 25.5% of respondents took extra work. Executives (CEOs)

160 The reference concerns the Aubry Laws.

were those who had been affected most. Therefore, a 35-hour work, with some exceptions, improved neither the lives of the officers not the lives of low-ranking employees. Of course, the latter have been enjoin the 35-hour work but under what conditions?" (Hatzopoulos, 2001, pp. 76–77).

Finally, a crucial observation on the French project of the widespread implementation of the 35-hour work, even without loss of pay, is that, besides being associated with other flexibilities, it relied solely on government subsidy with the rational that resources would be directed to enterprises to encourage employment rather than to passive extraction of unemployment benefits.

It should be noted that, regarding its impact on employment and no matter how it is evaluated, the French project was implemented in a country that compared to other shows rather positive features. First, France is the seventh among the top 15 countries in employment growth in recent years, meaning that there were 6 other countries ahead of it without having implemented the 35-hour work. Second, recent figures show that unemployment in France increased to 9.1% in September from 9% in August 2001. The most serious issue, however, is that unemployment in France increased for the first time in the last three years before June 2001, from the lowest point (8.7%) of 18 years that it was until then (Rise in Unemployment in France, 2001, p. 1).

The issue of the reduction of working time came in Greece by the GSEE as a request for a 35-hour working week without loss of pay in 1995. It was indeed characterized fundamental as it happened for the9-hour working day for five days a week. For the implementation of the measure trade unions accepted as a condition the formation of a sustainable social agreement between the state, employers and employees. According to their approach, direct implementation of the measure could be made in the fields of high productivity and profitability, whereas for SMEs unions, acknowledging as a problem the increase in labour costs, had argued that this could be addressed through government subsidy and transfer of resources – for example, through OAED (: National Organization for the Employment of the Labour Force), tax deductions tax reliefs (Mousouris, 1996b, pp. 22–23). From the employer's side there was a reaction, and it was argued that any implementation of the measure would burden the cost of production, that, combined with the "rigidities" in the labour market, it would lead to disinvestment and shift of funds to the informal economy, and that it would comprehensively undermine the country's progress towards the Economic and Monetary Union (EMU) (Mousouris, 1996b).

The issue, although it has been kept a "low" profile, has been maintained in the news to date. The social partners, despite the legislative developments of recent years in labour flexibility, insist on their views, whereas the state was negative in the proposed generalized and compulsory implementation of the 35-hour work without loss of pay. Today, in view of late employers' proposals to reduce weekly working days, any possible implementation of the 35-hour work without loss of pay is probably invalidated. More specifically, it is claimed that "the reduction of working time is an issue that is always in the news, however, a 35-hour work a week is costly, and, thus, serious issues are raised by the generalized mandatory implementation of such a measure. In earlier periods when the threefold: development – competitiveness – employment was the framework of the motto of the country, the state encouraged the social partners to agree upon the establishment of 35-hour work through bargaining. That was something that there was not fear of it in Greece then! "The state encouraged it, wished it and could have offered a good service towards this direction, by avoiding, nevertheless, at that stage to make this measure generalized[161]". Because the issue of implementation of a 35-hour work was proposed as a measure to combat unemployment, the government side argued that as far as the enhancement of employment was concerned, on the one hand, legislative measures for the structural organization of the labour market and the combined reduction and working time had already been taken, and, on the other hand, the implementation of numerous specific measures to foster employment had been initiated under the National Action Plan for Employment and the implement active policies, which boded well in dealing with the problem as they were operating in an environment governed by high growth and macroeconomic stability[162].

Earlier, the weekly working time was reduced from 48 to 44 and then to 40 hours without loss of pay. Nowadays, the evaluation of the proposed scheme of the obligatory implementation of 35-hour work, among other things, would have to take account of some findings that come out of national and international data. In Greece, 11.5% of Greek employees have already worked less than 35 hours a week, while the EU average is 8.4% (Gavroglou, 2001, p. 94). Indicative categories of employees in Greece who have obtained weekly working time of less than 40 hours through collective bargaining are: beauty consultants 38-hour work a week, teachers 21-hour work a week, civil servants 37.5-hour work a week, employees in shipbuilding zone 37.5-hour work a week, employees in

161 Part of the speech of the Minister of Labour and Social Security, Mr. D. Reppas, during the debate in the Parliament on a proposed law tabled by the left democratic party "Synaspismos" on the "Introduction of the 35 working-hour week and other provisions". See Greek Parliament, OABA, 2/4, 28-11-2001, BZ1128PX, p. 177.

162 op. cit., p. 168; National Action Plan for Employment, 2001, pp. 3–8; Simitis, 2001, pp. 2–5.

refineries of North Aegean 36.5-hour work a week, employees in waste collection in the Organizations of Local Authorities (OTA in Greek) 35-hour work a week, employees in cleaning in the OTA 32.5-hour work a week, miners 25-hour work a week, electricians 37.5 or 38-hour work a week, secondary school teachers 21-hour work a week for the first six years and 18-hour work a week for the last years, teachers of private foreign language institutions 18-hour work a week, engineers and stokers in mines, ships and tanks from 32 to 35-hour work a week,, kindergarteners in public education 15-hour work a week, nurses 27.5-hour work a week in winter and 36-hour work a week in summer, clinicians 37.5-hour work a week plus 6 calls per month, builders 38.45-hour work a week, employees of insurance companies 39-hour work a week, and bank employees 38.20-hour work a week (Karantinos, Ketsetzopoulou and Mouriki, 1997, pp. 146–147).

Moreover, in Greece 46% of Greek employees are self-employed. In fact, if it is taken into account that of the rest 54% 11.5% works less than 35 hours a week and 14.3% less than 40 hours a week, only 28% of employees would have been relevant the regulation under discussion (Gavroglou, 2001, pp. 120–121). Furthermore, should be borne in mind that, according to the 1998 Employment Report, economies with longer working hours have higher participation rates than those with shorter working hours, and this difference shows a substantial increasing trend. A typical case is that in the early 1980s, the employment rate was 70% in Japan, 66% in the USA, and 63% was for the average in the European Union, while the corresponding figures in 1997 were 74.5% in Japan, 74% in the USA, and 60.5% was for the average of the European Union. However, the lowest rate of the reduction of working time was in the USA, followed by Japan, whereas the greatest rate of reduction in working time over the other two countries was shown in the European Union. In other words, in countries where employment participation rate shows the largest increasing trend, working time has the least tendency to reduce or even negative trend. In the case even of Sweden, the reduction of working time in the period 1960–1996 was accompanied by the reduction in employment participation (Gavroglou, 2001, pp. 69–70).

There was a similar trend in Greece, as well. During the period 1974–1983 when working hours were being reduced from 48 to 40 a week, unemployment rose from 2% to 8%[163]. It is obvious that the reduction of weekly working time to 35 hours without loss of pay would have resulted in an increase in hourly labour costs by 14%. Such a development wouldn't have burdened evenly all enterprises. Studies

163 Mousouris, 1996b, p. 24. This was a key employers' side argument in Greece to support the negative position towards the 35-hour week.

on which the proposal is based refer to labour-intensive enterprises. However, it is not possible for enterprises to be clearly classified into categories based on the criterion "labour-intensive" in one sector or industry. Therefore, the implementation of the measure would have created inequality in terms of competition among the enterprises. Nevertheless, in addition to this, sectors and capital-intensive business, where labour costs represent only a small part of total production costs, would have been burdened much less than sectors and labour-intensive enterprises. In fact, this explains why it was possible for an agreement in the banking industry to be concluded and how a 35-hour work was adopted by the company Intracom.

The possibility of a universal compulsory implementation of the 35-hour work a week, if it hadn't led to bankruptcy a very good number of traditional SMEs, which cover much of the employment, it would certainly have put them in a hard test. It should be noted that, if the agricultural sector is excluded, only a small percentage of employees work in large enterprises more than 50 people (Vasileiou, 1996y, pp. 1–16; Gavroglou, 2001). The burden of SMEs would have jeopardized a very large part of the existing employment in the country, which these SMEs afford. Moreover, the implementation of measure in these companies would have had a negative impact on their earnings and might have resulted in a proportional reduction of their investments. In addition, 425,000 production units operate with fewer than 10 employees, whereas on average 2 people are employed by a unit. However, a 35-hour employment of two people leaves only 10 working hours a week, something that does not create a new 35-hour job. Such a contribution to employment might have been particularly small, and would have concerned mainly the creation of jobs of flexible employment. Finally, the proposed provision for a state subsidy for increasing labour costs would have been not simply a resources transfer but rather significant burden to public finances, which the state does not seem to be willing to take over.

7.5 External Quantitative Labour Flexibility-Flexible Forms of Employment: Formal and Informal Employment and Basic Types of Flexible Forms

Bringing to the fore essentially theories of internal and external labour markets, Atkinson outlines an idealized model of a flexible enterprise. He distinguishes between the central core of relatively permanent staff which is hardly replaceable and the periphery of temporary, casual employees with precarious jobs, who show high mobility within the labour market and who, compared with their peers, lack basic individual and collective rights and benefits. Central legitimizing element of the external quantitative flexibility is a direct adaptation to market requirements. The existence and development of the external quantitative flexibility may empirically be confirmed by: (a) the degree of decentralization of productive operational partnerships of the business, such as the use of materials supplied by the division into smaller regional units and outsourcing; (b) the industry and regional labour mobility and the employees' flows into and out of an enterprise; (c) the diachronic development and relative importance of different types of atypical forms of employment in business, industry, economy; (d) the speed of adjustment of the number of employees on changes in activity or business profitability; (e) conventional and legislation of employment protection, the individual and collective rights of employees; and, even compared to the past, (f) by the conditions of recruitment, utilization and redundancy of individual categories of employees.

The ideal flexible employment contract for employers would be "an employment contract, the terms of which could be reviewed every day" (Boyer, 1987, pp. 107–129, mainly pp. 109–111). The objective of external quantitative flexibility is the numerical adjustment of staff according to the business needs. This is only possible by removing the constraints of existing legislation or collective agreements with regard to freedom of hiring and firing. Some writers (Brunhes, 1989, pp. 23–28) called this external quantitative flexibility, in contrast with the internal quantitative flexibility which refers to changes in working hours without substantial changes in the number of employees in the business. The external quantitative flexibility is defined as the possibility to adjust the level of employment, that is, the number of employees, depending either on the conjectural or structural changes in the market for the products or services of the enterprise or on technological changes. It encourages both geographical mobility of the labour force depending on production needs and their employment so as to maximize its freer management, particularly its recruitment and dismissal, and its utilization within the context of flexible or atypical or special forms of employment (Daskalakis, 1995b, pp. 13–14).

One version of the external quantitative flexibility concerns employment flexibility. From the perspective of employment, flexibility is distinguished between into flexibility in terms of volume and size of employment and flexibility in the content and forms of employment (Kouzis, 2001, p. 44). First, as far as "flexibility in terms of volume" is concerned, it is focused on the idea of increasing the competitiveness of enterprises through policies to reduce labour cost, policies that are specialized in facilitating the "potential of dismissal" of overstaffing, through individual and mainly collective redundancies. This option is implemented with "flexibilization" of rules that are considered as rigid, and they either provide compensation in the event of termination of the individual employment contract or limit the possibility to reduce the number of staff, reducing redundancies or setting terms and conditions for their realization. "Flexibility of the content of employment" refers to the flexibility associated with a range of flexible or atypical or special forms of employment and is an individual expression of the businesses' adaptation to the needs of competition that requires cheaper labour costs.

Moreover, there is an alternative use of the terms "flexible", "special" and "atypical" forms of employment in the international and Greek literature. All these terms refer to the same phenomenon of those types of employment that diverge from classic, traditional model of full-time employment that still exists and is the principle subject of regulation of Labour Law (Kravaritou, 1987, p. 14). The expansion (DIMEL-GSEE, 1990, pp. 31 and 32) of flexible forms of employment observed in recent years is associated with an overall change in the structure of employment that have resulted from the new technological revolution, the restructuring of the production process, changes in production being expressed by the decline of industry and expansion of services, as well as the comprehensive reorganization of working time (ETUI, 1985a, pp. 119–149). The most important reason for the expansion of these forms of employment has been considered the economic crisis, recession and unemployment that makes not only the governments (Deligianni-Dimitrakou, 1989, p. 14) tolerate or promote flexible forms of employment as a solution but also same trade unions or employees themselves accept (ETUI, 1985a, p. 113 ff) these flexible forms of employment, under certain conditions.

At the same time, legislative interventions of governments in several European countries in this issue have been much affected by businesses' desired flexibility in conditions of the current crisis and by the argument that the dependent full-time paid employment and all the institutional nexus of the protection and organization of the labour market is too rigid (Kouzis, 1994, pp. 9–10 and 13–15), resulting in businesses' inability to reduce labour costs (Cordova, 1986, p. 648). These special forms of employment that are of a special type of relations are, as noted, a divergence from the typical form of employment (Toutziarakis, 1990, pp. 176–178), and either they may be covered institutionally or they are *de facto* situations (Cordova, 1986, pp. 647–641).

The typical form of employment occurred in industrial production, along with the development of massive – of large-scale – production units. Its development was linked with the development of the action of trade union, collective labour relations and institutions of Social and, primarily, of Labour Law (more specifically, with the development of collective bargaining and social security). Features of this formal type of employment (Kravaritou, 1990, pp. 229–231) are the employee: (a) to work for another person, be dependent on him/her, to get a wage or a salary; and, (b) have an employer, to have a full-time employment (currently 5 days x 8 hours working day) at the premises of the employer, and, in principle, for an undetermined period of time, that is, indefinitely.

This form of employment is subject to protection and guarantees of social, labour and social security legislation, which traditionally imposes obligations on the state and the employer, under which the employee is protected. Therefore, the formal form concerns the wage, dependent from an employer, full-time employment relationship (Mitsou, 1990, pp. 5–13 and 122–123) of indefinite time. On the contrary, atypical forms of employment are distinguished from the formal ones because they lack some of their features, which have just mentioned earlier.

Of about thirty atypical forms of employment that have been recorded internationally by national characteristics, they can be distinguished as important (Deligianni-Dimitrakou, 1989, pp. 146–147) – and depending on the features with which deviate from the formal model of employment – as follows:

a) The employment through agencies, lending employees, labour force on hand and subcontracting as main forms in which the existence of an employer cannot clearly be discerned; the existence of tripartite labour relations and the employee's dependence on several employers are often implied.
b) The work at home with piece-jobbing and teleworking (at home or in telecentres or tele-farmhouses) as forms in which employment is provided in premises that do not belong to the employer.
c) Part-time employment, casual employment, employment shifts, seasonal employment, intermittent employment, job rotation, altering employment sharing an employment, partial unemployment, suspension are key figures in which employment is not full-time job; it is not full-time employment of a 5-day working week or it is not an 8-hour full-time employment.
d) Fixed-term contracts, works contracts and employment contracts and training cum employment, as forms in which it is expected to provide employment for a specified duration and termination of the relationship with the occurrence of certain event, fixed time or upon the completion of certain project.

Nowadays, flexible forms of employment with their expansion are introducing a number of concerns that the interested parties are called upon to dealing with. Tripartite labour relationships (Koukiadis, 1974) developed in the case of employment through an agency and subcontracting (Evans and Walker, 1986, pp. 143–165), whereas, on the one hand, they are adaptable to the needs of each business and each employee, on the other hand, they often seem to cause legal, theoretical and practical problems. A special issue that should be mentioned is the difficulty to verify who the real employer is and whether s/he complies with her/his obligations. Temporary employment through fixed-term contracts – although it is considered functional within the context of the businesses' desired flexibility – has been "accused" that destabilizes employment and protection system for employees (ETUI, 1985a, pp. 103–110), since businesses are deliberated from obligations and restrictions (Casey, Dragendorf Heering and John, 1989, pp. 449–453) with the aid of it. Nevertheless, it should be noted that recent experience from abroad mentions the establishment of specific contracts under terms and in specific cases. Whether it is identified with self-employment or not, working "at home" is completely excluded from Labour Legislation and often operates without insurance coverage (DIMEL-GSEE, 1990, p. 258). Self-employment – which is often promoted systematically by the member-states (within projects) to create small businesses and in order to combat unemployment within programs (Commission of the European Communities, [1992]-1995, pp. 187–189) – is usually treated with caution by the employee's' side, which may, as shown by the European experience, accept it under certain conditions.

In reality, flexible forms of employment are not a new situation. They are elements that have been traditionally part of total employment, but today they are implemented to a significant extent, they are assuming a new special role in the modern diversified map of employment and a new institutional nexus of provision with content that meets the requirements of the principle of elasticity. In other words, they are elements that come from new technological and production conditions, new social equilibria and are now a real phenomenon of modern postindustrial society. Nowadays, given that: first, flexible forms of employment are neither a restricted phenomenon nor much more a hypothetical event; and, second, that the competition between traditional Labour Law and Post-Labour Law is in progress (Koukiadis, 1991a, p. 1), the problem with flexible form of employment is not only the wording of desires or theoretical postulates, but the search for institutional safeguards "through conventions", conventions that will form, enhance or will complete the nexus of regulation of flexible forms of employment, harmonizing the need for flexibility and the demand for social protection.

7.6 Part-time Employment

Part-time employment has many methodological problems in its conceptual definition (Labour Canada: Part-time work in Canada: Report of the Commission of Inquiry on Part-time Work, (1983), pp. 37–41; ILO, 1988), and this happens because there can be many sub-categories and combinations. Form of part-time, in a broad sense, could be considered in principle the reduced working time.

Nevertheless, and despite the fact that it is not full-time employment, many authors do not incorporate the reduced working time to part-time employment. Another subcategory rare solidarity or replacement contracts which essentially concern the recruitment of employees to perform work a few hours and, thus, supplementing the labour of certain categories of full-time employment labour force. Forms, however, of part-time employment are often considered to be the different types of labour, such as: shift work, rotation systems of daily, weekly and monthly work and the case of task and job sharing of a full-time position.

In the broader concept of part-time employment may fall "job rotation" too, which is recognized as a special form of part-time employment. More specifically, "job rotation" means reduced employment in which the employee is employed full-time but works fewer working days than those applicable in the business, based on calculating week, fortnight, month or year (Paragraph 2, Article 2, Law 2639/1998). It should be noted that job rotation may arise unilaterally by the employer in case of restrictions of his/her activities, bending of the business operations, and after s/he has bargained with legal representatives of employees (Makris, 1979, p. 24). Employees may also be placed in "suspension" by employers in case of restrictions of the latter's economic activities and so not to terminate the employment contract. The suspension of employees, in which they receive half pay, may not exceed three months a year. However, both suspension and job rotation are a unilateral manifestation of the employer's will rather than an agreement between employer and employee. In fact, the latter may only choose between redundancy and suspension or job rotation. In contrast, part-time employment is a product of the employee's free will, something that differentiates it from these two aforementioned types of employment[164].

As international literature shows, a definition of "part-time" employment to be mutually agreed upon has yet to be formulated. International experience has shown different views between the institutions of industrial relations on defining part-time time employment. Furthermore, there is no conceptual definition of part-time employment in Laws of different countries (ETUI, 1986, pp. 57–68). Instead, various and often contradictory definitions between them are often adopted depending on the situation and purpose.

One way to define the concept of part-time employment is what is used to measure by statisticians. It is about a statistical definition, which, although it is not legally binding, is the basis upon which research in measuring and mapping

164 To distinguish between the two forms of work and employment as well as of part time employment reference is made to Makris, 1979, pp. 24–25.

the phenomenon are based and social policy for part-time employment is made at national and international level. For this purpose, either the employees are asked whether they are part-timers or the number of hours of their employment is used as a criterion. In the former case, the measurement is based on employees' subjective perceptions, thus there is question of the validity of measurements, whereas in the latter case, as already mentioned, does not take into account differences between professions and in full-time hours among countries (van Bastelaer, Lemaitre and Pascal, 1997).

From a legal point of view, part-time employment is sometimes defined (Thurman and Trah, 1990, pp. 23–24; ILO, 1989, pp. 3–4.) as a daily or weekly employment, but shorter than normal or the statutory time or a predetermined limit of working hours (Tzekinis, 1986, p. 13). It once includes full-time employment for some days of the week or on weekends or by alternating weeks or days of the week. In addition, the seasonal full-time employment for a few months a year is often as part-time employment. In Great Britain (Scarff, 1982; ILO, 1989, pp. 127–128; Schoer, 1987, p. 83), part-time employees are considered those who work 30 hours a week or less, excluding meal breaks and overtime. Nevertheless, in order for part-time employees to rise individual employment rights, they should either be employed for at least 16 hours a week or have 5 and more years of continuous employment with the same employer, working more than 8 hours and less than 16 hours a week.

Within the framework of the definition that was adopted by the EEC (Council of the European Communities, 1982), part-time employment was considered to run on a regular basis, simply both the employer and the employee agree upon a shorter working hours than normal ones. What would be defined by the Law or by a collective labour agreement was considered as normal working hours. It could now be argued that, although there is no international definition, part-time employment usually concerns work up to 30 or 35 hours a week. According to the International Labour Organization (ILO) (1996) and the European Union (EU) (Council Directive 97/81/EC of 15 December 1997), a part-time employee is considered the employee whose normal hours of work, calculated on a weekly or maximum on an annual basis, are fewer than the normal hours of work if compared with those of a full-time employee. Employment in this context is "normal", that is, there is a formal, on-going, working relation. It is an employment that is paid and not independent (self-employment) or unpaid work. Working hours are "essentially" fewer (national laws often specify that they must be at least 20% shorter than full-time employment) (ILO, 1989, pp. 59–132). However, it should be taken into consideration that there are businesses that have reduced working hours compared with the statutory or contractual working hours.

Considering the approach that shows part-time employment as a concept dependent on full-time employment, it could be argued that in Greece, according to Law 2639/98, as full-time (normal) employment is considered this employment that is performed based on what is valid as full-time employment in the business, an employment that can be determined by applicable law or be derived from other sources, such as collective bargaining agreement or arbitration or labour regulation or operational habit, or even the individual employment contract. The legal time, then, is not the only and exclusive criterion for determining the concept of full-time (normal) employment. In addition, part-time employment differs both from the reduced working hours and from suspension. Moreover, distinguishing the concept of underemployment requires define a maximum limit of working hours (Makris, 1979, pp. 1–3). Those who will work a number of working hours in the maximum of full-time employment (e.g. 34 hours a week) can be considered as underemployed, if they wanted extra working hours but they found none, or as part-time employees, if they were not interested in additional employment

As a criterion, that is, to determine the concept of part-time employment is used the concept of maximum or minimum limits of weekly working hours that are established and implemented at national, mainly level. In Greece no such limit of working hours has been defined in which an employee falls into the regime of pat-time employment. Nevertheless, significant problems arise from such an approach to part-time employment. One problem is that the specific and differentiated schedules of full-time employment in certain sectors are not taken into account, such as those of many teachers that do not exceed 35 hours a week. At the same time, it is rather an issue to question that work up to 35 hours a week is part-time employment, once the request of European trade unions for 35-hour working week without loss of pay is a request that has been recently expressed with intensity.

In any case, the scope and nature of the various types of part-time employment has been the subject of intense debate between people involved with Law of Labour Relations[165]. Some consider these developments reasonable and expected (Cordova, 1986, pp. 641–642), since the legislation covering employment adapts to changes in economy and to new conditions of the free market[166]. Others

---

165 Kravaritou, 1990, pp. 231–232. An extra dimension of the impact of flexible forms of employment on employee representation structures are given by Lixouriotis, 1992, pp. 40–46.

166 Cordova, (1986), pp. 641–642. A view of a more radical questioning of special forms of employment is adopted by Mitropoulos, 1989, pp. 72–72.

believe that these new data reveal an escalating crisis in the system of regulation of labour relations (Papaioannou, 1991, pp. 172–175), that, that is, they (these data) call into question the model of formal employment and the entire system of labour protection that developed around it, as Labour and Insurance Law do not fully or adequately regulate these new forms in practice (Kravaritou, 1990, pp. 225–227, 234–235 and 259–260). Despite the existing inconsistencies, according to Law 2639 (Article 2) of 1998, part-time employment is defined as a form of work that is characterized by "regularity"; that is, the employee works a certain number of hours every day. This notion of regularity can define more fully part-time employment, preventing misunderstandings and delimiting clearly this form of labour.

By Law 1892 of 1990 an institutional framework governing part-time employment was formed, which was securing equivalent rights of full-time and part time employees. In short, by Law 2639 of 1998, we would say that the development of part-time employment was attempted to be encouraged through the expansion of the public sector, while increasing the proportion of allowances to full-time employment as well as the integration of rotation labour in it. The third attempt for employment flexibility in Greece was made by Law 2874 of 2000. This Law introduced a regulation that attempted to consolidate part-time employment, establishing the increment of the pay of part-time employees by 7.5%, if employed for a time less than four hours a day and are paid on the threshold of the minimum wage. The above measure aims to boost employment of new and unskilled labour force.

In 1975, the European Community (Makris, 1979, p. 9) part-time employees accounted for 9.4% of the employees. These rates differed significantly in their countries, starting from 4% in Denmark and reaching up to 17% in Ireland. The proportion of part-time employees in total male labour force was 1.9% versus 23.6% of total female employment, confirming the perception that women participate at a greater rate in part-time employment than men. The decade 1992–2002, the proportion of part-time employment in total employment increased in many of the countries of the European Union. In 1992, 14% of the total European labour force was part-time employees, rising to 18.1% by 2002 (Eurostat, 2003). The proportion of women working part-time was 33.5% (of total employment), nearly five times greater than that of men (6.6%).

Greece has the lowest percentage of part-time employment in the EU (4.0% in 2001), with downward trends (it was 5.8% in 1999, 4.5% in 2000). From information[167] referring to the development of part-time employees in one year (1995–

167 Data published in Employment in Europe 2001.

1996) it is shown that in Greece part-time employment is a transitional stage or a lobby for full-time employment. According to these figures, in Greece 49.0% of part-time employees in 1995 had moved to full-time employment in 1996, when the European average was only 19.4%[168].

Part-time employment seems to be in itself neither an expression of neo-liberal policies of deregulation of the labour market nor its diffusion is directly related to the amount of employees' salaries / wages. What is crucial is rather the way in which part-time employment is implemented, the rights and obligations that accompany it, and the social status ascribed to it in each country. Indeed, countries whose employment policies are not considered characteristically neoliberal or deregulated, such as Sweden and Germany, have high percentages of part-time (24.1% and 20.3% respectively)[169]. The percentage of part-time employment is high in deregulated Britain, but it is higher in the Netherlands (42%). Finally, in the most liberal labour market, the U.S., the proportion of part-time employment is not higher but lower than what the EU average is (13.0% vs. 17.9%).

Although temporary work in Greece is often treated as part-time employment and as an indicator for policy deregulation of the labour market, comparative data for its diffusion in the European Union does not seem to confirm this view. Temporary employment in Greece is lower than the EU average (12.6%), with small but steady upward trend since 1995 (9.4%) and lower than in 1990 (15%). The most striking feature is that temporary employment in the USA is lower at levels not only than the EU average but also than any other country in the European Union. Moreover, countries with regulatory tradition in industrial relations, such as Finland, Sweden, and France have temporary employment rates higher than the EU average, whereas the "deregulated" Britain has some of the lowest rates of temporary employment (6.8%).

As it occurs in part-time employment, so happens in temporary employment; it is a transitional solution for many employees as a form of employment. In Greece, between 1993 and 1997, 32.7% of temporary male employees and 25.5% of female employees switched to a permanent job within a year, while in the European Union, 31% of men and 29.1% women with temporary employment move to full-time employment within a year (Taylor, 2002). Is, however, temporary employment a form of complementary to regular employment of indefinite time or a substitute of it? Based on comparative data of 2000–2001, temporary

168 Employment Observatory Research-Informatics SA (P.A.E.-P.A.E.), (2003), Flexibility and Organization of Work: Empirical Evidence from Greece and the European Union, Working Papers, No. 9, March., op. cit.

169 Ibid.

employment has played a different role in the Member States of the European Union. In countries such as Ireland and Finland, and to a lesser extent in France and Spain, temporary employment functioned as a substitute, to some extent, of permanent employment. In contrast, in countries such as Germany, Luxembourg and the United Kingdom, temporary employment complemented the permanent one. In Greece, the correlation between temporary employment and employment in general has been positive, that is, temporary employment has been complementary to the regular employment[170].

7.7 Flexibility Regulation: Traditional Models and New Trends: Contractualization, Decentralization and Flexibility of Regulations

From the sources of Labour Law (Blanpain, 1986, p. 195; Leventis, 1981, pp. 47–51; Aliprantis, 1984, pp. 418–426), the practice has opted – in line with the recent European experience – the law and collective agreements (Paoli-Pelvey, 1993, pp. 419–421) to regulate flexible forms of employment and working time. This practice is based on two basic models (Rojot and Blanpain, 1994, pp. 5–6) that have been working in European countries in recent decades. It is about, first, the case of the model – which is classified as a *Laisez-Faire* model – which relied on collective bargaining, and, second, what is characterized as a model of state intervention and regulation.

On the one hand, the first model is found more in Great Britain and Denmark, within its context, regulations (Paoli-Pelvey, 1993, p. 398 par. 12 & pp. 419–420 par. 92) on working time – either in the form of traditional boundaries and constraints (duration of daily and weekly work, during holidays, public holidays, days of rest) or in the form of new flexible arrangements for employment – typically derive from a collective labour agreement, whereas corresponding state regulations, even if there are, either are scarce or are gradually abolished. On the other hand, the second model, that is, that of state regulation appears in one of the most representative forms in Portugal (Rojot and Blanpain, 1994, p. 6) nowadays. Under this model, the regulation of working time is the subject of state intervention (Spyropoulos, 1992, p. 17) and is implemented through the legislative activity of the national parliament to protect the employee according to Labour Law.

---

170 Employment Observatory Research-Informatics SA (P.A.E.-P.A.E.), (2003), Flexibility and Organization of Work: Empirical Evidence from Greece and the European Union, Working Papers, No. 9, March, op. cit.

In recent years with the development of all literature and practice of flexibility in working time and forms of employment, there have been substantial variations in the model of state intervention, which essentially consist of a trend of relative shrinkage of the regulatory role of the state for the expansion of autonomous regulatory power of agencies (Koukiadis, 1991a, p. 2) of employees and employers.

In other words, basic features of the two fundamental models patterns can be observed in the regulatory status of working time in almost all European countries nowadays, whereas these two traditional models no longer appear in pure form (Spyropoulos, 1992, p. 40). Practice shows that there are various combinations of the mechanisms of state and contractual regulation in different countries (Salamon, 1987, p. 222, mainly Index Nr 11.1). In this way, on the one hand, data from traditional ways of adjustment are used, but, on the other hand, the two aforementioned models appear changed or mutated. The wide variety of existing systems of regulating working time that is occurring in European countries may, therefore, be taken to constitute a scale (Rojot and Blanpain, 1994, p. 5) at both extremes of which could theoretically be placed- on the one and the other side respectively – the two traditional models of regulation of working time. An examination of sources (Blanpain, 1986, p. 195; Leventis, 1981, pp. 47–51) of Law regulating working time is conspicuous new mixed models (Rojot and Blanpain, 1994, p. 7) have started to prevail and are created by the reconstruction of elements of the traditional models of regulating working time and by the integration of new original regulatory structures in a complementary role.

These new mixed models rely first on legislation, produced normally by the national parliaments. These regulations, whereas in some cases of EU states they are regulations frameworks texts and in some other cases they are specific regulations, have the common feature that they are the key institutional nexus of working time (Kravaritou-Manitakis, 1986, p. 225) which has a clearly indicative protective character for the employee. Another common feature in various national cases is that this model is constantly being altered, giving an increasing regulatory scope in social dialogue (ILO, 1986, pp. 3–6), collective bargaining or other mechanisms of arbitration nature (de Roo and Jagtenberg, 1994, pp. 28–39) and certainly in more flexible arrangements (Paoli-Pelvey, 1993, p. 420 par. 97).

Collective agreements on the issues of flexibility, depending on the features, structure and role of collective bargaining in the context of national industrial relations systems (Commission of the European Communities, 1992, p. 4) of the Member States of the European Union are concluded at various levels – national, cross-industry, industry, operational, with emphasis on the industry, the enterprise and the production unit. The arrangements of a particular level complement those of the other and usually move from the general to the specific, forming in this way a complete series – or rather a pyramid – of mutually complementary arrangements which result from various levels of dovetailed bargaining.

These data confirm the view that the flexible arrangement of working time and employment is combined with a trend of contractualization but at the same time with decentralization of regulations (ETUI, 1990b, pp. 23–25, 43–44, 68–69 and. 35–36; Commission of the European Communities, 1992, pp. 74, 79, 80 and 82; Rojot and Blanpain, 1994, p. 9), which are now being conducted at increasingly low levels. The industry level (Wedderburn, 1985, p. 46 ff; Spyropoulos, 1990, p. 40) seems suitable for the formation only of a framework of arrangements and regulations, whereas more specialized arrangements and regulations have already formed configured at local, operational level, at exploitation level (Paoli-Pelvey, 1993, pp. 420–421, par. 98) or even on an individual basis (Spyropoulos, 1992, pp. 22–23 and 29).

7.8 Flexibility and Security (Flexicurity) in Employment: Is It Possible and Desirable a Greek Model?

The data presented here allow the comparison with those of empirical evidence for the European Union, giving the opportunity first to assess and clarify issues related to flexibility and security of labour in Greece. The phenomenon of insecurity is a key element of modern European society ([171]. According to research data ([172], in the fifteen old member states of the European Union, 30% of employees are employed on temporary and part-time employment contracts, whereas 10% of the total labour force is unemployed; that is, at least 40% of the world of wage labour is a status of flexible employment, with limited content of rights and pay or unemployment[173]. In the year 1999, in all countries of the EU, only 50% of new contracts do have the character of stable employment, with the remainder in temporary forms of employment (Commission Européenne, 1999). The diffusion of new forms of employment is reasonable to bring the increased mobility

171 See details in the Labour Market Yearbook 2002 PAEP SA, where there is a recording of the main data of the labour market in Greece as well as an overview of "qualitative" data of labour.

172 Employment Observatory Research-Informatics SA (P.A.E.-P.A.E.), 2003, Flexibility and Organization of Work: Empirical Evidence from Greece and the European Union, Working Papers, No. 9, op. cit.

173 Ibid.

of employees from one job to another and from one company to another, that is, instability of employment.

In Greece, employment stability remains high compared to the EU average. The available evidence suggests that in Greece the percentage of employees working "in this company/organization" for relatively few years are below the EU average, whereas the percentage of employees working in the "same company/organization" for several years is higher than the EU average. Thus, we see that 13.3% of employees were working "in the same company" for a year or less in Greece in 2000, compared to 19.7% of employees in the European Union. 16.7% of employees in Greece were working "in the same company" for 30 years and over, compared with 5.9% of employees in the European Union who was experiencing the same degree of stability in employment[174]

The precarious position in the labour market that continuously increases segments of the labour force is a new reality characterizing important parts of modern societies. The categories of unemployed, flexible employees with unstable status and second gear of employment as well as of employees with formal employment whose position in the labour market is threatened (Dauce, 1998, pp. 336–343) constitute a novel phenomenon that is constantly being expanded by the dynamic of modern developments and results in the formation of a binary model of labour. This development seems to have been decisively influenced by the fact that in recent years the theory according to which unemployment and low competitiveness are due mainly to the "rigidity" of the labour market have acquired many supporter in Europe.

According to this view, to enhance the competitiveness of economies and, thus, to combat unemployment effectively, rigidities in labour markets should be reduced; they should be reduced based on selectivity criteria, on social protection measures and on collective bargaining which should be decentralized (Spyropoulos, 1998, pp. 396–405). Most European countries began to adopt such policies, whereas at the same time international organizations began to suggest various degrees of flexibilization of the labour markets as a solution to the problem. In the last years flexibility of the labour market that has grown considerably. Nevertheless, different policies of flexibility haven't been able to solve the unemployment problem; on the contrary, they have created new problems such as increasing social inequalities (Spyropoulos, 1998, pp. 396–405). The phenomenon of the working poor and employees in "jobs in the secondary" labour market on unequal terms of social protection are very typical cases. For this reason it is

174 Employment Observatory Research-Informatics SA (P.A.E.-P.A.E.), 2003.

necessary to achieve a synthesis between the two seemingly opposite concepts of flexibility, on the one hand, and the security of employment, on the other hand (Javillier, 1994, pp. 533–550, esp. on p. 504).

The flexibility with employment security, that is, "flexicurity", is now a central – official policy of the European Union, not a policy of the Greek state, the Greek government or of the Greek Ministry of Employment. About a year ago, the Koukiadis Commission of "representative synthesis" was established by the Ministry of Employment to actively develop and propose a series of measures under the European Green Paper on "flexicurity". As known, the European Union gives priority to the issues of employment and cares for entrepreneurship, since it has set out to achieve the most competitive economy worldwide. As part of the official policy of the European Union, Member States should take specific measures. If it wants to continue to follow the course of the European Union, our country should also take such measures. The Koukiadis Commission resulted in proposals which have even been put to public consultation. Nevertheless, if the country disagrees with European policies or the specific European employment policy, this is an issue that should be discussed at the political level. But until today there has not been such an issue by the majority of political forces and especially the parties that are in power.

The EU policy on flexicurity in employment does not have one but several versions, as dictated by the European experience so far. It is a fact that flexicurity as a strategy to boost employment and stimulate entrepreneurship has been based on the experience of Denmark, which utilized economically and socially the "golden triangle": (a) ease of hiring – release; (b) replacement of wages of the unemployed; and (c) active policies of training and re-entry of the unemployed in the labour market. Thus, it has managed to have spectacular result for several years now, especially regarding the restrain of unemployment at low levels, and the preservation of social rights and the income of employees and the unemployed. It is also a fact that not all countries are the same, let alone Greece and Denmark, and there are also national peculiarities. In Denmark there are many differences in terms of economy, wage levels, labour relations, the level of unemployment benefits (90% of salary), the duration of the subsidy (up to 4 years) as well as the limit of collective redundancies (up 10%), compensation for redundancy (average wages of 13 weeks versus 29 in Greece), the effectiveness of retraining, the high level of the welfare state, the low presence of foreign investment, a lack of integration of the country in EMU. But it is also true that the policy of "flexicurity" is not limited to one version. There have already been several versions of this policy in Europe, which have been adopted in many cases by national trade unions, and the European Trade Union Confederation.

Greece can formulate its own "Greek model" on the issue of "flexicurity". Those who deny that the states of flexibility and insecurity must surround themselves with security policies need a strong persuasive argument that it has not been formulated so far. Of course, Greece is not Denmark; it has national particularities. But in Greece as part of a labour market that has been characterized by strong elements of flexibility in recent years strong arguments should be raised so that it can be argued that precarious situations do not need to assume security, situations that have been produced by modern economic reality for a great part of the active working population.

In a period where – as it is supported without questioning – the new labour market entrant would be forced to change job or career many times during his/her employment life, at a time when new production conditions create new data, raises the need to launch new incentives and recognition of new rights, at a time when the spectrum of unemployment is lurking and the mainstream labour market conditions raise the need for new forms of protection of employees in order for insecurity and inequality to be reduced, there is a need for a policy that ensures the rights of those employed under flexible forms, guarantees the principle of equal treatment for flexible employees, helps maintain employment even regardless of the content and location of employment, a policy that aims to maintain a tolerable income level regardless of the change of the subject of employment, a policy that seeks to ensure a secure system based on the strong subsidy for the unemployed, vocational education and training, and reintegration (in the labour market), thus facilitating labour mobility. There is a need for a policy that, among other things will aim at the employee's psychological safety – something that is equally important – against phenomena of precariousness and insecurity.

There is more flexibility in employment in Greece nowadays. It is a question whether as a society we will finally decide to "stare the truth in the face", the truth that is related to today's "Charter of Employment". Does this charter consist nowadays only of employees who work for eight hours for five days a week, who are full-time employed, or have an employment of indefinite duration, of the "normal-traditional" employment model which is now mainly confined to the public the wider public sector, only in certain businesses and only in certain locations, the protection of which is limited accordingly and the deficient social protection system and security as it was traditionally developed?

Full-time employment, full-time and lasting quality employment, for which I have advocated emotionally and politically, for which I have repeatedly written and argued in national, European and international scientific and political fora, it must certainly be maintained as the first objective as the first priority. At the same time, we must finally admit the reality that the Greek society, young people, students, families and our social surroundings face with. Most of our young people, like people of different ages are increasingly employed under flexible or other shapes. Some are part-timers. Others look for the solution to creating small businesses or individual businesses, of which only the fourth (1/4) will survive each year. Others are employed as employees through companies that hire employees or in recurrent stage programmes without insurance; others, in an obviously worse situation, work in "black" employment which occupies the highest percentage of total employment; others are employed as co-assisted and unpaid family members, who are hopefully 6.5% of total employment; and, finally, others are employed under a contracted project or service, whereas in fact they provide a dependent employment.

De facto flexibility is estimated 20% of the undeclared work; by the fact that recruitment is not carried out by the employment services but through social networks, friendly and cliental relationships. There is flexibility because the rules of labour law are not observed, there are not adequate controls, and these issues are not acclaimed firmly and immovably as the "first issue". There is additional flexibility because of the total of employment only 63% is about wage labour. Finally, there is the formal flexibility, flexible forms of employment and various forms of flexible working time arrangements, which have been regulated by various statutes in recent years, despite the fact that the special arrangements on working time have hardly been used by employees and employers. Employees in flexible employment have been covered even with social security. Yet, there have been no safety valves that will create conditions and hence security of permanent access to income, even in the form of unemployment benefits in retraining and employment, albeit in a new location. In view of these developments, it could not be argued that in Greece there is no flexibility. There is flexibility, without, however, security.

There has already been flexibility in redundancies in Greece today. First, in 98% of private sector enterprises restrictions do not apply to collective dismissals, because they are small and redundancies are free. There is also *de facto* flexibility that is ensured by the way that some giant (multinational) companies operate in the context of a globalized economy, companies whose investments are desirable and necessary for employment. More specifically, those which are able to form themselves the rules of the markets where they operate, they use different flexible forms, thus avoiding any notion of restrictions on collective redundancies.

Furthermore, there is flexibility because those companies which are under pressure, they either threaten or get relocated to neighboring countries, unless they are in Northern Greece, so they may prefer to transport cheap migrant labour for necessary shifts on a daily basis from these neighboring countries. Thus, the institution of restrictions on collective redundancies concern only few companies which are usually of Greek interests, can play a developmental role, but as a rule they operate in formal – obvious economy, receive significant pressure from competition from giant corporations which "breathe" on "their international markets" but also from small businesses which "breathe" with "informal" practices. For this type of business where the institution of the threshold for collective redundancies is reduced the Koukiadis Commission proposed the role that is currently reserved to management in the event of collective redundancies should be reviewed so that the Commission can actively intervene during bargaining, thus assisting the parties in finding out common solutions rather than to intervene in retrospect, after bargaining has failed, after creating faits accomplish have been created on the approval or prohibition of dismissal, something that it often exacerbates problems rather than solving them. That was the proposal of the Koukiadis Commission on the issue. It can be accepted, discussed about or even be rejected. Nevertheless, it cannot be used in any case as an argument so that the overall Commission proposals are discredited, proposals that have a specific target: situations of flexibility to be assumed with security.

In the Greek labour market there is flexibility, but there is no security. There is safety only for those "within the walls". Keeping this situation – that is, flexibility without security – is a *de facto* deregulation and leads to social fragmentation. The various forms of employment which are described above and which appear in the Greek labour market, as if they may be unpleasant or if they are not the best option for the employee, certainly aren't they theoretical constructions. On the contrary, they describe an existing reality in the Greek labour market today. They are real manifestations of flexibility which are thriving in the context of the dynamics of the modern economy but also in the spectrum of threat of unemployment for those who deal with a "snobbish" attitude the opportunity that may have for employment in such positions.

It is obvious that employees of these categories, even if they are not employed in undeclared work but in formal forms, lag far behind in terms of employment, social protection and security compared with employees of "normal – traditional" model of employment. In view of these data, will we continue to keep quiet about the reality of flexibility and maintain the provision of security as an exclusive privilege of the employees of "normal – traditional" labour model, that is, as a privilege for those "within the walls", or will we extend it for those "outside the walls" so that there will be indeed not only flexibility but also security? Does the maintenance of the existing situation today is a *de facto* deregulation of protection? Does the maintenance of such an unregulated situation in the labour market leads to an intense competition between different categories of employees? And further is this situation the required background for social fragmentation?

The Koukiadis Commission, considering the European experience and the particularities of the Greek labour market and economy, expressed and put to public consultation a number of proposals relevant to the limitation of insecurity and inequality within the existing labour relations, new rights and number of incentives that meet the new conditions of production, new protections for employees with already existing situations in the labour market. In other words, the Koukiadis Commission "dared" to raise the issue of flexibility enclosed with security in the labour market. Among the many important things that the aforementioned Committe proposed can be indicatively mentioned the following: Establishment of a "hard" core of social rights that will apply to the supply of labour, whatever its form may be. Fundamental guarantees of labour legislation related to freedom to associate, prohibition of discrimination, prohibition of child labour, health and safety as well as social security are proposed to be extended to the independent employment.

But as the reduced security of all previous categories of employees is in the precariousness of their own employment, extensive active labour market policies are proposed, extension of the unemployment benefit to almost all categories of employees and employees, the brave increase in unemployment benefits, the guarantee of a minimum subsistence, the design of a strategy to combat poverty, the development of a fair and effective system of successive insurance that will not "punish" but will support and encourage mobility for the benefit of employment and entrepreneurship, a series of measures against social security contribution by reducing non-wage labour costs with fewer taxes and levies, restricting arbitrary dismissals by introducing the principle of justified complaint, tackling upon undeclared work by intensified controls, enhancing and upgrading the operational capacity of the Labour Inspectorate in terms of infrastructure, equipment and staff, by co-operating even with the services of the Insurance Funds, the Internal Revenue Services (DOY in Greek) and National Organization for the Employment of the Labour Force (OAED in Greek) and by utilizing modern methods such as crosschecking of data.

Especially with regard to subsidization of unemployment, it is proposed the establishment of an Unemployment Fund of Self-Employed that will provide lump-sum compensations, the extension of unemployment insurance of the OAED to people who provide as main employment to employers with whom they are spouses or relatives of first or second degree, the reduction of strict requirements of regular unemployment benefit so that its protective provisions can cover new forms of employment, various combinations of continuation of full-time or part-time unemployment benefit along with employment, further social protection for employees in flexible forms of employment and the increase in unemployment benefits to two thirds of at least the minimum wage of an unskilled employee with their subsequent de-escalation so that the person will reintegrate into the labour market.

The Greek version of flexicurity, adopting measures designed to surround the existing flexicurity (flexibility with security) should essentially promise a "radical reform of social protection system", so that it can include those "outside the walls" for social cohesion and entrepreneurship. As already mentioned, there is flexibility in the Greek labour market, institutionalized or *de facto*, but without security. And this is reasonable since there are informal situations and since almost all social protection system is oriented towards "traditional – normal" model of employment on which it has been built, providing for this exact reason only to security to those "within the walls" nowadays. As a consequence, there is now need for a radical reform of the social protection system to include those "out of the wall", those who are affected by the new production conditions, those who are affected by the new but existing conditions in the labour market, those who are employed but not based on the traditional model of employment in order to provide them with security and support them in the continuous process of change.

However, the adoption of such measures, in addition to social and character development that has, also has large economic costs. Such a reform has very high economic cost, which, however, but both the state and businesses should be ready to bear, because such a cost for such a policy is necessary in order to establish a new social protection system capable of preventing disruption of social cohesion and release beneficial effects of flexibility for entrepreneurship, competitiveness and development. Yet, it is surprising both the systematic distortion of the Committee's proposals and the lukewarm treatment of its proposals, especially for the people who "lean over backwards" for entrepreneurship, competitiveness of the economy, the reform of the welfare state and the building of a new social model that will support development. Nevertheless, these proposals in practice maintain their relevance and continue to be subject to public consultation and a base of convergence of all powers of production, labour and politics who believe that development, competitiveness and entrepreneurship are necessary to rely on a modern and effective model of social protection.

7.9 Measures for Flexibility in the Labour Market and Employment after and under the Memorandum with the E.U. and the I.M.F.

Pursuant to the Memorandum, important reforms – changes related to employment conditions were made. Those changes essentially concern issues regarding individual contract and time limits of work. First, Law 3846/2010 "Guarantees for job security and other provisions" [FEK66/A' (Government Gazzette)], as amended by Law 3899/2010 "Urgent measures for the implementation of the support program of the Greek economy" (FEK 212/A'), adopted new rules and amendments were made to existing provisions of labour legislation concerning flexible forms of employment in order, on the one hand, for labour rights and the necessary flexibility in the labour market are safeguarded, and, on the other hand, for jobs to be maintained and expanded and for the economy's competitiveness to be improved.

Basic components of the provisions were: control, regulation and implementation of specific interventions for guarantees that were overlooked or that the reality revealed as absolutely necessary. By Law 3899/2010, in particular, a series of measures for labour market flexibility and simplification of the implementation of labour legislation were taken. As stated in the Explanatory Report on the new Law, the provisions of Chapter B' of Law 3899/2010 "Urgent measures for the implementation of the support programme of the Greek economy" provide, among others, regulations that seek to promote flexibility in the labour market, whose objective is to maintain and expand jobs and strengthen the competitiveness of Greek enterprises (Law Explanatory 3899/2010). More specifically, individual issues of part-time employment, job rotation, temporary employment as well as probationary employment period are regulated (Article 18, Law 3899/2010), whereas the simplification of the procedures for implementation of labour laws is provided.

In particular, the increase of part-time employment is aligned[175] with a corresponding pay of a comparable employee in proportion to the agreed working time. Until recently, it was provided[176] that the earnings of part-time employees increase by seven and a half percent (7.5%), provided that the hours of employment are less than four (4) hours a day. This increase is repealed by the new provision, so part-timer working for less than four (4) hours a day will be paid

175 By Paragraph 1, Article 18, Law 3899/2010, and it is amended accordingly, Paragraph 8, Article 38, Law 1892/1990, as replaced by Article 2, Law 3846/2010.

176 By Article 7, Law 2953/2000, this amended Article 38, Law 1892/1990.

more in absolute proportion to full-time employed[177]. It is also clarified[178] that the pay of the additional work of part-time employees for any additional hours worked beyond the agreed[179]. It was re-determined the way of computing the remuneration of part-timers, so their pay, including pay of any additional work beyond that has been agreed upon, can be commensurate with the remuneration of a comparable employee, that is, that of a full-time employee in equivalent job, without however increments.

Consequently, there is no provision[180] for the right plus fee if part-time employees are required to perform any work beyond their contract. The part-time employee ought to provide work, if s/he is able to do it, and his/her refusal would be contrary to good faith. It is provided, however, that the right of refusal to provide work, when this takes place in the usual way. Moreover, the increase of the salaries of part-time employees in seven and a half percent (7.5%) is repealed (Paragraph 1, Article 17, Law 3899/2010), since the hours of their employment is less than four (4) hours a day, something that was provided[181]. What was valid until recently, if a full-time employee worked more than what was designated by working hours, an extra payment / a bonus plus twenty-five percent (25%) (40-45 hours weekly). Furthermore, if a part-time employee was employed in addition to that provided for by the individual employment contract (reduced) time, it was first defined by Law 3846/2010[182] that's/he is entitled an increment of ten percent (10%). By the new regulation (Paragraph 2, Article 18, Law 3863/2010) this increment is abolished, so the part-time employee who will provide further work will now be entitled only with simple hourly wages.

It was also determined[183] that "job rotation is considered employment by fewer days a week or fewer weeks a month or fewer months a year, or a combination of these according to full-time work a day …". If his/her activities are limited, the employer may, instead of terminating the contract, impose rotation system of

177 In Paragraph 1, Article 18, Law 3899/2010.

178 Paragraph 2, Article 18, Law 3899/2010 and Paragraph 11, Article 38, Law 1892/1990, as replaced by Article 2, Law 3846/2010.

179 Law Explanatory 3899/2010.

180 According to Paragraph 2, Article 17, Law 3899/2010, which has replaced Paragraph 11, Law 3846/2010.

181 Paragraph, Article 2, Law 3846/2010, as it has replaced Paragraph 9, Article 38, Law 1892/1990.

182 In particular, by the provision of Paragraph 11, Article 38, Law 1892/1990, as amended by Law 3846/2010.

183 In Subparagraph 2, Paragraph 3, Article 2, Law 3846/2010.

employment in business, the duration of which shall not exceed nine (9) months – instead of six (6) months provided by old provisions – in the same calendar year (Paragraph 3, Article 17, Law 3899/2010), unless s/he previously informs and consults with the legal representatives of employees[184]. When the economic activity of the enterprise is reduced, the employer can unilaterally impose a rotating system of job rotation, that is, rotation periods of employment and non-employment. Two conditions are provided for the enforcement of job rotation, a substantial and procedural one: First, there must be a substantial reduction in activity of the business. Second, consultation with representatives of employees must take precedence, but it is not necessary to ensure that they tally. It should be noted that until 1998 the approval of the competent Labour Inspectorate was required, a condition which was subsequently removed (Article 2, Law 2639/1998), when it was replaced with the employer's obligation to simply notify the aforementioned authority about this decision. A maximum time limit on the duration of job rotation was also established[185], a limit which should not exceed six months in a calendar year. An increase in the maximum time duration of job rotation has been introduced[186] with the new provision, which now should not exceed nine (9) months a calendar year[187].

At the same time, the duration of employees' suspension is regulated[188] in nine (9) months, as the total duration of the employee's work in thirty six (36) months in the indirect employer, after which continuing to work in the indirect employer (Paragraph 4, Article 18, Law 3899/2010) makes the employment contract an employment contract of indefinite duration with the indirect employer. In particular, employees' time suspension in companies facing serious financial problems is expanded from 6 to 9 months. Labour through Temporary Employment Agency (EPA in Greek) is institutionalized[189]. Terms and conditions for the

184 In accordance with the provisions of the Presidential Decree 240/2006 (Government Gazzette-FEK 252/A΄) and Law 1767/1988 (Government Gazzette-FEK 63/A΄).

185 With the provision of Paragraph 3, Article 2, Law 1892/1990, as amended by Law 3846/2010.

186 In accordance with the provisions of Paragraph 3, Article 18, Law 3899/2010.

187 The Scientific Committee of the Parliament in its Report says: "since Article 2, Law 3846/2010 amended Article 38, Law 1892/1990, it would be entered in the header of the third paragraph of Article 18 that the fourth subparagraph of Paragraph 3, Article 38, as replaced by Article 2, Law 3846/2010, is amended".

188 With Paragraph 3, Article 18, Law 3899/2010, and it is replaced by Paragraph 3, Article 2, Law 3846/2010.

189 By Law 2956/2001 "Restructuring of THE OAED and Other Provisions" (Government Gazette-FEK 258/a/2001), as amended by Article 3, Law 3846/2010 and then amended by Law 3899/2010, too.

establishment and licensing of Temporary Employment Agency are determined so as employees' labour and insurance rights are secured, those rights that are available from the EPA to the indirect employer and protective regulations for these employees are introduced.

The maximum concession period of temporarily employed in the same indirect employer, without it being converted into a permanent contract with the indirect employer; it is formed into thirty-six (36) months, re-determined[190] (with possible extensions) in 36 months of 18 months that it is today. After 36 months the employee is deemed to have a permanent contract (with indefinite time) with the indirect employer. The new regulations (Paragraph 4, Article 18, Law 3899/2010) vary conditions concerning the permissible duration of the employee's concession by firms of temporary employment to indirect employers. The initial status[191] regulating the issue would allow only a renewal and the total duration was not allowed to exceed sixteen (16) months. Under the new wording of the provision[192], it is provided that the total period of employment of the employee by the indirect employer, including renewals, may not be greater than twelve months and, exceptionally, any excess of this duration, with a maximum of eighteen (18) months in the case the employee is to be replaced, whose contract for any reason is suspended. Nevertheless, with the new provision (Paragraph 4, Article 18, Law 3899/2010) the time limit of lending employees from firms of temporary employment has increased to thirty-six (36) months, a duration in which any renewals will be included.

In addition, issues related to termination of employment, warning time, the levels of compensation paid, manner and time of payment were regulated. A notice (i.e. warning time) to dismiss an employee on a permanent contract, who worked from 12 to 24 months, was re-determined as one month. In case of no notice, then severance (compensation for dismissal) pay of one month is provided. More analytically, a provision is institutionalized[193], according to which the notice is reduced in case of termination of the contract.

More specifically, the notice according to the seniority of the employee is formed as follows: (a) For employees who have served from twelve (12) months to two (2) years, a notice of one (1) month prior to the dismissal is required;

190 By Paragraph 4, Article 17, Law 3899/2010.

191 More specifically, the original wording of Article 22, Law 2956/2001.

192 As amended by the provisions of Article 3, Law 3846/2010.

193 By Paragraph 2, Article 74, Law 3863/2010 "New insurance system and related legislation, regulations on labour relations" (Official Gazette of the Ten/Government-FEK 115/I), as amended by Paragraph 5, Article 17, Law 3899/2010.

(b) For employees who have been employed from two (2) years completed up to five (5) years, a two-month notice before the dismissal is required; (c) For employees who have worked from five (5) years completed up to ten (10) years, a three-month notice before the dismissal is required; (d) For employees who have been employed from at least ten (10) years completed to fifteen (15) years, a four-month notice is required prior to dismissal; (e) For employees who have worked from fifteen (15) years completed to twenty (20) a five-month notice is required prior to termination of the contract or employment relationship. (f) For employees who have worked from twenty (20) years completed or more, a six-month notice before the termination of the contract or employment relationship is required. The particular levels paid by an employer to a dismissed in case of written notice of compensation are provided as follows[194]. When there was no use of written notice (according to the above), the provided by the aforementioned provisions compensation is paid by the employer to the dismissed.

The payment of compensation in instalments is also provided (Paragraph 3, Article 74, Law 3863/2010) with direct payment of compensation corresponding to the two-month remuneration during the dismissal and the payment of the remaining amount in bimonthly instalments, each of which may not be less than the two-month pay, unless the remaining amount for the repayment of the total of the compensation is less. The purpose of this provision is to facilitate – in relation to the time of payment of compensation – businesses that face serious financial problems due to the economic crisis and want to reduce their staff, but they shouldn't be brought to a definitive closure. At the same time, it was for the first time that the trial work period was regulated by law under the employment contract of indefinite duration.

More specifically, it is provided that the trial period will last up to 12 months, and the employment contract may be terminated without notice and without severance pay, unless otherwise agreed by the parties. Therefore, it is for the first time that the contract of a trial period is regulated (Paragraph 5, Article 17, Law 3899/2010), the duration of which is provided to be for 12 months. In particular, it is provided[195] that the employment with a contract of indefinite duration is considered as employment in probation for the first twelve (12) months from the date of effect, and may be terminated without notice and without severance pay, unless the interested parties agree. What was in effect until recently was that

194 From the relevant provisions of Laws 2112/1920 (Government Gazette-FEK No 67 1st) and 3198/1955 (Government Gazette-FEK 98 1st).

195 With an addition to Paragraph 2, Article 74, Law 3863/2010.

when an employee with an employment contract of indefinite duration, who has attained experience of two months (or two years), a one-month notice was required if the employee's employment contract was to be terminated.

And if a notice was preceded, the employer was required to pay a half-month compensation for the employee who had worked from two months to one year and one-month compensation for an employee who had worked from one year to four years. If there had been no notice, the employer would have to pay one-month compensation for an employee who had worked from one year to two years, two-month compensation for an employee who had worked from one year to four years. With the new provision (Paragraph 5, Article 18, Law 3899/2010) it is established the non-payment of compensation complaint / termination and there is no need for a prior notice if the employer terminates the employment contract within twelve months from the commencement of employment. Finally, Law 3863/2010 provides "an increase in the limit of dismissals in collective redundancies", as the limits beyond which the dismissals are considered a group have increased (Paragraph 1, Article 74, Law 3863/2010).

Meanwhile, new regulations substantially influenced time limits and the remuneration of labour, since the pay of overwork and overtime for employees was reduced (Paragraphs 10 & 11, Article 74, Law 3863/2010). More particularly, in businesses where contractual work hours to forty (40) hours a week are applicable, the employee may work five (5) additional hours a week (40-45), for five days and 8 hours a week, (40-48), for six days, and the hours are considered as overtime and remunerated by wages paid increased by 20%. Furthermore, employees who are employed overtime are entitled for every hour of lawful overtime upon completion of one hundred twenty (120) hours a year get a pay equal to the amount paid hourly plus forty per cent (40%). The increment for the legal overtime over one hundred twenty (120) hours a year is respectively 60%. Moreover, for each hour of overtime exceptionally every employee is entitled to get paid hourly plus eighty per cent (80%).

And finally, the new provisions have introduced processes and procedures to simplify the ways to provide the information to the relevant departments of the Ministry of Labour and Social Security, and, generally, to facilitate the monitoring of compliance with labour legislation.

Pursuant to the Memorandum, however, significant regulations on employment were introduced. More specifically, Law 3845/2010 (Government Gazette-FEK 65 A) "Measures for the implementation of the support mechanism for the Greek economy by the member states of the Eurozone and the International Monetary Fund" was established, as an institution, the "check reintegration" (Paragraph 4, Article 2, Law 3845/2010) in the labour market. So, every subsidized unemployed person is entitled to a "check reintegration" in the labour market, the monetary value of which equals the total amount that s/he is entitled to receive as unemployment benefit. It is also introduced the "possibility to get work experience for young people between 16 and 24 years of age" (Paragraph 6, Article 2, Law 3845/2010).

Thus, employers in the private sector who conclude contracts for work experience with unemployed persons 16-24 years of age, which last up to twelve (12) months, pay the recruited 80% of the minimum basic salary or wage as defined in each case by the National General Collective Labour Agreement and insure the pension sector, illness in kind and occupational risk of the IKA – ETAM (in Greek; Social Insurance Fund – Auxiliary Fund for Employees) while they themselves are entitled to get subsidized for insurance contributions by the OAED (: the National Organization for the Employment of the Labour Force). Measures, however, for new entrants to the labour market were established by Law 3863/2010 "New Insurance Scheme and related provisions, adjustments in labour relations" (Government Gazette-FEK 115 A). More specifically, this law has predicted (Paragraph 8, Article 74, Law 3863/2010) that new recruits under the age of 25, who are paid eighty-four per cent (84%) of the minimum basic salary or wage as defined in each case by the National General Collective Labour Agreement, the employers should be automatically included in the programme of the OAED to subsidize insurance premiums, which are payable by these new recruits.

The same Law (i.e. Law 3863/2010) also predicts special "protection of persons of 55-64 years of age from layoffs" (Paragraph 7, Article 74, Law 3863/2010). More specifically, a provision was introduced aiming exclusively to protect employees from 55 to 64 years of age, a provision that in the event of collective redundancies, the number of dismissed who are 55-64 years of age may not exceed ten per cent (10%) of the total number made redundant. At the same time, it was provided "the self-insurance of redundant of 55-64 years of age with the participation of the employer" (Paragraph 4, Article 74, Law 3863/2010). In particular, employees between 55 to 64 years of age, whose employment contract is terminated, regardless of whether it is collective or individual redundancies, if they remain unemployed, they have the right to self-insurance, the cost of which the employer ought to be involved with. Finally, "integration programmes of long-term unemployed to work in the public sector" were provided. In addition, under the same provision, the issue of Ministerial Decision to implement a programme for integration of the total of this category of dismissed in employment programmes for long-term unemployed of 55 to 64 years of age to work in the public sector.

Finally, Article 34 of Law 4024/27.10.2011 (Government Gazette 226, vol.: A), which was passed very recently (by the Greek Parliament on 20/10/2011), concerns on the Labour Reserve, which raised major political issue and which brought significant changes both to the status of employees employed both under private law in the public and broader public sector and, despite the fact that this may be a novelty, and to the status of employees under public law in the strict sense public sector. More specifically, under the new institution of labour redundancy, it is provided that the personnel of Compulsory and Secondary Education institutions which are merged or abolished are threatened with inclusion in the labour reserve scheme as from 1.1.2012. A key criterion will be seniority.

They are threatened especially those who have less experience. Under labour reserve status until retirement are those employees that complete 35 years of social security and earn pension entitlements as 31 December 2013. The positions where they used to work have been repealed. Furthermore, the Law provides for the elimination of vacant positions in the public sector, (the positions of) employees employed with contracts under private law of indefinite duration. Apart from the narrow public sector, the measure of abolishing vacant positions also affects employees in private entities (NPID in Greek, or Private Entity Law [PEL]). Those who join the labour reserve will take 60% of the basic salary (excluding bonuses), which they used to receive when they joined the reserve, for about 12 months. All premiums will be normally paid by the employee and the employer for the regular salary before redundancy. Those employees whose spouses have already joined this pre-retirement status or suspension are excluded from the labour reserve. Furthermore, any employee whose wife (or husband) or child living in the same house with him/her is disable of at least 67% and is included in the employee's income tax is excluded. Finally, people who are disabled of at least 67%, and have large families are also excluded.

7.10 Epilogue

The rapid integration of new technologies in the production process reverses any previous example of smooth adjustment of production process that had been prevailing for decades now through conventional technologies. The new technological production model changes completely the structure and the features of professional qualifications, labour market, working models and systems of education, training and social protection as they have been operating to date. It transforms economic and social constants, differentiates the concept of place and time, the value of work, structures of socialization and earning, overturns theories, analyses, values, ideologies and offers new perspectives to the concept and the duration of labour and biological life, new values and structures, new social hierarchies and priorities, a new social stratification and a new division in the work organization and in social time as a whole.

Nowadays, at the start of the new historical cycle that is brought by these changes, the picture of unemployment and poverty in Europe and worldwide anything but encouraging it is. An effective approach to the problem requires that attention be focused on a new phenomenon of economic life: that economic mixture does not create enough jobs to absorb the whole population seeking work any longer. In other words, the "iron law" of the new technological revolution will be valid according to which the change of the technological base of society as a whole destroys more jobs than it creates (Rifkin, 1996).

Thus, unemployment should not be treated as repetition of a traditional phenomenon in times of crisis and hardship or aggravation of international competition but as a phenomenon directly related to automation, due to which the economic mixture will take place in the future with less and less labour. This logically leads to the conclusion that the policy measures taken should create more jobs for each unit of output growth. As this finding will apply, as social inequalities will be maintained, as this new reality will supply society not only with unemployment but also with new opportunities that can be exploited for the development of human personality and communication, the demand for less working time, even if it is ground breaking in economic terms, will remain socially relevant and powerful (Rifkin, 1996, p. 391).

Flexibility in working time may be manifested in settlements and regulations concerning work day, work week, work year, or even the whole working life of the individual. The differentiation of work week, shift work and, especially, on Saturday and Sunday, the part-time, casual, seasonal or overnight employment, flexible working hours, most of flexible forms of employment and working time are definitely special aspects of the general issue of flexibility and shrinkage of time available for work. The shrinkage of working time and the expansion of flexible forms of employment and working time are parallel, interwoven with each other and enlarging phenomena, which are routed through the model of an either legislated flexibility or bargained and co-decided – through collective bargaining – flexibility or an individualized flexibility.

In any case, it is getting clear to the agencies and institutions of industrial relations in the member states of the European Union that the organization of working time and flexible forms of employment arrangements require regulations and arrangements balancing development needs and flexibility of enterprises with those consumers with individual and collective social-labour rights as well as with the effort to promote employment. Modern European countries –failing, under the pressure of financial difficulties of enterprises and the intensification of social problems, especially those of unemployment and poverty, to bear the cost of unilaterally policy making and proposing arrangements – attempt to pass "the responsibility" for finding the "golden mean" to interested parties, to the eminently versatile mechanism of collective bargaining, which anyway is an institution of co-decision, means of consensus and a political mechanism, a "barometer", of social relationships.

Nowadays, therefore, an alternative approach to flexicurity may be adopted, which, at least in terms of flexible forms of employment and working time, can lead to the formation, on the initiative of the state, of legal framework of regulations under which more specific contractual arrangements will grow, arrangements and regulations tailored to industrial, operational and individual production units. The combination of the minimum of state regulation in the social dialogue and the co-decision in regulating flexible forms of employment and organization of working time seems to be able to produce a complete institutional nexus of interlocking and mutually complementary regulations – which will provide, on the one hand, enterprises with harmonized and balanced ability to satisfy their demand and utilize labour flexibility, and, on the other hand, employees with minimum guarantees of individual and collective labour rights, and mainly safeguards that will restore these flexible forms of competitive factors of social rights and full-time employment in transformed forms of alternative expressions of social protection, in enhanced factors of the competitiveness of economy and, especially, in parameters of completion of full-time employment, thus stimulating total employment and preventing employment and social protection from being deregulated.

Instead of an Epilogue: Focusing into the Major Changes

A series of individual changes in the structure of the Greek system of collective bargaining will result in their decentralising at company level rather than at industry level which has been in effect up to date. Such regulations and changes have been both the elimination of overlapping provisions of collective employment agreements (CEAs) and the ineffective principle of favourable regulation combined with the introduction of the new institution of special company agreements. Equally important, if not the most important issue, are other measures adopted such as: the abolition of the institution of the extension of CEAs, a fact that leads to the creation of conditions of fierce competition between companies, fragmentation and competition among employees, multi-fragmentation of the market and to the deregulation of labour relations. This measure, combined with the former – that is, the decentralization at company level – intensifies the competition in the market and the multi-fragmentation in industrial relations.

Repeated legislative changes to the system of collective bargaining, starting from the initial Memorandum, the updated Memorandum up to the latest Memorandum have led to a complete restructuring of the system of collective bargaining. Up to the latest Memorandum, the system of collective bargaining was operational, since it had been making use, at a central level, of national bargaining to guarantee the minimum levels of protection and payment, while leaving flexibility so that the system of collective bargaining can be decentralised at the company level, but within a structured framework of industrial relationships that had ensured primarily decentralization at industry level. Collective bargaining labour agreements at industry level functioned as an "Umbrella" and underneath them there could be further decentralization and flexibility at the company level, while the regulations for confluence were providing the employee with adequate protection.

With repeated legislative changes that have occurred as a result of Memoranda first decentralization at industry level is removed. The abolition of the institution of expansion of collective bargaining labour agreements has led to conditions of multi-segmentation in regulating industrial relations by sector. It cancels the value and role of sectoral regulation. It creates conditions for wild and extreme competition. And as framed by the new institution of specific company agreements and the abolition of previous regime of the confluence of collective bargaining labour agreements, there have been forming institutional and potentially real conditions of further exacerbation of competition, further multi-fragmentation of industrial relations per a company and / or decollectivisation and individualization of industrial relations, meaning deregulation of industrial relations and labour protection framework. These data are exacerbated by an additional fact; there is not just the dramatic shrinkage of the minimum wage but the intervention of transnational legal abolition of the minimum wage as an institutional product of the constitutional recognition of collective autonomy.

By the end of the aftereffect, payments will be reduced automatically, that, the individual employment contract will be modified without the employee's consent. This would cause dramatic wage cuts in the private sector. The Memorandum states that the reduced wages will apply until a new contract, collective or individual. However, it is clear that employees will be forced to agree, at an individual level, on lower wages under the direct or indirect threat of dismissal. The inability of labour unions to sign an agreement is given within this new regime. This also becomes absolutely impossible due to another additional fact: that the recourse to arbitration is no longer feasible, since it requires the consent of employers and employees.

The reduction in the minimum wage – the effectiveness of which is to stimulate competitiveness of the economy is now openly questioned even by the most extreme neoliberal economists – has gripped a series of benefits and those people who are paid more than the minimum wage, and even unemployment benefits, which are calculated based on the minimum wage, something that has been forcing a large part of society in utter misery and ultimately social exclusion. The reduction (in the minimum wage) raises a serious constitutional issue, as the key core of Articles 22, Paragraph 2, and 23, Paragraph 1 of the Constitution, the precedence effect of International Labor Conventions 98 and 154 as well as the European Social Charter, fortifying collective autonomy.

Even those who were in favour of measures, they acknowledge that in medium term structural reforms will create favorable conditions for employment. Nevertheless, they together with the European Commission in its interim report acknowledge that the decision of the then government to proceed to a reduction in the minimum wage, bringing an overall impact on wages in order to improve competitiveness and increase employment of the young and unskilled employees, is expected to stand an obstacle to domestic demand, which in short term will affect negatively employment.

Finally, in the new Memorandum (Law 4046/2012), the implementation of which was the Cabinet Act (PYS in Greek) 6/28-2-2012, the arbitration is now available only on a voluntary basis. Thus, the arbitration system loses its mixed character and becomes voluntary, helping decisively overthrow the operational context of collective labour relations in Greece with other regulations. More specifically, this regulation – as it makes disappear any perspective of a framework of collective regulation at the "end of the street" of the bargaining "in any case", under great depression, unemployment and downturn bargaining power of the unions – leads to fatal decollectivisation and individualisation of industrial relations.

The previous status of collective bargaining – both maintaining the national collective employment agreement in a prominent position and ensuring the decentralisation at industry level – offered, on the one hand, conditions of decentralization and thus of flexibility, and, on the other hand, clauses of necessary social protection through minimum wages / minima. Today, with the emphasis on the decentralization at company level and the abolition of the provisions for concurrence – with the establishment of special employment agreements at company level, decentralisation at company level does not simply become flexible; it rather gets fragmented and liquify labour relations. At the same time, the minimum wage and protection, apart from the fact that they have already have been decreased legislatively, are being de-rooted, since collective autonomy is canceled by the Provisions of the new Memorandum and is provided in Annex (p. 801) of Law 4046/2012 that "the government as of July 2012 legislates the minimum wage in consultation with the social partners." This provision combined with that in Paragraph 7, Article 2 of Law 3845/2010 – that is, the ratifying Act of the First Memorandum that provides that the terms of any kind of collective employment agreements (CEAs) may diverge even from the national general employment agreement (EGSSE) (despite the fact that this executive decree might never have been issued) dislocates and deconstructs completely the collective bargaining system in Greecey.

With such an institutionally reformed framework of collective bargaining, this institution – when operating in an environment where in risk of poverty or exclusion is about the 37% of the general population, unemployment is about 28% and youth unemployment (18–24 age group) is near 58%, it is self-evident that as a political mechanism, reflecting the balance of power – will produce very poor results for employees. Ever more, after the repeated partial modifications that took place, eventually with the provisions of the new Memorandum, the previous system of mixed arbitration has been abolished; a system which, in spite of the fact that it featured bold elements of obligation, ensured that there would be no phenomena of unregulated labour relations. But within a context where society and employees are tested and unemployment has exploded to unprecedented heights, it is very doubtful whether and to what extent the institution of collective bargaining will operate; especially, when there is not even the prospect or the “threat” of arbitration “down the road”. According to the data of the new Memorandum, arbitration may be conducted only when both sides agree upon it. So, it is very likely that there may an increase in cases of failure to reach agreements and collective employment agreements, absence of collective arbitration rules (arbitral), thus there will be a transition to decollectivisation and individualisation of collective labour relations.

Consequently, the new landscape in industrial relations is characterized by an intense multi-fragmentation (decentralization at company level – each company has an individual status – either decollectivization and individualisation of labor relations – that is, absence of collective arrangements and conclusion of individual employment agreements or contracts), while the question of whether and how the state will intervene – certainly unconstitutionally – for the formation of a minimum wage will linger.

Indicative Bibliography

Aaronovitch, S., et al., (1981), The Political Economy of British Capitalism: A Marxist Analysis, Maidenhead, McGraw Hill.

Abentrot, B., (1976), Social History of European Labour Movement, (trans. Emi Manousi), Athens, Odysseus Publications. [Άμπεντροτ, Β., (1976), Κοινωνική Ιστορία του Ευρωπαϊκού Εργατικού Κινήματος, (μεταφρ. Αίμη Μανούση), Αθήνα, Εκδόσεις Οδυσσέας].

Addison J. and Siebert W., (1994), Recent development in social policy in the European Union, Industrial and Labor Relations Review, Vol. 48, No 1.

Advisory Conciliation and Arbitration Service (ACAS), (1979), "The ACAS Role in Conciliation, Arbitration and Mediation", London.

Advisory Conciliation and Arbitration Service (ACAS), (1980), Industrial Relations Handbook, HMSO.

Advisory Conciliation and Arbitration Service (ACAS), (1993), Information and Advice and Promoting Good Practice in informative edition "Promoting the Improvement of Industrial Relations", October.

Agallopoylos, P. and Travlos-Tzanetatos, D.A., Rapport Nationale, Grèce (1991). In XIII International Conference of Labour Law and Social Security, Athens.

Ahuja, M.K., and Carley, K.M., (1998), Network Structure in Virtual Organizations, Journal of Computer Mediated Communication (JCMC), [on line] 3 (4). Available: http: // www.ascusc.org/jcmc/vol3/issue4/ahuja.html.

Albeda, W., (1987), Recent Trends in Collective Bargaining in Netherlands, in Windmuller, J. P., et al, Collective Bargaining in Industrialized Market Economics: A Reappraisal, I.L.O., Geneva.

Aldrich, H., (1999), Organizations Evolving, Sage Publications Ltd, London.

Alesina, Alberto and George-Marios Angeletos, (2005), Fairness and Redistribution: Us vs. Europe, American Economic Review, 95.

Alexiadis, M., (1988), The Greek and International Scientific Naming of Folklore Studies, Kardamitsas Publications, Athens. [Αλεξιάδης, Μ., (1988), Η Ελληνική και Διεθνής Επιστημονική Ονοματοθεσία της Λαογραφίας, Εκδόσεις Καρδαμίτσα, Αθήνα].

Alexiadis, M., (2006), Modern Greek Folklore Studies: A Collection of Studies Institute of the Book, Kardamitsas Publications, Athens. [Αλεξιάδης, Μ., (2006), Νεωτερική Ελληνική Λαογραφία, Συναγωγή Μελετών, Ινστιτούτο του Βιβλίου, Εκδόσεις Α. Καρδαμίτσα, Αθήνα].

Aliprantis, N., (1979), The Nature and the Actors of Collective Bargaining, Destinctive Developments in Western-European Countries, Epitheorisi Ergatikou Dikeou (E.Erg.D.-Revew of Labour Law), vol. [Αλιπράντης, Ν., (1979), Η φύσις και οι φορείς των συλλογικών διαπραγματεύσεων, Χαρακτηριστικοί εξελίξεις εις τας δυτικοευρωπαϊκάς χώρας, Ε.Εργ.Δ., τ. 38].

Aliprantis, N., (1984), For the renewal of the theory of the Labour Law, Epitheorisi Ergatikou Dikeou (E.Erg.D.-Revew of Labour Law), v. 43, pp. 418–426. [Αλιπράντης, Ν., (1984), Για την Ανανέωση της θεωρίας του Εργατικού Δικαίου, Ε.Εργ.Δ., τ. 43].

Ambercrombie, N., Hill, St., Turner, Br. S., (1991), Dictionary of Sociology, (trans. A. Kantas & S. Kantas-ed. P. Terlexis), Athena, Pataki Editions. [Ambercrombie, N., Hill, St., Turner, Br. S., (1991), Λεξικό Κοινωνιολογίας, (μεταφρ. Α. Κάντας & Σ. Κάντας – επιμ. Π. Τερλεξής). Αθήνα, Εκδόσεις Πατάκη].

Analytis, N., (1991), Industrial Relations in Greece, Greek Industries Association Bulletin, No. 534, December. [Αναλυτής, Ν., (1991), Εργασιακές Σχέσεις στην Ελλάδα, Δελτίο Συνδέσμου Ελληνικών Βιομηχανιών, τεύχος 534, Δεκέμβριος].

Anderson, B., (1949), The Meaning of Scientific Management, Harvard Business Review, vol 28, n. 6.

Angelidis, M., (1993), The Theory of Rights in Modern Liberalism: Critical Issues on Rehabilitation Theories by Nozick, R., Rawls, J., and Dworkin, R., in Getimis P., and Gravaris, D., (1993), Welfare State and Social Policy: Contemporary Questioning, Athens, Themelio Publications. [Αγγελίδης, Μ., (1993), Η Θεωρία των Δικαιωμάτων στο Σύγχρονο Φιλελευθερισμό: Ζητήματα Κριτικής Ανακατασκευής στις Θεωρίες των Nozick, R., Rawls, J., και Dworkin, R., στο Γετίμης Π., και Γράβαρης, Δ., (1993), Κοινωνικό Κράτος και Κοινωνική Πολιτική: η Σύγχρονη Προβληματική, Αθήνα, Εκδόσεις Θεμέλιο].

Annual Report (2000), Greek Economy and the Employment, Reports (2), Institute of Labour G.S.E.E.-A.D.E.D.Y, Athens.

Antonopoulou, M., (1991), Theory and Ideology in the Thought of Classical Sociology, Athens, Papazisis Editions. [Αντωνοπούλου, Μ., (1991), Θεωρία και Ιδεολογία στη Σκέψη των Κλασσικών της Κοινωνιολογίας, Αθήνα, Εκδόσεις Παπαζήση].

Argyle, M., (1972), Social Psychology of Work, Harmonds-Worth, Penguin.

Argyris, C., (1964), Integrating the Individual and the Organization, John Wiley & Sons.

Argyros, St., (1991), President of SEB, Robert Spyropoulos, State Executive Committee and President of GSEE IN.E. GSEE, and Vasso Papandreou, Greek EEC Commissioner, in the conference held on the 31.10.91 Department of International and Economic Studies, Athens University of Economics on “Employee Relations since 1992”. [Αργυρός, Στ., (1991), Πρόεδρος ΣΕΒ, Ροβέρτος Σπυρόπουλος: μέλος της Εκτελεστικής Επιτροπής της ΓΣΕΕ και Πρόεδρος του ΙΝ.Ε.-ΓΣΕΕ και Βάσω Παπανδρέου Ελληνίδα Επίτροπος στην ΕΟΚ, στη συζήτηση που διοργάνωσε, στις 31.10.91 το Τμήμα Διεθνών και Οικονομικών Σπουδών του Οικονομικού Πανεπιστημίου Αθηνών με θέμα: «Εργασιακές Σχέσεις μετά το 1992»].

Articles 1-11 of Law 2150/1993 “National Labour Institute and other provisions” FEK/98 / issue A′ of the 16th of June 1993.

Articles 14-18 of Law 1876/1990 “On Free Collective Bargaining”, in the book, “The New Ways of Solving Collection Labour Disputes”, Edition of the Legal Society of Northern Greece, Nr 14, Thessaloniki, 1992.

Artinopoulou, B., (1998), School Violence and Social Exclusion. Recent Trends in Research and Response. Proceedings of the Conference: Education and Social Exclusion, Athens. [Αρτινοπούλου, Β., (1998), Σχολική Βία και Κοινωνικός Αποκλεισμός,. Πρόσφατες Τάσεις στην Έρευνα και την Αντιμετώπιση. Πρακτικά Συνεδρίου με Θέμα: Εκπαίδευση και Κοινωνικός Αποκλεισμός, Αθήνα].

Artinopoulou, B., (2000), Treatment of Juvenile Offenders. Neoconservative Trends and Standards. I Epochi 13, June 18, 2000. [Αρτινοπούλου, Β., (2000), Μεταχείριση Ανηλίκων Παραβατών. Νεοσυντηρητικές Τάσεις και Πρότυπα. Η Εποχή, 13, 18 Ιουνίου 2000].

Assessment of the Work of the OMED 1992–2001 and Action Planning for 2002, (January 2002), Organization for Mediation and Arbitration, OMED, Athens.

Atkinson, A., (1986), Employment Flexibility in Internal and External Labour Markets, Institute of Manpower Studies, University of Sussex, Brighton, March.

Babas, S., (1990), Labour and Social Relations, Athens, Nea Skepsi Publications. [Μπαμπάς, Σ., (1990), Εργασία και Κοινωνικές Σχέσεις, Αθήνα, Εκδόσεις Νέα Σκέψη].

Babalis, Th., (2005), Children of Single Parent Families, Atrapos Publications, Athens. [Μπαμπάλης, Θ., (2005), Παιδιά Μονογονεϊκών Οικογενειών, Εκδόσεις Ατραπός, Αθήνα].

Babounis, Ch., (2007), Local Government and State, Vanyas Publications, Thessaloniki. [Μπαμπούνης, Χ., (2007), Τοπική Αυτοδιοίκηση και Κράτος, Εκδόσεις Βάνιας, Θεσσαλονίκη].

Babounis, Ch., (2008), Aspects of Local Authorities in the Greek Government, Administrative Organization, Population, Education, Papazisis, Athens. [Μπαμπούνης, Χ., (2008), Όψεις της Τοπικής Αυτοδιοίκησης στο Ελληνικό Κράτος, Διοικητική Οργάνωση, Πληθυσμός, Εκπαίδευση, Εκδόσεις Παπαζήση, Αθήνα].

Bagnoli, Marc and Susan Watts, (2003), Selling to socially responsible consumers: Competition and the private provision of public goods, Journal of Economics and Management Strategy, 12.

Bain G.S., - Clegg, H.A., (1974), A strategy for Industrial Relations Research in Great Britain, British Journal of Industrial Relations, March, Vol XII, No I.

Bamber, G. and Cordova, E., (1993), Collective Bargaining, in Blanpain, R. and Engels, C., (eds.), Comparative Labour Law and Industrial Relations in Industrialized Market Economies, 5th and revised edition, Deventer-Boston.

Banoutsos, H., (1996), Anthropocentric Production Systems: Their Importance for the less industrialized countries of Europe, in Liodakis G., (ed.), Society, Technology and Restructuring of Production Papazisis, Athens. [Μπανούτσος, Η., (1996), Ανθρωποκεντρικά Συστήματα Παραγωγής: η σημασία τους για τις λιγότερο βιομηχανικά αναπτυγμένες χώρες της Ευρώπης, στο Λιοδάκης Γ., (επιμ), Κοινωνία, Τεχνολογία και Αναδιάρθρωση της Παραγωγής, Εκδόσεις Παπαζήση, Αθήνα].

Barbash, J., (1964), The Elements of Industrial Relations, British Journal of Industrial Relations, Vol. II, No. I.

Baron, R.A., (1986), Behavior in Organizations, Allyn & Bacon, Inc., Boston.

Bauman, Z., (2002), (trans.: K. D. Geormas), Labour, Consumerism and the new poor, Metehmio Editions, Athens. [Μπάουμαν, Ζ., (2002), (μετ.: Κ. Δ. Γεώρμας), Η Εργασία ο Καταναλωτισμός και οι Νεόπτωχοι, Εκδόσεις Μεταίχμιο, Αθήνα].

Behrend, H, (1963), The Field of Industrial Relations, British Journal of Industrial Relations, Vol. I, No 3, October.

Bell, D., (1960), The End of Ideology, The Free Press, in Walker, C. Technology, Industry and Man, McGraw-Hill Company.

Bell, D., (1974), The Coming of Post-Industrial Society: A Venture in Social Forecasting, London, Heinemann.

Bendix, R., (1963), Work and Authority in Industry: Ideologies of Management in the Course of Industrialization, Harper and Row, New York.

Bessant, J., Bowen, J., Dickson, K., Marsh, J., (1981), The Impact of Microelectronics, Frances Pinter.

Bessant, J., (1989), Microelectronics and Change at Work, I.L.O., Geneva.

Blackburn, Ph., Coombs, R. and Green, K., (1985), Technology, Economic Growth and the Labour Process, MacMillan.

Blain, A.N.J. and Gennard, J., (1970), Industrial Relations Theory - A Critical Review, British Journal of Industrial Relations, Vol. VIII, No 3, November.

Blauner, R., (1964), Alienation and Freedom, Chicago University Press.

Blanpain, R., (1986), Legal and Contractual Limitations to Working Time, Leuven, February, in Dahrendorf, R., Kohler, E., and Poitet, E., (1986), New Forms of Work and Activity, Documentation, European Foundation of Living and Working Conditions, Dublin, Colloquim, Brussels.

Blanpain, R., (1987), Recent Trends in Collective Bargaining in Belgium, in Windmuller, J. P., et al, Collective Bargaining in Industrialized Market Economics: A Reappraisal, I.L.O., Geneva.

Blanpain, R. and Koukiadis, I., (1993), The Community Law Labor Before and After Maastricht, Paratiritis Publications, Thessaloniki. [Blanpain, R., και Κουκιάδης, I., (1993), Το Κοινοτικό Δίκαιο της Εργασίας, Πριν και Μετά το Μάαστριχ, Εκδόσεις Παρατηρητής, Θεσσαλονίκη].

Blumberg, P., (1968), Industrial Democracy: The Sociology of Participation, London, Constable.

Bolin, B., (1987), Trade Unions and the Crisis, in Spyropoulos, G., (eds), Trade Unions Today and Tomorrow, Vol. I, Trade Unions in a Changing Europe, Work and Society, No 6, European Centre for Work and Society, Maastricht, Presses Interuniversitaires Europeennes.

Bonefeld, W., & Holloway, J., (1991), Post Fordism and Social Form, A Marxist Debate on the Post Fordist State, Macmillan, London,

Boyer, R., & Coriat, B., (1986), Technical Flexibility and Macro-stabilization, Preliminary Insights, Communication at the Conference on Innovation Diffusion, Venice 17-21.03.1986, (nimeo).

Boyer, R., (1979), La Crise Actuelle: Une Mise en Perspective Historique, Critiques d' Economie Politique, n. 7-8.

Boyer, R., (1987), Labour Flexibilities: Many Forms, Uncertain Effects, Labour and Society, Vol. 12, No. 1, January.

Brannen, P., (1983), Authority and Participation in Industry, London, Bastford.

Brannen, P., et al, (1976), The Worker Directors, London, Hutchinson.

Braverman, H., (1974), Labour and Monolopoly Capital, The Degradation of Work in the Twentleth Century, Monthly Review Press.

Bright, R.J., (1958), Automation and Management, Boston Division of Graduate School of Business Administration, Harvard University.

Brown, H., (1981), The Individual in the Organisation, στο Salaman, G., και Thompson, K., (eds), Control ar Ideology in Organisations, London, Open University.

Brunhes, B., (1989), La flexibilité du travail: Réflexions sur les modèles européens, Problemes économiques, no 2125, 17.05.1089.

Bultje, R., van Wijk, J., (1998), Taxonomy of virtual organizations, based on definitions, characteristics and typology. VO – Newsletter, 2(3).

Burgess, Ch., (1985), Skill Implications of New Technology, Employment Gazette, October. Burn, J.M. and Ash, C., (2000), Knowledge management strategies for virtual organizations, Information Resources Management Journal, 13 (1).

Burns, T. and Stalker, G. M., (1961), The Management of Innovation, Tavistock Publications.

Caire, G., (1987), Recent Trends in Collective Bargaining in France, in Windmuller, J. P., et al, Collective Bargaining in Industrialized Market Economics: A Reappraisal, ILO. Geneva.

Casey, B., Dragendorf, R., Heering, W. and John, G., (1989), Temporary Employment in Great Britain and the Federal Republic of Germany, International Labour Review, Vol. 128, No 4.

Castells, M., (2000), Materials for an explanatory theory of the network society, British Journal of Sociology, 51 (1).

Chamberlain, N.W. and Kuhn, J.W., (1965), Collective Bargaining, Mc Graw Hill.

Chelnt, D., (1995), Models of democracy, Stachy Publications, Athens. [Χελντ, Ντ., (1995), Μοντέλα δημοκρατίας, Εκδόσεις Στάχυ, Αθήνα].

Chinoy, E., (1955), Automobile Workers and the American Dream, Doubleday, New York.

Chitiris, L. (1994), Organizational Behavior, Interbooks Publications. [Χυτήρης, Λ., (1994), Οργανωσιακή Συμπεριφορά, Εκδόσεις Interbooks].

Chitiris, L. (ny), Basic Principles of Management, ELKEPA. [Χυτήρης, Λ., (χ.χ.), Βασικές Αρχές Διοίκησης (Μάνατζμεντ), ΕΛΚΕΠΑ].

Choidas, F.G., (1997), The Working Hour-Hose Wraps Europe Kyriakatiki Elefterotypia, Economy, International, October 19. [Χοϊδάς, Φ.Γ., (1997), Το Ωράριο-Λάστιχο Τυλίγει την Ευρώπη, Κυριακάτικη Ελευθεροτυπία, Οικονομία, Διεθνή, 19 Οκτωβρίου].

Christodoulou, D., (1992), Flexible Specialization and Postindustrial Management, Thessaloniki. [Χριστοδούλου, Δ., (1992), Εύκαμπτη Εξειδίκευση και Μεταβιομηχανικό Μάνατζμεντ, Θεσσαλονίκη].

Christoforatos, Ch., (1989), Elasticity in Labour Relations, From Confrontation of Co-operatives to Social Consensus, Epitheorisi Ergatikou Dikeou (E.Erg.D.-Revew of Labour Law), v. 48. [Χριστοφοράτος, Χ., (1989), Η Ελαστικότητα στις Εργασιακές Σχέσεις. Από την Αντιπαράθεση των Κοινωνικών Εταιριών στη Συναίνεση, Ε.Εργ.Δ., τ. 48].

Clarke, O., (1984), Collective Bargaining and the Economic Recovery, in OECD Observer, (Paris, Organization for Economic Cooperation and Development), July.

Clegg, H., (1960), A New Approach to Industrial Democracy, Oxford, Blackwell.

Clegg, H., (1975), Pluralism in industrial relations, British Journal of Industial Relations, XIII, (3).

Clegg, S.R., (1990), Modern Organizations: Organization Studies in the Post-modern World, Sage Publications.

Clegg, S., & Sewell, G., (2001), Social Conflict, Organizational, in Baltes, P., and Smelser, N. (Eds.), The international encyclopedia of social and behavioral sciences, Elsevier, Oxford.

Cockburn, C., (1983), Brothers, Pluto, London.

Cohen, P.S., (1968), Modern Social Theory, Heinemann, London

Cole, G.D.H., (1972), Self Government in Industry, (introduction by J.G. Corina), London, Hopkinson.

Commission Européenne, (1999), L' emploi en Europe 1992–1999, (publication annuelle), Emploi et affaires sociales, Bruxelles.

Commission of the European Communities COM (91) 511 final, Brussels (1991). The First Report on the Implementation of the Community Charter of Fundamental Social Rights of Workers.

Commission of the European Communities, (1992), Annual Report of the European Industrial Relations Observatory in Europe, Directorate-General, V/1466/92, V. [Επιτροπή των Ευρωπαϊκών Κοινοτήτων, (1992), Ετήσια Έκθεση του Ευρωπαϊκού Παρατηρητηρίου των Εργασιακών Σχέσεων στην Ευρώπη, Γενική Διεύθυνση V, V/1466/92].

Commission of the European Communities, [1992]-1995, (regularly published), Employment Observatory Trends, Brussels, Directorate General for Employment, Industrial Relations and Social Affairs.

Conflict and consent in work, available at: http://www.oup.co.uk/pdf/bt/fincham/Chapter10.pdf.

Constitution and Labor Relations, Lectures-Interventions and Debates of the Third Congress of EDEKA, Epitheorisi Ergatikou Dikeou (E.Erg.D.-Revew of Labour Law), Athens. [«Σύνταγμα και Εργασιακές Σχέσεις», Εισηγήσεις-Παρεμβάσεις και Συζητήσεις από το Γ΄ Πανελλήνιο Συνέδριο της Ε.Δ.Ε.Κ.Α., Έκδοση της Ε.Εργ.Δ., Αθήνα].

Cordova, E., (1985), New Forms and Aspects of Atypical Employment Relationships, General Report, 11th International Congress of the International Society for Labour Law and Social Security, Caracas, September.

Cordova, E., (1986), From Full-Time Wage Employment to Atypical Employment: A Major Shift in the Evolution of Labour Relations? International Labor Review, I.L.R. (International Labor Review), Vol. 125, November-December.

Cordova, E., (1993), Collective Bargaining, in Blanpain, R. and Engels, C., Comparative Labour Law and Industrial Relations in Industrialized Market Economies, 5th and revised edition, Deventer-Boston, vol. 2.

Coria, M., (1985), Science, Engineering and Capital, Discontinuity, Athens. [Κοριά, Μ., (1985), Επιστήμη, Τεχνική και Κεφάλαιο, Ασυνέχεια, Αθήνα].

Coriat, B., (1980), The Restructuring of the Assembly Line: a New Economy of Time and Control, Capital and Class, n. 11.

Coriat, B., (1990), L' atelier et le robot-essai sur le fordisme et la production de masse a l' âge électronique, Ch. Bourgois.

Coser, L., (1956), The Functions of Social Conflict, Routledge & Kegan Paul, London.

Coser, L., (1965), Georg Simmel, Prentice Hall, Englewood Cliffs, NJ.

Council Directive 97/81/EC of 15 December 1997 concerning the Framework Agreement on part-time work concluded by UNICEF, CEEP and the ETUC - Annex: Framework agreement on part-tíme work, Official Joumal L 014, 20/01/1998 P. 0009- 0014.

Council for Science and Society, (1981), New Technology: Society, Employment and Skill, (GSS Report).

Council of the European Communities, (1982), Proposal for a Council Directive on Voluntary Part-Time Work, January 1982.

Cressey, P., Eldridge, J., and MacInnes, J., (1985), Just managing: Authority and Democracy in Industry, O.U.P.

Crouch, C., (1982), The Politics of Industrial Relations (2nd edition), Fontana.

Crozier, M., (1963), The Bureaucratic Phenomenon, The University of Chicago Press.

Dahl, R., (1957), The Concept of Power, Behavioral Science II, July.

Dahrendorf, R., (1957), Soziale Klassen und Klassenkunflikte in der industriellen Gessellschaft, Enke Stuttgart, Germany.

Dahredorf, R., (1958), Out of Utopia: Toward a Reorganization of Sociological Analysis, American Journal of Sociology, LXIV (1).

Dahrendorf, R., (1959), Class and Class Conflict in Industrial Society, Stanford University Press, Stanford.

Dahrendorf, R., (1966), Gesellschaft und Demokratie in Deutschland, Piper, Munich, Germany.

Dahrendorf, R., (1968), Class and Class Conflict in Industrial Society, Routledge & Kean Paul, London.

Dahrendorf, R., (1972), Konflikt und Freiheit auf dem Weg zur Dienstklassengesellschaft, Piper, Munich, Germany.

Daskalakis, D., (1989a), The Problem of Theory in Industrial Relations and Dunlop's Systemic Approach, Public Sector, April, No. 43, Athens. [Δασκαλάκης, Δ., (1989a), Το Πρόβλημα της Θεωρίας στις Εργασιακές Σχέσεις και η Συστημική Προσέγγιση του Dunlop, Δημόσιος Τομέας, Απρίλιος, τεύχος 43, Αθήνα].

Daskalakis, D., (1989b), Current research directions in industrial relations, Hellenic Sociological Bulletin, No. 19, Athens. [Δασκαλάκης, Δ., (1989b), Σύγχρονες κατευθύνσεις της έρευνας των εργασιακών σχέσεων, Δελτίο Ελλήνων Κοινωνιολόγων, τεύχος 19, Αθήνα].

Daskalakis, D., (1989c), Modern dimensions of industrial democracy and participation, Dimosios Tomeas (: Public Sector), No. 46-47, Athens. [Δασκαλάκης, Δ., (1989c), Σύγχρονες διαστάσεις της βιομηχανικής δημοκρατίας και συμμετοχής, Δημόσιος Τομέας, τεύχος 46-47, Αθήνα].

Daskalakis, D., (1991a), Paper presented in the Seminar Training of Mediators-Arbitrators of OMED, Athens, Nov. 16, Royal Olympic Hotel. [Δασκαλάκης, Δ., (1991b), Εισήγηση στο Σεμινάριο Επιμόρφωσης των Μεσολαβητών-Διαιτητών του Ο.ΜΕ.Δ., Αθήνα, 16 Νοεμβρίου, Ξενοδοχείο Royal Olympic].

Daskalakis, D., (1991b), A promising new framework for arbitration in labor relations, Oikonomikos Tachidromos (: The Economist), January 10, 2 F. (1914), 10.01.91, Athens. [Δασκαλάκης, Δ., (1991β), Ένα ελπιδοφόρο νέο πλαίσιο για τη διαιτησία στις εργασιακές σχέσεις, Οικονομικός Ταχυδρόμος, 10 Ιανουαρίου Φ. 2 (1914), Αθήνα].

Daskalakis, D., (1992), Institutional Innovation: The new model of mediation and arbitration in collective labor disputes. Newsletter, published by the Institute of Labour GSEE, Vol. 18–19, August-September, Athens. [Δασκαλάκης, Δ., (1992), Θεσμική καινοτομία: Το νέο μοντέλο μεσολάβησης και διαιτησίας στις συλλογικές διαφορές εργασίας. Ενημερωτικό Δελτίο, έκδοση του Ινστιτούτου Εργασίας της Γ.Σ.Ε.Ε., τεύχος 18-19, Αύγουστος-Σεπτέμβριος, Αθήνα.

Daskalakis, D., (1993), The Labour Status of the Personnel of Public Enterprises, Direction: Professor: K. Mavrias, Forward: Professor J. Koukiadis, Ant. N. Sakkoulas Editions, Constitution-Management-Policy, Nr 10, Athens-Komotini. [Δασκαλάκης, Δ., (1993), Το Εργασιακό Καθεστώς του Προσωπικού των Δημοσίων Επιχειρήσεων, Εκδόσεις Αντ. Ν. Σάκκουλα, Σειρά: Σύνταγμα-Διοίκηση-Πολιτική, Ν. 10, Αθήνα-Κομοτηνή].

Daskalakis, D., (1994), The Evolution of Collective Bargaining, Epitheorisi Ergatikou Dikeou (E.Erg.D.-Revew of Labour Law), vol. 53, Athens. [Δασκαλάκης, Δ., (1994), Η Εξέλιξη των Συλλογικών Διαπραγματεύσεων, Ε.Εργ.Δ., τ. 53].

Daskalakis, D., (1995a), The Collective Autonomy in Modern Industrial Society: The Collective Bargaining Experience in European Countries, Series: Publications of Labour Law and Social Security, Direction: Professor J.

Koukiadis, Sakkoulas Editions, Thessaloniki. [Δασκαλάκης, Δ., (1995a), Η Συλλογική Αυτονομία στη Σύγχρονη Βιομηχανική Κοινωνία - Η Εμπειρία των Συλλογικών Διαπραγματεύσεων στις Ευρωπαϊκές Χώρες, Εκδόσεις Σάκκουλα, Θεσσαλονίκη].

Daskalakis, D., (1995b), Regulation of Flexible Forms of Employment and Organisation of Working Time, Ant. N. Sakkoulas, Athens-Komotini. [Δασκαλάκης, Δ., (1995b), Η Ρύθμιση των Ευέλικτων Μορφών Απασχόλησης και Οργάνωσης του Χρόνου Εργασίας, Εκδόσεις Αντ. Ν. Σάκκουλα, Αθήνα-Κομοτηνή].

Daskalakis, D., (2000), Foreword to Labour and Labour Relations, Ant. N. Sakkoulas Editions, Athens-Komotini. [Δασκαλάκης, Δ., (2000), Προλεγόμενα για την Εργασία και τις Εργασιακές Σχέσεις. Εκδόσεις Αντ. Ν. Σάκκουλα, Αθήνα-Κομοτηνή].

Daskalakis, D. (2004a): Policies for the Reinforcement and the Protection of Labour: Current Trends in the Policies for the Labour Market, the Social Security and the Protection of Labour, Ant. N. Sakkoulas Editions, Athens-Komotini. [Δασκαλάκης, Δ., (2004a), Πολιτικές Ενίσχυσης και Προστασίας της Εργασίας, Εκδόσεις Αντ. Ν. Σάκκουλα, Αθήνα-Κομοτηνή].

Daskalakis, D., (2004b), Basic Principles of Sociology, Athens-Komotini, Ant. N. Sakkoulas. [Δασκαλάκης, Δ., (2004b), Βασικές Αρχές Κοινωνιολογίας, Αθήνα-Κομοτηνή, Εκδόσεις Αντ. Ν. Σάκκουλα].

Daskalakis, D., (ed.), (2009a), Poverty, Social Exclusion and Childhood, Ant. N. Sakkoulas Editions, Athens-Komotini. [Δασκαλάκης, Δ., (2009a), Φτώχεια, Κοινωνικός Αποκλεισμός και Παιδική Ηλικία, Εκδόσεις Αντ. Ν. Σάκκουλα, Αθήνα – Κομοτηνή].

Daskalakis, D., (2009b), Industrial Relations, Forward: Professor J. Koukiadis, Ant. N. Sakkoulas Editions, Athens-Komotini. [Δασκαλάκης, Δ., (2009b), Βιομηχανικές Σχέσεις, Πρόλογος: Καθηγητής Ι. Κουκιάδης, Εκδόσεις Αντ. Ν. Σάκκουλα, Αθήνα – Κομοτηνή].

Daskalakis, D., (2009c), Industrial Sociology, Forward: Professor V. Filias, Ant. N. Sakkoulas Editions, Athens-Komotini. [Δασκαλάκης, Δ., (2009b), Βιομηχανική Κοινωνιολογία, Πρόλογος: Καθηγητής Β. Φίλιας, Εκδόσεις Αντ. Ν. Σάκκουλα, Αθήνα – Κομοτηνή].

Daskalakis, D., (2010), Introduction to Modern Sociology, Series: Modern Social Sciences – Theory and Practice, Direction & Forward: Professor V. Filias, Papazisis Editions, Athens. [Δασκαλάκης, Δ., (2010), Εισαγωγή στη Σύγχρονη Κοινωνιολογία, Πρόλογος: Καθηγητής Β. Φίλιας, Εκδόσεις Παπαζήση, Αθήνα].

Daskalakis, D. and Givalos, M. (eds.), (2011a), Childhood and the Child's Rights, Livanis Editions, Athens. [Δασκαλάκης, Δ., και Γκίβαλος, Μ., (επιμ.) (2011a),

Παιδική Ηλικία και τα Δικαιώματα του Παιδιού, Εκδόσεις Α.Α.Λιβάνη, Αθήνα].

Daskalakis, D., (2011b), Industrial Sociology and Industrial Relations, Ant. N. Sakkoulas Editions, Athens-Komotini. [Δασκαλάκης, Δ., (2011b), Βιομηχανική Κοινωνιολογία και Βιομηχανικές Σχέσεις, Εκδόσεις Αντ. Ν. Σάκκουλα, Αθήνα – Κομοτηνή].

Daskalakis, El, (2009), Psycho-social Factors of School Indifference. The Case of Corfu, PhD Thesis, Panteion University of Social and Political Sciences, Department of Psychology, Athens. [Δασκαλάκης, Ηλ., (2009), Ψυχοκοινωνικοί Παράγοντες της Σχολικής Αδιαφορίας. Η Περίπτωση της Κέρκυρας, Διδακτορική Διατριβή, Πάντειο Πανεπιστήμιο Πολιτικών και Κοινωνικών Επιστημών, Τμήμα Ψυχολογίας, Αθήνα].

Data of "Labour Inspectors", (2001), Ministry of Labour and Social Security, December, Athens, Greece.

Data of the Supreme Labour Council, (2001), Ministry of Labour and Social Security, December, Athens, Greece.

Daubler, W., (1980), Industrial Relations and Law in the Federal Republic of Germany (Trans. by M. Travlos-Tzanetatos), E. Erg. D., v. 39. [Daubler, W., (1980), Εργασιακές Σχέσεις και Δίκαιο στην Ομοσπονδιακή Δημοκρατία της Γερμανίας (Μετάφραση Δ. Τραυλού-Τζανετάτου), Ε. Εργ.Δ., τ. 39].

Dauce, N., (1998), Quand la precarité redessine le marché de l'emploi, "Le monde du travail", Paris, La Découverte.

Davenport, T.H. and Pearlson, K., (1998), Two cheers for the virtual office, Sloan Management Review, 39(4).

Davidow, W. H. and Malone, M. S., (1992), The virtual corporation, New York, Harper Collins Publishers.

Davidsson, P. and Honig, B., (2003), The Role of Social and Human Capital among Nascent Entrepreneurs, Journal of Business Venturing 18(4).

Davis, L., (1962), The Effects of Automation on Job Design, Industrial Relations, v. 2, n. 1, October.

Davis, L., (1963) Applying Technology to Social Problems, New Society, January 13, in de Neubourg, Ch., (1990), Unemployment and Labour Market Flexibility: The Netherlands, World Employment Programme, ILO, Geneva.

de Roo, An. and Jagtenberg, R., (1993), Settling Labour Disputes in Europe, Duventer/Boston, Kluwer.

De Sanctis, G. and Monge, P., (1998), Communication Processes for Virtual Organizations JCMC, 3, 4.

de Neubourg, Ch., (ed.), (1990), Unemployment and Labour Market Flexibility: The Netherlands, World Employment Programme, ILO, Geneva.

Deaton, D.R., and Beaumont, "P.B., (1980), The determinants of bargaining structure: some large scale survey evidence for Britain", 'British Journal of Industrial Relations", vol XVIII.

Dees, J. G. (1998), "Enterprising nonprofits: What do you do when traditional sources of funding fall short?", Harvard Business Review, Jan.-Feb.

Delamotte, Y, (1987), The Evolution of Law and the Collective Labour Relations in France from 1981 to 1986 (Trans. by Sofia Mitsou), E. Erg. D., Vol 46, Issue 13. [Delamotte, Y, (1987), Η Εξέλιξη του Δικαίου και των Συλλογικών Εργασιακών Σχέσεων στη Γαλλία από το 1981 μέχρι το 1986 (Μετάφραση Σοφίας Μήτσου), Ε.Εργ.Δ, τ. 46, τεύχος 13].

Deligianni-Dimitrakou, C., (1989), Labor market flexibility as a Source of Conflict Between National and International Labour Standards, Epitheorisi Ergatikou Dikeou (E.Erg.D.-Revew of Labour Law), Volume 48, Issue 4. [Δεληγιάννη-Δημητράκου, Χ., (1989), Η Ευκαμψία της Αγοράς Εργασίας ως Πηγή Συγκρούσεων Ανάμεσα σε Διεθνείς και Εθνικούς Κανόνες Εργασίας, Ε.Εργ.Δ., τόμος 48, τεύχος 4].

Delkos, N., (2009), Milestones in the Development of Trade Union Movement in Greece, Emporiki Bank Employees Association, Youth Workers Conference, Athens, 14-15 March. [Δέλκος, Ν., (2009), Ιστορικοί Σταθμοί στην Ανάπτυξη του Συνδικαλιστικού Κινήματος στην Ελλάδα, Σύλλογος Εργαζομένων Εμπορικής Τράπεζας, Διημερίδα Νέων Εργαζομένων, Αθήνα, 14-15 Μαρτίου].

Democratic Political Dialogue, Hellenic Centre for Political Research, Panteion University, Lectures and Working Papers 1.

Department of International Relations, Conclusions concerning tripartite consultations at the national level on economic and social policy, kps/kk-3237N. [Τμήμα Διεθνών Σχέσεων, Συμπεράσματα αναφορικά με τις τριμερείς διαβουλεύσεις σε εθνικό επίπεδο για την οικονομική και κοινωνική πολιτική, κψ/κκ-3237Ν].

Deppe, F., (1996), Trade Unions and Labour Relations in the European Union, in Social Policy and Social Dialogue in the Perspective of the Economic-Monetary Union (EMU) and the Europe of Citizens, Kritiki publications and European Cultural Centre of Delphi. [Deppe, F., (1996), Συνδικάτα και Εργασιακές Σχέσεις στην Ευρωπαϊκή Ένωση, στο Κοινωνική Πολιτική και Κοινωνικός Διάλογος στην προοπτική της οικονομικής-Νομισματικής Ένωσης και η Ευρώπη των Πολιτών, Εκδόσεις Κριτική και Ευρωπαϊκό Πολιτιστικό Κέντρο Δελφών].

Dickens, L., (1991), National Paper presented in the 13th World Congress of Labour Law and Social Security, Athens, September 18-21, [Dickens, L., (1991), Εθνική Εισήγηση στο 13° Παγκόσμιο Συνέδριο Εργατικού Δικαίου και Κοινωνικής Ασφάλισης, Αθήνα, 18-21 Σεπτεμβρίου].

Dictionary of Social Sciences (1972), Industrial Sociology, UNESCO, Nikas-Tegopoulos, Athens, 1st vol. [Λεξικό Κοινωνικών Επιστημών, (1972), Βιομηχανική Κοινωνιολογία, UNESCO, Νίκας-Τεγόπουλος, Αθήνα, τ. 1ος].

Diebold, J., (1952), Automation: The Advent of the Automatic Factory, New York: D. Van Nostrand Co, Inc.

DIMEL-GSEE (1990), "The Modern Greek Employee", research by DIMEL-GSEE, December 1989 - January 1990. [ΔΗΜΕΛ-ΓΣΕΕ, (1990), «Ο Σύγχρονος Έλληνας Εργαζόμενος», έρευνα ΔΗΜΕΛ-ΓΣΕΕ, Δεκέμβριος 1989 - Ιανουάριος 1990].

Donovan Commission, (1965–68), Report of Royal Commission on Trade Unions and Employers' Associtations, HMSO.

Doukakis, Nt.–L., (1988), Labour Relations: Economy and Institutions, Odysseas Publications, Athens. [Δουκάκης Ντ.-Λ., (1988), Εργασιακές Σχέσεις, Οικονομία και Θεσμοί, Εκδόσεις Οδυσσέας, Αθήνα].

Drayton, W., (2002), The Citizen Sector: Becoming as Entrepreneurial and Competitive as Business, California Management Review, 44(3).

Droukopoulos, B., (1987), Art, Technique and Technology: Human Nature and mechanization, in Art and Technology, Proceedings, Athens, Ypsilon. [Δρουκόπουλος, Β., (1987), Τέχνη, Τεχνική και Τεχνολογία: Ανθρώπινη Φύση και Μηχανοποίηση, στο Τέχνη και Τεχνολογία, Πρακτικά Συνεδρίου, Αθήνα, Ύψιλον].

Dubin, R., (1954), Constructive aspects of industrial conflict, in Korhauscr, A., Dubin, R. and Ross, A.M., (eds.), Industrial Conflict, Mac Graw Hill.

Dubin, R., (1956), Industrial Workers' World: A study of the Central Life Interest of Industrial Workers, Social Problems, 3 (1).

Duguit, L., (1991), Traite de Droit Constitutionnel, Vol. I, Paris.

Dukakis, D. L. (1988), Employee Relations, Economy and Institutions, Odysseas Publications, Athens. [Δουκάκης, Ντ. Λ., (1988), Εργαυιακές Σχέσεις, Οικονομία και Θεσμοί, Εκδόσεις Οδυσσέας, Αθήνα].

Dunlop, J.T., (1958), Industrial Relation Systems, Carbondale, Southern Illinois UP.

Durkheim, E., (1893/1960), The Division of Labour in Society, (G. Simpson, Trans.) New York, The Free Press.

Dyer-Witheford, N., (1999), Cyber Marx: Cycles and Circuits of Struggle in High-Technology Capitalism. University of Illinois Press.

Easton, D., (1958), The perception of authority and political change, in C. J. Friedruch (Ed.), Authority, Cambridge, Harvard University Press.

Employment Observatory Research-Informatics SA (P.A.E.-P.A.E.), (2003), Flexibility and Organization of Work: Empirical Evidence from Greece and the

European Union, Working Papers, No. 9, March, Athens. [Παρατηρητήριο Απασχόλησης Ερευνητική-Πληροφορική Α.Ε. (Π.Α.Ε.-Π.Α.Ε.), (2003), Ευελιξία και Οργάνωση της Εργασίας: Εμπειρικά Στοιχεία από την Ελλάδα και την Ευρωπαϊκή Ένωση, Κείμενα Εργασίας, Νο 9, Μάρτιος, Αθήνα].

Epstein, C., (2003), WorldWideWhale.Globalisation/Dialogue of Cultures? Cambridge Review of International Affairs, 16 (2).

ESC (1999), Social Dialogue in South East Europe, ESC, April, No. 29.

ETUI (European Trade Union Institute), (1979), A Reduction of Working Hours in Western Europe-Part One: The Present Situation, Brussels.

ETUI (European Trade Union Institute), (1980), The Reduction of Working Hours in Western Europe, Second Part: Analysis of the Social and Economic Consequences, Brussels.

ETUI (European Trade Union Institute), (1981), Redesigning Jobs: Western European Experiences.

ETUI (European Trade Union Institute), (1982), Negotiating Technological Change, Brussels.

ETUI (European Trade Union Institute), (1985a), Flexibility and Jobs-Myths and Realities, Brussels.

ETUI (European Trade Union Institute), (1985b), Trade Union Alternative: Flexibility through the Joint Regulation of Change in Flexibility and Jobs-Myths and Realities, Brussels.

ETUI (European Trade Union Institute) (1986), Flexibility of Working Time in Western Europe, Brussels.

ETUI (European Trade Union Institute), (1989), The Impact of Microelectronics on Employment in Western Europe in the 1980s. European Trade Union Institute, Brussels.

ETUI (European Trade Union Institute), (1990a), The role of economic and social councils in Western Europe, Brussels.

ETUI (European Trade Union Institute), (1990b), Employees' representation and rights in the workplace in Western Europe, Brussels.

ETUI (European Trade Union Institute), (1990c), Collective Bargaining in Western Europe in 1989 and Prospects for 1990, Brussels.

ETUI (European Trade Union Institute) (1992), The European Dimensions of Collective Bargaining After Maastricht, Brussels.

Etzioni, A., (1961), A Comparative Analysis of Complex Organizations, New York, Free Press.

Etzioni, A., (1964), Modern Organizations, Englewood Cliffs, New Jersey, Prentice-Hall.

The Changing Face of Work, (1988), Dublin, European Foundation for the Improvement of Living and Working Conditions.

European Foundation for the Improvement of Living and Working Conditions, (2002), European Industrial Relations Observatory, Eironline, 35-Hour Working Week. Law Adopted, Country: France, 1st of February, Available at: / http://www.eirofound.ie 1998/06/feature/FR 9806113F.html

Eurostat, (2003), Reconciling work and family life in the EU25 in 2003: Employment rates lower and part-time rates higher for women with children. Higher employment rates for men with children, 49/2005, 12 April 2005.

Evans, Al. and Bell, J., (1986), Emerging Themes in Flexible Work Patterns, in Curson, Ch., (ed.), Flexible Patterns of Works, by Institute of Personnel Management, London.

Evans, A. and Walker, L., "Sub-contracting", in Curson, Ch., (ed.), (1986), "Flexible Patterns of Work", Institute of Personnel Management, London.

Evans, A., (1973), Flexibility in Working Life, OECD, Paris.

Express (newspaper), (2001), Rising Unemployment in France on November 20, Athens. [Εξπρές (εφημερίδα), (2001), Άνοδος της Ανεργίας στη Γαλλία, 20 Νοεμβρίου, Αθήνα].

Fakiolas, R., (1978), Labour Trade Unionism in Greece, Athens, Papazisis. [Φακιόλας, Ρ., (1978), Ο Εργατικός Συνδικαλισμός στην Ελλάδα, Αθήνα, Εκδόσεις Παπαζήση].

Fakiolas, R., (1985), The Greek Trade Unions: Past Experience, Present Problems and Future Outlook, in Spyropoulos, G., (eds.), (1985), Trade Unions Today and Tomorrow, Trade Unions in a Changing Europe, Work and Society, Maastricht, Presses Interuniversitaires Europeennes.

Farnham, D. and Pimlott, J., (1983), Understanding Industrial Relations, (2nd ed.), Cassell.

Fasoulis, K., (2001), Quality in human resources management Education (Critical approach to the system of "Total Quality Management" – DOP (Top), "Review of Scientific and Educational Affairs", Edition of the Pedagogical Institute, No. 4. [Φασούλης, Κ., (2001), Η ποιότητα στη διοίκηση του ανθρώπινου δυναμικού της Εκπαίδευσης, (Κριτική προσέγγιση στο σύστημα «Διοίκησης Ολικής Ποιότητας»- ΔΟΠ (Τοπ)., «Επιθεώρηση Επιστημονικών και Εκπαιδευτικών Θεμάτων», Έκδοση του Παιδαγωγικού Ινστιτούτου, τεύχος 4].

Fasoulis, K., (December 2008-May 2009), The Right to Education and the Equal Educational Opportunities. Ideological Approaches and Conceptual Clarifications "Comparative and International Education Review ", Issue 11-12. [Φασούλης, Κ., (Δεκέμβριος 2008-Μάϊος 2009), Το Δικαίωμα στην

Εκπαίδευση και οι ίσες Εκπαιδευτικές Ευκαιρίες. Ιδεολογικές Προσεγγίσεις και Εννοιολογικές Αποσαφηνήσεις, «Συγκριτκή και Διεθνής Εκπαιδευτική Επιθεώρηση», τεύχος 11-12].

Feraroti, F., (Eds), (n.y.), The Classics of Sociology, (TRANS, Kostas Katiforis et al.) Athens, Odysseas Publications. [Φεραρότι, Φ., (επιμ.), (χ.χ.), Οι Κλασσικοί της Κοινωνιολογίας, Αθήνα, (μεταφ. Κώστας Κατηφόρης κ.α.), Αθήνα, Εκδόσεις Οδυσσέας].

Ferner, A., (1987), Enterprise and the Politics of Commercialism: Changing Industrial Relations in British and Spanish Railways, Work, Employment and Society, vol 1, n. 2.

Filias, B.I. (1974), Problems of Social Transformation, Studies, Modern Problems, Papazisis, Athens. [Φίλιας, Β.Ι., (1974), Προβλήματα Κοινωνικού Μετασχηματισμού, Μελέτες, Σύγχρονα Προβλήματα, Εκδόσεις Παπαζήση, Αθήνα].

Filias, B.I. (1976), Max Weber: Systematic Sociology and Methodology (An introduction to his work), Nea Synora Publications, A. Livanis, 2nd ed., Athens. [Φίλιας, Β.Ι., (1976), Μάξ Βέμπερ: Συστηματική Κοινωνιολογία και Μεθοδολογία, (μία εισαγωγή στο έργο του), Εκδόσεις Νέα Σύνορα, Α. Λιβάνης, β΄έκδοση, Αθήνα].

Filias, B.I. (1978), Social Systems, and Courses on Sociology Publications, Nea Synora Publications, A. Livanis, Athens. [Φίλιας, Β.Ι., (1978), Κοινωνικά Συστήματα, και Μαθήματα Κοινωνιολογίας, Εκδόσεις Νέα Σύνορα, Α. Λιβάνης, Αθήνα].

Filias, B.I. (1980), Aspects of Conservation and Change of Social System, Volume A, Publications, Nea Synora Publications, A. Livanis, Athens. [Φίλιας, Β.Ι., (1980), Όψεις της Διατήρησης και της Μεταβολής του Κοινωνικού Συστήματος, Τόμος Α΄, Εκδόσεις Νέα Σύνορα, Α. Λιβάνης, Αθήνα].

Filias, B.I. (1988), Social Systems in the 20th Century, Volume I, Sociological and Anthropological Library, 21, Gutenberg Publications, Athens. [Φίλιας, Β.Ι., (1988), Κοινωνικά Συστήματα στον 20ο Αιώνα, Τόμος Α΄, Κοινωνιολογική και Ανθρωπολογική Βιβλιοθήκη, 21, Εκδόσεις Gutenberg, Αθήνα].

Filias, B.I. (1994), Sociology of the Economy, Volume I, Library of Social Science and Social Policy, 39, Gutenberg Publications. [Φίλιας, Β.Ι., (1994), Κοινωνιολογία της Οικονομίας, Τόμος Α', Βιβλιοθήκη Κοινωνικής Επιστήμης και Κοινωνικής Πολιτικής, 39, Εκδόσεις Gutenberg].

Fjalestad, J., Introduction, in Fossum, E., (eds), (1983), Computerization of Working Time, Norwegian Computing Centre, Ellis Horwood Limited.

Flanders, A., (1968), Collective Bargaining: A Theoretical Analysis, British Journal of Industrial Relations, Vol. VI.

Flanders, A., (1984), The Tradition of Voluntarism, British Journal of Industrial Relations, November, 12.

Fligstein, N., (1998), Is Globalization the Cause of the Crises of Welfare State, pp. 6–8, in Conference Papers Reading Material, ETUI Working Paper- SPS n. 98/5. Conference: Globalization, European Economic Integration and Social Protection, European University Institute, European Forum, Center for Advanced Studies.

Flogaitis, S., (2010), Administrative Law, (collective work: Apostolos Gerontas, Sotiris A. Lytras, Prokopis Pavlopoulos, Glykeria Siouti, Spiros Flogaitis), Sakkoulas Editions, Athens, 2nd Edition. [Φλογαΐτης, Σ., (2010), Διοικητικό Δίκαιο (συλλογικό: Απόστολος Γέροντας, Σωτήρης Α. Λύτρας, Προκόπης Παυλόπουλος, Γλυκερία Σιούτη, Σπύρος Φλογαΐτης), Εκδόσεις Σάκκουλα, Αθήνα, 2η Έκδοση].

Flogaitis, S., (1987), The Greek Administrative System, Ant. N. Sakkoulas Editions, Athens-Komotini. [Φλογαΐτης, Σ., Το Ελληνικό Διοικητικό Σύστημα, Αθήνα, Εκδόσεις Αντ. Ν. Σάκκουλα, Αθήνα-Κομοτηνή].

Flogaitis, S., (1987), Modern Aspects of State Interventionism, Ant. N. Sakkoulas Editions, Athens-Komotini. [Φλογαΐτης, Σ., Σύγχρονες όψεις κρατικού παρεμβατισμού, Αθήνα, Εκδόσεις Αντ. Ν. Σάκκουλα].

Fong, C., (2001), Social Preferences, Self-Interest and the Demand for Redistribution, Journal of Public Economics 82(2).

Ford, H., Mass Production, Encyclopaedia Britannica, 22nd ed., vol. 15.

Foster, O., (1978), History of the World Trade Union Movement, Editions Hellenic Book Company, (Trans. L.K.-M.D.), Vol. A & B. [Φόστερ, Ο., (1978), Ιστορία του Παγκόσμιου Συνδικαλιστικού Κινήματος, Εκδόσεις Εταιρεία Ελληνικού Βιβλίου, (Μεταφρ. Λ.Κ.-Μ.Δ.), Αθήνα, τόμ. Α΄& Β΄].

Fox, A., (1971), A Sociology of Work in Industry, Collier Macmillan, London.

Fox, A., (1973), Industrial relations: A critique of pluralist ideology, in Child, J., (ed.), Man and Organization, Allen and Unwin, London.

Fox, A., (1974), Beyond Contract: Work, Power and Trust Relations, Faber, London.

Fox, A., (1975), Collective Bargaining, Flanders and the Webbs, British Journal of industrial Relations, vol. XIII, no.2.

Fox, A., (1985), History and Heritage. The Social Origins of the British Industrial Relations System, G. Allen & Unwin, London - Boston.

Freddi, G. and Bjorkman, J., (1989), Controlling Medical Professionals, Sage.

Frege, C., (2005), The Discourse of Industrial Democracy: Germany and the US Revisited, Economic and Industrial Democracy, Vol. 26 (1).

Friedman, G., (1984), Where is Humanity going? (trans. M. Lomi), Athens, Kalvos Publications. [Friedman, G., (1984), Που Τραβά η Ανθρώπινη Εργασία; (μτφ: Μ. Λώμη), Αθήνα, Εκδόσεις Κάλβος].

Fromm, E. (1975), The Human Figure in Marx, (TRANS L. Karaztas), Athens, Boukoumanis Publications. [Φρόμ, Ε., (1975), Η Εικόνα του Ανθρώπου στον ΜΑΡΞ, (Μετάφραση Λ. Καρατζάς), Αθήνα, Εκδόσεις Μπουκουμάνης].

Gabriel, C., (1995), Cultural View of Organisations, in Tsivakou, P., Action and System, Athens, Themelio Editions. [Γαβριήλ, Γ., (1995), Πολιτισμική Θεώρηση των Οργανώσεων, στο Τσιβάκου, Π., Δράση και Σύστημα, Αθήνα, Εκδόσεις Θεμέλιο].

Gallie, D., (1978), In Search of the Working Class: Automation and Social Integration in the Capitalist Enterprise, Cambridge University Press.

Gavroglou, St. P., (2001), "Reduction of Working Time and Employment: Approaches, Implementations and Findings", in Work Organisation and New Forms of Employment in Greece and Europe, Library: 1, National Labour Institute, Sakkoulas Editions, Athens-Thessaloniki. [Γαβρόγλου, Στ. Π., (2001), Μείωση του Χρόνου Εργασίας και Απασχόληση: Προσεγγίσεις, Εφαρμογές και Διαπιστώσεις, στο Οργάνωση της Εργασίας και Νέες Μορφές Απασχόλησης στην Ελλάδα και την Ευρώπη, Βιβλιοθήκη: 1, Εθνικό Ινστιτούτο Εργασίας, Εκδόσεις Σάκκουλα, Αθήνα-Θεσσαλονίκη].

Geary, D., (1988), The European Labour Movement (1848–1939), (TRANS-EDS: Tasos Darveris), Paratiritis Publications, Thessaloniki. [Geary, D., (1988), Το Ευρωπαϊκό Εργατικό Κίνημα 1848–1939, (Μετάφραση – επιμέλεια: Τάσος Δαρβέρης), Εκδόσεις Παρατηρητής, Θεσσαλονίκη].

General Confederation of Greek Labour, History, Memory Pages. www.gsee.gr [Γενική Συνομοσπονδία Εργατών Ελλάδας, Ιστορία, Σελίδες Μνήμης. www.gsee.gr]

Georgakopoulou, B., (1991), Labor flexibility, Definitions, Concept, Classification and Basic Forms, June, during the investigation the EEC - GSEE - Ministry of Labour entitled "Flexibility and New Employment Relations" [Γεωργακοπούλου, Β., (1991), Ευελιξίες της Εργασίας, Ορισμοί, Έννοια, Ταξινόμηση και Βασικές Μορφές, Ιούνιος, στα πλαίσια της έρευνας Ε.Ο.Κ. - Γ.Σ.Ε.Ε. - Υπουργείου Εργασίας με τίτλο: «Ευελιξίες και Νέες Εργασιακές Σχέσεις»].

Georgakopoulou, B., (1996a), Business flexibility and Labour, Labour Institute of GSEE, Design I.N.E., GSEE, Issue 5 [Γεωργακοπούλου, Β., (1996a), Ευελιξίες της Επιχείρησης και της Εργασίας, Ινστιτούτο Εργασίας της Γ.Σ.Ε.Ε., Μελέτες Ι.Ν.Ε., Γ.Σ.Ε.Ε, Τεύχος 5].

Georgakopoulou, B., (1996b), Working Time Reduction and Employment, paper presented in the Seminar organized by the OMED, May 17-19,

Athens – Kavouri. [Γεωργακοπούλου, Β., (1996b), Μείωση Χρόνου Εργασίας και Απασχόληση, Εισήγηση σε Σεμινάριο του Ο.ΜΕ.Δ, 17-19 Μαΐου, Αθήνα – Καβούρι].

Georgakopoulou. B., (1998), Working Time Reduction and Employment, Introduction and Basic Parameters of the Issue in Modern Conditions in OTOE, Reduction of Working Time: Studies on the Application of the 35-hour week in the Banking Sector, Athens, INE-OTOE. [Γεωργακοπούλου. Β., (1998), Μείωση Χρόνου Εργασίας και Απασχόληση, Παρουσίαση και Βασικές Παράμετροι του Ζητήματος στις Σύγχρονες Συνθήκες, στο ΟΤΟΕ, Η Μείωση του Χρόνου Εργασίας: Μελέτες για την Εφαρμογή του 35ωρου στον Τραπεζικό Κλάδο, Αθήνα, ΙΝΕ-ΟΤΟΕ].

Gephart, R.P., (1996), Management. Social Issues, and the Postmodern Era, in Boje, D.M.,

Gephart, R.P. and Thatchenkery, T.J., (eds.), Postmodern Management and Organization Theory, Thousand Oaks, Calif., Sage Publications.

Gergen, K. J., (1992), Organization Theory in the Postmodern Era, in Reed, M., and Hugues, M., (eds.), Rethinking organization: New directions in organization theory and analysis, London, Sage.

Gershung, J. and Miles, I., (1983), The New Service Economy: The Transformation of Employment in Industrial Societies, Frances Pinter.

Gershyny, J., (1986), Lifestyle, Economic Structure and Time Use, in Dahrendorf, R., Kohler, E. and Poitet E., New Forms of Work and Activity, Documentation, European Foundation of Living and Working Conditions, Dublin, Colloquium, Brussels.

Giannakourou, S., (1996), The experience of social dialogue in the Mediterranean countries of the European Union, Review of Industrial Relations. [Γιαννακούρου, Σ., (1996), Η εμπειρία του κοινωνικού διαλόγου στις μεσογειακές χώρες της Ευρωπαϊκής Ένωσης, Επιθεώρηση Εργασιακών Σχέσεων].

Giannakourou, S., (2001), Function and Evolution of institutionalized social dialogue at national level, in Social dialogue and Collective Bargaining in the United Europe, Ant. N. Sakkoula, Athens-Komotini. [Γιαννακούρου, Σ., (2001), Λειτουργία και εξέλιξη του θεσμοθετημένου κοινωνικού διαλόγου σε εθνικό επίπεδο στο Κοινωνικός διάλογος και συλλογικές Διαπραγματεύσεις στην Ενωμένη Ευρώπη, Εκδόσεις Αντ. Ν. Σάκκουλα, Αθήνα-Κομοτηνή].

Giannitis, T., (1993), Markets and Globalization Effects on Technological Organization of Greek Economy, in Liodakis, G., (ed.), Society, Technology and Restructuring of Production Symposium Proceedings, University of Crete, October 1992. [Γιαννίτσης, Τ., (1993), Παγκοσμιοποίηση Αγορών και Επιπτώσεις στην Τεχνολογική Οργάνωση της Ελληνικής Οικονομίας, στο Λιοδάκης, Γ., (επιμ.), Κοινωνία, Τεχνολογία και Αναδιάρθρωση της Παραγωγής, Πρακτικά Συμποσίου, Πολυτεχνείο Κρήτης, Οκτώβριος 1992].

Giddens, A., (1979), The Class Structure of the Advanced Societies, London, Hutchinson.

Giddens, A., (1989), Introduction to Sociology, (ed. - prologue by Koniavitis, Th. / Trans. by Triantafillopoulou Ntina), Odysseus Publications, 3rd ed., Athens. [Giddens, A., (1989), Εισαγωγή στην Κοινωνιολογία, (επιμέλεια - πρόλογος Κονιαβίτης, Θ./ μεταφρ. Τριανταφυλλοπούλου Ντίνα), Εκδόσεις Οδυσσέας, έκδοση γ΄, Αθήνα].

Giddens, A., (2002), Sociology (Trans. and ed. by Tsaousis, D.), Gutenberg Publications, Athens. [Giddens, A., (2002), Κοινωνιολογία, (μετάφραση-επιμέλεια Τσαούσης, Δ.), Εκδόσεις Gutenberg, Αθήνα].

Gill, J., (1969), One Approach to the Teaching of Industrial Relations, British Journal of Industrial Relations, Vol. VII, Nr 2.

Gill, C., (1985), Work, Unemployment and the New Technology, Cambridge: Polity Press.

Gill, C., (ny), New Technology: Its Effect on Work Organization, Paper for El ASM Workshop Brussels, 5th-6th November.

Giugni, G., (1983), Three Lectures, Guarantees of Freedom of Association in the Italian and Comparative Law, Articles EDEK, v. 14. [Giugni, G., (1983), Τρεις Διαλέξεις, Οι Εγγυήσεις της Συνδικαλιστικής Ελευθερίας στο Ιταλικό και Συγκριτικό Δίκαιο, Δημοσιεύματα ΕΔΕΚΑ, τ. 14].

Giugni, G., (1987), Recent Trends in Collective Bargaining in Italy, in Windmuller, J. P., et al., Collective Bargaining in Industrialized Market Economies: A Reappraisal, ILO, Geneva.

Gkivalos, M., (2005), Science, Knowledge and Method, revised 2nd ed. Paradoseis 9, Nisos, Greece. [Γκίβαλος, Μ., (2005), Επιστήμη, Γνώση και Μέθοδος, β΄έκδοση αναθεωρημένη, Παραδόσεις 9, Νήσος, Αθήνα].

Gladstone, Al., (1984), Voluntary Arbitration of Interest Disputes, A practical guide ILO, Geneva.

Glenn, E.N. and Felberg, R.L., (1977), Degraded and Deskilled: The Proletarialization of Clerical Work, Society for the Study of Social Problems, 25.

Gorz, A., (1982), Ferewell to the Working Class, London, Pluto.

Goutos, Chr., (1985), Industrial Relations of the Constructors in mainland Greece after 1800, Athens. [Γκούτος, Χ., (1985), Εργασιακές Σχέσεις των Οικοδόμων στη Χερσαία Ελλάδα μετά το 1800, Αθήνα].

Goutos, Chr., (1988), Trade Unionism in the Greek state from 1834 to 1914, Volume I, Athens. [Γκούτος, Χ., (1988), Ο Συνδικαλισμός στο Ελληνικό κράτος 1834–1914, Τόμος Α', Αθήνα].

Goutos, Chr. - Leventis, G., (1988), Labor Legislation, DEN Publications, 7th ed., Athens. [Γκούτος, Χ. - Λεβέντης, Γ., (1988), Εργατική Νομοθεσία, έκδοση ΔΕΝ, 7η, Αθήνα].

Grote, R. J., (1985), Tripartism and European Integration, in Spyropoulos, G., (ed.), Trade Unions Today and Tomorrow, vol I, Presses Interuniversitaires Europeennes Maastricht.

Guest, R., (1955), Men and Machines: An Assembly-line Worker Looks at his Job, Personnel, XXXI.

Habermas, J., (1981), Theorie des kommunikativen Handels, Suhrkamp, Frankfurt am Main, Germany.

Handy, L. J., (1968), Absenteeism and Attendance in the British Coal Mining Industry, British Journal of Industrial Relations, Vol. IV, No. 1.

Haralambos, M., (1990), Sociology: Themes and Perspectives, Bell and Hycan.

Harbison, F.H., (1954), Collective Bargainig and American Capitalism, in Kornhauser, A., Dubin, R. and Ross, A.M., (eds.), Industrial Conflict, McGraw Hill, New York.

Harrington, J., (1991), Organizational structure and information technology, Prentice Hall International Group.

Hartley, J., and Kelly, J., (1986), "Psychology and industrial relations: from conflict to cooperation?" Journal of Occupational Psychology, Vol. 59.

Harvey, D., (1995), Globalization in Question, Rethinking Marxism, 8.

Hatzopoulos, A, (2001), The Pros and Cons of Working Time Reduction, Athens, Oikonomikos Tachidromos, November 24. [Χατζόπουλος, Α., (2001), Τα Υπέρ και τα Κατά της Μείωσης του Χρόνου Εργασίας, Αθήνα, Οικονομικός Ταχυδρόμος, 24 Νοεμβρίου, σ. 76-77.].

Hayek, F.A., (1979), The Mirage of Social Justice, Vol. 13.

Heckscher, Ch., (1994), Defining the post-bureaucratic type, in Heckscher, Ch., and Donnellon, A., (eds.), The Post-Bureaucratic Organization: new perspective on organizational change, Thousand Oaks, Calif., Sage.

Held, D., (1995), (trans. Mariana Tziantzi), Models of Democracy, 1rst edition, Stahi Editions, Athens. [Ντέιβιντ Χέλντ, (1995), (μετ. Μαριάννα Τζιάντζη), 1η έκδοση, Αθήνα, Εκδόσεις Στάχυ].

Herzberg, F., (1966), Work and Nature of Man, World Publishing Company.

Heydebrand, W., (1999, October), The network metaphor as Key to the Analysis of Complex Production and Service Relations in a Global Economy. Stuttgart: Akademie für Technikfolgenabschätzung in Baden-Wurttemberg, No 149, http://www.ta-akademie.de.

Hinterscheid M., (1985), The Role of Trade Unions in the Coming Decade: The Point of View of the European Confederation of Trade Union, in Spyropoulos, G., (ed.), Trade Unions Today and Tomorrow, Vol. I, Trade Unions in a Changing Europe, Work and Society, No 6, European Centre for Work and Society, Maastricht, Presses Interuniversitaires Europeennes.

Hirsch, J., (1993), Fordism and post-Fordism: the present social crisis and its consequences, in Holloway, J., and Bonefeld, W., (eds.), Fordism and Social Form, Athens, Exantas Publications. [Hirsch, J., (1993), Φορντισμός και Μεταφορντισμός: η παρούσα κοινωνική κρίση και οι συνέπειες της, στο Holloway, J., και Bonefeld, W., (eds), Μεταφορντισμός και Κοινωνική Μορφή, Αθήνα, Εκδόσεις Εξάντας].

Hirst, P., and Zeitlin, J., (1991), Flexible Specialization versus Post-Fordism, Economy and Society, 20 (1).

Hoidas, F. G., (in Greek) (1997), The Opening Hours-Tire Covers Europe, Athenean Newspaper "Kiriakatiki Eleftherotipia", Economy, International Affairs, 19 of October, pp. 19/115.

House, R., and Widgor, L., (1967), Herzberg's Dual Factor Theory of Job Satisfaction and Motivation: A Review of the Evidence and a Criticism, Personnel Psychology, 20(4).

Hunt, J., (1998), Hours Reduction as Work-sharing, in Brooking Papers on Economic Activity, Washington, D.C.

Hyman, R., (1975), Industrial Relations: A Marxist Introduction, Macmillan, London.

ILO (International Labor Organization), (1975), The Freedom of Association, Workers' Training Courses, Series of Labour Training Courses (Trans. by A. Kyriakopoulos), Athens. [Διεθνές Γραφείο Εργασίας, (1975), Η Συνδικαλιστική Ελευθερία, Σειρά Μαθημάτων Εργατικής Εκπαιδεύσεως, (Μετάφραση Α. Κυριακόπουλου), Αθήνα].

ILO (International Labor Organization), (1977), Collective Bargaining in Industrialized Countries, Recent Trends and Problems, Vienna Symposium, 2-9 November, Labour-Management Relations Series, No. 56.

ILO (International Labor Organization), (1980), Conciliation and Arbitration Procedures in Labour Disputes, A Comparative Study, Geneva, Ch. 4th: Bipartite Arrangements for Preventing and Setting Disputes.

ILO (International Labor Organization), (1973), Conciliation in Industrial Disputes, A Practical Guide, International Labor Office (ILO), Geneva, (Trans. by the OMED).

ILO (International Labour Organization), (1975), The Freedom of Association, Workers Training Course (trans. by A. Kyriakopoulos). [Διεθνές Γραφείο

Εργασίας (Δ.Γ.Ε.), (1975), Η Συνδικαλιστική Ελευθερία, Σειρά Μαθημάτων Εργατικής Εκπαιδεύσεως, (μετάφραση Ανδρέα Κυριακόπουλου), 3η έκδοση].

ILO (International Labor Organization), (1981), Workers' Participation in Decisions Within Undertakings, Geneva.

ILO (International Labor Organization), (1984a), World Labour Report.

ILO, (International Labor Organization) (1984b), Working-Time, Reduction of Work, Weekly Rest and Holidays with Pay, General Survey by the Committee of Experts on the Application of Conventions and Recommendations, International Labour Conference, 70th Session, Geneva.

ILO (International Labor Organization), (1986), Flexibility in Working Time, in Conditions of Work Digest, Geneva, Vol. 5 (2).

ILO (International Labor Organization)), (1988), Working Time Issues in Industrialised Countries, "Documents Considered in the Tripartite Symposium 1988 on Working Time Issues in Industrialized Countries", Geneva, 17-25 October.

ILO (International Labor Organization), (1989), Conditions of Work Digest, Part-time Work, Volume 8, 1/1989.

ILO (International Labor Organization), (1996), "Convention Concerning Part-time Work", Convention No I, 75, 1994, and International Labour Conventions and Recommendations 1977 - 1995, Geneva, Available on: http://www.ilo.org

ILO (International Labor Organization), (2003) Commission on Trade Unions' Freedom, 332nd Report – Case 2261/2003.

Industrial Conflict in the Contemporary Business World, 123HelpMe.com, 14 April 2009 Available at: http://www. 123HelpMe.com /asp?id=149869.

Ingham, G. K., (1967), Organizational Size, Orientation to Work and Industrial Behaviour, Sociology, 1 (3).

International Association of Virtual Organizations – http://www.mnsinc.com

Ioannou, Ch., (1988), Wage policy, collective bargaining and strike activity in Greece, Review of Social Research, EKKE publications, No. 68. [Ιωάννου, Χρ., (1988), Πολιτική μισθών, συλλογικές διαπραγματεύσεις και απεργιακή δραστηριότητα στην Ελλάδα, Επιθεώρηση Κοινωνικών Ερευνών, έκδοση Ε.Κ.Κ.Ε., τεύχος 68].

Ioannou, Ch., (1989), Wage Employment and Trade Unionism in Greece, Medeteranean Founfation Studies, Athens. [Ιωάννου, Χ., (1989), Μισθωτή Απασχόληση και Συνδικαλισμός στην Ελλάδα, Ίδρυμα Μεσογειακών Μελετών, Αθήνα].

Ioannou, Ch., (1992), Economic Adjustment in labor relations are "Kathimerini" daily newspaper 14.02.92. [Ιωάννου, Χρ., (1992), Οικονομική Προσαρμογή στις εργασιακές σχέσεις, Εφημερίδα Καθημερνή 14.02.92].

Ioannou, Ch., (1998), The Future of Trade Unions, Labour Relations Review, No 12. [Ιωάννου, Χρ., (1998), Το Μέλλον των Συνδικάτων, Επιθεώρηση Εργασιακών Σχέσεων, τ. 12].

Jackson, M.P., (1985), Industrial Relations, 3rd ed., Croom Helm, London.

Jacobs, A., (1993), Conciliation, Mediation and Arbitration, ın Industrial Disputes, Part II, Synthesis report, International Conference, The Resolution of Industrial Disputes, The use and the Development of Conciliation and Mediation Procedures, October, Dublin, Ireland.

Jaffee, D., (2001), Organization Theory: Tension and Change, Mc Graw-Hill International Editions.

Jansen, W., Steenbakkers, W. and Jagers, H., (1999), Electronic commerce and virtual organizations, Organizational Virtualness and Electronic Commerce, 1(1) (a special issue).

Jarvenpaa, S. L. and Leidner, D. E., (1994), The global network organization of the future: Information management opportunities and challenges, Journal of Management Information Systems, 10 (4).

Javillier, J.C., (1994), Le droit international du travail entre pragmatisme et creativité, Libre propos d'un juriste du travail, Revue Internationale du travail, 133, 4, pp. 533–550.

Jellinek, G., (1976), AllgcmcincSlaaslslchre, 3rd edition.

Jessop, B., (1994), Post Fordism and the State, in Amin, A., (ed.), Post Fordism, a Reader, Blackwell, Oxford.

Jessop, B., (1978), Capitalism and Democracy: The Best Possible Political Shell,, in Littlejohn, G., Smart, B., Wakeford, J., Yuval-Davis, N., (eds), Power and the State, Croom Helm, London.

Jessop, B., Bonnett, K., Bromley, S., Ling, T., (1984) Authoritarian Populism, Two Nations and Thatcherism, New Left Review, I/147, September-October.

Jones, D., (1980), Producer Co-operatives in Industrialized Western Economies, British Journal of Industrial Relations, 18 (2).

Kahn-Freund, O., (1983), Labour and the Law, 3rd edition, London, Stevens & Sons.

Kakaboura, P., (2008), Narratives of Life, The Biographical Approach to Modern Folklore Research, Atrapos Publications. [Κακάμπουρα, Ρ., (2008), Αφηγήσεις Ζωής, Η Βιογραφική Προσέγγιση στη Σύγχρονη Λαογραφική Έρευνα, Εκδόσεις Ατραπός].

Kallinikos, G., (1995), The Age of Information - Texts and Objects in the post-industrial society, in Tsivakou, I., (1995), Action and System, Themelio Publicatios. [Καλλίνικος, Γ., (1995), Η Εποχή των Πληροφοριών - Κείμενα και Αντικείμενα στη Μεταβιομηχανική Κοινωνία, στο Τσιβάκου, I., (1995), Δράση και Σύστημα, Εκδόσεις Θεμέλιο].

Kalyvis, A., (2005), Demassification: A Curse for Trade Unions, "Kathimerini" Newspaper (10.05.2005). [Καλύβης, Α., (2005), Πληγή για τα Συνδικάτα η Απομαζικοποίηση, Εφημερίδα «Καθημερινή» (10.05.2005)].

Kandas, A., (1995), Organizational - of Industrial Psychology, Ellinika Grammata Publications, Athens. [Κάντας, Α., (1995), Οργανωτική - Βιομηχανική Ψυχολογία, Εκδόσεις Ελληνικά Γράμματα, Αθήνα].

Kandas, A., (1998), Industrial-Organizational Psychology, Ellinika Grammata, Athens. [Κάντας, Α., (1998), Οργανωτική-Βιομηχανική Ψυχολογία, Εκδόσεις Ελληνικά Γράμματα, Αθήνα].

Kanellopoulos, Ch., (1990a), Utilization of the Personnel by Developing staff and Improving Organization, Athens. [Κανελλόπουλος, Χ., (1990), Αξιοποίηση Προσωπικού με Ανάπτυξη Στελεχών και Βελτίωση Οργάνωσης, Αθήνα].

Kanellopoulos, Ch., (1990b), Management - Effective management in companies, organizations, services, Athens. [Κανελλόπουλος, Κ.Χ., (1990), Μάνατζμεντ - αποτελεσματική διοίκηση σε επιχειρήσεις, οργανισμούς, υπηρεσίες, Αθήνα].

Kanellopoulos, L. (1992) Speech by the President of the GSEE. Formal Opening of the OMED, November 15, Hotel Royal Olympic, Athens. [Κανελλόπουλος, Λ., (1992), Χαιρετισμός του Προέδρου ΓΣΕΕ, Πανηγυρική Εναρκτήρια Ημερίδα Ο.ΜΕ.Δ., 15η Νοεμβρίου, Ξενοδοχείο Royal Olympic, Αθήνα].

Karagiorgas, D., (1981), Public Economics, (Volume 1) Papazisis, Athens. [Καράγιωργας, Δ., (1981), Δημόσια Οικονομική, (τόμος 1), Εκδόσεις Παπαζήση, Αθήνα].

Karakatsanis, A., (1980), Labor Law, Vol. BII, Athens. [Καρακατσάνης, Α., (1980), Εργατικό Δίκαιο, Τόμος ΒΙΙ, Αθήνα].

Karakatsanis, A., (1985), Labor Law, Vol. B/II. [Καρακατσάνης, Α., (1985), Εργατικό Δίκαιο, Τόμος Β/ΙΙ].

Karakatsanis, A., (1992), Collective Labor Law, Ant. N. Sakoulas, Athens-Komotini. [Καρακατσάνης, Α., (1992), Συλλογικό Εργατικό Δίκαιο, Αντ. Ν. Σάκκουλας, Αθήνα-Κομοτηνή].

Karantinos D., Ketsetzopoulou, M. and Mouriki A. (1997) Flexible Employment and Labour Minimization Time Trends, Developments, Prospects, National Institute of Labour Studies: 1, Athens. [Καραντινός Δ., Κετσετζοπούλου Μ., Μουρίκη Α. (1997), Ευέλικτη Απασχόληση και Ελαχιστοποίηση του Χρόνου Εργασίας - Τάσεις, Εξελίξεις, Προοπτικές, Εθνικό Ινστιτούτο Εργασίας, Μελέτες: 1, Αθήνα].

Kardelj, E., (1976), Socialist Self-management in Yugoslavia, International Review of Administrative Science, 42, (2).

Karmin, M.W. and Sheler, J.L., (1982), Jobs: A Million that will never come back, U.S. News and World Report.

Kassalow, E., (1977), Industrial Conflict and Consensus in the United States and Western Europe: A Comparative Analysis, Industrial Relations Research Association, 30th Annual Proceedings, December.

Kassimatis, Gr., (1980), Constitutional Law II, The Operations of the State, Issue A. [Κασσιμάτης, Γρ., (1980), Συνταγματικό Δίκαιο II, Οι Λειτουργίες του Κράτους, Τεύχος Α'].

Kassimatis, Gr, (1932), Collective labor agreement as an institution of contemporary law, Athens. [Κασσιμάτης, Γρ., (1932), Η συλλογική σύμβασις εργασίας ως θεσμός του σύγχρονου δικαίου, Αθήνα].

Kassimatis, K., (1991), Research on Social Characteristics of Employment, Study I, The Choice of Profession, National Centre for Social Research (EKKE in Greek). [Κασιμάτης, Κ., (1991), Έρευνα για τα Κοινωνικά Χαρακτηριστικά της Απασχόλησης, Μελέτη I, Η Επιλογή του Επαγγέλματος, Εθνικό Κέντρο Κοινωνικών Ερευνών (ΕΚΚΕ)].

Katrivesis, N., (2005), The European Strategy for Vocational Education and Training in Tsobanoglou, G.O., Korres, G. and Giannopoulos, I., Social Exclusion and Inclusion Policies. Papazisis. [Κατριβέσης, Ν., (2005), Η Ευρωπαϊκή Στρατηγική για την Επαγγελματική Επιμόρφωση και Κατάρτιση, στο Τσομπάνογλου, Γ.Ο., Κορρές, Γ., και Γιαννοπούλου, Ι., Κοινωνικός Αποκλεισμός και Πολιτικές Ενσωμάτωσης, Εκδόσεις Παπαζήση].

Katsanevas, Th, (1994), The Modern Trade Union Movement in Modern Greece, Livani Publications, Athens. [Κατσανέβας, Θ., (1994), Το Σύγχρονο Συνδικαλιστικό Κίνημα στην Ελλάδα, Εκδόσεις Λιβάνη, Αθήνα].

Katsanevas, Th. et al., (1995), Labour Relations, Stamoulis Publications, Athens - Piraeus. [Κατσανέβας, Θ. και συν., (1995), Εργασιακές Σχέσεις, Εκδόσεις Α. Σταμούλης, Αθήνα – Πειραιάς].

Katsanevas, Th., (1997), Labour Economics and Industrial Relations, Stamoulis Publications. [Κατσανέβας, Θ., (1997), Οικονομική της Εργασίας και Εργασιακές Σχέσεις, Εκδόσεις Σταμούλη].

Katz, R., (1960), Towards a More Effective Enterprise, Harvard Business Review, September-October.

Kaufman, B., (1982), The Determinants of Strikes in the United States, 1900–1977, Industrial and Labor Relations Review, 35 (4).

Kazakos, A., (in Greek) (1998), The Arbitration on Collective Disputes on Interests According to the Law 1876/90, Sakkoulas Editions, Thessaloniki. [Καζάκος, Α., (1998), Η Διαιτησία Συλλογικών Διαφορών Συμφερόντων κατά το Ν. 1876/90, Εκδόσεις Σάκκουλα, Θεσσαλονίκη].

Keller B. and Sorries B., (1997), The new social dialogue: procedural structuring, first results and perspectives, Industrial Relations Journal, European Annual Review.

Kernberg, O.F., (1998), Ideology, Conflict and Leadership in Groups and Organizations, Yale University Press, London.

Kerr, C., Dunlop, J., Harbison, F., Myers, C., (1962), Industrialism and Industrial Man, Heineman, London.

Kilroy-Silk, R., (1970), Contemporary Theories of Industrial Democracy, Political Quarterly, April, Vol 41(2).

Kioukas, D., (1994), Organization of Interests in Greece, Exantas Publications, Athens. [Κιούκιας, Δ., (1994), Οργάνωση συμφερόντων στην Ελλάδα, Εξάντας, Αθήνα].

Kioukas, D., (1996), The European social model in the current context: Europe and Greece, Review of Industrial Relations, 3/96. [Κιούκιας, Δ., (1996), Το Ευρωπαϊκό κοινωνικό πρότυπο στη σημερινή συγκυρία: Ευρώπη και Ελλάδα, Επιθεώρηση Εργασιακών Σχέσεων, 3/96].

Kioulafas, K., (1992), Employees' Mobility in the Greek Labour Market, Special Studies, 20, IOBE. [Κιουλάφας, Κ., (1992), Η Κινητικότητα των Εργαζομένων στην Ελληνική Αγορά Εργασίας, Ειδικές Μελέτες, 20, ΙΟΒΕ].

Kochan, Th.A., Mckersie, R. and Capelli, P., (1984), Strategic Choice and Industrial Relations Theory, Industrial Relations, Winter, 23(1).

Kolb, D. M. and Putnam, L. L., (1992), The Dialectics of Disputing, in Kolb, D.M., and Bartunek, I. M., (εds.), Hidden Conflict in Organizations, Sage Publications, Newbury Park.

Kolyva, B. and Koutsafti, M., (1997), Design for Creating National Centre for Vocational Guidance (EKEP), National Institute of Labour, (5) studies. [Κολυβά, Β., και Κουτσαυτή, Μ., (1997), Μελέτη Εφαρμογής για τη Δημιουργία Εθνικού Κέντρου Επαγγελματικού Προσανατολισμού (ΕΚΕΠ), Εθνικό Ινστιτούτο Εργασίας, (5) μελέτες].

Konstantopoulou, Ch., (1986), Towards a Sociology of Labour, Publishing Kyriakides. [Κωνσταντοπούλου, Χ., (1986), Για μια Κοινωνιολογία της Εργασίας, Εκδόσεις Κυριακίδη].

Konstantopoulou, Ch., (1994), Towards a Sociology of Labour, Publications Paratiritis, Thessaloniki. [Κωνσταντοπούλου, Χ., (1994), Για μία Κοινωνιολογία της Εργασίας, Εκδόσεις Παρατηρητής, Θεσσαλονίκη].

Kontrarou, G., (1991), Unconstitutional is the Law for the Collective Bargaining, Athenean Daily Newspaper "TO VIMA", 03.11.1991, p. D2, Economy. [Κοντράρου, Τζ., (1991), Αντισυνταγματικός ο νόμος για τις ελεύθερες διαπραγματεύσεις, το ΒΗΜΑ, 3-11-91, σ. Δ2 Οικονομία].

Kornhauser, A., Dubin, R. and Ross, A. M., (eds.), (1954), Industrial Conflict, McGraw-Hill Book Company, New York.

Koskinas, K., (1995), The Politics of Labour, Simeon Publications [Κοσκινάς, Κ., (1995), Η Πολιτική της Εργασίας, Εκδόσεις Συμεών].

Kotsaridas, D., (1999), The Question of Union Representation, Enimerosi (: Bulletin), INE-GCGL, issue Nr 48-49, Athens. [Κοτσαρίδας, Δ., (1999), Το ζήτημα της Συνδικαλιστικής Εκπροσώπησης, Ενημέρωση ΙΝΕ-ΓΣΕΕ, 48-49, Αθήνα].

Koukiadis, I., (1974), Tripartite Relations from Labour Provision, Thessaloniki. [Κουκιάδης, Ι., (1974), Τριμερείς Σχέσεις εκ Παροχής Εργασίας, Θεσσαλονίκη].

Koukiadis, I., (1981), Labor Law, Collective Labour Relations, Paratiritis Publications, Thessaloniki. [Κουκιάδης, Ι., (1981), Εργατικό Δίκαιο, Συλλογικές Εργασιακές Σχέσεις, Εκδόσεις Παρατηρητής, Θεσσαλονίκη].

Koukiadis, I., (1982), Relations Between Constitution and Labour Law, EDEKA Publications, vol.12 [Κουκιάδης, Ι., (1982), Σχέσεις Συντάγματος και Εργατικού Δικαίου, Δημοσιεύματα ΕΔΕΚΑ, τ. 12].

Koukiadis, I, (1991a), The Principle of Elasticity and the Evolution of Labour Law, Epitheorisi Ergatikou Dikeou (E.Erg.D.-Revew of Labour Law), issue Nr 50. [Κουκιάδης, Ι., (1991a), Η Αρχή της Ελαστικότητας και η Μετεξέλιξη του Εργατικού Δικαίου, Ε.Εργ.Δ., τ. 50.]

Koukiadis, I, (1991b), Ways of Regulating Collective Labour Disputes, XIII World Congress of Labour Law and Social Security, 19 September, Athens. [Κουκιάδης, Ι., (1991b), Οι Τρόποι Ρύθμισης των Συλλογικών Διαφορών Εργασίας, XIII Παγκόσμιο Συνέδριο Εργατικού Δικαίου και Κοινωνικής Ασφάλισης, 19 Σεπτεμβρίου, Αθήνα].

Koukiadis, I, (1992a), The new concept of collective bargaining and new mediation and arbitration procedures, in "New ways of resolving collective labor disputes" Legal Society of Northern Greece, vol 14, Thessaloniki. [Κουκιάδης, Ι, (1992α), Η νέα αντίληψη για τις συλλογικές διαπραγματεύσεις και οι νέες διαδικασίες μεσολάβησης και διαιτησίας, στο «Οι νέοι τρόποι επίλυσης των συλλογικών διαφορών εργασίας», Εταιρεία Νομικών Βορείου Ελλάδος, τ. 14, Θεσσαλονίκη].

Koukiadis, I., (1992b), The new concept of collective bargaining and new mediation and arbitration procedures, Enimerotiko Deltio (Informative Issue) of IN.E. (Labour Institute) of G.C.G.L. (General Confederation of Greek Labour), issue 14, April, Athens. [Κουκιάδης, Ι., (1992β), Η νέα αντίληψη για τις συλλογικές διαπραγματεύσεις και οι νέες διαδικασίες μεσολάβησης και διαιτησίας, Ενημερωτικό Δελτίο ΙΝ.Ε.-ΓΣΕΕ, Αθήνα].

Koukiadis, I., (1992c), Introduction, in New Ways for the Resolution of Collective Labour Disputes, Sakkoulas Editions, Thessaloniki, [Κουκιάδης, Ι., (1992c), Εισαγωγή, στο "Οι νέοι τρόποι επίλυσης των συλλογικών διαφορών εργασίας", Εκδόσεις Σάκκουλα, Θεσσαλονίκη].

Koukiadis, I, (1992d), The First Meeting of Mediators-Arbitrators and Representatives of the Parties, November 1991, House of Mediators – Arbitrators of the OMED, Edition of the Organization for Mediation and Arbitration (OMED), Athens. [Κουκιάδης, Ι., (1992d), Πρώτη συνάντηση των Μεσολαβητών - Διαιτητών και των εκπροσώπων των μερών, Νοέμβριος 1991, στη Γραφεία Ο.ΜΕ.Δ., Έκδοση του Οργανισμού Μεσολάβησης και Διαιτησίας (Ο.ΜΕ.Δ.), Αθήνα.

Koukiadis, I., (1993), Introductory speech by the President of the OMED at the Reception of the representatives of employers, workers and the Ministry of Labour, in "Institutional framework of collective bargaining, mediation and arbitration", OMED Publications. p. 16 [Κουκιάδης, Ι., (1993), Εισαγωγική ομιλία του Προέδρου του Ο.ΜΕ.Δ., ενώπιον εκπροσώπων εργοδοτών, εργαζομένων και Υπουργείου Εργασίας, στο «Θεσμικό πλαίσιο συλλογικών διαπραγματεύσεων, μεσολάβησης και διαιτησίας», έκδοση Ο.ΜΕ.Δ.].

Koukiadis, I. (1996), Political and social dialogue. A necessary condition for a modern development policy, Athens, OMED Educational Seminar, June 21-23. [Κουκιάδης, Ι. (1996), Πολιτικός και κοινωνικός διάλογος. Αναγκαίος όρος μιας σύγχρονης αναπτυξιακής πολιτικής, Αθήνα, Εκπαιδευτικό Σεμινάριο Ο.ΜΕ.Δ., 21-23 Ιουνίου].

Koukiadis, I., (1993), Introductory speech by the President of the OMED at the Reception of the representatives of employers, workers and the Ministry of Labour, in "Institutional framework of collective bargaining, mediation and arbitration", OMED Publications. [Κουκιάδης, Ι., (1993), Εισαγωγική ομιλία του Προέδρου του Ο.ΜΕ.Δ., ενώπιον εκπροσώπων εργοδοτών, εργαζομένων και Υπουργείου Εργασίας, στο «Θεσμικό πλαίσιο συλλογικών διαπραγματεύσεων, μεσολάβησης και διαιτησίας», έκδοση Ο.ΜΕ.Δ.].

Koukiadis, I. (1996), Political and social dialogue. A necessary condition for a modern development policy, OMED Educational Seminar, June 21-23. [Κουκιάδης, Ι. (1996), Πολιτικός και κοινωνικός διάλογος. Αναγκαίος όρος μιας σύγχρονης αναπτυξιακής πολιτικής, Εκπαιδευτικό Σεμινάριο Ο.ΜΕ.Δ., 21-23 Ιουνίου].

Koukiadis, I., (1997), Labor Law - Collective Labour Relations, Sakkoulas Publications, Thessaloniki. [Κουκιάδης, Ι., (1997), Εργατικό Δίκαιο - Συλλογικές Εργασιακές Σχέσεις, Εκδόσεις Σάκκουλα, Θεσσαλονίκη].

Koukiadis, I., (1999), Labor Law-Collective Labour Relations, 2nd vol., Sakkoulas Publications, Thessaloniki. [Κουκιάδης, Ι., (1999), Εργατικό Δίκαιο-Συλλογικές Εργασιακές Σχέσεις, Τόμος 2ος, Εκδόσεις Σάκκουλα, Θεσσαλονίκη].

Koukoules, G., (1983), Towards a History of Greek Trade Union Movement. Odysseus Publications, Athens. [Κουκουλές, Γ., (1983), Για μία Ιστορία του Ελληνικού Συνδικαλιστικού Κινήματος, Αθήνα, Εκδόσεις Οδυσσέας].

Koukoules, G., (1985), L' Evolution des Rapports Collectives du Travail en Grande Bretagne, vol. II.

Koukoules, G., (1985), Collective bargaining in Greece, Trade Union Review, vol 3, Athens. [Κουκουλές, Γ., (1985), Οι Συλλογικές Διαπραγματεύσεις στην Ελλάδα, Συνδικαλιστική Επιθεώρηση, τ. 3, Αθήνα].

Koukoules, G. and Tzanetakos, B., (1986), Trade Union Movement 1981–1986, The Great Opportunity lost, Odysseus Publications, Athens. [Κουκουλές, Γ., και Τζανετάκος, Β., (1986), Συνδικαλιστικό Κίνημα 1981–1986, Η Μεγάλη Ευκαιρία που Χάθηκε, Εκδόσεις Οδυσσέας, Αθήνα].

Koukoules, G., (1998), Yearbook of Labour, Athens, Panteion University Press. [Κουκουλές, Γ., (1998), Επετηρίδα Εργασίας, Αθήνα, Πανεπιστημιακές Εκδόσεις Παντείου].

Koukoules, G., (1994), Greek Unions: Financial Self-Reliance and Dependence, Odysseus Publications, Athens. [Κουκουλές, Γ., (1994), Ελληνικά Συνδικάτα: Οικονομική Αυτοδυναμία και Εξάρτηση, Εκδόσεις Οδυσσέας, Αθήνα].

Koumandou, Ir., (1994), Development-Competitiveness. Effects on Employment, National Industrial Conference, Hotel HILTON, 1-2 March, Athens. [Κουμάντου, Ειρ., (1994), Ανάπτυξη-Ανταγωνιστικότητα. Επιδράσεις στην Απασχόληση, Πανελλήνιο Βιομηχανικό Συνέδριο, Ξενοδοχείο HILTON, 1-2 Μαρτίου, Αθήνα].

Kourmatzis, I., (1987), Economy and Politics in the Theory of Transition, The Greek Case, Aichmi. [Κουρματζής, Θ., (1987), Οικονομία και Πολιτική στη Θεωρία της Μετάβασης, Η Ελληνική Περίπτωση, Αιχμή].

Koutsibou, E., (2000), Mediation in the context of the OMED, Educational Seminar of the OMED, OMED, Volos. [Κουτσιμπού, Ε., (2000), Η Μεσολάβηση στα πλαίσια του Ο.ΜΕ.Δ., Εκπαιδευτικό Σεμινάριο Ο.ΜΕ.Δ., Ο.ΜΕ.Δ., Βόλος].

Kouzis, G., (1992), The New Industrial Relations at the Heart of the Policies of Flexibility IN.E.-G.S.E.E. Bulletin, No. 12-13. [Κουζής, Γ., (1992), Οι Νέες Εργασιακές Σχέσεις στο Επίκεντρο των Πολιτικών Ευελιξίας, Δελτίο ΙΝ.Ε.-Γ.Σ.Ε.Ε., τεύχος 12-13].

Kouzis, G., (1993), On social dialogue in "14 Texts for the Left", Erodios Publications, Athens. [Κουζής, Γ., (1993), Περί κοινωνικού διαλόγου, στο 14 Κείμενα για την Αριστερά, Εκδόσεις Ερωδιός, Αθήνα].

Kouzis, G., (1994), White Bible, Employment and Industrial Relations, Newsletter IN.E-GSEE., No. 36-37, February-March. [Κουζής, Γ., (1994), Λευκή Βίβλος, Απασχόληση και Εργασιακές Σχέσεις, Ενημερωτικό Δελτίο ΙΝ.Ε-Γ.Σ.Ε.Ε., τεύχος 36-37, Φεβρουάριος-Μάρτιος].

Kouzis, G., (2000), Industrial relations and social dialogue, in Kouzis, G. - Robolis S. (eds.) Issues of Social Dialogue, Gutenberg, Athens. [Κουζής, Γ., (2000), Εργασιακές σχέσεις και κοινωνικός διάλογος, στο Κουζής, Γ., Ρομπόλης, Σ., Ζητήματα κοινωνικού διαλόγου, Gutenberg, Αθήνα].

Kouzis, G. and Robolis, S. (eds.) (2000), Issues of social dialogue, Gutenberg, Athens. [Κουζής, Γ. - Ρομπόλης Σ. (2000), Ζητήματα κοινωνικού διαλόγου, Gutenberg, Αθήνα].

Kouzis, G., (2001), Industrial Relations and European Integration: Flexibility and deregulation or upgrading of work? Studies I.N.E. GSEE-ADEDY, Issue 14, Athens. [Κουζής, Γ., (2001), Εργασιακές σχέσεις και ευρωπαϊκή ενοποίηση: Ευελιξία και απορρύθμιση ή αναβάθμιση της εργασίας; Μελέτες Ι.Ν.Ε. Γ.Σ.Ε.Ε-ΑΔΕΔΥ, Τεύχος 14, Αθήνα].

Kouzis, G., (2002), Changes in labor relations in Greece, in Work: Developments, Analysis, Documentation, Essays on Labor Relations, Panteion University, Institute of Urban Environment and Human Resources, Athens. [Κουζής, Γ., (2002), «Οι αλλαγές στις εργασιακές σχέσεις στην Ελλάδα», στο Εργασία: Εξελίξεις, Αναλύσεις, Τεκμηρίωση, Αφιέρωμα στις Εργασιακές Σχέσεις, Πάντειο Πανεπιστήμιο, Ινστιτούτο Αστικού Περιβάλλοντος και Ανθρώπινου Δυναμικού, Αθήνα].

Kouzis, G., (2005), Trade Union Movement in Greece, "Enimerosi" Magazine GSE. [Κουζής, Γ., (2005), Το Συνδικαλιστικό Κίνημα στην Ελλάδα, Περιοδικό «Ενημέρωση» ΓΣΕΕ].

Kravaritou, G., (1987), New Forms of Employment and New Problems, Athens, "Eleftherotipia Newspaper", 11.18.1987, p. 14. [Κραβαρίτου, Γ., (1987), Νέες Μορφές Απασχόλησης και Νέα Προβλήματα, "Εφημερίδα Ελευθεροτυπία", 18.11.1987].

Kravaritou, G., (1990), The New Forms of Employment and Transient Employment, Epitheorisi Ergatikou Dikeou (E.Erg.D.-Revew of Labour Law), Volume 49, Issue 6. [Κραβαρίτου, Γ., (1990), Οι Νέες Μορφές Πρόσληψης και το Πρόσκαιρο της Απασχόλησης, Ε.Εργ.Δ., τόμος 49, τεύχος 6].

Kravaritou-Manitakis, Y., Repercussions of the New Forms of Work on Labour Law and Social Security, Faculty of Law, University of Thessaloniki, April 1986 in New Forms of Work and Activity.

Kremalis, K., (1976), The Obligations Part of Collective Labour Agreements. [Κρεμαλής, Κ., (1976), Το Ενοχικό Μέρος των Συλλογικών Συμβάσεων Εργασίας].

Koutsibou, E., (2000), Mediation in the context of the OMED, Educational Seminar of the OMED, OMED, Volos. [Κουτσιμπού, Ε., (2000), Η Μεσολάβηση στα πλαίσια του Ο.ΜΕ.Δ., Εκπαιδευτικό Σεμινάριο Ο.ΜΕ.Δ., Βόλος].

Labour Centre of Thessaloniki (EKTH), History of Greek Unions. Available at: http://trade-unions.macedonia.gr/tue. [Εργατικό Κέντρο Θεσσαλονίκης (ΕΚΘ), Ιστορία των Ελληνικών Συνδικάτων. Διαθέσιμο στο: http://trade-unions.macedonia.gr/tue].

Labour Institute GSEE-AD.E.D.Y. (2000), Annual Report: "The Greek Economy and Employment" Reports (2). [Ινστιτούτο Εργασίας Γ.Σ.Ε.Ε.-ΑΔ.Ε.Δ.Υ. (2000), Ετήσια Έκθεση «Η Ελληνική Οικονομία και η Απασχόληση», Εκθέσεις (2)].

Lamprinidis, L. (1993), Restructuring the production process through Subcontracting Relations, Liodakis, G., (ed.) Society, Technology and Restructuring of Production, Symposium Proceedings, University of Crete, October 1992 Papazisis. [Λαμπρινίδης, Λ., (1993), Αναδιάρθρωση της Παραγωγικής Διαδικασίας μέσω των Υπεργολαβικών Σχέσεων, στο Λιοδάκης, Γ., (επιμ.) Κοινωνία, Τεχνολογία και Αναδιάρθρωση της Παραγωγής, Πρακτικά Συμποσίου, Πολυτεχνείο Κρήτης, Οκτώβριος 1992, Εκδόσεις Παπαζήση].

Lash, S., and Urry, J., (1987), The End of Organized Capitalism, Cambridge, Polity Press.

Laudon, K.C. and Laudon, J. P., (1998), Management Information Systems-New Approaches to Organization and Technology, 5th edition, U.S.A., Prentice Hall International, Inc.

Law 2874/2000, FEK 286/29.12.2000/ Vol. A'.

Leenders, R., van Engelen, J. and Kratzer, J., (2003), Virtuality, communication and new product team creativity: a social network perspective, Journal of Engineering and Technological Management, 20.

Legal Society of Northern Greece (1992), New Ways of Settlement of Collective Labour Disputes, No. 14, Thessaloniki. [Εταιρεία Νομικών Βορείου Ελλάδος, (1992), Οι Νέοι Τρόποι Επίλυσης των Συλλογικών Διαφορών Εργασίας, Νο. 14, Θεσσαλονίκη].

Leontsini, El.G., (2001), Lifelong education of the citizen and political dimension, in Harris, K.P., Petroulakis, N.B. and Nicodemus, S., (eds.), Continuing education and lifelong learning: International Experience and Greek perspective, Proceedings of the 9th International Pedagogical Conference of the Educational Society, Volos, 1999, Atrapos Publications, Athens. [Λεοντσίνη, Ελ.Γ., (2001), Η διά βίου εκπαίδευση του πολίτη και η πολιτική της διάσταση, στο Χάρης, Κ.Π., Πετρουλάκης, Ν.Β., και Νικόδημος, Σ., (εκδ.), Συνεχιζόμενη εκπαίδευση και διά βίου μάθηση: Διεθνής εμπειρία και ελληνική προοπτική, Πρακτικά του Θ΄Διεθνούς Παιδαγωγικού Συνεδρίου της Παιδαγωγικής Εταιρείας Ελλάδος, Βόλος, 1999, Εκδόσεις Ατραπός, Αθήνα].

Leontsinis, G., (2003), Theoretical and Methodological Issues of History of Teaching and the Environment, "Institute of the Book – Kardamitsas" Publications, Athens. [Λεοντσίνης, Γ., (2003), Θεωρητικά και Μεθοδολογικά Ζητήματα

Διδακτικής της Ιστορίας και του Περιβάλλοντος, Εκδόσεις «Ινστιτούτο του Βιβλίου – Καρδαμίτσα», Αθήναι].

Leventis, G., (1976), The Citizen's Social Rights of, ToS (The Constitution), (134), Athens. [Λεβέντης, Γ., (1976), Τα Κοινωνικά Δικαιώματα του Πολίτη, ΤοΣ (Το Σύνταγμα), (134), Αθήνα].

Leventis, G., (1981), Collective Autonomy and State Intervention in Labour Law, Ant. N. Sakkoulas Publications, Athens-Komotini. [Λεβέντης, Γ., (1981), Συλλογική Αυτονομία και Κρατικός Παρεμβατισμός στο Εργατικό Δίκαιο, Εκδόσεις Αντ. Ν. Σάκκουλα, Αθήνα-Κομοτηνή].

Leventis, G., (1986), Labour Law. Volume I, Trade Union Law, Strike, Athens, Bulletin of Labour Legislation. pp. 376–381. [Λεβέντης, Γ., (1986), Εργατική Νομοθεσία. Τόμος Α΄, Συνδικαλιστικό Δίκαιο, Απεργία, Αθήνα, Δελτίο Εργατικής Νομοθεσίας, σελ. 376-381].

Leventis, G., (2007), Collective Labor Law, Athens. [Λεβέντης, Γ., (2007), Συλλογικό Εργατικό Δίκαιο, Αθήνα].

Levitas, R., (2004), The Concept of Social Exclusion and the Durkheimean Hegemony, in Petmetzidou, M., Papatheodorou, C., (eds.) Poverty and Social Exclusion, Scientific Society for Social Policy, Exantas Publications. [Levitas, R., (2004), Η Έννοια του Κοινωνικού Αποκλεισμού και η Ντυρκεμιανή Ηγεμονία, στο Πετμετζίδου, Μ., και Παπαθεοδώρου, Χ., (επιμ.), Φτώχεια και Κοινωνικός Αποκλεισμός, Επιστημονική Εταιρεία Κοινωνικής Πολιτικής, Έξαντας].

Lévy, P., (1997), Cyberculture, Editions Odile Jacob-Editions du Conseil de l'Europe.

Lévy, P., (1999), Potential Reality: The philosophy and culture of cyberspace, (trans. by M. Karachalios), Athens, Kritiki. [Lévy, P., (1999), Δυνητική Πραγματικότητα: η φιλοσοφία του πολιτισμού και του κυβερνοχώρου, (μτφρ. Μ. Καραχάλιος), Αθήνα, Εκδόσεις Κριτική].

Lewis, I. D. and Weigert, A., (1985), Trust as a social reality, Social Forces, 63(4).

Lewis, R., (1983), Collective Labour Law, in Bain, G.S., (ed.), Industrial Relations in Britain, Blackwell, Oxford.

Liodakis, G., (ed.) (1993), Society, Technology and Restructuring of Production. Symposium Proceedings, University of Crete, Papazisis Publications [Λιοδάκης, Γ., (1992), (επιμ.), Κοινωνία, Τεχνολογία και Αναδιάρθρωση της Παραγωγής, Πρακτικά Συμποσίου, Πολυτεχνείο Κρήτης, Εκδόσεις Παπαζήση].

Liodakis, G., (1993), The Theory of Economic Regulation and Flexible Specialization, Its Critique and Relevance in the Case of Greece, in Liodakis, G., (ed.), Society, Technology and Restructuring of Production. Symposium Proceedings, University of Crete, Papazisis Publications [Λιοδάκης, Γ., (1993), Η θεωρία της οικονομικής ρύθμισης και της ευέλικτης εξειδίκευσης, Η κριτική τους και η σημασία τους στην περίπτωση της Ελλάδας, στο Λιοδάκης, Γ., (επιμ.), Κοινωνία, Τεχνολογία και Αναδιάρθρωση της Παραγωγής, Πρακτικά Συμποσίου, Πολυτεχνείο Κρήτης, Εκδόσεις Παπαζήση].

Lipietz, A., (1994), Post Fordism and Democracy, in Amin, A., (1994), Post Fordism, a Reader, Oxford, Blackwell.

Lipset, M., (1960), Political Man, Doubleday, New York.

Lixouriotis, G., (1992), Collective Labour Relations, Social Interlocutors in Collective Bargaining. Laboratory of Comparative and European Labour Law. Law School University of Thrace. Library of Labor Law and Social Security, vol 1. [Ληξουριώτης, Γ., (1992), Συλλογικές Εργασιακές Σχέσεις, Οι Κοινωνικοί Συνομιλητές στις Συλλογικές Διαπραγματεύσεις. Εργαστήριο Συγκριτικού και Ευρωπαϊκού Εργασιακού Δικαίου Νομικής Σχολής Πανεπιστημίου Θράκης. Βιβλιοθήκη Εργατικού Δικαίου και Κοινωνικής Ασφάλειας, τ. 1].

Lixouriotis, I., (1995), Fundamentals of the OMED's Mediation Procedure, Educational Programme of the OMED. [Ληξουριώτης, Ι., (1995), Βασικά Στοιχεία της Διαδικασίας Μεσολάβησης του Ο.ΜΕ.Δ., Εκπαιδευτικό Πρόγραμμα Ο.ΜΕ.Δ.].

Lixouriotis, I., (1996a), Arbitration as the Ultimate Procedure for the Resolution of Collective Labour Disputes under the OMED, Educational Programme of the OMED. [Ληξουριώτης, Ι., (1996a), Η Διαιτησία ως Ύστατη Διαδικασία Επίλυσης Συλλογικών Διαφορών Εργασίας στο Πλαίσιο του Ο.ΜΕ.Δ., Εκπαιδευτικό Πρόγραμμα Ο.ΜΕ.Δ.].

Lixouriotis, I., (1996b), Public Dialogue with Law 2224/1994, Training Programme of the OMED. [Ληξουριώτης, Ι., (1996b), Ο Δημόσιος Διάλογος μετά τον Νόμο 2224/1994, Εκπαιδευτικό Πρόγραμμα Ο.ΜΕ.Δ.].

Lockwood, D., (1975), Sources of Variation in Working Class, Images of Society, London, Routledge and Kegal Paul.

Lukes, S., (1974), Power: A Radical View, Macmillan, London.

Lutz, B. and Schmidt, G., (1977), Industriesoziologie, in Konig, R., (Hg), Handbuch der empirischen Sozialoforschung, Bd 8, Stuttgart.

Lyberaki, A. (1991) Flexible specialization: Crisis and Restructuring in Small Industry, Gutenberg. [Λυμπεράκη, Α., (1991), Ευέλικτη Εξειδίκευση: Κρίση και Αναδιάρθρωση στη Μικρή Βιομηχανία, Gutenberg.].

Lyberaki, A. and Mouriki, A., (1993), The Quiet Revolution, Metaichmio Publications, Athens. [Λυμπεράκη, Α., και Μουρίκη, Α., (1993), Η Αθόρυβη Επανάσταση, Εκδόσεις Μεταίχμιο, Αθήνα].

Lymperopoylos, K. (1991) Dynamics of Groups and Creativity. Papazisis. [Λυμπερόπουλος, Κ., (1991) Δυναμική των Ομάδων και Δημιουργικότητα, Εκδόσεις Παπαζήση].

Lymperopoylos, K., (1990), Labour from Authoritarianism to Participation. Papazisis. [Λυμπερόπουλος, Κ., (1990), Η Εργασία από τον Αυταρχισμό στη Συμμετοχή, Εκδόσεις Παπαζήση].

Lytras, A. and Koskinas, K., (1993), Labour and Class in Society, Technology and Restructuring of Production, Technical University of Crete, October 1992. [Λύτρας, Α., και Κοσκινάς, Κ., (1993), Εργασία και Τάξη, στο Κοινωνία, Τεχνολογία και Αναδιάρθρωση της Παραγωγής, Πολυτεχνείο Κρήτης, Οκτώβριος 1992].

Lytras, A., (2000), Society and Labour, The role of social classes, Series: Modern Social Sciences-Theory and Practice, Papazisis. [Λύτρας, Α., (2000), Κοινωνία και Εργασία, Ο ρόλος των κοινωνικών τάξεων, Σειρά: Σύγχρονες Κοινωνικές Επιστήμες-Θεωρία και Πράξη, Εκδόσεις Παπαζήση].

Lytras, A., (2007), Analyses of social structure, social organization and policy in the twenty-first century, Papazisis, Athens. [Λύτρας, Α., (2007), Αναλύσεις περί κοινωνικής δομής, Κοινωνική οργάνωση και πολιτική στον εικοστό πρώτο αιώνα, Εκδόσεις Παπαζήση, Αθήνα].

Lytras, A. and Prontzas, E., (2006), Farming in Greece. Society, Production and Ownership 1951, Series: Modern Social Sciences-Theory and Practice, Papazisis, Athens. [Λύτρας, Α., και Πρόντζας, Ε., (2006), Η Αγροτική Εκμετάλλευση στην Ελλάδα. Κοινωνία, Παραγωγή και Ιδιοκτησία το 1951, Σειρά: Σύγχρονες Κοινωνικές Επιστήμες-Θεωρία και Πράξη, Εκδόσεις Παπαζήση, Αθήνα].

Lytras, A., (2008), Political Strategy for Social Classes, Analytical Essays, Papazisis, Athens. [Λύτρας, Α., (2008), Πολιτική Στρατηγική για τις Κοινωνικές Τάξεις, Αναλυτικά Δοκίμια, Εκδόσεις Παπαζήση, Αθήνα.

Lytras, P. (1992), Labour Relations, INTERBOOKS, Athens [Λύτρας, Π., (1992), Εργασιακές Σχέσεις, INTERBOOKS, Αθήνα]

Maclanes, J., (1985), Conjuring up Consultation, British Journal of Industrial Relations, Vol. 23, No. I.

Makris, G., (1979), Part-time Employment in the EEC Countries and Prospects for Development in Greece, OAED (: National Organization for the Employment of the Labour Force). [Μακρής, Γ., Η Μερική Απασχόληση στις Χώρες της ΕΟΚ και οι Προοπτικές για Ανάπτυξη στην Ελλάδα, ΟΑΕΔ.].

Malinvaud, E., (1998), Les cotisations sociales à la charge des employeurs, Conseil d' analyse économique, Paris.

Mamford, L., (1997), Art and technique, Nisides Publicatios, Athens. [Μάμφορντ, Λ., (1994), «Τέχνη και Τεχνική», (1997), Τέχνη και τεχνική, Εκδόσεις Νησίδες , Αθήνα.

Tomson, E.P. (1994), Time, Work Discipline and Industrial Capitalism, Nisides Publications, Thessaloniki. [Τόμσον, Ε.Π., (1994), Χρόνος Εργασιακή Πειθαρχία και Βιομηχανικός Καπιταλισμός, Εκδόσεις Νησίδες, Θεσσαλονίκη].

Manesis, A., (1980a), Institutional crisis of liberal democracy and the Constitution, Current Issues, vol 8, p 22. [Μάνεσης, Α., (1980α), Η Κρίση των Θεσμών της Φιλελεύθερης Δημοκρατίας και το Σύνταγμα, Σύγχρονα Θέματα, τ. 8, σ. 22].

Manesis, A., (1980b), Constitutional Law I, Sakkoulas Editions, Athens-Thessalomiki. [Μάνεσης, Α., (1980b), Συνταγματικό Δίκαιο I, Εκδόσεις Σάκκουλα, Αθήνα-Θεσσαλονίκη].

Manitakis, A., (1987), Collective Autonomy as a Civil Right and as a Constitutional Institution, in "Constitution and Labour Relations," Third Congress of the Society of Labour Law and Social Security (E.D.E.K.A.), Special Edition of Epitheorisi Ergatikou Dikeou (E.Erg.D.-Revew of Labour Law). [Μανιτάκης, Α., (1987), Η συλλογική αυτονομία ως δικαίωμα των πολιτών και ως Συνταγματικός θεσμός, στο «Σύνταγμα και Εργασιακές Σχέσεις, "Τρίτο Συνέδριο του της Εταιρείας Δικαίου Εργασίας και Κοινωνικής Ασφάλισας (Ε.Δ.Ε.Κ.Α.), Ειδική Έκδοση του περιοδικού Επιθεώρηση Εργατικού Δικαίου (Ε.Εργ.Δ.)].

Manwarning, T., (1981), The Trade Union Response to New Technology, Industrial Relations Journal, 12 (4).

Margerison, C.J., (1961), What do we Mean by Industrial Relations? A Behavioral Science Approach, British Journal of Industrial Relations, Vol. VIII, No. 2, July.

Marginson, P., (1992), European Integration and Transnational Management-Union Relations in the Enterprise, British Journal of Industrial Relations, Vol. 30, No. 4.

Marglin, S., (1976), What Do Bosses Do, in Gorz, A., (eds.), The Division of Labour, London, Harvester Press.

Markman, H., (1984), The Role of Industrial Relations in Coping with the Labour Implications of Technical Change: A Trade Union Perspective.

Markovic, M., (1975), Self-management, Epikourios Publishing, Athens. [Μάρκοβιτς, Μ., (1975), Αυτοδιαχείριση, Εκδόσεις Επίκουρος, Αθήνα].

Marks, G., (1986), Neocorporatism and Incomes Policy in Western Europe and North America, Comparative Politics, April, Vol. 18, No. 3.

Marsden, D., (1978), Industrial Democracy and Industrial Control in West Germany, France and Great Britain, DE, Research Paper no Mayo, E., (1960), The Human Problems of an Industrial Civilization, New York.

Marx, K., (1983), Capital I., Capital: A Critique of Political Economy; Volume I, Lawrence & Wishart, London.

Marx, K. (1975), (trans. Babis Grammenos), Economic and Philosophical Manuscripts, Athens, Glaros Publications. [Μαρξ, Κ., (1975), (μετφρ: Μπάμπης

Γραμμένος), Οικονομικά και Φιλοσοφικά Χειρόγραφα, Αθήνα, Εκδόσεις Γλάρος].

Maslow, A., (1970), Motivation and Personality, New York, Harper and Row.

Matthaiou, D., (2000), Globalization, Knowledge Society and Lifelong Education. New Determinants of Educational Work, "New Education", v. 93, Athens. [Ματθαίου, Δ., (2000), Παγκοσμιοποίηση, Κοινωνία της Γνώσης και δια Βίου Εκπαίδευση. Νέες Ορίζουσες του Εκπαιδευτικού Έργου, «Νέα Παιδεία, τ. 93, Αθήνα].

Matthaiou, D., (2007), Quality in Education - Ideological Determinants, conceptualization and Policies - A comparative approach, "Review of Educational Affairs", Issue 13. [Ματθαίου, Δ., (2007), Ποιότητα στην Εκπαίδευση – Ιδεολογικές Ορίζουσες, Εννοιολογήσεις και Πολιτικές – Μία Συγκριτική Θεώρηση, «Επιθεώρηση Εκπαιδευτικών Θεμάτων», Τεύχος 13].

Mavrogordatos, G., (1988), Between the Hard and the Rock Place. Professional organizations in today's Greece, Odysseus Publications. [Μαυρογορδάτος, Γ., (1988), Μεταξύ Πιτυοκάμπτη και Προκρούστη. Οι επαγγελματικές οργανώσεις στη σημερινή Ελλάδα, Εκδόσεις Οδυσσέας].

Mayo, E., (1945), The Social Problems of an Industrial Civilization, Harvard University Press.

McCabe, D., and A. Wilkinson, (1998), The Rise and Fall of TQM': The Vision, Meaning and Operation of Change, Industrial Relations Journal, Vol. 29 (1).

McGregor, D., (1960), The Human Side of Enterprise, New York, McGraw Hill.

McWilliams, Abagail and Donald Siegel, (2001), Corporate social responsibility: A theory of the firm perspective, Academy of Management Review, 26(1).

Mediation and Arbitration-OMED, (2002), Report on the Project of the OMED. 1992–2001and Action Planning 2002, January, Athens. [Οργανισμός Μεσολάβησης και Διαιτησίας-Ο.ΜΕ.Δ., (2002), Απολογισμός Έργου του Ο.ΜΕ.Δ. 1992-2001 και Προγραμματισμός Δράσης 2002, Ιανουάριος, Αθήνα].

Meraklis, M., (1981), Notes on Folklore, issue A, Meaning and Purpose of Folklore, Ioannina. [Μερακλής, Μ., (1981), Σημειώσεις Λαογραφίας, τεύχος Α΄, Έννοια και Σκοπός της Λαογραφίας, Ιωάννινα].

Meraklis, M., (2007), Greek Folklore, Social Formation – Customs - Folk Art, Odysseus Publications, 2nd edition, Athens. [Μερακλής, Μ., (2007), Ελληνική Λαογραφία, Κοινωνική Συγκρότηση-Ήθη και Έθιμα-Λαϊκή Τέχνη, Εκδόσεις Οδυσσέας, 2η έκδοση, Αθήνα].

Merton, R., (1957), Social Theory and Social Structure, The Free Press, in Walker, C., Technology, Industry and Man, The Age of Acceleration, McGraw-Hill.

Miller, D., (1983), The Correlates of Entrepreneurship in Three Types of Firms, Management Science, 29.

Miller, D.C. and Form, W. H., (1951), Industrial Sociology, New York, Harper Bros.

Mills, C.W., (1948), New Men of Power, America's Labor Leaders, Harcourt Brace, New York.

Mills, C.W., (1956), The Power Elite, Oxford University Press, New York.

Ministry of Labour and Social Security (1997), Social Dialogue, Development - Competitiveness - Employment: Confidence Pact of the Government and social partners in Towards 2000, November 10, Offprint Ministry of Labour and Social Security, Appendix II, Athens. [Υπουργείο Εργασίας και Κοινωνικών Ασφαλίσεων, (1997), Κοινωνικός Διάλογος, Ανάπτυξη - Ανταγωνιστικότητα - Απασχόληση: Σύμφωνο Εμπιστοσύνης Κυβέρνησης και Κοινωνικών Εταίρων στην Πορεία προς το 2000, 10 Νοεμβρίου, Ανάτυπο Υπουργείου Εργασίας και Κοινωνικών Ασφαλίσεων, Παράρτημα II, Αθήνα].

Ministry of Labour and Social Security (2000), National Action Plan for Employment, May, pp. 48–49. [Υπουργείο Εργασίας και Κοινωνικών Ασφαλίσεων, (2000), Εθνικό Σχέδιο Δράσης για την Απασχόληση, Μάιος].

Ministry of Labour and Social Security (2001a), National Action Plan for Employment, Working Document, April, Athens, pp. 3–8. [Υπουργείο Εργασίας & Κοινωνικών Ασφαλίσεων, (2001), Εθνικό Σχέδιο Δράσης για την Απασχόληση, Κείμενο Εργασίας, Απρίλιος, Αθήνα].

Ministry of Labour and Social Security (2001b), Elements of the Labour Inspectorate, December, Athens. [Υπουργείο Εργασίας και Κοινωνικών Ασφαλίσεων, (2001), Στοιχεία Σώματος Επιθεωρητών Εργασίας, Δεκέμβριος, Αθήνα].

Ministry of Labour and Social Security (2001c), Reply to the Questionnaire of the European Commission, Council of Experts in Employment and Social Security, December, Athens. [Υπουργείο Εργασίας και Κοινωνικών Ασφαλίσεων, (2001), Απάντηση σε Ερωτηματολόγιο της Ευρωπαϊκής Επιτροπής, Συμβούλιο Εμπειρογνωμόνων Απασχόλησης και Κοινωνικής Ασφάλισης, Δεκέμβριος, Αθήνα].

Ministry of Labour and Social Protection (2006), National Strategy Report on Social Protection and Social Inclusion 2006–2008, September. [Υπουργείο Απασχόλησης και Κοινωνικής Προστασίας, (2006), Εθνική Έκθεση Στρατηγικής για την Κοινωνική Προστασία και την Κοινωνική Ένταξη 2006-2008, Σεπτέμβριος].

Mitropoulos, A., (1985), The Trade Union Action in the Enterprise, Law and Policy, reprint from issue Nr 8 of 1984. [Μητρόπουλος, Α., (1985), Η Συνδικαλιστική Δράση στην Επιχείρηση, Δίκαιο και Πολιτική, Ανάτυπο από το τεύχος 8 του 1984].

Mitropoulos, A., (1989), Theoretical Aspects of the Trade Union Movement, Athens-Komotini, Ant. N. Sakkoulas Editions. [Μητρόπουλος, Α., (1989),

Θεωρητικά Ζητήματα του Συνδικαλιστικού Κινήματος, Αθήνα-Κομοτηνή, Αντ. Ν. Σάκκουλας].

Mitropoulos, A., (1991), Neoliberalism and Degradation of Labour, Tolidis Publications. [Μητρόπουλος, Α., (1991), Νεοφιλελευθερισμός και Υποβάθμιση της Εργασίας, Εκδόσεις Τολίδη].

Mitsou, Tr, (1971), Regulation of collective labour disputes in Greece. [Μήτσου, Τρ., (1971), Η ρύθμιση των συλλογικών διαφορών εργασίας στην Ελλάδα].

Mitsou, Tr., (1981), Trade Unions and the Exercise of Trade Unions' Rights in Greece, Offprint from Epitheorisi Ergatikou Dikeou (E.Erg.D.-Revew of Labour Law), EDEKA Publications, v. 10, pp. 6–7. [Μήτσου, Τρ., (1981), Τα Συνδικάτα και η Άσκηση των Συνδικαλιστικών Δικαιωμάτων στην Ελλάδα, Ανάτυπο από την Ε.Εργ.Δ., Δημοσιεύματα ΕΔΕΚΑ, τ. 10].

Mitsou, Tr., (1982), The Constitutional Foundations of Labour Law, Off-print of Epitheorisi Ergatikou Dikeou (E.Erg.D.-Revew of Labour Law), EDEKA Publications, issue 13. [Μήτσου, Τρ., (1982), Οι Συνταγματικές Βάσεις του Εργατικού Δικαίου, Ανάτυπο από την Ε.Εργ.Δ., Δημοσιεύματα Ε.Δ.Ε.Κ.Α., τ. 13].

Mitsou, Tr. (in collaboration with Tsatiris, G., and Papadimitriou, C.), (1990), Le travail atypique et sa protection sociale en Gréce, pp. 5–13, 122–123. Unpublished report for the EP, March. [Μήτσου, Τρ. (σε συνεργασία με τους Τσατήρη, Γ., και Παπαδημητρίου, Κ.), (1990), Le travail atypique et sa protection sociale en Gréce, Ανέκδοτη έκθεση για την Ε.Κ., Αθήνα, Μάρτιος].

Monat, J. and Hedra Safarti, (1986), Workers' Participation: A Voice in Decisions, 1981–1985, ILO, Geneva.

Montgomery, D., Wiesman, D. and DeCaro, P. & W., (2001), Towards a code of ethics for organizational communication of professionals: a working proposal. American Communication Journal, 5 (1), Fall, http://acjournal.org/holdings/vol5/iss1/special/ montgomery.html

Moore, W.E., (1951), Industrial Relations and the Social Order, Rev. ed. New York, MacMillan.

Moskov, K., (1988), Introduction to the History of the Working Class Movement, The Shaping of National and Social Consciousness in Greece, Athens, Kastaniotis Publications. [Μοσκώφ, Κ., (1988), Εισαγωγικά στην Ιστορία του Κινήματος της Εργατικής Τάξης, Η Διαμόρφωση της Εθνικής και Κοινωνικής Συνείδησης στην Ελλάδα, Αθήνα, Εκδόσεις Καστανιώτη].

Mousouris, Ar., (1996a), Social Dialogue. Determining the priorities of Greek society, Selection, April, pp. 32–37. [Μουσούρης, Άρ., (1996), Κοινωνικός Διάλογος. Για τον καθορισμό των προτεραιοτήτων της ελληνικής κοινωνίας, Επιλογή, Απρίλιος, σελ. 32-37].

Mousouris, Ar., (1996b), 35-hour Work – A solution to handle unemployment or a Bomb on the Foundations of Economics?, Selection, February. [Μουσούρης, Α., (1996), 35ωρη Εργασία - Λύση για την Αντιμετώπιση της Ανεργίας ή Βόμβα στα Θεμέλια της Οικονομίας;, Επιλογή, Φεβρουάριος].

Mouzelis, N., (1991), Organization and Bureaucracy, (trans. by E. Sofoulis), Mathioudaki-Andronopoulou Publications, Athens. [Μουζέλης, Ν., (1991), Οργάνωση και Γραφειοκρατία, (μτφρ. Ε. Σοφούλη), Εκδόσεις Μαθιουδάκη-Ανδρονοπούλου, Αθήνα].

Nascent Entrepreneurs, Journal of Business Venturing, 18, pp. 301–331.

National Confederation of Greek Commerce http://www.esee.gr/ellEtisíaEkthesiEm Poήoul2002/261.shtm1#toP [Εθνική Συνομοσπονδία Ελληνικού Εμπορίου http://www.esee.gr/ellEtisíaEkthesiEmPoήoul2002/261.shtm1#toP

Natsopoulos, D. (n.y), Handbook of Industrial and Human Relations, Paratiritis Publications, Thessaloniki. [Νατσόπουλος, Δ., (χ.χ.), Εγχειρίδιο Βιομηχανικών Ανθρώπινων Σχέσεων, Εκδόσεις Παρατηρητής, Θεσσαλονίκη].

Neuhauser, P. G., Bender, R. and Stromberg, K.L., (2000), Culture.Com: Building Corporate Culture in the Connected Workplace, Canada, John Wiley & Sons Ltd.

Nicholaou-Smokovitis, L. (1987b), New Institutions in Industrial Relations. Participation and Self-management. Papazisis, Athens. [Νικολάου-Σμοκοβίτη, Λ., (1987β), Νέοι Θεσμοί στις Εργασιακές Σχέσεις. Συμμετοχή και Αυτοδιαχείριση, Εκδόσεις Παπαζήση, Αθήνα]

Nicholaou-Smokovitsis, L. (1990), Organizations, Management and Society, Stamoulis Publications, Athens. [Νικολάου-Σμοκοβίτη, Λ., (1990), Οργανισμοί, Διοίκηση και Κοινωνία, Εκδόσεις Σταμούλη, Αθήνα].

Nicholaou-Smokovitis, L. (1994), Sociology, Society and Social Life, Stamoulis Publications, Athens-Piraeus. [Νικολάου-Σμοκοβίτη, Λ., (1994), Κοινωνιολογία, Κοινωνία και Κοινωνική Ζωή, Εκδόσεις Σταμούλη, Αθήνα-Πειραιάς].

Nichols, T., (1969), Ownership, Control and Ideology, London, Allen & Unwin.

Nikolouzos, L. (GSEBEE representative: Representative of the General Confederation of Professionals, Manifacturerers, Mercants of Greece), (1991), Paper presented at the Seminar Training of Mediators-Arbitrators of the OMED, held on 16 November at Royal Olympic Hotel. [Νικολούζος, Λ., (εκπρόσωπος ΓΣΕΒΕΕ), (1991), Εισήγηση στο Σεμινάριο Επιμόρφωσης των Μεσολαβητών-Διαιτητών του Ο.ΜΕ.Δ., που πραγματοποιήθηκε την 16η Νοεμβρίου, στο Ξενοδοχείο Royal Olympic].

Ntasios, L., (1991a), Labour Procedural Law, Collective Labour Relations, Volume II / II. [Ντάσιος, Λ., (1991a), Εργατικό Δικονομικό Δίκαιο, Συλλογικές Εργασιακές Σχέσεις, Τόμος Β/ΙΙ].

Ntasios, L., (1991b), Labour Procedural Law, Collective Labour Relations, Volume IV., par. 5. [Ντάσιος, Λ., (1991b), Εργατικό Δικονομικό Δίκαιο, Συλλογικές Εργασιακές Σχέσεις, τόμος IV].

Nohria, N., and Berkley, J.D., (1994), The virtual organization: bureaucracy, technology, and the implosion of control, Chapter 5, in Heckscher, C. and Donnellon, A. (Eds.): The Post-Bureaucratic Organization: New Perspectives on Organizational Change, Sage Publications, Thousand Oaks, California.

OKE, (1999), Social dialogue in South-eastern Europe. Opinion of the OKE, April, no. 29 [ΟΚΕ, (1999), Κοινωνικός διάλογος στη Νοτιοανατολική Ευρώπη, Γνώμη της ΟΚΕ, Απρίλιος, αρ. 29].

OMED, (1993a), Developments in the Countries of the Community in Working Time Issues. Trans. into Greek by the OMED. [Ο.ΜΕ.Δ. (1993), Εξελίξεις στις Χώρες της Κοινότητας σε Θέματα Χρόνου Εργασίας, Μετάφραση στην Ελληνική].

OMED, (1993b), Economic and Social Councils of the Member Countries of EEC, OMED, Athens. [ΟΜΕΔ, (1993), Οικονομικές και κοινωνικές επιτροπές των χωρών-μελών Ε.Ο.Κ.].

OECD, (1986), Flexibility in the Labour Market: "The Current Debate", Paris.

OECD, (1998), Maintaining Prosperity in an Ageing Society, OECD Publishing, Paris. DOI: http://dx.doi.org/10.1787/9789264163133-en

Offe, C., (1981), The Attribution of Public Status to Interest Groups: Observations on the West German Case, in Berger, S. (ed.), Organizing Interests in Western Europe, Cambridge: Cambridge University Press.

Offe, C., (1993), Society of Labor, States 1, Athens, Nisos Publications. [Offe, C., (1993), Κοινωνία της Εργασίας, Πολιτείες 1, Αθήνα, Εκδόσεις Νήσος].

Government Gazette (FEK) 6/A711-1-1983.

Government Gazette (FEK) 179/A718-10-1985.

Paleologos, N., (2006), Employment and Trade Unions in the 21st Century, Athens, Studies-INE-GSEE. [Παλαιολόγος, Ν., (2006), Εργασία και Συνδικάτα στον 21ο Αιώνα, Αθήνα, Μελέτες-ΙΝΕ-ΓΣΕΕ].

Palmer, J. W. and Speier, C., (1997), A typology of virtual organizations: an empirical study, in Gupta, J., (ed.), Proceedings of the Association for information systems, Americas Conference, Indianapolis.

Panagiotopoulou, P., (1990), Presentation of Key Theoretical Direction of Sociology of Organization: Introduction to Sociology of Organization, Department of Business Administration, University of the Aegean. [Παναγιωτοπούλου, P., (1990), Παρουσίαση των Κυριότερων Θεωρητικών Κατευθύνσεων της Κοινωνιολογίας της Οργάνωσης, στο Εισαγωγή στην Κοινωνιολογία της Οργάνωσης, Τμήμα Διοίκησης Επιχειρήσεων Πανεπιστημίου Αιγαίου].

Panagiotopoulou, P., (1997), Communication in organizations: the evolution of theories of organizations and communicative dimensions. Kritiki, Athens. [Παναγιωτοπούλου, P., (1997), Η επικοινωνία στις οργανώσεις: η εξέλιξη των θεωριών των οργανώσεων και οι επικοινωνιακές τους διαστάσεις. Εκδόσεις Κριτική, Αθήνα].

Panteli, N. and Dibben, M.R., (2001), Revisiting the nature of virtual organizations: reflections on mobile communication systems, Futures, 33(5).

Paoli-Pelvey, Ch., (1993), Working Time, in Blanpain, R. and Engels, C., Comparative Labour Law and Industrial Relations in Industrialized Market Economies, 5th rev. ed., Deventer-Boston, Kluwer Law & Taxation Publishers.

Papadimitriou, K., (1991), Rapport National, in XIII International Conference of Labour Law and Social Security. [Παπαδημητρίου, K., (1991), Παγκόσμιο Συνέδριο Εργατικού Δικαίου και Κοινωνικής Ασφάλισης].

Papadimitriou, K., (1992), Collective Labour Relations and Labour Dispute Resolution, vol. A, Settlement of Collective Labour Disputes (conciliation-mediation-arbitration), Ant. N. Sakkoulas Editions, Athens-Komotini. [Παπαδημητρίου, K., (1992), Συλλογικές Εργασιακές Σχέσεις και Επίλυση Διαφορών Εργασίας, τ. Α΄, Η Επίλυση των Συλλογικών Διαφορών Εργασίας (συμφιλίωση-μεσολάβηση-διαιτησία), Εκδόσεις Αντ.Ν. Σάκκουλας, Αθήνα-Κομοτηνή].

Papadimitriou, Z., (1992), Development Prospects Anthropocentric Production Systems in Greece: The Case of Textile and Apparel, Contemporary Issues, 48, Athens. [Παπαδημητρίου, Z., (1992), Προοπτικές Ανάπτυξης Ανθρωποκεντρικών Συστημάτων Παραγωγής στην Ελλάδα: Η Περίπτωση της Κλωστοϋφαντουργίας και Ένδυσης, Σύγχρονα Θέματα, 48, Αθήνα].

Papadimitriou, Z., (1996), Sociological Analects, Aspects of Modern Industrial Society, University Studio Press. [Παπαδημητρίου, Z., (1996), Κοινωνιολογικά Ανάλεκτα, Όψεις της Σύγχρονης Βιομηχανικής Κοινωνίας, University Studio Press].

Papaioannou, Ath., (1991), "Deregulation" of Labour Law and "Elasticity" of Labour Relations, Neoliberalism and the Challenge of Labour Law, Epitheorisi Ergatikou Dikeou (E.Erg.D.-Revew of Labour Law), vol. 5, Volume 50. [Παπαϊωάννου, A., (1991), Η «Απορρύθμιση» του Εργατικού Δικαίου και η «Ελαστικότητα» των Εργασιακών Σχέσεων, Ο Νεοφιλελευθερισμός και η Αμφισβήτηση του Εργατικού Δικαίου, Ε.Εργ.Δ., τ. 5, τόμος 50].

Papaioannou, Ath., (1996), The agencies of social dialogue at national level, Congress by the EDEKA, Plan of Recommendation, November, Piraeus. [Παπαϊωάννου, Αθ., (1996), Οι Φορείς του Κοινωνικού Διαλόγου σε Εθνικό Επίπεδο, Συνέδριο Ε.Δ.Ε.Κ.Α., Σχέδιο Εισήγησης, Νοέμβριος, Πειραιάς].

Papaioannou, Ath., (1997), The institutionalization of social dialogue at national level in Greece, Review of Labour Law, vol. 56, vol. 20. [Παπαϊωάννου, Αθ., (1997), Η θεσμοποίηση του κοινωνικού διαλόγου σε εθνικό επίπεδο στην Ελλάδα, Επιθεώρηση Εργατικού Δικαίου, τομ. 56, τεύχ. 20].

Papalexandri, N., (1990), "Organizational Development", in Kanellopoulos, C. (ed.), Utilization of the Personnel by Beveloping Officers and Improving the Organization, International Publishing. [Παπαλεξανδρή, Ν., (1990), «Οργανωτική Ανάπτυξη», στο Κανελλόπουλος, Χ., Αξιοποίηση Προσωπικού με Ανάπτυξη Στελεχών και Βελτίωση Οργάνωσης, International Publishing].

Pararas, P. (1981), Legislative Content Acts of the President of the Republic, Athens. [Παραράς, Π., (1981), Αι Πράξεις Νομοθετικού Περιεχομένου του Προέδρου της Δημοκρατίας, Αθήνα].

Parsons, T., (1958), Authority, Legitimation and Political Action, in Friedrich, C., (1958), Authority, Cambridge Mass.

Parsons, T., (1964), The Social System, Routledge and Kegan Paul, London.

Pateman, C., (1970), Participation and Democratic Theory, Cambridge University Press.

Pavlopoulos, Pr., (2013), The Public Law in the constellation of economic crisis, A.A. Livanis Publications, Athens. [Παυλόπουλος, Πρ., Το δημόσιο δίκαιο στον αστερισμό της οικονομικής κρίσης, Εκδοτικός Οίκος Α.Α. Λιβάνη, Αθήνα].

Pavlopoulos, Pr., (2010), Administrative Law, (collective work: Apostolos Gerontas, Sotiris A. Lytras, Prokopis Pavlopoulos, Glykeria Siouti, Spiros Flogaitis), Sakkoulas Editions, Athens, 2nd Edition. [Παυλόπουλος, Πρ., Διοικητικό Δίκαιο (συλλογικό: Απόστολος Γέροντας, Σωτήρης Α. Λύτρας, Προκόπης Παυλόπουλος, Γλυκερία Σιούτη, Σπύρος Φλογαΐτης), Εκδόσεις Σάκκουλα, Αθήνα, 2η Έκδοση].

Pavlopoulos, Pr., (1983), Administrative Science Lessons, Ant. N. Sakkoulas, Athens. [Παυλόπουλος, Πρ., Μαθήματα Διοικητικής Επιστήμης, Εκδόσεις Αντ. Ν. Σάκκουλα, Αθήνα].

Pazarzi, E., (2001), Sociology, Volume A, The Sociological Theory, G. Benos Publications, Athens. [Παζαρζή, Ε., (2001), Κοινωνιολογία, τόμος Α΄, Η Κοινωνιολογική Θεωρία, Εκδόσεις Γ. Μπένου, Αθήνα].

Peck, J. and Tickell, A., (1994), Searching for a New Institutional Fix: the After-Fordism Crisis and the Global-Local Disorder, in Amin, A., (ed.) (1994), Post-Fordism, a Reader, Oxford, Blackwell.

Petrinioti, X., (1985), State and Labor Relations, Political Economy of Industrial Relations, Papazisis. [Πετρινιώτη, Ξ., (1985), Κράτος και Εργασιακές Σχέσεις, Η Πολιτική Οικονομία των Εργασιακών Σχέσεων, Εκδόσεις Παπαζήση].

Petrinioti, X., (1989), Labor Markets, Papazisis, Athens. [Πετρινιώτη, Ξ., (1989), Αγορές Εργασίας, Εκδόσεις Παπαζήση, Αθήνα].

Petrou, M., (1988), The Nature of Collective Bargaining, Epitheorisi Ergatikou Dikeou (E.Erg.D.-Revew of Labour Law), issue Nr 47.

Piore, M., Sabel, C., (1984), The Second Industrial Divide: Possibilities for Prospectivity, Basic Books, New York.

Piperopoulos, G., (1994), Sociology, Art of Text, Thessaloniki. [Πιπερόπουλος, Γ., (1994), Κοινωνιολογία, Art of Text, Θεσσαλονίκη].

Piperopoulos, G., (1997), Sociology, Ellinka Grammata Publications, Athens. [Πιπερόπουλος, Γ., (1997), Κοινωνιολογία, Ελληνικά Γράμματα, Αθήνα].

Pizzorno, A., Interests and Parties in Pluralism, in Berger, S., Organizing Interests in Western Europe, Cambridge University Press, Cambrigde.

Poitet, F., (1987), The Changing Face of Work, Researching and Debating the Issues, European Foundation for the Improvement of Living and Working Conditions, Paris.

Pool, M., (1975),Workers' Participation in Industry, R.K.P.

Poulantzas, N., (1968), Pouvoir Politique et Classes Sociales, Maspero, Paris.

Poulantzas, N., (1969), The Problem of the Capitalistic State, New Left Review, vol. 58, November/December.

Prontzas, E. (ed.) (2003), The Banking Trade Unionism after Dictatorship, The Archive of G. Anomeritis 1974–1985, Historical Archive of the Rural Bank. Series Documents Edition. [Πρόντζας, Ε., (επιμ.) (2003), Ο Τραπεζικός Συνδικαλισμός στη Μεταπολίτευση, Το Αρχείο του Γ. Ανωμερίτη 1974-1985, Ιστορικό Αρχείο Αγροτικής Τράπεζας, Σειρά Έκδοση Τεκμηρίων].

Prontzas, E., (1999), Economic Nationalism: An Essay on Modern Greek History, "History and Culture", 11, University Studio Press / Expression, Thessaloniki. [Πρόντζας, Ε., (1999), Οικονομικός Εθνικισμός, Δοκίμιο στη Νεοελληνική Ιστορία, «Ιστορία και Πολιτισμός», 11, University Studio Press/ Έκφραση, Θεσσαλονίκη].

Psalidopoulos, M. (no year), International Conflict and Economic Thought, International Trade and the National Interest of 17th-20th Century, Metamesonikties Publications, Athens. [Ψαλιδόπουλος, Μ., (χ.χ.), Διεθνής Σύγκρουση και Οικονομική Σκέψη, Διεθνές Εμπόριο και Εθνικό Συμφέρον 17ος – 20ος Αιώνας, Μεταμεσονύκτιες Εκδόσεις, Αθήνα].

Psalidopoulos, M., (1997), Economic Theory and Social Policy, Aeolus Publications. [Ψαλιδόπουλος, Μ., (1997), Οικονομικές Θεωρίες και Κοινωνική Πολιτική, Αίολος].

Psimitis, M., (1999), Corporatist mediation and social control, Ellinika Grammata Publications, Athens. [Ψημίτης, Μ., (1999), Κορπορατιστική διαμεσολάβηση και κοινωνικός έλεγχος, Ελληνικά Γράμματα, Αθήνα].

Psimmenos, I. and Skamnakis, C., (2008), Migrant Domestic Work and Social Protection, The Case of Women from Albania and Ukraine Series: Sociology and Work Papazisis, Athens. [Ψημμένος, Ι., και Σκαμνάκης, Χ., (2008), Οικιακή Εργασία Μεταναστριών και Κοινωνική Προστασία, Η Περίπτωση των Γυναικών από την Αλβανία και την Ουκρανία, Σειρά: Κοινωνιολογία και Εργασία, Εκδόσεις Παπαζήση, Αθήνα].

Rada, J., (1980), The Impact of Microelectronics: A Tentative Appraisal of Information Technology, ILO.

Ramondt, J.J., (1979), Workers Self Management and its Constraints: The Yugoslav Experience, British Journal of Industrial Relations, March, 17, 1.

Ramsay, H., (1977), Cycles of Control, Sociology, Vol. 11, No. 3, September.

Raphael, M., (1991), Sociological Theory, Background and Prospects, Stamoulis, Piraeus. [Ραφαήλ, Μ., (1991), Κοινωνιολογική Θεωρία, Αναδρομή και Προοπτικές, Εκδόσεις Σταμούλης, Πειραιάς].

Reagle, J.M., (1996), Trust in electronic markets. First Monday, 1(2), August 5, http://www.firstmonday.org/issues/issue2/markets/index.html

Rideau, Al., (1988), Sociology of Work, in Kaznev, G., and Viktorof, D., Key Issues Sociology and Sociological Dictionary, (Trans. N. Psiroukis), Kastaniotis-Epikerotita Editions, Athens. [Ριντώ, Αλ., (1988), Κοινωνιολογία της Εργασίας, στο Καζνέβ, Ζ., και Βικτόρωφ, Ντ., Βασικά Θέματα της Κοινωνιολογίας και Κοινωνιολογικό Λεξικό, (μεταφρ. Ν. Ψυρούκης), Εκδόσεις Καστανιώτης-Επικαιρότητα, Αθήνα].

Reed, M., (1992), The Sociology of Organizations: Themes, Perspectives and Prospects, London, Harvester Wheatsheaf.

Reinermann, H., (1996), Virtual Organizations. Informatika, (Slovenia), Vol 1.

Report of the Commisariat Generl du Plan, (2001), June.

Labour Canada: Part-time work in Canada: Report of the Commission of Inquiry on Part-time Work, (1983), Ottawa, Ontario.

Report of the Scientific Department of the Chamber of Deputies on the Bill "Urgent Measures for the Implementation of the Programme of Support for the Greek Economy": Report of the Bill, "Approval of the mid-term budgetary Strategy 2013-2016-Urgent implementing measures of n. 4046/2012 and of the mid-term th Framework budgetary Strategy 2013-2016",

B' Directorate of Scientific Studies, Department of Legal Elaboration of Pojects and Introduction of Ptotasewn Laws, Greek Parliament. ["'Έκθεση επί του Νομοσχεδίου, "'Έγκριση Μεσοπρόθεσμου Πλαισίου Δημοσιονομικής Στρατηγικής 2013-2016 - Επείγοντα μέτρα εφαρμογής του ν. 4046/2012 και του Μεσοπρόθεσμου Πλαισίου Δημοσιονομικής Στρατηγικής 2013-2016", Β' Διεύθυνση Επιστημονικών Μελετών, Τμήμα Νομοτεχνικής Επεξεργασίας Σχεδίων και Πτοτάσεων Νόμων, Βουλή των Ελλήνων].

Reppas, D., (2001), Extract from the speech of the Minister of Labour and Social Security Minister during the debate in the House bill, tabled by the Coalition for the "Establishment of 35-hour working week and other provisions", Proceedings of the House, OABA, 2/4, 28-11-2001, VZ1128RCH. [Ρέππας, Δ., (2001), Απόσπασμα της ομιλίας του Υπουργού Εργασίας και Κοινωνικών Ασφαλίσεων, κ. κατά τη συζήτηση στη Βουλή πρότασης νόμου που κατέθεσε ο Συνασπισμός για την «Καθιέρωση της 35ωρης εβδομαδιαίας εργασίας και άλλες διατάξεις», Πρακτικά Βουλής, ΟΑΒΑ, 2/4, 28-11-2001, ΒΖ1128ΡΧ].

Rifkin, J., (1995), The End of Labour and its Future, Nea Synora (trans.) - A. A. Livanis, Athens. [Rifkin, J., (1995), Το Τέλος της Εργασίας και το Μέλλον της, Νέα Σύνορα (μεταφρ.) - Α.Α. Λιβάνη, Αθήνα].

Rigatou, Al., (2000), Dialogue or epilogue in labour relations? Some thoughts on Social Dialogue, Labour Law. E. Erg. Dikaiou, vol. 59, issue 20. [Ρηγάτου, Αλ., (2000), Διάλογος ή επίλογος στις εργασιακές σχέσεις; Πρώτες σκέψεις για τον κοινωνικό διάλογο, Επιθεώρησις Εργατικού Δικαίου, τόμ. 59, τεύχ. 20].

Rise in Unemployment in France, (2001), Efimerida Express (: Newspaper Express), 20th November, p. 1.

Robbins, R., (1995), Organizational Behavior, Englewood Cliffs, Prentice Hall.

Robertson, K., (2000), Work transformation: integrating people, space and technology, Facilities, 18(10-12).

Robinson, D., (1973), Incomes Policy and Capital - Sharing in Europe, Croom Helm.

Robolis S. and Kollias G. (1998) Social dialogue in Greece, in Yearbook of Labour, Panteion University Press. [Ρομπόλης Σ. - Κολλιάς Γ. (1998), Ο κοινωνικός διάλογος στην Ελλάδα, Επετηρίδα Εργασίας, Πανεπιστημιακές Εκδόσεις Παντείου].

Rojot, J., (1991), "Legislative and Contractual Restriction of Working Time in the Member States of the European Community: A Modernization", Final Report, European Community Network of Experts on Working Time, 15.10.1991, University of Paris I - Pantheon Sorbonne - Developments in the Countries of the Community on Working Time Issues, trans. in Greek by the OMED, 1993. [Rojot, J., (1991), Νομοθετικές και Συμβατικές Οριοθετήσεις του Χρόνου Εργασίας στα Κράτη-Μέλη της Ευρωπαϊκής Κοινότητας:

Ένας Εκσυγχρονισμός, Τελική Εισήγηση, Ευρωπαϊκό Κοινοτικό Δίκτυο Εμπειρογνωμόνων για το Χρόνο Εργασίας, 15-10-1991, Πανεπιστήμιο Paris I. - Pantheon Sorbonne. Εξελίξεις στις Χώρες της Κοινότητας σε θέματα Χρόνου Εργασίας, Μετάφρ. στην Ελληνική - Ο.ΜΕ.Δ., 1993].

Rojot, J. and Blanpain, R., (1994), Legal and Contractual Limitations to Working Time in the European Community Member-States, General Report, 1st Draft, March.

Romagnoli, U., (1989), Deregulation and Sources of Labour Law, (trans. I. Lixouriotis), Epitheorisi Ergatikou Dikeou (E.Erg.D.-Revew of Labour Law), v. 48. [Romagnoli, U., (1989), Η Απορρύθμιση και οι Πηγές του Εργατικού Δικαίου, (Μετάφρ. Ι. Ληξουριώτης), Ε.Εργ.Δ., τ. 48].

Romanias, G., (1996), It is still possible to measure social convergence, Trade Union Review, December. [Ρωμανιάς, Γ., (1996), Κι όμως είναι εφικτή η μέτρηση της κοινωνικής σύγκλισης, Συνδικαλιστική Επιθεώρηση, Δεκέμβριος].

Romer, P., (1994), Preferences, Promises, and the Politics of Entitlement, in Fuchs, V.R. (Ed.), Individual and Social Responsibility: Child Care, Education, Medical Care, and Long-Term Care in America. University of Chicago Press, Chicago and New York, pp. 195–228.

Rosanvallon, P., (1982), Self-Management: The Future of Socialism, Andromeda, Athens. [Rosanvallon, P., (1982), Αυτοδιαχείριση: Το Μέλλον του Σοσιαλισμού, Ανδρομέδα, Αθήνα].

Rose, M., (1985), Economic nationalism versus class solidarity: the perspectives of active trade union members, in Spyropoulos, G., Trade unions today and tomorrow. Vol. 1, Presses Interuniversitaires Europeennes, Maastricht.

Ross, N.S., (1958), Organized Labour and Management: The U.K., in Hugh-Jones, E.M., (eds), Human Relations and Modem Management, North Holland, Elsevier.

Ross, A.M. and Hartman, P.T., (1960), Changing Patterns of Industrial Conflict, Wiley, New York.

Roussis, G., (1983), Socialization of the means of production from the Marxist point of view, Radical Newspaper, F. 7.9.1983, p 140. [Ρούσσης, Γ., (1983), Κοινωνικοποίηση των μέσων παραγωγής από τη μαρξιστική άποψη, Εφημερίδα Ριζοσπάστης, Φ. 7-9 1983, σ. 140].

Roussis, G. (1983), Workers' participation: Attendance: Class struggle and class collaboration? Synchroni Epochi Publications. [Ρούσης, Γ. (1983), Συμμετοχή των εργαζομένων: Ταξική πάλη ή ταξική συνεργασία;, Εκδόσεις Σύγχρονη Εποχή].

Rowe, Chr., (1986), People and Chips, The Human Implications of Information Technology, Paradigm Publishing, London.

Ruccio, D., (1989), Fordism on a World Scale: International Political Dimensions of Regulation, Review of Radical Political Economics, 21/1.

Sakellaropoulos, Th., (1993), European Welfare State or National Social Policies? The European Social Space after Maastricht, in Getimis, P. and Gravaris, D., Welfare State and Social Policy: Contemporary Questioning, Themelio Publications, Athens. [Σακελλαρόπουλος, Θ., (1993), «Ευρωπαϊκό Κοινωνικό Κράτος ή Εθνικές Κοινωνικές Πολιτικές; Ο Ευρωπαϊκός Κοινωνικός Χώρος μετά το Μάαστριχτ», στο Γετίμης, Π., και Γράβαρης, Δ., (1993), Κοινωνικό Κράτος και Κοινωνική Πολιτική: η Σύγχρονη Προβληματική, Εκδόσεις Θεμέλιο, Αθήνα].

Sakellaropoulos, Th., (1999), Seeking the New Welfare State, in Sakellaropoulos, Th. (ed.), The Reform of the Welfare State, Vol. A., Scientific Library, Kritiki publications. [Σακελλαρόπουλος, Θ., (1999), «Αναζητώντας το Νέο Κοινωνικό Κράτος», στο Σακελλαρόπουλος, Θ., (επιμ.), Η Μεταρρύθμιση του Κοινωνικού Κράτους, τομ. Α., Επιστημονική Βιβλιοθήκη, Εκδόσεις Κριτική].

Salamon, M., (1987), Industrial Relations-Theory and Practice, Prentice Hall International, London.

Sapir, Z., Labor and Employment Relations in Russia, Commune / Conflicts, vol 7. [Σαπίρ, Ζ., Εργάτες και Εργασιακές Σχέσεις στη Ρωσία, Κομμούνα/ Αντιπαραθέσεις, τ. 7].

Sayer, A., (1986), New Developments in Manufacturing: The Just-in-Time System, Capital and Class, 30.

Sayles, C.R., (1958), Behavior of Industrial Work Groups, New York, Wiley.

Scarff, Elisabeth A.E., (1982), A Report on Part-time Employment in Britain.

Schmitter P., (1974), Still the Century of Corporatism? Review of Political Studies, Vol. 36, No 1.

Schmitter, P., (1997), The corporatist Sisyphus: past, present and future, European University Institute, Florence.

Schneider, E.V., (1957), Industrial Sociology, McGraw-Hill, New York.

Schoer, K., (1987), Part-lime Employment: Britain and West Germany, Cambridge Journal of Economics, March, vol 11, no 1.

Scott, J.F. and Homans, G.C., (1947), Reflections on the Wildcat Strikes, American Sociological Review, Vol. 12, June.

Shepard, J.M., (1970), Automation and Alienation: a Study of Office and Factory Workers, MIT Press, Cambridge, Mass and London.

Shorter, E. and Tilly, C., (1974), Strikes in France, 1830-1968, Cambridge University Press, Cambridge.

Simitis, K., (2001), Speech during the "Pre-Agenda Discussion" in the Parliament on: "Social and Economic Situation of the Country", 12 November, House

Minutes. [Σημίτης, Κ., (2001), Ομιλία στην «Προ Ημερησίας Διατάξεως Συζήτηση» στη Βουλή με θέμα: Η Κοινωνική και Οικονομική Κατάστασης της Χώρας, 12 Νοεμβρίου, Πρακτικά Βουλής].

Sisson, K., (1993), Transnational Industrial Relations in Europe, presented in International Conference organized by the European Commission and the Irish Labour Relations Commission on the Resolution of Industrial Disputes., Dublin Castle, Dublin, Ireland, 5-6 October, (A Report on the Conference prepared by Antony Kerr).

Skiadas, C. (1990), An Approach to the Concept of Technology, in the Conference: "Culture and Technology", 2-3 of December 1989, Hania, Polytechnic School of Krete, Parousiasi Publications. [Σκιαδάς, Χ., (1990), Μία Προσέγγιση της Έννοιας της Τεχνολογίας, στο «Κουλτούρα και Τεχνολογία», 2-3 Δεκεμβρίου 1989, Χανιά, Πολυτεχνείο Κρήτης, Εκδόσεις Παρουσίαση].

Smith, J. H., (1961), Industrial Sociology, Paris, UNESCO.

Snyder, D., (1977), Early North American Strikes: A Reinterpretation, Industrial and Labor Relations Review, 30 (3).

Soisson, J.P. (Minister of Labor), (1990), Employment and Training, France in Fighting Unemployment and Managing structural change, The role of active manpower policies, Report on an International Trade Union Seminar, held by the OECD, Paris, 29-31 January, TUAC-OECD Publications, Paris.

Sorge, A., Warner, M., Hartmann, G. and Nicholas, I., (1981), Microelectronics and Manpower in Manufacturing: Applications of Computer Numerical Control in Great Britain and West Germany, Research Report.

Sparrow, P.R., (2000), New employee behaviours, work designs and forms of work organization: what is in store for the future of work? Journal of Managerial Psychology, 15 (3).

Spyropoulos, G., (1955), The International Recognition and Protection of Freedom of Association, Epitheorisi Ergatikou Dikeou (E.Erg.D.-Revew of Labour Law), issue Nr 14. [Σπυρόπουλος, Γ., (1955), Η Διεθνής Αναγνώριση και Προστασία της Συνδικαλιστικής Ελευθερίας, Ε.Εργ.Δ., τ. 14].

Spyropoulos, G., (1956), La liberté syndicale, Librairie générale de droit et de jurisprudence (L.G.D.J.), Paris.

Spyropoulos, G., (1977), Multinational and International Employment Relations in the European Economic Area, EDEKA Publications. [Σπυρόπουλος, Γ., (1977), Πολυεθνικές και Διεθνείς Εργασιακές Σχέσεις στον Ευρωπαϊκό Χώρο, Δημοσιεύματα Ε.Δ.Ε.Κ.Α.].

Spyropoulos, G., (ed.) (1985a), Trade Unions Today and Tomorrow, Vol. I, Trade Unions in a Changing Europe, Work and Society, No 6, European Centre for Work and Society, Maastricht, Presses Interuniversitaires Europeennes.

Spyropoulos, G., (1985b), The Role of Trade Unions in a Changing World, in Spyropoulos, G., (ed.), Trade Unions Today and Tomorrow, Vol. I, Trade Unions in a Changing Europe, Work and Society, No 6, European Centre for Work and Society, Maastricht, Presses Interuniversitaires Europeennes.

Spyropoulos, G., (1985c) Internationalization of Economy: a New Challenge to Trade Unions, in Spyropoulos, G., (ed.), Trade Unions Today and Tomorrow, Vol. I, Trade Unions in a Changing Europe, Work and Society, No 6, European Centre for Work and Society, Maastricht, Presses Interuniversitaires Europeennes.

Spyropoulos, G., (1987), Labour Relations and Economic Crisis in Southern European countries, Epitheorisi Ergatikou Dikeou (E.Erg.D.-Revew of Labour Law), issue Nr 46, p. 6–7. [Σπυρόπουλος, Γ., (1987), Εργασιακές Σχέσεις και Οικονομική Κρίση στις Χώρες της Νότιας Ευρώπης, Ε.Εργ.Δ., τ. 46].

Spyropoulos, G., (1987–1988), Negotiation Collective Transnational on International, Review Hellenique de Droit International.

Spyropoulos, G., (1988), Collective bargaining and the International Experience, Some Reflections on the evolution of institutions in Greece, Epitheorisi Ergatikou Dikeou (E.Erg.D.-Revew of Labour Law), v. 47. [Σπυρόπουλος, Γ., (1988), Οι Συλλογικές Διαπραγματεύσεις και η Διεθνής Εμπειρία, Μερικές Σκέψεις για την Εξέλιξη του Θεσμού στην Ελλάδα, Ε.Εργ.Δ., τ. 47].

Spyropoulos, G., (1992), New Trends in Collective Bargaining in European Countries, Paper presented at the seminar of the OMED. held on 6 and 7 July. [Σπυρόπουλος, Γ., (1992), «Νέες Τάσεις των Συλλογικών Διαπραγματεύσεων στις Ευρωπαϊκές Χώρες», Εισήγηση στο εκπαιδευτικό σεμινάριο του Ο.ΜΕ.Δ. που πραγματοποιήθηκε στις 6 και 7 Ιουλίου].

Spyropoulos, G. (1996) The European experience in collective bargaining, Epitheorisis Employment Law, vol. 55, issue 8. [Σπυροπουλος, Γ. (1996), Η ευρωπαϊκή εμπειρία στο χώρο των συλλογικών διαπραγματεύσεων, Επιθεώρησις Εργατικού Δικαίου, τόμ.55, τευχ.8].

Spyropoulos, G., (1998a), Industrial Relations: Developments in Greece, Europe and the International Arena, Ant. N. Sakkoulas Editions, Athens-Komotini. [Σπυρόπουλος, Γ., (1998α), Εργασιακές Σχέσεις. Εξελίξεις στην Ελλάδα, την Ευρώπη και τον Διεθνή Χώρο, Εκδόσεις Αντ. Ν. Σάκκουλα, Αθήνα-Κομοτηνή].

Spyropoulos, G., (1998b), The Social Dialogue in the European Union, Epitheorisi Ergatikou Dikeou (E.Erg.D.- Revew of Labour Law), Vol. 57, issue Nr 1. [Σπυρόπουλος, Γ., (1998β), Ο Κοινωνικός Διάλογος στην Ευρωπαϊκή Ένωση, Επιθεώρησις Εργατικού Δικαίου, τόμος 57, τεύχ. 1].

Spyropoulos, G., (1999), Syndicalism in the throes of change, Epitheorisis Labour Law, vol. 58. Issue 2. [Σπυρόπουλος, Γ., (1999), Ο συνδικαλισμός στη δίνη των αλλαγών, Επιθεώρησις Εργατικού Δικαίου, τόμ. 58. τεύχος 2].

Spyropoulos, G., (2000), Impact of economic globalization on the development of labour relations, Epitheorisis Employment Law, vol. 59, issue. 1. [Σπυρόπουλος, Γ., (2000),Επιπτώσεις της παγκοσμιοποίησης της οικονομίας στην εξέλιξη των εργασιακών σχέσεων, Επιθεώρησις Εργατικού Δικαίου, τόμ.59, τευχ. 1].

Staboulis, M., (2000), The Mediation Process, Seminar held by the OMED, OMED, Naoussa. [Σταμπουλής, Μ., (2000), Η Διαδικασία Μεσολάβησης, Εκπαιδευτικό Σεμινάριο Ο.ΜΕ.Δ., Ο.ΜΕ.Δ., Νάουσα].

Stalin, J., Leninism in Theory and Practice. Dialectical and Historical Materialism, Anagnostidis. [Στάλιν, Ι., Λενινισμός στη Θεωρία και Πράξη. Διαλεκτικός και Ιστορικός Υλισμός, Αναγνωστίδης].

Stanton, Er. S., (1988), Realistic Management. Key to High Productivity, Rural Cooperative Publishing, Thessaloniki. [Stanton, Er. S., (1988), Ρεαλιστικό Μάνατζεμεντ. Κλειδί για την Υψηλή Παραγωγικότητα, Αγροτικές Συνεταιριστικές Εκδόσεις, Θεσσαλονίκη].

Stassinopoulou, O., (1992), Welfare State, Publications Gutenberg, Sociological and Anthropological Library Series: Social Policy / 1. [Στασινοπούλου, Ο., (1992), Κράτος Πρόνοιας, Εκδόσεις Gutenberg, Κοινωνιολογική και Ανθρωπολογική Βιβλιοθήκη, Σειρά: Κοινωνική Πολιτική/1].

Statistical History of the United States from Colonial Times to the Present, Stamford, CT, Fairfield Publishers, 1965.

Stavrou, S. (1993), Organization and Labour Protection, University Lectures, Ziti. [Σταύρου, Σ., (1993), Οργάνωση και Προστασία της Εργασίας, Πανεπιστημιακές Παραδόσεις, Ζήτη].

Stavroulakis, D., (1993), Quality Circles in Greek companies. Reproduction of Japanese and Western standard in Liodakis, G., (ed.), Society, Technology and Restructuring of Production Symposium Proceedings, University of Crete, October 1992 Papazisis Publications. [Σταυρουλάκης, Δ., (1993), Κύκλοι ποιότητας σε ελληνικές επιχειρήσεις. Η αναπαραγωγή του Ιαπωνικού και του Δυτικού προτύπου, στο Λιοδάκης, Γ., (επιμ.), Κοινωνία, Τεχνολογία και Αναδιάρθρωση της Παραγωγής, Πρακτικά Συμποσίου, Πολυτεχνείο Κρήτης, Οκτώβριος 1992, Εκδόσεις Παπαζήση].

Steeck, W., (1984), Co-determination: the Fourth Decade, International Yearbook on Organizational Democracy, John Wiley.

Stergiou, Agg., (1988), The Employer's Obligation for Negotiations in French Law, Epitheorisi Ergatikou Dikeou (E.Erg.D.-Revew of Labour Law), v. 47.

[Στέργιου, Αγγ., (1988), Η Υποχρέωση Εργοδότη για Διαπραγματεύσεις στο Γαλλικό Δίκαιο, Ε.Εργ.Δ., τ. 47].

Strinati, D., (1982), Capitalism, the State and Industrial Relations, London, Croom Helm.

Svolos, A. and Vlachos, G., (1954), The Constitution of Greece, vol. A. p. 94. [Σβώλος, Α., - Βλάχος, Γ., (1954), Το Σύνταγμα της Ελλάδος, τ. Α'].

Svolos, A., (1958), The Forced Expropriation towards the restoration of Landless Farmers from a Constitutional and Financial view, in Svolos, A., Nomike Melete (: Legal Studies), Vol. B. [Σβώλος, Α., (1958), Η Αναγκαστική Απαλλοτρίωσις προς Αποκατάστασιν Ακτημόνων Γεωργών υπό Συνταγματικήν και Οικονομικήν Άποψιν, Σβώλου, Αλ., Νομικαί Μελέται, τ. Β΄].

Symon, G., (2000), Information and communication technologies and the network organization: A critical analysis, Journal of Occupational Psychology, 73.

Szell, G., (1988), Participation, workers' control and self-management Sage Publications.

Szell, G. and C. J. Lammers, (1989), International Handbook of Participation in Organizations: Volume I: Organizational Democracy: Taking Stock: For the Study of Organizational Democracy, Vol 1, OUP Oxford.

Szell, G., et al., (eds.), (1992), Labour relations

Szell, G., (1994), Participation, Workers' Control and Self Management, Critical review of the major trends and contributions, (trans. and ed. by Nicholaou-Smokovitis L.) Papazisis, Athens. [Szell, G., (1994), Συμμετοχή, Εργατικός Έλεγχος και Αυτοδιαχείριση, Κριτική Επισκόπηση των Σημαντικότερων Τάσεων και Συνεισφορών, (μετάφραση-επιμέλεια Νικολάου-Σμοκοβίτη, Λ.), Εκδόσεις Παπαζήση, Αθήνα].

Szell, G., (eds), (2001), New Democracies and Old Societies in Europe, (Work - Technology - Organization - Society), Peter Lang AG.

Szell, G., Chetty, D., Chouraqui, Al., (eds.), (2002), Participation, Globalisation & Culture: International and South African Perspectives, (Work - Technology - Organization - Society), Peter Lang AG

Szell, G., et al., (eds.), (2003), The Injustice at Work: An International View on the World of Labour and Society, (Work - Technology - Organization - Society), Peter Lang AG.

Szell, G., Bosling, C.-H., Hartkemeyer, J., Ehlert, W., Sünker, H., (eds.), (2005), Labour, Globalisation and the New Economy, in transition in Eastern Europe Berlin, New York: W. de Gruyter.

Szell, G., (ed), (2006), Corporate Social Responsibility in the EU and Japan, Peter Lang AG.

Szell, G., et al., (eds.), (2007), Education, Labour & Science: Perspectives for the 21st Century, Paperback – 1 Nov 2007, by Gyoergy Szell (Author), Peter Lang AG.

Szell, G., and Y. Kim, (eds.), (2011), Economic Crisis and Social Integration (Comparative Regional Integration Studies, Peter Lang GmbH.

Tahar, G., (1985), La Réduction de la Durée du Travail, La Découverte, Paris.

Tapscott, D., and Caston, A., (1993), Paradigm Shift, N.Y., McGraw-Hill.

Taylor, F., (1911), The Principles of Scientific Management, Harper and Brothers, New York.

Theodorou, E.Th., (1983), Trade Union Law, Tolidis Publications, Athens. [Θεοδώρου, Ε.Θ., (1983), Συνδικαλιστικό Δίκαιο, Εκδόσεις Τολίδη, Αθήνα].

Therborn, G., (1984), The prospects of labour and the transformation of advanced capitalism, in Socialism in the world (Beograd), Nr. 44.

Salaman, G., and Thompson, K., (ed.) (1982), Control and Ideology in Organisations, London, Open University Press.

Thompson, P., (1983), The Nature of Work, An Introduction to Debates on the Labour Process, London, Macmillan.

Thompson, P. and McHugh, D., (1995), Work Organizations: a Critical Introduction, 2nd edition, London, MacMillan.

Thurman, J.E. and Trah, G., (1990), Part-time Work in International Perspective, International Labour Review, Vol. 129, Nr 1, pp. 23–24.

Tilly, R., (1970), Popular Disorders in Nineteen Century Germany, Journal of Social History, No. 1, pp. 25–30.

Timasheff, N and Theodorson, G., (1979), History of Sociological Theories, (trans. D.G. Tsaousis), Sociological Library, Gutenberg Publications. [Timasheff, N, και Theodorson, G., (1979), Ιστορία Κοινωνιολογικών Θεωριών, (μεταφρ. Δ. Γ. Τσαούση), Κοινωνιολογική Βιβλιοθήκη, Εκδόσεις Gutenberg].

Toutziarakis, J., (1990), Flexibility of Working Time and the Crisis of the Regular Employment Relationship, Epitheorisi Koinonikon Ereunon (: Social Research Review) EKKE (: National Centre for Social Research), issue 76, pp. 176–193, [Τουτζιαράκης, Γ. (1990) Η Ελαστικοποίηση του Χρόνου Εργασίας και η Κρίση της Κανονικής Σχέσης Εργασίας, Επιθεώρηση Κοινωνικών Ερευνών, EKKE, τ. 76].

Trade Union Congress, (1979), Employment and Technology, Macdermott and Chant Ltd.

Travicca, B., (1997), The design of the Virtual Organization: A research model. Association for Information Systems, Proceedings of the Americas Conference on Information Systems.

Travlos-Tzanetatos, D. (1977), Labour Law and Industrial Society, Ant. N. Sakkoulas Editons. [Τραυλός-Τζανετάτος, Δ., (1977), Εργατικό Δίκαιο και Βιομηχανική Κοινωνία, Εκδόσεις Αντ. Ν. Σάκκουλα, Αθήνα- Κομοτηνή].

Travlos-Tzanetatos, D., (1980), Strike and Risk for the Operation of the Exploitation, Ant. N. Sakkoulas, Athens – Komotini. [Τραυλός-Τζανετάτος, Δ., (1985), Απεργία και Κίνδυνος Λειτουργίας της Εκμετάλλευσης, Εκδόσεις Αντ. Ν. Σάκκουλα, Αθήνα – Κομοτηνή].

Travlos-Tzanetatos, D., (1984), Trade Union Action in the Enterprise and Constitution, Ant. N. Sakkoulas Editons, Athens - Komotini. [Τραυλός - Τζανετάτος, Δ., (1984), Η Συνδικαλιστική Δράση στην Επιχείρηση και το Σύνταγμα, Εκδόσεις Αντ. Ν. Σάκκουλα, Αθήνα – Κομοτηνή].

Travlos-Tzanetatos, D. (1986), Neoliberalism and Labor Relations, in Travlos-Tzanetatos, D. (ed.), Labor Law and Policy, Ant. N. Sakkoulas, Athens - Komotini. [Τραυλός-Τζανετάτος, Δ., (1986), «Νεοφιλελευθερισμός και Εργασιακές Σχέσεις», στο Τραυλός-Τζανετάτος, Δ., (επιμ.), Εργατικό Δίκαιο και Πολιτική, Εκδόσεις Αντ. Ν. Σάκκουλα, Αθήνα – Κομοτηνή].

Travlos-Tzanetatos, D. (1990), The Labour Law at a Critical Point, Athens, Odysseas Publications. [Τραυλός-Τζανετάτος, Δ., (1990), Το Εργατικό Δίκαιο σε Κρίσιμη Καμπή, Αθήνα, Εκδόσεις Οδυσσέας].

Travlos-Tzanetatos, D. (1991), the Employee's Loan in Consortia (groups of companies), Ant. N. Sakkoulas, Athens - Komotini. [Τραυλός-Τζανετάτος, Δ., (1991), ο Δανεισμός Εργαζομένου στους Ομίλους Επιχειρήσεων, Εκδόσεις Αντ. Ν. Σάκκουλα, Αθήνα – Κομοτηνή].

Trebilcock, An., et al., (1994), Towards Social Dialogue: Tripirtite Cooperation in National Economic and Social Policy-making, ILO, Geneva.

Trist, E., Higgin, G, Murray, H., and Pollock, A., (1963), Organizational Choice, London, Tavistock.

Tsaousis, D., (1983), The Human League, Gutenberg. [Τσαούσης, Δ., (1983), Η Κοινωνία του Ανθρώπου, Gutenberg].

Tsekouras, Th., (1989), From Taylorism to New Production Technologies, Theses, v. 29. [Τσεκούρας, Θ., (1989), Από τον Τεϋλορισμό στις Νέες Τεχνολογίες της Παραγωγής, Θέσεις, ν. 29].

Tsivakou, I., (1995a), Action and System, Athens, Themelio Publications. [Τσιβάκου, Ι., (1995α), Δράση και Σύστημα, Αθήνα, Εκδόσεις Θεμέλιο].

Tsivakou, I., (1995b), Organization and Power. A Course of Rupture and Reconstitution of the Collective, in Tsivakou, I., (1995), Action and System, Athens, Themelio Publications. [Τσιβάκου, Ι., (1995β), Οργάνωση και Εξουσία. Μία πορεία Διάσπασης και Επανασυγκρότησης του Συλλογικού, στο Τσιβάκου, Ι., (1995), Δράση και Σύστημα, Αθήνα, Εκδόσεις Θεμέλιο].

Tsobanoglou, G. and Economou, Th., (2005), Social Policy for Social Inclusion: Education, Training and Lifelong Sustainability Working in Tsobanoglou, G.O., Korres, G. and Giannopoulos, I., Social Exclusion and Inclusion Policies, Papazisis Publications. [Τσομπάνογλου, Γ., και Οικονόμου, Θ., (2005), Κοινωνική Πολιτική για την Κοινωνική Ενσωμάτωση: Εκπαίδευση, Διά Βίου Κατάρτιση και Αειφορία Εργασίας, στο Τσομπάνογλου, Γ.Ο., Κορρές, Γ., και Γιαννοπούλου, Ι., Κοινωνικός Αποκλεισμός και Πολιτικές Ενσωμάτωσης, Εκδόσεις Παπαζήση].

Tsobanoglou, G., (2008), Enhancing sustainable communities: The role of social capital, the social economy and local partnerships in Tsobanoglou, G. (ed.) (2008), The Emergence of Social Economy, The Road Sustainable Employment in a Europe of Active Citizens Papazisis, Athens. [Τσομπάνογλου, Γ., (2008), Ενισχύοντας τις βιώσιμες κοινότητες: Ο ρόλος του κοινωνικού κεφαλαίου, της κοινωνικής οικονομίας και των τοπικών συμπράξεων, στο Τσομπάνογλου, Γ., (επιμ.) (2008), Η Ανάδυση της Κοινωνικής Οικονομίας, Ο Δρόμος της Βιώσιμης Απασχόλησης σε μία Ευρώπη Ενεργών Πολιτών, Εκδόσεις Παπαζήση, Αθήνα].

Turner, H.A., (1969), Is Britain Really Strike Prone? Cambridge UP, Cambridge.

Tzekinis, Ch., (1984), Industrial Relations and Development, Athens, Papazisis Publications. [Τζεκίνης, Χρ., (1984), Εργασιακές Σχέσεις και Ανάπτυξη, Αθήνα, Εκδόσεις Παπαζήση].

Tzenkinis, Ch., (1984), Employee participation in Business Administration, Athens, Organization of Labour Force Employment (O.E.L.F.). Τζεκίνης, Χρ., (1984), Η συμμετοχή των εργαζομένων στη διοίκηση των επιχειρήσεων, Αθήνα, Οργανισμός Απασχολήσεως Εργατικού Δυναμικού (Ο.Α.Ε.Δ.)].

Tzekinis, Ch., (1986), Problems and Prospects Part-Time Employment, Ministry of Labour, OAED (: Manpower Employment Organisation) editions, Athens, January. [Τζεκίνης, Χρ., (1986), Προβλήματα και Προοπτικές της Μερικής Απασχόλησης, Υπουργείο Εργασίας, έκδοση Ο.Α.Ε.Δ., Αθήνα, Ιανουάριος].

Tzevelekakis, I., (1974), The State Economic Planning in terms of public law, n.p. [Τζεβελεκάκης, Ι., (1974), Ο Κρατικός Οικονομικός Προγραμματισμός εξ απόψεως δημοσίου δικαίου, χ.ε.].

U.S. Department of Labor, (1979), The Employment and Training Report of the President, Washington, D.C.

U.S. Labor Law and the future of Labor – Man agement Cooperation, (1986), U.S. Department of Labor, Bureau of Labor Management Relations and Cooperative Programmes, BLMR 104.

Vagias, Ant., (1991), The Consensual Element in Regulating Economic Collective Disputes in Greek Law, Epitheorisi Ergatikou Dikeou (E.Erg.D.-Revew of Labour Law), issue Nr 50. [Βάγιας, Α., (1991), Το συνεναιτικό στοιχείο στη ρύθμιση των οικονομικών συλλογικών διαφορών κατά τον ελληνικό νόμο, ΕΕργΔ, 50].

Vais, I., (1978), Freedom of Association and Protection of Trade Union Freedoms, Scientific Journal "The Constitution" (ToS). [Βαής, Θ., (1978), Συνδικαλιστική Ελευθερία και Προστασία Συνδικαλιστικών Ελευθεριών, Επιστημονικό Περιοδικό το Σύνταγμα (ΤοΣ)].

van Bastelaer, A., Lemaitre, G. and Pascal, M., (1997), The definition of part-time work for the purpose of international comparisons, Labour Market and Social Policy, Occasional Papers-no. 22, Paris, Organization for Economic Cooperation and Development, OECD/GD (97) 121.

Vasileiou, St. (1996), Reduction of Working Time and SMEs, Paper presented in the Seminar O.ME.D., May 18. pp. 1–16. [Βασιλείου, Στ., (1996), Η Μείωση του Χρόνου Εργασίας και οι ΜΜΕ, Εισήγηση σε Σεμινάριο του Ο.ΜΕ.Δ., 18 Μαΐου].

Vasileiou, Th. and Stamatakis, N., (1992), Dictionary of Human Sciences, Gutenberg. [Βασιλείου, Θ., και Σταματάκης, Ν., (1992), Λεξικό των Επιστημών του Ανθρώπου, Gutenberg].

Vlachos, G., (1979), Sociology of Human Rights, Athens, Papazisis Publications. [Βλάχος, Γ., (1979), Κοινωνιολογία των Δικαιωμάτων του Ανθρώπου, Αθήνα, Εκδόσεις Παπαζήση].

Voulgaris, G., (1994), Liberalism, Conservatism, Welfare State 1973-1990, Themelio Publications. [Βούλγαρης, Γ., (1994), Φιλελευθερισμός, Συντηρητισμός, Κοινωνικό Κράτος 1973-1990, Εκδόσεις Θεμέλιο].

Waddock, S. A., (1988), Building Successful Social Partnerships, Sloan Management Review 29(4).

Walker, C., (1950), The Problem of the Repetitive Job, Harvard Business Review, V. 28, n. 3, May.

Walker, C., (1966), Technology, Industry and Man: The Age of Acceleration, McGraw Hill.

Walker, C.R. and Guest, R., (1952), Man on the Assembly Line, Cambridge, Mass, Harvard University Press.

Walker, C.R. and Guest, R.H., (1957), The Man on the Assembly Line, Yale University Press, New Haven.

Wallace, S.L., (1999), Social Entrepreneurship: The Role of Social Purpose Enterprises in Facilitating Community Economic Development, Journal of Development Entrepreneurship 4.

Walters, D., (2000), Virtual Organizations: new lamps for old? Management Decision, 38 (6).

Warner, J., (1999), Information Society or Cash Nexus? A study of the United States as a copyright haven. Journal of the American Society for Information Science, 50, 5.

Watson-Manheim, M. B., Chudoba, K. M., and Crowston, K., (2002), Discontinuities and continuities: a new way to understand virtual work. Information Technology and People, 15 (3).

Webb, Sidney and Beatrice, (1902), Industrial Democracy, Longman, London.

Weber, M., (1964), The Theory of Social and Economic Organizations, trans. A. M. Henderson and T. Parsons, introduction by T. Parsons, Glencoe, Free Press.

Wedderburn, L., (1985), The New Industrial Relations Laws in Great Britain, Labor and Society, Vol. 10, January.

Weiss, E., (1996), Creating a new civilization: the politics of the third wave. Harvard Journal of Law and Technology, 9, 1.

White, G., (1982), Technological Changes and Employment: A Review of Some Implications for Company and Union Policies, in Bekemans, L., European Employment and Technological Change, European Centre for Work and Society, Maastricht.

Whyte, W., (1955), Money and Motivation, Harper and Row, in Walker, C., Technology, Industry and Man, McGraw-Hill Company.

Wiesenfeld, B. M., Raghuran, S. and Garud, R., (1998), Communication patterns as determinants of organizational identification in a virtual organization, JCMC, 3(4), June, http://www.ascusc.org/jcmc/vol13/issue4/wiesenld.html

Windmuller, J. P., et al, (1987), Collective Bargaining in Industrialized Market Economics: A Reappraisal, ILO, Geneva.

Witte, J., (1980), Democracy, Authority and Alienation at Work: Workers' Participation in an American Corporation, Chicago, University of Chicago Press.

Wood, S., (eds.) (1982), The Degradation of Work?, London, Hutchinson.

Woodward, J., (1980), Industrial Organization Theory and Practice, Oxford University Press.

XIII Congres Mondial de droit du travail et de la sécurité sociale, Athènes 1991, Thème I, Rapports Nationaux.

XIII International Conference of Labour Law and Social Security, Athens, 1991, 1st Topic, Rapports National.

Xirotiri-Koufidou, S., (1995), Personnel Management, Kyriakidis Bros Publications. [Ξηροτύρη-Κουφίδου, Σ., (1995), Διοίκηση Προσωπικού, Εκδόσεις Αδελφών Κυριακίδη].

Zack, Ar., (1980), Understanding, Fact Finding and Arbitration in Public Sector, U.S. Department of Labor, Labor Management Services Administration, 3rd Edition.

Zack, A.M., (1985), Public Sector Mediation, the Bureau of National Affairs, Inc. Washington D.C.

Zolotas, X. (1978), Inflation and Monetary Target, Bank of Greece, Archive Studies and Lectures (38). [Ζολώτας, Ξ., (1978), Πληθωρισμός και Νομισματικός Στόχος, Τράπεζα της Ελλάδος, Αρχείον Μελετών και Ομιλιών (38)].

Zorbas, C. (1996) The role of social partners at Community level and new procedures introduced by the Agreement on social policy, in Social Policy and Social Dialogue in the Perspective of the Economic-Monetary Union (EMU) and the Europe of Citizens Kritiki Publications and European Cultural Centre of Delphi. [Ζορμπάς, Γ., (1996), Ο ρόλος των κοινωνικών εταίρων στο κοινοτικό επίπεδο και οι νέες διαδικασίες που θεσπίστηκαν με τη συμφωνία για την κοινωνική πολιτική στο Κοινωνική πολιτική και κοινωνικός διάλογος στην προοπτική της οικονομικής νομισματικής ένωσης και της «Ευρώπης των πολιτών», Εκδόσεις Κριτική και Ευρωπαϊκό Πολιτιστικό Κέντρο Δελφών].

Zwass, V., (1991), Electronic commerce: structure and issues. International Journal of Electronic Commerce, 1(1).

Abbreviations Index

ADEDY: Supreme Administration of Greek Civil Servants Trade Unions or Greek Civil Servants' Union (Reuters)	ΑΔΕΔΥ (ADEDY): Ανώτατη Διοίκηση Ενώσεων Δημοσίων Υπαλλήλων
GESASE: General Confederation of Agricultural Associations in Greece	ΓΕ.ΣΑ.ΣΕ (GE.SA.SE): Γενική Συνομοσπονδία Αγροτικών Συλλόγων Ελλάδος
GSEVEE: General Confederation of Professional Graftsmen and Traders in Greece	ΓΣΕΒΕΕ (GSEVEE): Γενική Συνομοσπονδία Επαγγελματιών Βιοτεχνών Εμπόρων Ελλάδος
GSEE or GCGL General Confederation of Greek Labour	ΓΣΕΕ (GSEE): Γενική Συνομοσπονδία Εργατών Ελλάδος
CNT (Conseil National du Travail): National Labour Council of Belgium	CNT: Εθνικό Συμβούλιο Εργασίας του Βελγίου
DEK (CVRIA): Court of Justice of the European Union	Δ.Ε.Κ. (DEK): Δικαστήριο των Ευρωπαϊκών Κοινοτήτων
DEKOs: Public Utility Organizations	Δ.Ε.Κ.Ο. (DEKO): Δημόσιες Επιχειρήσεις Και Οργανισμοί
IMF: International Monetary Fund	ΔΝΤ (DNT): Διεθνές Νομισματικό Ταμείο
ILO: International Labour Organization	ΔΟΕ (DOE): Διεθνής Οργανισμός Εργασίας
IRS (or DOY, in Greek): Internal Revenue Service	ΔΟΥ: Δημόσια Οικονομική Υπηρεσία

EGSSE: National General Collective Agreements	Ε.Γ.Σ.Σ.Ε. (EGSSE): Εθνικές γενικές συλλογικές συμβάσεις εργασίας
EESE: National Confederation of Hellenic Commerce	Ε.Ε.Σ.Ε. (EESE): Ένωση Εμπορικών Συλλόγων
EESSE or SELCAs: Special enterprise-level Collective Agreements	Ε.Ε.Σ.Σ.Ε. (EESSE): Ειδικές Επιχειρησιακές Συλλογικές Συμβάσεις Εργασίας
EIE (or NIL in English): National Institute of Labour	E.I.E. (in Greek): Εθνικό Ινστιτούτο Εργασίας
EKEP: National Resource Center for Vocational Guidance	Ε.Κ.Ε.Π. (ΕΚΕΡ): Εθνικό Κέντρο Επαγγελματικού Προσανατολισμού
EKEPIS: National Accreditation Center for Continuing Vocational Training	Ε.Κ.Ε.Π.Ι.Σ. (EKEPIS): Εθνικό Κέντρο Πιστοποίησης Δομής Συνεχιζόμενης Επαγγελματικής Κατάρτισης
EPA: National Observatory of Employment	Ε.Π.Α. (EPA): Εθνικό Παρατηρητήριο Απασχόλησης
ESAP: National Council of Development and Productivity	Ε.Σ.Α.Π. (ESAP): Εθνικό Συμβούλιο Ανάπτυξης και Παραγωγικότητας
EPA: Temporary Employment Agency	ΕΠΑ (EPA): Εταιρείας Προσωρινής Απασχόλησης
ESEE National Confederation of Hellenic Commerce	ΕΣΕΕ (ESEE) Εθνική Συνομοσπονδία Ελληνικού Εμπορίου
IGEE: Private employment agencies	Ι.Γ.Ε.Ε. (IGEE): Ιδιωτικά γραφεία ευρέσεως εργασίας
IKA-ETAM: Social Insurance Fund – Auxiliary Fund for Employees	IKA-ETAM: Ίδρυμα Κοινωνικών Ασφαλίσεων – Ενιαίο Ταμείο Ασφάλισης Μισθωτών

INE: Labour Institute	INE (INE): Ινστιτούτο Εργασίας
KEK: Centres for Vocational Training	K.E.K. (KEK): Κέντρα Επαγγελματικής Κατάρτισης
KPA: Employment Promotion Centres	K.Π.A. (KPA): Κέντρα Προώθησης της Απασχόλησης
KEDKE: Central Union of Municipalities and Communities of Greece	ΚΕΔΚΕ (KEDKE): Κεντρική Ένωση Δήμων και Κοινοτήτων Ελλάδας
SMEs: Small and medium-sized enterprises or SMBs: Small and medium-sized businesses	MME: Μικρομεσαίες επιχειρήσεις
NPID (or PEL): Private Entity Law (USLegal)	Ν.Π.Ι.Δ. (NPID) Νομικό Πρόσωπο Ιδιωτικού Δικαίου
OAED: National Organization for the Employment of the Labour Force	Ο.Α.Ε.Δ. (OAED): Οργανισμός Απασχόλησης Εργατικού Δυναμικού
OKE or ESC: Economic and Social Committee	O.K.E. (OKE): Οικονομική και Κοινωνική Επιτροπή
OMED: Organization for Mediation and Arbitration	Ο.Μ.Ε.Δ. (OMED): Οργανισμός Μεσολάβησης και Διαιτησίας
ODEPES: Special Resources Management Agency of Labour Unions	ΟΔΕΠΕΣ (ODEPES) Οργανισμός Διαχειρίσεως Ειδικών Πόρων Εργασιακών Σωματείων
OEK: Employees' Housing Organization **Note**: Initially, this Organization was known with two acronyms in Greek. Now, it is known with OEK.	ΟΕΚ ή ΟΕΕ Οργανισμός Εργατικής Κατοικίας ή Οργανισμού Εργατικής Εστίας **Σημείωση**: Τώρα αυτός ο Οργανισμός είναι γνωστός με το πρώτο ακρωνύμιο.

EMU: Economic Monetary Union	ONE: Οικονομική Νομισματική Ένωση
OTA: Organization of Local Authorities	OTA: Οργανισμός Τοπικής Αυτοδιοίκησης
PA.SE.GE.S: Pan-Hellenic Confederation of Unions of Agricultural Co-operatives	ΠΑΣΕΓΕΣ (PA.SE.GE.S): Πανελλήνια Συνομοσπονδία Ενώσεων Αγροτικών Συνεταιρισμών
PNP: Ordinance(s)	ΠΝΠ (PNP):- Πράξη Νομοθετικού Περιεχομένου
SEPE: Agency of Labour Inspection or Labour Inspection Authority	Σ.ΕΠ.Ε. (SEPE): Σώμα Επιθεώρησης Εργασίας
sse: collective labour agreements	σ.σ.ε. (sse): συλλογικές συμβάσεις εργασίας
SEV: Association of Greek Industrialists	ΣΕΒ (SEV): Σύνδεσμος Ελληνικών Βιομηχανιών
SEO 115: "115 Collaborating Labour Organizations"	ΣΕΟ 115 (SEO 115): "115 Συνεργαζόμενες Εργατοϋπαλληλικές Οργανώσεις"
SKEEE: Council for Social Control of Labour Inspection	ΣΚΕΕΕ (SKEEE): Συμβούλιο Κοινωνικού Ελέγχου Επιθεώρησης Εργασίας
SKOP: Council of Social and Economic Policy	ΣΚΟΠ (SKOP): Συμβούλιο Κοινωνικής και Οικονομικής Πολιτικής
TKE: Department of Social Inspection	Τ.Κ.Ε. (TKE): Τμήμα Κοινωνικής Επιθεώρησης
TSAs: Local Employment Pacts	Τ.Σ.Α. (TSA): Τοπικά Σύμφωνα Απασχόλησης

About the Author

Dr. Dimosthenis Daskalakis is a Professor of Sociology (Industrial Sociology and Industrial Relations) at National and Kapodistrian University of Athens.

In March 2014 he was elected as **Dean of the School of Education in National and Kapodistrian University of Athens**.

Since January 1st 2013 up to the 31st of August, 2014 Professor Dr. Dimosthenis Daskalakis has been the **President of the Faculty of Pedagogy in Primary Education (P.E.)** and **Member of the Senate** at the National and Kapodistrian University of Athens.

He is **Head of the "Observatory for the Study of Childhood" of the Social Sciences Research Laboratory** of the Faculty of Pedagogy in P.E. at National and Kapodistrian University of Athens. He is also **Head of the Direction 'Sociology of Labour, labour market policies-minorities-childhood'** in the Postgraduate Studies Programme of the same Faculty.

He served as Deputy President of the Faculty of Pedagogy in P.E. at National and Kapodistrian University of Athens and as Director of the Human Studies Sector of the above mentioned Faculty for two years. His research interests focus on the following subject matters: a) new technologies – work – education; b) social inequalities and discriminations in work, education, society and social change; and c) sociology of childhood, minorities, poverty and social exclusion. He has been teaching in three postgraduate studies programmes at the National and Kapodistrian University of Athens, and he also taught in two postgraduate programmes at Panteion University of Athens for a number of years in the past.

He is a member of International Sociological Association, Greek Society for Labour Law and Social Security, and an honorary member of Greek Sociologists' Society.

As an expert, he has participated in high level Councils and Experts' Committees and especially in the Committee of Labour and Social Security Experts of the Ministry of Labour, in the Central Health Council as well as in joint Expert's Committees of the Social Partners. He has also represented Greece in many informal and formal fora of the European Union and other international organizations.

Career

He has served as researcher in the National Labour Institute, as a member and Director of the Organization for Mediation & Arbitration (OMED) for the settlement of collective labour disputes, as an External Expert of the General

Confederation of Greek Labour (GSEE) and the Labour Institute of the GSEE (INE-GSEE) and as an Expert of the National Confederation of Hellenic Commerce (ESEE), while he has participated in many Councils and Committees of Special Experts.

He has participated as a special expert in high-level councils and committees and, more specifically, in the Council of Experts on Employment and Social Security of the Ministry of Labour and Social Security, the Supreme Labour Council (ASE), the Central Health Council (KESY), in the Board of Directors of the Organization for Mediation & Arbitration (OMED) and of National Organization for the Employment of the Labour Force (OAED), as well as in Joint Committees of Experts of the social partners. Furthermore, he has represented Greece in many informal and formal fora of the European Union and other international organizations.

Public posts he has been appointed in:

2010–2011: General Secretary of the Ministry of Labour and Social Security and President of the Supreme Labour Council.

1998–2000 and 2002–2004: General Secretary of the General Secretariat of Social Security in the Ministry of Labour and Social Security and President of the Social Security Council.

2001–2002: Member of the National Radio-Television Council

2001: President of the National Labour Institute

1997–1998: Vice-Governor of the Organization of Agricultural Social Security (OGA)

Arbeit, Bildung & Gesellschaft
Labour, Education & Society

Herausgegeben von Prof. Dr. György Széll, Prof. Dr. Heinz Sünker, Dr. Anne Inga Hilsen und Dr. Francesco Garibaldo

Bd. 1 György Széll (ed.): Corporate Social Responsibility in the EU & Japan. 2006.

Bd. 2 Katja Maar: Zum Nutzen und Nichtnutzen der Sozialen Arbeit am exemplarischen Feld der Wohnungslosenhilfe. Eine empirische Studie. 2006.

Bd. 3 Daniela De Ridder: Vom urbanen Sozialraum zur kommunikativen Stadtgesellschaft. 2007.

Bd. 4 Heinz Sünker / Ingrid Miethe (Hrsg.): Bildungspolitik und Bildungsforschung: Herausforderungen und Perspektiven für Gesellschaft und Gewerkschaften in Deutschland. 2007.

Bd. 5 Anja Bastigkeit: Bildungsbiographie und elementarpädagogische Bildungsarbeit. 2007.

Bd. 6 Antônio Inácio Andrioli: Biosoja versus Gensoja. Eine Studie über Technik und Familienlandwirtschaft im nordwestlichen Grenzgebiet des Bundeslandes Rio Grande do Sul (Brasilien). 2007.

Bd. 7 Russell Farnen / Daniel German / Henk Dekker / Christ'l De Landtsheer / Heinz Suenker (eds.): Political Culture, Socialization, Democracy, and Education. Interdisciplinary and Cross-National Perspectives for a New Century. 2008.

Bd. 8 Francesco Garibaldo / Volker Telljohann (eds.): New Forms of Work Organisation and Industrial Relations in Southern Europe. 2007.

Bd. 9 Anne Marie Berg / Olav Eikeland (eds.): Action Research and Organisation Theory. 2008.

Bd. 10 György Széll / Carl-Heinrich Bösling / Ute Széll (eds.): Education, Labour & Science. Perspectives for the 21st Century. 2008.

Bd. 11 Francesco Garibaldo / Philippe Morvannou / Jochen Tholen (eds.): Is China a Risk or an Opportunity for Europe? An Assessment of the Automobile, Steel and Shipbuilding Sectors. 2008.

Bd. 12 Yunus Dauda: Managing Technology Innovation. The Human Resource Management Perspective. 2009.

Bd. 13 Jarmo Lehtonen / Satu Kalliola (eds.): Dialogue in Working Life Research and Development in Finland. 2009.

Bd. 14 György Széll / Werner Kamppeter / Woosik Moon (eds.): European Social Integration – A Model for East Asia? 2009.

Bd. 15 Benedicte Brøgger / Olav Eikeland (eds.): Turning to Practice with Action Research. 2009.

Bd. 16 Till Johannes Hoffmann: Verschwendung. Philosophie, Soziologie und Ökonomie des Überflusses. 2009.

Bd. 17 Denis Harrisson / György Széll / Reynald Bourque (eds.): Social Innovation, the Social Economy and World Economic Development. 2009.

Bd. 18 Werner Weltgen: Total Quality Management als Strukturierungsaufgabe für nachhaltigen Unternehmenswandel. 2009.

Bd. 19 György Széll / Ute Széll (eds.): Quality of Life and Working Life in Comparison. 2009.

Bd. 20 Francesco Garibaldo / Volker Telljohann (eds.): The Ambivalent Character of Participation. New Tendencies in Worker Participation in Europe. 2010.

Bd. 21 Richard Ennals / Robert H. Salomon (eds.): Older Workers in a Sustainable Society. 2011.

Bd. 22 Christoph Sänger: Anna Siemsen – Bildung und Literatur. 2011.

Bd. 23 Nam-Kook Kim: Deliberative Multiculturalism in Britain. A Response to Devolution, European Integration, and Multicultural Challenges. 2011.

Bd. 24 Mirella Baglioni / Bernd Brandl (eds.): Changing Labour Relations. Between Path Dependency and Global Trends. 2011.

Bd. 25 Rüdiger Kühr: Japan`s Transnational Environmental Policies. The Case of Environmental Technology Transfer to Newly Industrializing Countries. 2011.

Bd. 26 Francesco Garibaldo / Dinghong Yi (eds.): Labour and Sustainable Development. North-South Perspectives. 2012.

Bd. 27 Francesco Garibaldo / Mirella Baglioni / Catherine Casey / Volker Telljohann (eds.): Workers, Citizens, Governance. Socio-Cultural Innovation at Work. 2012.

Bd. 28 Simone Selva: Supra-National Integration and Domestic Economic Growth. The United States and Italy in the Western Bloc Rearmament Programs 1945-1955. Translation by Filippo del Lucchese, revision by Simone Selva. 2012.

Band 29 György Széll / Roland Czada (Hrsg.): Fukushima. Die Katastrophe und ihre Folgen. 2013.

Band 30 Siqi Luo: Collective Bargaining and Changing Industrial Relations in China. Lessons from the U. S. and Germany. 2013.

Band 31 Litsa Nicolaou-Smokoviti / Heinz Sünker / Julia Rozanova / Victoria Pekka Economou (eds.): Citizenship and Social Development. Citizen Participation and Community Involvement in Social Welfare and Social Policy. 2013.

Band 32 Christ'l De Landtsheer / Russell F. Farnen / Daniel B. German / Henk Dekker / Heinz Sünker / Yingfa Song / Hongna Miao (eds.): E-Political Socialization, the Press and Politics. The Media and Government in the USA, Europe and China. 2014.

Band 33 Jukka M. Krisp / Michael Szurawitzki (eds.): Doctoral Experiences in Finland. 2014.

Band 34 Dimosthenis Daskalakis: Greek Labour Relations in Transition in a Global Context. 2015.

www.peterlang.com

www.ingramcontent.com/pod-product-compliance
Ingram Content Group UK Ltd.
Pitfield, Milton Keynes, MK11 3LW, UK
UKHW020834290926
15470UKWH00004B/1332

9 783631 666579